Ft Worth Public Library

3 1668 02328 4943

◁ Y0-CAY-399

92 CONWAY
ALLEN, RAYE VIRGINIA
GORDON CONWAY: FASHIONING A
NEW WOMAN

NOV 1 3 1997

AMERICAN STUDIES SERIES

William H. Goetzmann, Editor

GORDON CONWAY
Fashioning a New Woman

GORDON CONWAY

Fashioning a New Woman

Raye Virginia Allen

Foreword by
William H. Goetzmann

University

of Texas Press

Austin

Photographs of drawings and duplicates of archival photographs by Wm. Edmund Barrett.

Reproduction of the color plates has been made possible by the generosity of the Neiman Marcus Foundation, the Fashion Industry Council, Charles W. Flynn, the Stanley and Linda Marcus Foundation, Mrs. Eugene McDermott, Mary Munger Cassidy, and Terrell and Evelyn Allen.

Copyright © 1997 by the University of Texas Press
All rights reserved
Printed in the United States of America

First edition, 1997

Requests for permission to reproduce material from this work should be sent to Permissions, University of Texas Press, Box 7819, Austin, TX 78713-7819.

♾ The paper used in this publication meets the minimum requirements of American National Standard for Information Sciences—Permanence of Paper for Printed Library Materials, ANSI Z39.48-1984.

Library of Congress Cataloging-in-Publication Data

Allen, Raye Virginia.
    Gordon Conway : fashioning a new woman / by Raye Virginia Allen ; foreword by William H. Goetzmann. — 1st ed.
        p.   cm. — (American studies series)
    Includes bibliographical references and index.
    ISBN 0-292-70459-3 (alk. paper). — ISBN 0-292-70470-4 (pbk. : alk. paper)
    1. Conway, Gordon, 1894–1956.   2. Women costume designers—United States—Biography.   3. Fashion illustrators—United States—Biography.   I. Title.   II. Series.
TT505.C65A43   1997
741.6′72′092—dc21
[B]   96-45862

Previously published and archival material reproduced by permission as follows:

Gordon Conway Collection and Archive: copyrighted artwork, archival photographs, and quotes from archival materials courtesy the late Olive Johnson Allen and Dr. and Mrs. Harvey Waldo Allen, Fredericksburg, Virginia. A large number of these images are part of the Gordon Conway Collection at the Theatre Arts Collection, Harry Ransom Humanities Research Center, The University of Texas at Austin.

Gordon Conway drawings from *Vogue*. Courtesy *Vogue*. Copyright © 1917 (renewed 1945) by The Condé Nast Publications Inc.

Gordon Conway drawings from *Vanity Fair*. Courtesy *Vanity Fair*. Copyright © 1918, 1919 (renewed 1946, 1947) by The Condé Nast Publications Inc.

Stills from the films *The Return of the Rat, The Good Companions, Soldiers of the King, It's a Boy, I Was a Spy, Channel Crossing, Sunshine Susie, Love on Wheels, Rome Express, There Goes the Bride, Friday the Thirteenth, Falling for You, Just Smith, The Man from Toronto,* and *After the Ball* by courtesy of The Rank Organisation Plc. Source: BFI Stills, Posters, and Designs.

Stills from *Confetti* courtesy Turner Entertainment Co.

Stills from *High Treason, The Midshipmaid, Night of the Party, The Constant Nymph, Britannia of Billingsgate, White Face, Waltz Time,* and *Orders Is Orders.* Source: BFI Stills, Posters, and Designs.

Cover art: *Presentation drawing, untitled, Paris or London, ca. 1924, featuring a redheaded woman in profile draped in an orange embroidered shawl, which closely resembles Gordon Conway's Spanish shawl deposited in the Theatre Arts Collection, Harry Ransom Humanities Research Center, University of Texas at Austin. Labeled a self-portrait by some authorities, this unpublished drawing was the title image for the 1980 exhibition "That Red Head Gal." From the private collection of the artist's family. Courtesy of Dr. and Mrs. Harvey W. Allen.*

Title page: *Self-caricature of Gordon Conway, 1920, printed in selected U.S. and Continental newspapers, 1920–1924.*

WITH GRATITUDE

for their help, love, and encouragement,
I dedicate this book
to my husband, H. K. Allen,
and our three children and their families:

Henry Kiper "Ki" Allen, Jr., and Kay Barnes Allen
Judith Allegra Allen
Henry Kiper Allen III

Irvin McCreary "Mac" Allen

Raye Virginia "Ginger" Allen Cucolo and
Anthony Arthur "Tony" Cucolo III
Anthony Allen "Tony-Allen" Cucolo
Raye McCreary "Mackie" Cucolo
Abigail Lee "Abbie" Cucolo

and in loving memory of my parents,
Irvin Paul McCreary and
Mary Vivian Arnold McCreary.

Catalogues, posters, advertisements of all types . . . they contain the poetry of our epoch.

Guillaume Apollinaire

CONTENTS

Color sections follow pages 12 and 188.

FOREWORD
William H. Goetzmann

This book is about a lady who dealt in dreams. It is an important book because the dreams that Gordon Conway created—visions of café society, fashion, glamour, wealth, chic with just a touch of cheek, wanton abandon, mysterious women in mythical narratives, motorcars, elegance even in animals, expensive cabarets, jazz music, and, above all, the spice of the exotic—provided images that seemed to make an exciting lifestyle accessible to middle-class people in both the United States and Europe. In nearly five thousand finished drawings that appeared in some twenty-six magazines like *Vanity Fair, Vogue,* the *Tatler,* and *Eve,* as well as in newspapers and on posters; in costumes and set designs for 119 stage productions, and in forty-seven films, Gordon Conway created a consumer society on the wild side—largely addressed to women. As her boss, Frank Crowninshield, editor of *Vanity Fair,* explained, the "happy dreams and illusions are built up for them by the advertising pages. Such pages spell romance to them. They are magic carpets on which they ride out to love, the secret gardens into which they wander in order to escape the workaday world and their well-meaning husbands." He added that, "after a single hour's reading of the advertising pages, 10,000,000 housewives, salesgirls, telephone operators, typists, and factory workers see themselves daily as *femmes fatales,* as Cleopatra, as Helen of Troy . . ." In so doing they became New Women and often goddesses.

Even if most of what Gordon Conway, "that red-headed gal" from Dallas, New York, Paris, and London, portrayed was unattainable—indeed, sometimes ridiculous—it gave women a sense of self-worth and sexual attractiveness. It also provided a sense of humor, frivolity, and flapper smart-aleckiness that was largely lacking among the suffragists. If the stern women's movements of the early twentieth century aimed to drag males into the world of equality, Conway's females enticed them into it. She herself was one of the first woman set designers and a regular illustrator for major magazines. No housebound, frumpy Myra Babbitt, Gordon Conway was always where the action was on both sides of the Atlantic. She had stature, intelligence, and, most of all, respect. People liked her for all her qualities, especially for her grace under pressure—that ellusive quality that her contemporary, Ernest Hemingway, was always looking for but never found. Of course, she was an unusual woman, which makes her story almost as compelling as his.

Gertrude Stein, guru of the Paris avant-garde, had warned the young Hemingway about women like Gordon, who probably crossed paths with the writer at Sylvia Beach's bookstore in Paris. Whether she was referring to Hadley Hemingway or Pauline Pfeiffer, his fashion writer girlfriend, Stein asserted, "You can either buy clothes or pictures. . . ." She added, "But it's not you buying clothes so much. It's your wife always." This was, of course, a characteristic degree of malice that went with her efforts at dominating the avant-garde with her money and her brother's taste. Handouts on the Rue de Fleurus spelled hegemony—and a place in the histories of literature and the "higher" arts. Though Gordon Conway undoubtedly crossed paths with *Vogue* writer Pauline Pfeiffer as she chased Hemingway on the Left Bank, and she possibly glimpsed Sara Murphy and Picasso on the beach at Cap d'Antibes, her salons were not theirs.

However, just as salon culture had a life of its own, so too did the middle-class café and couturier society of Gordon Conway. It was admittedly a consumer culture, a creature of capitalism—materialism not metaphysics, style not substance, movie star dreams that became Macy's realities. Vicarious pleasures at public glamour spots rather than the crabbed culture that Edith Wharton wrote about were all part of the new freedom that Condé Nast and like-minded publishers brought to the fore.

Most studies of "consumption communities" sermonize for some unfathomable reason about *American* materialism. Gordon Conway's activities indicate that as the new glamour became accessible, materialism became ubiquitous in both Europe and the United States. Locked-up aristocratic wealth, as Daniel Boorstin has observed, gave way to a focus on the standard of living in cultures, as we see in this book, on both sides of the Atlantic. This phenomenon is now worldwide. It is necessary dogma for any would-be ruling party in virtually every country in the world. In that sense, Gordon Conway's work was importantly political.

But what of her work? In an age of illustration, Conway produced very high and sophisticated art. Clearly influenced by the Orientalism of the Ballets Russes, the decadence of Beardsley, the elegance of Barbier, Bakst's eroticism, the imagination of the young St. Petersburg refugee Erté, the Spaniard Zamora, the vogue for Japanese prints, and a number of fashion, costume, and stage designers, Gordon Conway partook of a cosmopolitan art world of moder-

nity that has largely escaped the attention of "great artist" art historians and the horde of contemporary postmodern critics. The latter, however, should be greatly interested in Gordon Conway's art, which is not elitist and is full of cultural clues. Disciples of Lacan, Derrida, Jameson, and certainly the great Baudrillard could romp through the carnival of her works, which, of course, have meaning as yet untapped.

The spare linear beauty as well as the stunning color that characterizes Gordon Conway's art is perhaps too obvious to mention. Besides the above-cited influences, Conway clearly mastered the Japanese vision even as she displayed the excesses of Persian, Byzantine, Russian, African, and flapper styles. About the same time that Josephine Baker was mesmerizing Paris audiences and Picasso was reveling in the beauties of Third World art, Gordon Conway began to adopt its motifs—and then exaggerate them. Though she was not an anthropologist or a traveler to exotic lands, she brought "the other" into the world of popular culture fully as much as the jazz musicians who came to give a name to her age. As her amazing "Jazz Lint" drawings indicate, in Gordon Conway's imagination, "life was a cabaret."

PREFACE AND ACKNOWLEDGMENTS

The story of this book is an odyssey that began during the Thanksgiving holidays of 1982 in Washington, D.C., when I met Gordon Conway's cousin, the late Olive Johnson Allen of Fredericksburg, Virginia. Having once established that the families of my husband, H. K. Allen, and her husband, Marshall E. Allen, were not related, the two couples acknowledged our Texas roots and mutual acquaintances.

The conversation turned to Gordon Conway's art and archive from the early part of the century, which I had viewed at a 1980 exhibition entitled "That Red Head Gal" at the Octagon House of the American Institute of Architects Foundation. Because of the popular and critical response to the traveling exhibition in Washington, D.C., Dallas, Chicago, and Los Angeles, Olive Johnson Allen was convinced that the artwork should be available to research students and the public alike. She was in the process of contacting various cultural institutions and art authorities to discuss the placement of the material in a museum or library and asked me to help in locating research centers specializing in the fields of costume design and illustrative art. The next step in the endeavor was an on-site inspection of the private collection, then located in an archival studio at "Pembroke," outside of Orange, Virginia.

Olive Johnson Allen knew that I was commuting between Washington, D.C., and Austin, Texas, to pursue post-MA graduate studies in the field of American Civilization at the University of Texas. Indicating that exclusive research use of the materials—including the soon-to-be-copyrighted drawings—might be possible, she asked if I would consider changing my proposed dissertation topic to a study of the artwork and era of Gordon Conway. My answer on the spot was without hesitation "I will." Research notes quickly evolved into a book manuscript. My encounter with the original artwork and archive had convinced me immediately that the material had great merit and that the story of Gordon Conway should be told to a wider audience. This experience launched what was to become a twelve-year research project and analysis of the commercial art and costume design career and the life and times of Gordon Conway (1894–1956). The odyssey that began so spontaneously continues to this day with the same commitment and enthusiasm.

The research journey has taken me from one state to the next, from this continent to another, from enormous research libraries to tiny movie houses featuring silent films, and to amateur auctions of between-the-world-wars collectibles and down alleys to flea markets full of old magazine pages and film stills. I could not have created this book were it not for scores of people and institutions who encouraged my effort and unselfishly helped me along the way. The long thank-you list that I have been assembling through the years includes:

Dr. Harvey Waldo Allen and Carolyn Allen for their permission to reproduce images from their private collection; for their donation of the Gordon Conway materials to the Harry Ransom Humanities Research Center, University of Texas at Austin (Theatre Arts Collection); for their family's concern about my research and this illustrated biography; and for continuing Olive Johnson Allen and Marshall E. Allen's dedication to the legacy of Gordon Conway.

William H. Goetzmann, the Jack S. Blanton, Sr., Professor of American History at the University of Texas at Austin, former director of the American Civilization Program, and a Pulitzer Prize–winning historian, for his unique vision and insistence on quality. I appreciate Dr. Goetzmann's encouragement since the inception of this book and his evaluation that Gordon Conway was a "brilliant artist." I am grateful for his invaluable intellectual inspiration, ideas and practical advice, editing numerous drafts of the manuscript, including the book in his American Studies Series, and providing the Foreword to this illustrated biography.

Wm. Edmund Barrett for the excellent photographic documentation of over five hundred images, including Gordon Conway's drawings, personal photographs, and archival materials, and for helping with my research.

Walt and Roger Reed, Illustration House, Inc., New York, for the loan of the Jon Whitcomb drawing transparency and the private collection of business letters of Heyworth Campbell, and for inspiring me about American illustration.

Jacques and Marguerite Barzun for their interest in my book from the beginning of my research, for Jacques' helpful letter about his early years at Condé Nast publications, and for Marguerite's identification of Gordon Conway's drawings and graphic reproductions in the Metropolitan Museum of Art.

Alan and Karen Jabbour for Alan's ideas and editorial recommendations and for Karen's support.

Grace Jones for her observations, advice, encouragement, and remarkable fashion leadership.

Stanley Marcus for his intellectual insight, good taste, social conscience, and continuing interest in my research.

The professors, curators, and staffs of the following programs and institutions and the independent scholars and cultural authorities (for the specific departments and collections, see A Note on Sources):

Harry Ransom Humanities Research Center, University of Texas at Austin: Melissa Miller and Charles Bell.

American Studies/Civilization Program, University of Texas at Austin, faculty: William S. Stott, Jeffrey L. Meikle, and former faculty member Suzanne Shelton Buckley.

Department of Theatre and Dance, University of Texas at Austin, faculty: Coleman A. Jennings and Susan Tsu.

Fine Arts Library, University of Texas at Austin: Janine Jacqueline Henri, Art Librarian.

Mary Marcelle Hamer Hull, University of Texas at Arlington Libraries.

David J. Francis, Chief, Motion Picture, Broadcasting and Recorded Sound, Library of Congress.

Patrick Loughney, Head, Moving Image Section, Motion Picture, Broadcasting and Recorded Sound, Library of Congress.

Beverly Brannan, Prints and Photographs Division, Library of Congress.

American Folklife Center in the Library of Congress and Archive of Folk Culture staff Peter Bartis and Gerry Parsons.

Walter Zvonchenko, Music Division, Library of Congress.

American Institute of Architects Foundation, Inc., and Octagon House Museum: Research Library and Audio Visual Department, and those associated with the 1980 exhibition "That Red Head Gal: Fashions and Designs of Gordon Conway, 1916–1936": Jeanne Butler Hodges, Wm. Edmund Barrett, David Schaff, and Tony Wren, as well as Charles Spencer, John Crain, and Edward Maeder.

Michael W. Monroe, former Curator-in-Charge, Renwick Gallery of the National Museum of American Art, Smithsonian Institution.

Nancy Hanks, former Chairman, National Endowment for the Arts.

Alan Fern, Director, National Portrait Gallery.

National Museum of Women in the Arts: Wilhelmina "Billie" Cole Holladay, Founder and Chairman of the Board; Elizabeth Stafford Hutchinson, Board; and staff Rebecca Phillips Abbott, Director, Krystyna Wasserman, and Brett Topping.

Tom Allen and the Washington, D.C., Writers Center.

Janet Anderson, for encouraging words during the early years of this project.

William K. Everson, New York University, Film Studies.

Charles Silver, Supervisor, Film Study Center, Museum of Modern Art.

Harriet G. Warkel, Indianapolis Museum of Art; Sally Yerkovich, Museum of the City of New York; American Film Institute staff, Washington, D.C.; National Cathedral School staff, Washington, D.C.; Audrey S. Gilbert, "The Archives" of Preble County, Ohio; Director, Maidenform Museum/New York; and Ann Townsend, Trust for Museum Exhibitions, Washington, D.C.

Paul Wagner and Nina G. Seavey.

The Condé Nast Publications Inc.: Diana Edkins, Permissions Editor; Cynthia Cathcart, Librarian; and Jeanne Ballot Winham, former secretary to Frank Crowninshield.

Louis A. Rachow, Curator and Librarian, The Walter Hampden–Edwin Booth Theatre Collection and Library at the Players Club, New York.

The Shubert Archive: Maryann Chach, Research Archivist.

Society of Illustrators Museum of American Illustrators: Terry Brown, Fred Taraba, and Jill Bossert, exhibition coordinator in 1985 of "America's Great Women Illustrators: 1850–1950."

The Art Students League of New York: Lawrence Campbell, Archivist.

Fashion Institute of Technology: Mary Direnzo, Reference Assistant.

New York Public Library for the Performing Arts at Lincoln Center, The Billy Rose Theatre Collection staff.

American Studies Association: selected members, especially Alice Sheppard Klak and Michelle Bogart.

Costume Society of America: selected members, especially Elizabeth Ann Coleman, Costume Institute, Houston Museum of Art; Polly Willman, Costume Conservator, National Museum of American History; and Richard Martin, Director, and Harold Koda, Costume Institute, Metropolitan Museum of Art.

Agnes de Mille and Michael Bolloten for detailed letters describing British musical theater in the 1920s and early 1930s.

Authorities on the Interview List in the Selected Bibliography and donors for the color reproductions.

In Great Britain, my appreciation to individual cultural authorities, the staff of numerous divisions in the British Film Institute (BFI), and those granting permission for research and/or reproduction of film stills:

Special gratitude for the remembrances of Gordon Conway by the extraordinary mother-and-daughter pair who generously gave permission to reproduce their images and gave of their time and energy on behalf of this biography: Dorothy Dickson and Lady Dorothy Quayle (Dorothy Hyson).

The invaluable help through the years of:

Eric Braun.

Gary Chapman.

Elizabeth Heasman.

Elizabeth Leese.

Stella Mary Newton.

Martin Marix-Evans.

Christopher Robson.

Valerie Ripley.

Catherine A. Surowiec.

British Film Institute: especially Elaine Burrows and Janet Moat as well as Gillian Hartnoll, Tessa Forbes, Markuu Salmi, and former associate Michelle Snapes Aubert.

A special thank you to the family of Michael Balcon, British film industry pioneer, and his brother, production assistant Chandos Balcon, for their help and generosity: Jonathan Balcon, Jill Balcon Day-Lewis, Rosalind Balcon, and Vicky Balcon Taylor.

Appreciation also to Michael Thornton, Philip Kemp, Anthony Mendleson, Sidney Cole, and John Bly; Elaine Hart of *The Illustrated London News* Picture Library; Savoy Theatre management; Victoria and Albert Museum's Costume Division and Theatre Museum staffs; and staff of Mander and Mitchenson Theatre Collection.

Permissions related to British film research: Jonathan Balcon, for access to the Aileen and Michael Balcon Collection, BFI; Kathy Lendech, Turner Entertainment Co.; and Rank Organisation/Rank Film Distributors Ltd., Managing Director Fred Turner, Contracts Manager Ray Jenkins, and Graham Newman, as well as George J. Helyer, Teresa Ross, and former associate Graham Howell.

In Lausanne, Switzerland, my appreciation to the astute, generous, and dedicated historians of the city, Louis and Miriam Polla, and to the authorities and institutions they introduced to me: Les Archives de la Ville de Lausanne, Marcel Ruegg; Musée Historique de Lausanne; Bibliothèque Cantonale et Universitaire; and the family of Annibale Galdini for their affection and concern for "Villa Claire."

Historic Fredericksburg Foundation, Inc., Board of Directors, especially 1990 members Kitty McKann and William B. Denis.

Joanna Catron, Curator in 1990, "Red, Hot & Southern: The International Fashions and Designs of Gordon Conway, 1916–1936," Belmont, The Gari Melchers Memorial Gallery, Fredericksburg, Virginia.

Micheline Barrere, "Mount Sion," Caroline County, Virginia.

Ron Tyler, Director, Texas State Historical Association and Center for Studies in Texas History.

Douglas E. Barrett, Managing Editor, *The New Handbook of Texas*.

Dallas Public Library, Texas/Dallas History and Archives, Joan L. Dobson.

Baylor University Libraries, Toni Nolen.

Mildred Padon, Layland Museum, Cleburne, Texas.

A Salado contingent: Tyler Fletcher, the late Thelma Fletcher, Elizabeth Silverthorne, and A. C. and Judy Greene.

Temple Public Library, Reference Department, Lupe Macias.

Kenny M. Yauk, Ken's Texas Camera, Temple, Texas.

Friends and colleagues, and even strangers, from all over the United States who have been advocates for this book project: Betty Jane Acker Addington, Evelyn Wemple Allen, Ron Amey, Carol Armbruster, Jasper H. Arnold III, Steven M. L. Aronson, Betty Beale, Randy Bryan Bigham, Gray Boone, Ann Brinkerhoff, Barbara Jester Burris, Bob and Lajuana Carabasi, John Cope, Shirley Leach Courtney, William H. "Deacon" Crane, Kendall Curlee, Jay DuBose, Charles C. Eldredge, Eleni Sakes Epstein, Benjamin Faber, "Didi" Fitzpatrick, Merry A. Foresta,

Andrea Foster, Joe B. Frantz, William Glade, David Gould, Sylvia Grider, Lee Hall, Judith Lynne Hanna, Mary Margaret Holt, Conover Hunt, Nancy Baker Jones, Rue Judd, Margaret Kaplan, Ed Kendrew, Gloria Korngold, Fred Korth, Penne Korth, Eleanor Lambert, Joe Linz, Florence Lowe, Judith McCulloh, Hope Ridings Miller, Michael Mullins, Mernie Myers Northrup, Mary-Stuart Montague Price, Anne-Imelda M. Radice, Paul Reinhardt, Peter Riva, Rosemary Allen Roach, Mary Beth Rogers, Lee "Teeny" Russell, Gary Scott, Margy P. Sharpe, Robert Skinner, Jr., Arnold and Jillian Steiner Sandrock, Ann Sheffield, Fred and Shirley Steiner, Lonn Taylor, St. John and Mary Terrell, Eleanor Tufts, Decherd Turner, Amanda Vaill, Stephen Weil, Frankie Welch, and Vicky Wilson.

Friends and associates who searched files, proofread pages, processed notes, made telephone calls, and wrote letters:

Jacqueline Downs for being there at the very beginning of my research with a thorough knowledge of the Gordon Conway materials and for compiling for Olive Johnson Allen the inventory of the collection and archive, an inventory I have used many times.

Mike and Kim Szydlowski, my stalwart research assistants in Woodberry Forest, Virginia, who, for over a decade, researched every detail and followed through on every request. A special thank you for their resourcefulness, intellect, and good spirit that greatly informed this book.

Other assistants: Barbara Brewer Burton, William Thomas "Tom" and Oscar "Oscie" Coghill, Shelley Cunningham, Marie Henderson, Howard Hooper (Director, Oakland Cemetery, Dallas), Selena Hoyle, Winnie Jenkins, John Kelly, Florence Melford, Juanita Coghill Noel, Pat Roeder, Eleanor Sreb, and Sherrie Thornton.

I am especially grateful to Stanley Marcus, who recognized Gordon Conway's sense of color as a major strength of her artwork, and who inspired other donors to join the Stanley and Linda Marcus Foundation in underwriting the beautiful thirty-two color reproductions in this book: the Neiman Marcus Foundation, the Fashion Industry Council, Charles W. Flynn, Mrs. Eugene McDermott, and Mary Munger Cassidy. Thank you also to Terrell and Evelyn Allen for contributing to the effort.

University of Texas Press current and former staff, whose concern, patience, and expertise have improved this book, especially Joanna Hitchcock, Ali Hossaini, Jr., Zora Molitor, Laura Bost, Louise Saxon, Jack Kyle, Betsy Williams, Tayron Tolley Cutter, Charlotte Harris, Sherry Solomon, Lois Rankin, Nancy Bryan, Keri North, and Heidi Haeuser. A word of gratitude to my sponsoring editor, Frankie Westbrook, who recognized the importance of the art, life, and times of Gordon Conway, and whose vision, inspiration, criticism, and good cheer bolstered my confidence and commitment to the telling of this story. Her admonition from a January 25, 1993, meeting, "State the obvious," hangs over my computer in big, bold letters and continues to instruct me. I close with a special thank you to Madeleine Williams and Carolyn Cates Wylie for their help, accuracy, precision, logic, and reliability, which not only greatly improved the text but made a pleasant experience out of the final stages of this odyssey.

A final word to the reader: I apologize ahead of time for omissions and mistakes I may have made inadvertently and welcome comments and corrections to the text.

Raye Virginia Allen
June 1996

NOTE TO THE READER

Except as otherwise noted, all illustrations are reproductions of works by Gordon Conway now in the Harry Ransom Humanities Research Center, The University of Texas at Austin (HRHRC/UT) Theatre Arts Collection, or a private collection. Most of Conway's drawings were executed in tempera and/or gouache, watercolor, and pen and ink, and often were mixed media accented with pencil, chalk, crayon, and/or metallic media. (Conway very rarely worked in oil.) The author's list of dimensions of these drawings is deposited in the HRHRC/UT with the Comprehensive Bibliography by the author (Com/Bib/RVA).

GORDON CONWAY
Fashioning a New Woman

PART ONE

BIOGRAPHY

THE ARTIST WHO DRAWS BY EAR

On the morning of September 10, 1915, a chic, attractive redhead breezed into the office of Heyworth Campbell, art director of *Vogue* and *Vanity Fair*. The young woman was Gordon Conway; she was twenty years old. She walked with an agility and a briskness that belied the image of women who had endured the posture of deference, discretion, piety, and caution during the decades of the Victorian era. Gordon, with her olive complexion and blue-green eyes, was decked out as usual in the latest Parisian style—even in the midst of World War I—with accessories from Neiman-Marcus, the exclusive department store in Gordon's hometown of Dallas.

Each gesture of Gordon Conway, each entrance was custom-made for the occasion. Tall, svelte, and sophisticated, she bore herself with the confidence and flair of the figures illustrated in the Condé Nast periodicals. In fact, she appeared to be the prototype of the *Vogue* and *Vanity Fair* magazines' special kind of New Woman. As the precursor to the freedom- and fun-loving flapper of the 1920s, this New Woman of the teens declared her individuality, publicly displayed a sense of humor, took liberties with American middle-class social mores, dedicated herself to a career, and cultivated a certain kind of "look."

The term "New Woman" originally had appeared during the feminist efforts of the nineteenth century. Later, during the teens in Greenwich Village, the "New Woman" took on a more political—socially radical—cast. Borrowing elements from these types of New Women, but discreetly avoiding blatant use of the term, the Condé Nast publications recast the concept into their own mold. The publisher, editors, staff, and readers of *Vogue* and *Vanity Fair* had been influenced by the New Woman radical fringe but repackaged the concept for more consumer-oriented and fashion-conscious women and men. In addition to the goal of establishing a lucrative business, the desire to change the look and lifestyle of the American woman drove Condé Nast. He promoted certain feminist issues consistent with his belief that women could better their lot by acquiring buying power. Actually, a similar dictum had been proclaimed as early as 1852 by feminist-pioneer Elizabeth Cady Stanton, when she proclaimed "Go out and buy!" as an act of individuality and independence.[1]

Condé Nast set the stage for the new feminine roles in the culture when he purchased and revitalized *Vogue* in 1909. He proclaimed women could accomplish anything. Nast showcased chic costumes in stylish settings that became an inspiration and guide as well as a seductive temptation for women in search of new looks and new lifestyles. This modern woman of the Nast periodicals took on another dimension in the premier issue of *Vanity Fair* in March 1914. Frank Crowninshield's first editorial listed among the magazine's aims: "For women we intend to do something in a noble and missionary spirit, something which, so far as we can observe, has never been done for them by an American magazine. We mean to make frequent

Pastel portrait by Porter Woodruff of Gordon Conway, Paris, August 16, 1924.

appeals to their intellects. We dare to believe that they are, in their best moments, creatures of some cerebral activity; we even make bold to believe that it is they who are contributing what is most original, stimulating, and highly magnetized to the literature of our day, and we hereby announce ourselves as determined and bigoted feminists." [2]

This New Woman was no less revolutionary in her impact on American culture than the other types of New Women during the first two decades of the

Another Porter Woodruff full-length portrait of Gordon Conway alongside a photograph of her in the identical ensemble, New York City, 1918. These two images reflect Conway's flair and sense of style toward the end of World War I.

century. Such a woman might not demonstrate with the suffragists, but would stand on the sidewalk and cheer during their marches on Fifth Avenue. She might not join Crystal Eastman in sociological research, but would agree with the legislation that resulted. She was not jailed with Emma Goldman, but was aware of Goldman's anarchist protestations. She did not write for *The Masses* like Inez Haynes Irwin Gillmore and Louise Bryant, but she would discuss the issues presented in the publication and follow the lives of these personalities at the revolutionary press. She might not distribute Margaret Sanger's birth-control pamphlets in public, but she would study the information and contribute to Sanger's legal defense fund. Not a political radical, this New Woman considered herself an independent woman and advanced thinker. Except for Prohibition laws, she stood on the law-abiding side of public protest. The "revolution" this New Woman participated in was social and cultural, but a revolution nevertheless.

Because the term "New Woman" has multiple and often contradictory meanings, it needs clarification. Since the beginning of the feminist movement in the mid-nineteenth century, the concept has expanded and become amorphous. It has been applied to many types of women. For example, early observers applied the term to such pioneers and activists as Elizabeth Cady Stanton, Frances Willard, and Susan B. Anthony. The term continues to be used today, as evidenced by the title of *New Woman* for a popular women's magazine.[3] For the purpose of this study, elements shared in common with other types of New Women include accelerated physical, social, mental, and emotional activities for women that led to increased political and legal independence and freedom. Work—outside the home and in the marketplace—provided a new status for women, whether through volunteerism and consumer power or as wage-earners and property owners. Finally, self-confidence, education, intelligence, and self-expression were highly valued characteristics of early 1900s' New Women.

The gradations of meaning often contribute to a

misunderstanding of the concept, especially when linked to the appearance or "look" of a New Woman. In August 1895, an article and illustration in the *New York World* addressed this confusion: "A great deal had been said about the new woman, but nobody, until to-day, has had the opportunity of looking her in the face. . . . [This sketch] is a composite of the new woman. . . . It is faithfully made up of twelve excellent likenesses of the twelve most prominent new women in the world. . . . [it is] a strong face. . . . a stern, unyielding face." The journalist argued that the composite face of the New Woman "indicates character and progress. . . . [and an] 'intellectual-looking person' whom men would probably rather not wed." Pragmatic leaders in the women's movement perceived that the rising power of the media could be appropriated for feminist goals. They judged that the representations of the New Woman would be more persuasive if the characteristics of "charm" and "beauty" were added to the image. According to Martha Banta, a noted authority on female images, by 1900 the "American Girl declare[d] herself truly new. . . . [with] up-to-date poses that portrayed vigor of body and mind. . . . The feminist per se had only an independent mind to display, but the young woman who was physically active appeared to state her bodily and mental freedom through the clothes she wore and the poses she struck. . . . the feminist had to dress her ideas, and her inner convictions in order to let them be expressed . . . by the surface she presented." Thus, the "strong look" of the determined New Woman—who fought for real changes in American society—joined forces with the "Beautiful Charmer," the "Outdoor Girl," and the "fun-loving girls."[4] This combination of qualities—this new female package—quickly gained the approval of the general public and growing consumer market.

At the turn of the century Condé Nast anticipated these cultural, social, and economic shifts that led to his first marketing triumph at *Collier's Weekly,* before he launched his vast publishing empire. In addition to making a profit, he dreamed of creating a special American woman in *Vogue* and *Vanity Fair.* He built his magazine and pattern business around the new trends of promoting beauty and leisure products and services for the New Woman. Basically, his feature articles supported his advertisements, making ordinary women believe they could be extraordinary if they used these products and services. Like most journalistic expression, the Nast publications both followed a trend and directed a trend.

Editor Frank Crowninshield reinforced the dream of Condé Nast by describing the role of image making at the magazines. He stressed that for American women "those happy dreams and illusions of theirs are built up for them by the advertising pages. Such pages spell romance to them. They are magic carpets on which they ride out to love, the secret gardens into which they wander in order to escape the monotony of their workaday world and the banality of their well-meaning husbands." He pointed out that "after a single hour's reading of the advertising pages, 10,000,000 housewives, salesgirls, telephone operators, typists, bookkeepers, and factory workers daily see themselves as *femmes fatales,* as Cleopatra, as Helen of Troy, or even as Ninon de L'Enclos, who, at age seventy-five, was still deriving an ecstasy from her love affairs." Crowninshield added that "romance, to women, is very often only another name for *morale.* The American woman feels that she can be a better wife, a better worker, if she can only believe that glamour is to be her lot. She wants to nourish the illusion that, with the right kind of face cream, or mouth wash, and a little aid from the beauticians, she will be-

Publicity stills for High Treason, *1929. The shocked expression of the older woman reflects the attitude of thousands who disapproved of the New Woman who smoked, used cosmetics, worked at the typewriter, and dressed in non-traditional clothing like the pants and boots worn by the younger woman.*

come a creature whom Dante would have loved and Casanova would have died for. . . . All these things does a woman sigh for. And miraculously enough, all these things can she have—and have them very inexpensively."[5]

This type of New Woman—which Gordon Conway represented in both life and art—attracted a wide range of positive public response along with controversy and protest. Two antithetical points of view, presented through the dialogue of characters in the novels of Zane Grey and Edna Ferber, deserve brief comment. (Interestingly, the talents of the two novelists were celebrated on the pages of *Vanity Fair* during the early part of the century. Both writers were extremely popular, indicating the mixed reception given the New Woman in the United States.)

In his 1921 novel, *The Call of the Canyon,* Western writer Zane Grey portrayed the "young women of modern times" as the ruination of America, and pre-

dicted that if American women as a race "don't change, they're doomed to extinction." He feared that if these women triumphed, "money . . . [would] become God in America." Grey carefully distinguished the once "normal girls," now turned of "materialistic mind," from more radical types that he described as "the new-woman species, the faddist . . . [and] the reformer." He excoriated "the modern feminist unrest [as] speed-mad, excitement-mad, fad-mad, dress-mad, or . . . *un*dress-mad, culture-mad." Grey abhorred the kind of woman who "gadded, danced, dressed, drank, smoked, motored. . . . [and craved] the excitement and glitter of the city." He warned that the "rotten crowd" of females in this "set are idle, luxurious, selfish, pleasure-craving, lazy, useless, work-and-children shirking, absolutely no good."[6]

Zane Grey argued that the "extreme of style in dress. . . . [was] Immoral!" These "decorated" women were "slaves to the prevailing mode. . . . slaves to fashion [with] open-work silk stockings, skirt to [the] knees, gowns without sleeves or bodices." He complained "that style for women's clothes has not changed for the better. In fact, it's worse than two years ago in Paris and later in New York." To reverse this "moral lapse of the day" in dress, Zane Grey chastised his female characters and readers alike: "Where will you women draw the line?" He worried about the influence of these women on the next generation: the "youngsters go to the dark motion-picture halls . . . [that] make vampires of our girls. . . . These young adolescent girls ape . . . [the New Women on the screen] and wear stockings rolled under their knees below their skirts and use a lip stick and paint their faces and darken their eyes and pluck their eyebrows." [7]

The females also suffered from "*knowing too much.*" He warned that "city women [were] standing at street corners distributing booklets on birth control . . . [and] great magazines print no page or picture without its sex appeal." Indeed, Zane Grey believed that these New Women were "the devil's angels." [8] His text reflected much the same bias as many religious and moral-reform campaign tracts of the period. The warnings in Grey's book reinforced legislation introduced in Congress, which, if passed, would have controlled the way this kind of New Woman looked and behaved.

In contrast, Edna Ferber created fictional characters who championed the New Woman in her novels, short stories, and plays. The heroine of her 1915 novel, *Emma McChesney & Co.,* is both a determined businesswoman and an avid consumer of beauty and luxury items, including clothes. The story revolved around the career and life of this self-made woman who began work at eighteen years of age for a nationally known petticoat manufacturer in New York. Though a divorced single mother who supported, trained, and schooled her only child, Emma McChesney progressed from an office worker with skills as a fabric-cutter to a partner in the firm. The book featured all kinds of women, including dour, dumpy, docile, domestic, and traditional women, but primarily focused on New Women like Emma McChesney during the middle of the teens. Other women described by Edna Ferber were affluent, fashionable, and energetic characters, who worked hard as volunteers on behalf of suffrage, war-work, and charities. Still another group was represented by Emma McChesney's future daughter-in-law, who was a clever advertising copy-writer making four thousand dollars a year in New York. Independent, smart, resourceful, slim, and chic, this young woman won applause—and customers—for one of Mrs. McChesney's innovative designs. While she modeled this radical new line, the young new woman struck "a magazine-cover attitude" and won over hundreds of buyers who attended the first American designers style show. This fictional show, interestingly, sponsored by the "Society for the Promotion of American Styles for American Women," corresponded to an actual event in New York in November 1914. [9]

Very soon after World War I began in Europe, *Vogue* sponsored a benefit "Fashion Fete" that showcased the original designs of New York houses, previously unable to compete with the seasonal showings of Parisian haute couture collections. Since freelance modeling was an unknown profession at that time in the United States, models were taken from dressmakers in the city. This landmark fashion event aided the widows and orphans of French soldiers, and was enthusiastically supported by New York's high society. The style show recast the concept of the tableau vivant and set the pattern for consumer and advertising staged events and gala spectacles in the decades to follow. [10]

Edna Ferber's New Women were working women of

all types: "women in offices, women in stores, women in hotels—chambermaids, clerks, buyers, waitresses, actresses in road companies, women demonstrators, occasional traveling saleswomen, women in factories, scrubwomen, stenographers, models—every grade, type and variety of working woman, trained and untrained." The dreams of these working women echoed those of Mrs. McChesney's employees—especially the "Italian, German, Hungarian, [and] Russian . . . machine-girls" in the workroom who aspired to better pay, hours, and conditions, as well as the opportunity to advance in the system.[11]

These fictional young women often copied Emma McChesney's stylish clothes and sophisticated carriage. Ferber noted that with astute budgeting and use of lay-away plans, these workers managed to squeeze enough money from their wages to buy cosmetics, leisure services, and garments in the latest style. Rather than appear a drudge from the Bronx, each young woman looked so smart and stylish that she "might have passed for a millionaire's daughter. . . . They wore their clothes with a *chic* that would make the far-famed Parisian *ouvrière* look dowdy and down at heel in comparison. Upper Fifth Avenue, during the shopping and tea-hour, has been sung, painted, vaunted, boasted. Its furs and millinery, its eyes and figure, its complexion and ankles have flashed out at us from ten thousand magazine covers, have been adjectived in reams of Sunday-supplement stories."[12]

Magazine covers and feature stories described in Ferber's 1915 novel served as a working women's guide to the New Woman look. They were emblematic of periodicals that reflected and shaped Gordon Conway's life and work. For the next two decades, Gordon Conway illustrated female figures for the print media that Ferber's protagonist, Mrs. McChesney, and company would have emulated. They were female proto-

types that Zane Grey declared dangerous to American womanhood. Also for two decades, Gordon dressed actresses who played New Woman roles on the stage and screen—roles requiring costumes that Grey would have labeled salacious and immoral. In spite of Zane Grey and other detractors, however, the New Woman—and the look—prevailed.

A key point in distinguishing this New Woman from other types was her appearance. The packaging was paramount in the process of identification. Pointing out an important shift in the culture during this period, Frederick Lewis Allen—an authority on the 1920s—claimed that "the most conspicuous sign of what was taking place was the immense change in women's dress and appearance."[13] The New Woman was defined by certain looks and gestures: what her face and body looked like; what clothes she wore; what pose she struck; and what roles she played, or aspired to play, in the culture. Such an outlook added a visual and aesthetic dimension to women—real or imagined. No longer bound by restrictions of drab and unimaginative uniforms, she was free to choose her own distinctive attire. Novelists define fictional characters by describing clothes and demeanor. Costume designers likewise delineate stage and screen roles by the art of costuming. Naturally, the New Woman expected to be dressed for the part, to be costumed for her new roles, especially in public. One role was performed in the act of trade—on the stage of the marketplace, on the consumers' platform, where buying and selling evolved into a tightly structured ritual. Now the New Woman was part of a congenial "consumption community." She too became the central figure of bright, tony, and cosmopolitan vignettes featured in the mass media. Insight into this woman, her image, and her newly found public visibility is reinforced by a page of sketches featuring Gordon Conway and several famous women in a spring 1922 issue of *Eve: The Lady's Pictorial.* The caption captured the essence of the New Woman by proclaiming that these female "celebrities . . . believe that 'as you wear—so you are.'" [14]

When Gordon Conway launched her career in September 1915, she shared the professional goals of the youthful female staff at the Condé Nast publications. A few months before Gordon's first assignment, her friend Dorothy Rothschild Parker began her literary career at *Vogue,* and soon proceeded to *Vanity Fair,* where she felt more comfortable. The preceding summer had been full of talk about professional careers for women, especially at one East Coast spot where Dorothy, future husband Eddie Parker, Thorne Smith, Yale beaus, and Gordon and her mother vacationed. The two young women had become friends years before at the resorts near Branford, Connecticut, where Gordon and her mother, Tommie Johnson Conway, had visited regularly since August 1911. Like Gordon, Dorothy possessed a fashionable flair and chic look. This look was both extolled by *Vogue* and its advertisers and lampooned by the *Vanity Fair* editorial staff, who welcomed social satirists like Dorothy Parker. Unlike Gordon, who never questioned it, Dorothy remained ambivalent in her private life about this female image à la mode. Other colleagues shared as well an ambivalence toward this kind of appearance and lifestyle while they earned a living in popular print and film media. Nevertheless, Dorothy adopted "the look" early on, just like most young women on the Condé Nast staff who were training as professional writers, editors, advertising specialists, public relations trainees, models, photographers, illustrators, and designers.

Not only did Gordon look like the figures of the New Woman that appeared in the *Vogue* and *Vanity Fair* photographs and illustrations, but her drawings were replete with female images resembling the magazine artwork. A mimic by nature, she drew like an actress playing different roles with a brush. As spontaneous as a performer in a game of charades, she could present many styles and artistic genres on paper, sketching them wherever she happened to be—at such unlikely spots as picnic grounds or hotel suites. Such a talent long had amused family and friends in letters and cards. In a period when illustration was all the rage, friends wondered why she did not pursue illustration as a career. In 1915 Gordon announced with blithe assurance her intention to become an artist. Indeed, she became an artist in spite of herself. A career begun almost as a lark would become a source of stress and ambivalence as she struggled to balance her personal and professional lives.

Gordon had sketched intermittently for years, but it had never been a serious ambition. Before World War I, at school in Dallas, at the National Cathedral School in Washington, D.C., and at Villa Claire in Lausanne, she had taken the usual art lessons, along with instruction in piano, ballet, and French—the education expected of a young woman of breeding and culture in the early part of the century. Certain family members and friends predicted this Dallas debutante would become a concert pianist or a professional dancer. Not until the first three months of 1914—during a series of art lessons in Rome—was she encouraged to think of herself as having a special talent for drawing.

A few months later that year, Gordon's schooling and meanderings across Europe with her mother and Dallas friends was brought to an end by the outbreak of World War I. However, it was six weeks after the August 1914 declaration of war before Gordon and her mother could sail home. In New York, she took up her life among the artistic and moneyed members of Man-

Self-caricature as Gordon Conway's signature on a Christmas card, 1920–1921.

hattan's café society, and resumed her usual rounds of theater openings, movie matinees, shopping sprees, house parties, costume balls, midnight soirées, and travels to East Coast haunts. It was an incident at a social occasion in the summer of 1915 that changed the course of Gordon's life—indeed, it would never be the same again. At a dinner party at a resort in Indian Neck (near Branford, Connecticut) Gordon was provided with the nudge she needed to launch a professional career in art. Mystery writer Rufus Gilmore was so impressed with the sketches she made on a menu card that he insisted on mailing them to his friend Heyworth Campbell, who was not only a distinguished illustrator and commercial art authority but also the art director of *Vogue* and *Vanity Fair.* Gilmore praised the young woman's talent and assured Campbell that Mrs. Conway had ample financial means to provide her daughter with the best of schooling, since Gordon "has had little . . . instruction so far."[15]

Heyworth Campbell responded on August 17, 1915, that "this artist unquestionably has ability. . . . these sketches suggest lots of personality." He offered to advise Gordon but hoped that she would "retain this distinctive style that should in a very little while be applicable to the general magazines and to advertisers illustrations."[16] During their first meeting Campbell urged Gordon to forget about embarking on a long, formal course in a traditional art school whose academic rules might spoil her unique style. To colleagues in the New York world of the print and advertising media, he declared that "Gordon has talent, temperament, imagination, and originality." He extolled her individual style, and repeated that "about all any art school could do for her now is to flatten that all out and make her do things like the rest of the students."[17] Except for occasional classes at the Art Students League and sessions with critics, Gordon's untutored hand and her refusal to use models became trademarks of her career. *Vanity Fair* soon labeled Gordon as the artist "who draws by ear!"[18]

Leaping from anonymity onto the pages of *Vogue* and *Vanity Fair,* Gordon Conway was one day a social butterfly, and the next a professional illustrator and designer. All of a sudden, there she was on the pages and stages of the most noted entertainment media in New York. It all seemed so effortless, a fortuity that two decades later may have amazed the artist as she found herself struggling to cope with career burnout and bad health.

From that auspicious meeting with Heyworth Campbell in September 1915, Gordon Conway launched a successful career in commercial graphic art. Her art opens a window onto the era at the same time that it acts as a mirror of the artist herself. Between the two world wars, in New York, London, and Paris, Gordon's drawings celebrated the independent and glamorous New Woman. Her art translated the life of the beau monde into indelible images for the print, stage, and screen media, which then made that world seem available to most women. Gordon's professional career, from 1915 to her untimely retirement in 1937, lasted a mere twenty-two years, not quite one-third of her lifespan of sixty-two years. Compared to eight decades of work by Erté (Romain de Tirtoff), who lived to be ninety-seven, or the forty-eight-year career of Eric (Carl Oscar August Erickson), perhaps the most famous of the Condé Nast illustrators, the output of Gordon Conway's brief two decades of creation is astonishing.

The career years of Gordon Conway differ dramatically from her early life and from her years of eclipse. Her achievements and contributions can best be understood by dividing her life into three periods of roughly twenty years each.

From Dallas Dance Recitals to Tango Teas in Rome: 1894–1915

The early years found Gordon a devoted daughter and young arbiter of taste in the social and cultural worlds of Dallas, Washington, D.C., and New York, as well as during European travels with her mother, Tommie, which included schooling at Villa Claire in Lausanne, Switzerland, and in Rome prior to World War I. Following the death of her father in 1906, she began the regular habit of keeping a diary. Gordon Conway did not apply her intelligence in the various schools she sporadically attended, but she collected a vast array of friends whom she would succeed in keeping for a lifetime. During this period the family was quite well off financially. Leading a peripatetic life, she joined her mother in a strenuous and hectic schedule of travels, weekly theater and movie attendance, and parties. Her devotion to her mother began when Conway was a young child and remained a central feature of her life.

An Artist à la Mode: 1915–1937

The professional career of Gordon Conway is best viewed in two stages: the New York period from 1915 to 1921, and the European period from 1921 to 1936. The New York period highlights her success as an illustrator, caricaturist, and silhouette and poster artist for magazines, newspapers, books, advertisements, and other forms of print media from handbills to billboards. In 1916 she began costume, set, and graphic design work for the newly respectable cabaret and nightclub entertainment field. Her stage commissions expanded in 1917 to include the legitimate theater with a focus on the burgeoning Broadway musical comedy. Gordon's European career developed after her December 1920 marriage to Blake Ozias and the couple's subsequent move to London and Paris in February 1921. Tommie Conway soon joined the pair while Ozias worked in assorted business ventures on the Continent. Gordon maintained studios in both capitals until her divorce in 1927, when she and her mother settled in London. Conway clients were drawn from the European publishing and entertainment industries as well as from the growing American community on the Continent. This period of her work is characterized by a more polished, sophisticated, and streamlined style. She continued working in most of the genres of illustration and design that had brought her acclaim in New York, adding film costume design in 1927. Between 1931 and 1934, costume design and wardrobe management for the British film industry

IMAGE TWO
New Body

1. *Costume design for Dorothy Dickson,* Peggy-Ann, *London, 1927, that evidences Gordon Conway's skill at portraying movement.*

2. *Tear sheet of "Her Latest Dance Frock?,"* The Tatler, *October 27, 1926. Gordon Conway's New Women bare more skin and become more daring.*

3. *Costume design*, Pins and Needles, *"Hat scene," 1921–1922. This lively young woman sports a plunging neckline, shows her knees under a fitted bloomer skirt, and prances in high boots on the top of a bandbox.*

4. *Poster of Dorothy Dickson in* Patricia, *1924. The svelte and graceful actress dances with the shadows of New Women like herself.*

5. *Drawing for* The Tatler, *August 6, 1930. This New Woman lounges on public beaches and is dressed to undress for the new fad of sunbathing.*

IMAGE THREE
New Energy

6. Presentation drawing, ca. 1924. This redhead celebrates the Jazz Age as though every night were New Year's Eve.

7. *Presentation drawing or magazine proposal in the "Jazz Lint series," ca. 1924–1928, repeats the Jazz Age motif of revelry and abandon.*

8. *Poster, program cover, and sheet music cover,* Wonder Bar, *London, 1930, delineate Jazz Age motifs.*

9. Proposal for set design,
Wonder Bar, *London, 1930.*

*10. Costume designs for "In the
Caucasus" scene,* New Princes' Frivolities, *London, 1924. The mixed-
race dance team contorts and twists
in brief, colorful costumes.*

IMAGE FOUR
Night Owl

11. *Cover for program, menu, and promotional graphics,* Midnight Follies, *Club Daunou, Paris, 1924. This New Woman serenades the midnight moon.*

12. *Presentation drawing, Paris, 1924. This young woman begins her nocturnal outings long after the stars come out.*

13. *Cover for* Eve, *September 12, 1928. This woman cele-brates at a costume ball to the wee hours of the morning.*

14. *Cover for* Eve, *January 9, 1929. As the sun comes up, this night owl smokes one last cigarette in an Art Moderne chair—a replica of a chair that belonged to Gordon Conway.*

15. Drawing for The Tatler, *November 13, 1929. This New Woman retires in style around 4:00 A.M. to a bedroom much like Gordon Conway's own, with a Conway-designed bed as pictured in the drawing.*

16. Drawing for The Tatler, *October 22, 1930. In a draped boudoir, this New Woman, attired in satin and fur, awaits a late-night visitor.*

dominated her career. She was named "Dress De-signer" in 1932 by the Gaumont-British Picture Cor-poration that also included Gainsborough studios. Gordon has the distinction of serving as the head of the first autonomous wardrobe department in British film history and as one of the few female film-production executives in the world at that time.

Debilitated by the demands and long arduous hours of the motion picture industry, combined with the frenetic social schedule inherited from the first period of her life, she suffered severe exhaustion and a heart attack. By late 1933 bad health forced her to withdraw from the film executive position as she completed her thirty-ninth year of life. She limited her work to musical revue design and magazine and advertising illustration between 1934 and early 1936, when she and her mother sailed for New York. Between 1936 and 1937 Gordon made a half-hearted attempt to rebuild her career in New York, but declining health and the acquisition through her father's estate of an ancestral home drew her to Tidewater Virginia. At the beginning of her professional life, she worked mainly for the challenge and excitement, but after financial losses sustained during the Depression, her fees were the major source of income for her and her mother.

Fulfillment of a Father's Dream: 1937–1956

Gordon retired to a quiet country life where her creative talents were channeled into the restoration, decoration, and landscaping of the eighteenth-century Conway family estate of Mount Sion in Caroline County, Virginia. She made a modest living by managing the 427 acres efficiently. As a pioneer historic preservationist, she mounted a campaign that saved Mount Sion and neighboring historic buildings from the encroachment of Camp A. P. Hill prior to World War II. She lived her days outdoors, from feeding chickens to planning the color contrasts in her flower gardens. She abandoned diary-keeping in 1942 just after the nation entered World War II. Throughout this nineteen-year period she entertained frequently and kept in touch with a vast network of friends all over the world. The last years brought illness to both Gordon and her mother. Gordon's death was caused by a spate of painful malignancies that drained away the last three years of her life.

Tommie Johnson Conway outlived her daughter by four years, but she was afflicted with high blood pressure long before Gordon's death. From 1956 to 1960, Tommie Conway was cared for by her great niece, Olive Johnson Allen, a native of Paris, Texas, then living in Lubbock. Tommie Conway died from a series of strokes on May 28, 1960, and was buried in Dallas next to her husband and Gordon, whose body had been moved to Oakland Cemetery.

Not only did Gordon's cousin Olive Allen care for Mrs. Conway, but she and husband Marshall Allen lovingly looked after Mount Sion. In the dank basement she discovered massive trunks holding Gordon's entire collection of drawings and a complete record of the artist's career, as well as a lifetime of memorabilia and the personal wardrobes of both women. She retrieved from the mass of mildewed material around 1,200 original drawings and an archive of graphic reproductions, film stills, press books, letters, diaries, personal photographs, and scrapbooks. For many years, she oversaw the preservation of this archive until her son Dr. Harvey W. Allen and his wife Carolyn assumed the responsibility. In 1992 Dr. and Mrs. Allen

02328 4943
FORT WORTH PUBLIC LIBRARY

generously donated most of the collection and archive to the Harry Ransom Humanities Research Center (Theatre Arts Collection) at the University of Texas at Austin.

During her twenty-two-year professional career, Gordon Conway created around five thousand finished drawings, including illustrations for at least twenty-six publications and thirty-three advertising clients. She costumed forty-seven films. Whether filling an assignment for one or for scores of drawings, she designed graphics and costumes for at least 119 stage productions for both theater and cabaret. The appendix to this study ("Catalogue Raisonné: A Reference Guide to the Artwork and Career of Gordon Conway") provides evidence of her prolific output—averaging six finished drawings a week. That translated into hundreds of stunning and original ensembles, which informed and entertained thousands of women and men between the world wars.

The discovery of this material restored the lost accomplishments of a celebrated woman artist and renowned New Woman of the 1920s and 1930s. Gor-don Conway's drawings reintroduce lively images of freedom-loving flappers and glamorous urban sophisticates that entertain as much today as in that era long ago. The oeuvre preserves Gordon Conway's cutting-edge innovations in commercial art and costuming, and reveals the shifts in the fields of illustration and design of the time. It recalls as well the period's exciting social changes in the United States and Western Europe. In preserving this record, Gordon Conway seemed to know what she was about. She explained to friends during her Virginia years that she had saved the art and the record of her career for future generations interested in illustration, graphic design, costume for stage and screen, fashion and leisure advertisement, and the world of the early twentieth century. Capturing the essence of the discovery, the curator of a 1990 Gordon Conway exhibition in Fredericksburg, Virginia, observed that the artist "put her extensive archives in order and safekeeping at Mount Sion, where her colorful record of a time gone by remained, as if sealed in a time capsule, until the public was ready for her dazzling re-appearance." [19]

CHAPTER ONE

DECEMBER'S CHILDREN

Origins and Precedence

Gordon Conway was born and reared in Texas as the only child of wealthy and socially prominent parents. She was the ninth generation of Conways descending from Edwin Conway, the son of Edwin Connaway of Worcestershire, England. She would be the last of that line. Edwin Conway emigrated to colonial America, where he received thousands of acres through a crown land grant issued about 1681 in the area along the fall line of the major tidal rivers of Virginia. His son Francis was born in 1697 in Richmond County and served as one of the earliest justices of nearby Caroline County, established in 1727. Francis Conway became a tobacco planter and warehouse owner on the Rappahannock River, as well as a grower of corn, flax, wheat, oats, and barley. Around 1722, he initiated a Conway tradition when he built a sturdy cypress clapboard Colonial manor house surrounded by black walnut, oak, holly, and dogwood trees amid his crop-filled and timber-lined acres. Eight miles south of Fredericksburg, founded in 1728, the estate of Mount Sion became a mecca to the Conways, the only family to inhabit the house until Gordon's death on June 9, 1956. To Gordon and her father, Mount Sion was a revered spot that became a haven to the artist when she retired in 1937.[1]

Francis Conway married Rebecca Catlett in 1718. Among their seven children was Eleanor Rose Conway, called Nelly, whose marriage to Colonel James Madison, Sr., took place in the parlor of Mount Sion before the handcarved mantelpiece on September 13, 1749. Their first son, James Madison—the Father of the Constitution and the fourth President of the United States—was born on March 16, 1751, while Nelly Conway Madison was on a maternity visit to her mother's home.[2]

Gordon's father, John Catlett Conway, was born to Catlett and Selina Frances Fitzhugh Conway at Mount Sion on December 30, 1854. As a boy he witnessed the death and devastation of the two battles of Fredericksburg during the Civil War. Within two hundred yards of the Conway home, Robert E. Lee's troops established their second line of defense during the final battle. In 1883 Conway moved to Texas, where he established a lucrative lumber business during the building explosion in the Lone Star State. When Gordon was barely eleven years old, her father died of pneumonia at age fifty-two on January 12, 1906, at St. Paul's Sanitarium in Dallas. The dean of St. Matthew's Episcopal Cathedral, where the Conways were communicants, officiated at the funeral service in the family home. Conway was buried in the Oakland Cemetery family plot, which would become the final resting place in 1960 for both Gordon and her mother.

Gordon's mother, Tommie Johnson Conway, also was descended from patriarchs of American leadership, the Samuel Adams family. The Johnsons first settled near Braintree, Massachusetts, in 1632, before moving to the western part of Virginia, where in 1844

Joseph Johnson became the first governor elected by a vote of the people. This Johnson line then moved from Osceola, Missouri, to Texas, where Tommie Johnson was born in Whitesboro on December 29, 1870, as Effie Mae Johnson, a name chosen by her mother, Mary Jane Utterbach Johnson. Her father, Thomas Benton Johnson, detested the name, as would his daughter, and ordered it never to be spoken. He ordained that the baby girl be called "Tom." The name was spelled alternately throughout her life as "Tommye" or "Tommie." Friends recall that the command rarely was breached for fear of retribution from Thomas Johnson's spirit and the ire of "Miss Tommie." When her father died about 1880, Tommie and her mother moved to Paris, Texas, and on to Cleburne, where she would meet and marry John Catlett Conway and give birth to Gordon.

Children of December

Gordon Conway's parents married on December 21, 1891, at the Episcopal Church of the Holy Comforter, which was the site of their first meeting. Olive Johnson Allen recalled that "one Sunday morning in the spring, Uncle Jack admired Aunt Tom in the church choir as she began her solo." No sooner had the soprano notes been sounded than Jack Conway turned to his business partner and whispered, "I want to meet that girl."[3] Conway added that he would marry the pretty woman within the year. With the prediction realized, the couple honeymooned in high style in the French Quarter of New Orleans over the Christmas and New Year's holiday. And they celebrated their own December birthdays, with hers on the twenty-ninth and his on the thirtieth. Three years later, on

December 18, 1894, Gordon arrived. With Gordon's birthday, her parents' birthdays, and their wedding anniversary all in December, the month had an almost mythical significance for the three. As though it had been ordained, twenty-six years later, Gordon was married on December 11, 1920, to Blake Ozias, who had been born on December 2, 1881, in Lewisburg, Ohio. Throughout Gordon's life, December stood both as a time of decision and a time of celebration.

The county seat of Johnson County, Cleburne was blessed with an abundance of timber that gave rise to John Conway's prosperous lumberyard chain. Gordon Conway's father first established a business called Conway-Craig, to which he added a lumber enterprise named Conway and Leeper—a model for branches with resident partners in Canton, Denton, Greenville, Mansfield, Midlothian, and Waxahachie. Conway also owned a wholesale lumber center in Dallas and the Quarles Lumber Company in Fort Worth. In Cle-

John C. Conway and Tommie Johnson Conway, Cleburne, Texas, ca. 1894.

Gordon Conway and Tommie Johnson Conway, Cleburne, Texas, ca. 1898. Conway's reverence for her mother was a constant theme throughout her lifetime.

burne, from 1891 to 1899 Conway served as a city alderman and was elected mayor from 1899 to 1901.

On February 24, 1895, Gordon was christened in the Episcopal church of her parents by the Bishop of the Northern Texas Diocese. The church members recently had built a beautiful "countryside Gothic" frame structure down the street from the Conway home. The name "Gordon" had been selected by John C. Conway for a male or female offspring long before her birth in honor of an ancestral line in Virginia. Gordon found the name quite useful during her professional years as a woman artist, and in New Woman fashion continued to use her maiden name after marriage.

Gordon lived her first five years in an 1892 Queen Anne–style frame house accented with exotic fish-

scale shingles. As a little girl Gordon was treated like an adult, often attending her parents' social functions, like the Lotus Club balls with ladies garbed in elaborate gowns à la mode and men attired in full evening dress. With dance orchestras brought in from various cities, the club members' "dance cards were filled for Cotillions, waltzes, two steps and Shottisches." One such ball in August 1897 entertained leaders of "the smart set" on the Conways' long side porch gracefully edged by a hand-carved balustrade. The surprise party flowed from the porch to the parlor and into the octagonal-shaped dining room, inspiring local press praise: "dreamy music, scintillating electric lights, together with the magnificent costumes of the ladies. . . . [produced] one of the most brilliant affairs of the season." An artifact from such a soirée, found by a sub-

Conway home in Cleburne, Texas, ca. 1898.

sequent owner, reveals Gordon's parents' tastes and expenses: a graceful French wine bottle with a label custom-designed with the Conway name and marked with the price of ten dollars.[4]

The Conways supported the Episcopal church, including its Preaching Missions, and Tommie Conway worked with the church women in providing an exhibition of the "finest and most expensive collection of art and curios ever displayed in Cleburne." The church women entertained the community with concerts, pantomimes, and tableaux in the local opera house. One costumed musicale presented to a packed audience brought "frequent bursts of applause . . . and enthusiastic encores" when Tommie Conway presented an array of songs. News coverage often reported "little Miss Conway" as a special guest. The church boasted among its members all the mayors of Cleburne between 1894 and 1904, including John C. Conway. His terms were highlighted by such civic improvements as a public sewage system, a public free school, and city parks. He engineered a controversial plan to prevent overcrowding on market days by carving out space near the courthouse square where six hundred wagons could be parked with horses left in full harness.[5] His community service, especially to outdoor spaces, was always a source of pride for Gordon.

Before the end of his 1900–1901 term, John C. Conway established residence in Dallas and settled the family into a boarding house near the corner of Ross and Harwood, where he built a showplace for his two stars in a neighborhood known as "Silk Stocking Row" and the "Fifth Avenue" of Dallas. While he supervised the construction, Tommie Conway planned the decor for the home that they moved into in 1902. The mansion joined others built between 1880 and 1900—all homes, save one, vanished since the early 1930s from the Dallas cityscape. A historian recaptured the now forgotten grandeur of Ross Avenue as "an almost uninterrupted, two-mile Gilded Age promenade lined with French chateaus, Gothic mansions, Italianate palazzi, large spreading shade trees, and manicured gardens, all animated by the hushed clatter of liveried coachmen."[6] Gordon would be an attentive witness to it all.

While John C. Conway expanded his lumber business and invested in real estate in the rapidly developing city, Dallas society embraced the family. According to Gordon's former classmates, the Conways joined with the Colonel J. T. Trezevant family as the leaders of the "so-called 400 in Dallas, members of the beau monde."[7] Opening a window onto this era in Dallas was a publication by the same name that painstakingly chronicled the exhaustive doings of Dallas society. The wife of the editor of the *Dallas Morning News,* Mrs. Hugh Nugent Fitzgerald, published *Beau Monde,* a weekly that claimed to be "the Prayer Book of the Texas' Smart Set, and is read by all men and women who think!" Filled with upscale advertisements appealing to a developing consumer class, the journal was dedicated to "Music, Art, Literature, and Current Gossip and Society." Another weekly journal competing for the same elite readership, the *Dallas Society News,* made similar claims: a "chronicle with new ideas. . . . [on] pleasures and frivolities [of] The Theatre, Humor, Concerts, Opera, Architecture, Photography, Sport, [and] Cartoons."[8]

Founded around 1895, *Beau Monde* mirrored Belle Epoque Dallas. In flowery and exuberantly high-toned language, the editor reported not only on Dallas high society but also on the international social set and arts world. With equal assurance, editors of these periodicals could report Gordon and Eva Trezevant's departure in 1912 for the Lausanne finishing school of Villa Claire and blithely announce another departure of an Enrico Caruso or a George M. Cohan. Of course, the Dallas doings often were conventionally middle-class, reflecting attitudes, values, and behavior in other parts of the Lone Star State. But strains of urban café society like the Conway salon were creeping in and influencing segments of Dallas society. While much of the social, religious, domestic, and familial environment in Dallas was mainstream, the rearing of Gordon and her friends was not. In counterpoint, Protestant evangelists preached to enormous revival meetings against the sins of dancing, playing cards, alcohol, smoking, gambling, petting, going to the movies, women's makeup, and the extravagance of luxuries. In the Texas Bible Belt around the turn of the century, Episcopalians like the Conways often were thought to be dangerously swayed by "Romishness," ritual, and riches, full of big-city and foreign influences. Gordon's upbringing was judged dangerously avant-garde and frightfully cosmopolitan, except within this small circle in Dallas.

The exception rested with the group of sophisti-

cates around Gordon and her mother, a circle more tightly knit after John Conway's death in 1906. At the time, Tommie Conway was a young, lively, beautiful, and fashionable thirty-six years old. In 1907 she expanded her role as an arbiter of taste in the city that boasted to be the wealthiest and most populous in the state and home to more first-class retail stores than any other city in Texas. That same year of 1907 celebrated the opening of the swank Neiman-Marcus department store that rose to institutional status, promulgating fashion à la mode and the art of the good life.[9]

When Tommie Conway received a postcard addressed simply "The Merry Widow, Dallas, Texas," the post office delivery was immediate; there could be no doubt that it was intended for the glamorous Mrs. Conway at her residence at 315 Ross Avenue.[10] A childhood friend of Gordon's remembered that "Mrs. Conway had sparkly eyes and personality sticking out all over her. Exciting, she was!" The friend recalled that after John Conway died, the house was full of beaus, the most notable of whom were the prominent and debonair attorney Tom L. Camp and the Right Reverend Harry Tunis Moore, Dean of St. Matthew's Cathedral and future Bishop of the Diocese of North Texas. The friend remembered Mrs. Conway "all decked out in a bright red evening dress, and she wore red tights to match, and of course, red shoes, beautiful red slippers . . . She had the prettiest feet and legs anybody ever had . . . Yes, tiny feet." After many years, the friend remained amazed by the profusion of sixty to seventy pairs of shoes that she had witnessed in Mrs. Conway's closet at Mount Sion, as well as by the dozens in the Ross Avenue dressing-room that was also "full of shoes—all colors. As young girls, Gordon and I loved to peek at all those shoes."[11]

The Conway mansion was sold in July 1920, six

months before Gordon's wedding, and demolished in the early 1930s to make room for a tire store. The site is now the grounds of the Dallas Museum of Art.

Dallas Abroad

During her early years in Dallas, Gordon adored paintings and drawings. She enjoyed the arts of theater, symphony music, opera, ballet, modern dance, sculpture, architecture, poetry, and literature. She also loved movies, though film in that day was suspect entertainment and championed as an art only by a few visionaries. In the display of clothes, the decorative arts, and handcrafted possessions, Gordon advocated an understated style—an extension of her parents' cultivated tastes, though Tommie Conway's private party and fashion theatrics might appear to the contrary. Gordon possessed innate good taste and a sense of quality craftsmanship encouraged by John Conway and his fortune. Department stores and artisans in New York and St. Louis and burgeoning Dallas retail establishments like Neiman-Marcus informed this understated consumer taste long before the oil boom gave birth to the glaring extravagances of the Texas new-rich.

As to education, Gordon's attendance was sporadic at the private schools of Cowart Hall and St. Mary's College Preparatory School, sponsored by St. Matthew's Cathedral. Private lessons in the arts filled an irregular schedule during her Dallas residence and later when she attended the National Cathedral School in Washington, D.C. Lessons in piano, elocution, dance, and drawing, as well as French, Italian, and Spanish, were sprinkled between concerts at the Opera House in Dallas, recitals at St. Mary's, plays at the Majestic, and exhibitions at the local museum. A childhood friend, Margaret Page Elliott, recalled that "Gordon was as graceful as a fawn. She was not a beauty like her mother in a classic way, but she could just toss an old shawl around her shoulders and look as glamorous as all get-out. If the rest of us tried that, we'd look like rough-dried laundry hanging on a clothesline." She remembered the dance recitals with the fancy costumes, like brisk white ruffled costumes on Gordon and Eva Trezevant as they floated across the stage at Mrs. John Priestly Hart's Terpsichore Hall.[12]

Most certainly, Gordon loved to dance, from ballet to round dancing—but ballroom dancing became her passion. A lifelong friend who made her debut with Gordon reminisced about those nights on Dallas dance floors, when the boys couldn't wait to dance with Gordon. Her chum averred that one such partner, J. C. Tennison, led Gordon in a one-step around many a stage, where the couple's agility and sense of rhythm thrilled spectators and everyone said they could have been exhibition dancers like Vernon and Irene Castle. The former debutante also remembered the evening of November 6, 1914, at the Columbian Country Club, when eleven friends came out at the thirty-first Idlewild Ball. Leading the grand march on the arm of Leven Jester, Gordon stepped out carrying American Beauty roses and wore a yellow satin and lace fur-trimmed ankle-length gown, a contrast to the traditional white floor-length attire. Gordon had purchased this couture gown in the latest Parisian style on her way home from Europe after World War I had begun in August. That this debutante celebration was held three months into the war did not dampen the spirit of the revelers, for they were convinced like thousands of citizens that the military skirmish in Europe would be over by Christmas. Indeed, the fighting would be over by Gordon's birthday in December. In Dallas—as in other American towns—citizens felt that the United States should not be involved in foreigners' squabbles. The Idlewild couples whirled past five hun-

Caricature of Gordon Conway by Sylvio Duarte, Rome or Lausanne, 1914.

dred guests and around the statues, foliage, and fountains shimmering with artificial moonlight and the glow from cherry-blossom chandeliers.[13] The chateau-garden theme of the evening displayed a romantic and popularized view of French culture, while the citizens of France fought for their lives and traditions back home. The death and destruction all seemed so far away.

Gordon and Tommie Conway were two among the thousands of middle- and upper-class Americans in Europe prior to World War I. A sizable number of Texans traveled and lived on the Continent, a pattern that continued after the war. During the Conway women's two lengthy sojourns in Europe before and after the Great War, they hosted many a floating salon of Dallasites. These informal delegations were in frequent touch with Gordon and Tom and located the pair wherever they were. The two women seemed to be unofficial ambassadors to the world of the beau monde, providing a cultural clearing house and social mecca for the Dallas crowd. Years later, one Dallas acquaintance—who traveled with his parents and friends to the 1925 Paris exhibition introducing the style now called Art Deco—recalled that even as a young boy he was awestruck by Mrs. Conway's classic beauty and arresting presence, as well as by the glamour and sophistication of Gordon and Tom's lifestyle.

For some Europeans who followed the international press, the two women symbolized the American dream for aspiring middle-class Continentals determined to combine centuries of history, culture, good taste, and pleasure with American affluence and material conveniences. The mother and daughter were part of a small but definite movement of American expatriates who had inherited the pioneering spirit of their ancestors, who crossed the ocean to this virgin land in search of freedom from European polit-ical, religious, and social oppression. This group now felt, rightly or wrongly, that their personal freedoms were being squelched by protestations from the pulpit and a reformer mindset prevalent in the Progressive Era that led to such social, economic, and political idiocies as Prohibition. They yearned to escape these sanctimonious moral judgments and self-righteous attitudes that were attacked frequently in such publications as *The Smart Set* magazine. This contingent represented a new kind of reverse pilgrim, returning across the Atlantic on luxury liners to discover Continental pleasures and tasteful living ridiculed in rural and religious America. In Europe, the once profligate and extravagant lifestyle of the aristocracy—thought by the Puritans, often correctly, to be corrupt and depraved—was being democratized, reined in, and adapted by an aspiring middle class. Also, the life of the Continental beau monde that attracted these ex-patriates was possible for less money than a mundane and unimaginative life at home. The mass-print press, movie industry, and commerce were quick to rein-force and shape the aspirations of this segment of so-ciety, while shrewdly linking the desires to an upscale version of the American dream.

Following Gordon's sporadic schooling in Washing-ton, D.C., Gordon and Tommie Conway were joined by other Dallas passengers when they sailed early in August 1912 on the *Kronprinzessin Cecilie,* the newest of the famous foursome of German luxury ships built during the heyday of Atlantic travel and immigration at the turn of the century. Their Continental stay from August 1912 to September 1914 provided Gor-don with partial schooling at Villa Claire in Lau-sanne. This stay exposed Gordon to a variety of artis-tic expression, from the Old Masters to the shocking new Modernists. While New York's cultural world was

reeling from the Armory Show of February 1913, Gor-don witnessed the new rebels firsthand, albeit with a skeptical eye. Though she would later be influenced by such art innovations, at the age of eighteen, Gor-don reacted to a Cubist and Futurist exhibition in Munich in August 1913 with the diary entry "Ridicu-lous!" Gordon's aversion to Modernism modified dur-ing the weeks ahead, when a visit to a Futurist gallery in Rome produced no expression of derision in her diary.[14] Throughout her career she collected *pochoirs,* prints, and lithographs by and books about such mod-ern art pioneers as Aubrey Beardsley and Egon Shiele, as well as artists who designed costumes and sets for Diaghilev and the Ballets Russes, like Georges Lepape, Erté, Georges Barbier, and Léon Bakst.

In early 1914, Gordon's cluster of academic portrai-ture lessons with "Sr. Paveda" in Rome was eclipsed by the meanderings of a carefree spring and summer. She and her mother, with their chums from Dallas,

Gordon Conway (second from left) and friends at the races in Rome, 1913.

Untitled watercolor from Conway's art lessons in Rome, 1914, sharply contrasts to her style and delineation of women one year later.

the frantic scramble home. Gordon worried on August 3 that the group "decided to stay in Lausanne for we can't get out of Switzerland."[15] On August 4 German troops crossed the Belgian border for an attack on Liège. Great Britain declared war on Germany, and World War I began.

On that same August 4, Gordon sequestered herself in the Conway suite at the Hotel Royal on the Avenue d'Ouchy, during a heavy day-long rainstorm. Concerned about her many beaus from all over the world, she confided to the diary pages: "I am very sad on account of the war. . . . for Germany is fighting and Renee [sic] is there. . . . there is a revolution in Paris and Anibal is there. Silvio is stuck in France." She remembered the well-mannered and disciplined young men in smartly tailored uniforms at their Rome barracks just a few months before. Gordon sensed that the war would consume her favorite Italian beaus— Prince Fabrizio Colonna and his brothers, and Prince Francesco Ruspoli and his brother Constantine. She lamented that "Italy is thinking of fighting, and Fabrizio and Ruspoli and the others will fight."[16] She had met most of this "bounty of beaus" through the renowned boys' academy l'Institut Auckenthaler, called "La Villa," which coordinated activities with her girls' school of Villa Claire. She counted as friends young men from France, Portugal, Spain, England, Austria, Germany, and Italy, as well as from Greece and Egypt, and from as far away as Argentina and Brazil. She was clearly concerned about all of them.

With an ambivalent statement uncharacteristic of Gordon Conway, she confronted herself on paper: "If I could go as a nurse, to which country shall I go?"[17] (Written between the lines was the tormenting puzzle of why there had to be fighting among these people— people she had observed and liked, and who so easily could live side by side in everyday harmony.) The

crisscrossed Europe on yet another holiday spree. With the Austrian Archduke Franz Ferdinand's murder in Sarajevo on June 28, the group encountered hesitant assurances of safety from their Swiss hotel concierge and the consulate. To the Dallasites, however, such international assassinations seemed to come and go. The travelers judged the bombastic nationalistic rhetoric and spotty fighting would be short lived, and, in any case, Americans would not join the fray. For a while the Dallasites proceeded with their plans. The summer was filled with even more tango teas, tennis and high tea, walks on the quai and in the Bois, and shopping at Parisian couturiers. In truth, however, it was an uneasy July.

By early August, the group received warnings that the Kaiser's aggression should be judged serious, but they proceeded on an Alpine outing regardless. After only two days in St. Moritz, where Gordon loved meandering through the Maloja Pass and visiting the famous Cresta Bob Run, the Conways' entourage learned that a war was beginning and took emergency departure on the last train to Zurich. Back in Lausanne, Gordon and her mother rallied with friends for

next day, Gordon's international cast of boyfriends in Lausanne began to disperse for enlistment in the military units of their native countries. She reported in her diary that a group drove to nearby Morges to witness "the rest of the Swiss army leave for the war. . . . There were 10,000 men and it was most impressive. They said a prayer and took the oath." [18]

As beaus scattered to fight on different sides, Gordon found herself sitting up all the way on a jammed train for a nineteen-hour fitful rail ride from Geneva to Paris. That fateful August 23 turned out to be a chilling game of musical chairs, a frightening contest of will and wit. She and her mother jumped from railroad cars to platforms, leapt from track to track, scrambled over discarded luggage, pushed through hordes of people, stumbled up and down scores of steps, took turns standing up, and fell into seats. Amid the chaos and delays, they grieved over lifeless bodies. They halted for notes from wounded soldiers, scribbled addresses for family messages, took photographs of the destruction, and passed out kerchiefs, cigarettes, film, and fruit. Gordon gasped on arrival that "Paris is changed! There's no one on the streets and lights are not burning." [19] Not surprisingly, like other Parisian businesses, couturiers and artisans feared their investments would be lost; they hurriedly notified hotel staff about special sale prices to tourists before the war escalated. Though anxious about their escape and as though in a surreal dream, Gordon and Tom purchased sample ensembles and stood for fittings of the latest gowns à la mode at Worth, Patou, and Poiret. The ritual of shopping somehow eased the anxiety building up during their four days fraught with governmental red-tape transactions that delayed their train trip to the coast to catch the Channel ferry to England.

In the early evening of September 16, 1914, Gordon and Tom sailed on the RMS *Olympic* from Liverpool to New York. The crowded ship encountered very rough weather the first four days and was one of the roughest crossings Gordon would experience in eight voyages across the Atlantic. She explained that they "had to go so far north to get out of the way of two German men of war that were after us." Adding to the excitement, a fire broke out, and the ship "ran into an English cruiser in the night." As the ocean liner rocked in a heavy sea, her diary entry that they "took the *Titanic* route home!" typified the ironic twist to Gordon's sense of humor. She envisioned the weird paradox of escaping from World War I on this sister ship to the *Titanic,* only to die in a repeat of the 1912 sea tragedy. [20]

Though the ship was running dark with all portholes painted black, levity crept into the daily routine. Gordon gathered with other returning Americans for chatty luncheons served on the upper deck and relished the games of shipboard golf with young men on the stern. The late night watches on the deck scanning the inky horizon until dawn were shared with brand new friends. At the beginning of the cruise Gordon and an array of dance partners slid across the pitching floor. Late in the crossing when the sea suddenly turned to glass, this teenage American girl took the weather change as a good omen and danced the night away. Gordon was like most carefree returning Yankees who thought the war only a brief hiatus. With a kind of hedonistic abandonment, the ritual of ballroom dancing helped dispel lingering anxieties. Gordon and her fellow passengers may have shuddered when recalling a report two years before that the *Titanic*'s dance orchestra continued to play for the doomed passengers as the ocean liner slipped into a grave of freezing water, but the *Olympic*'s cruise officers and guests still poured onto the dance floor. On that autumn evening in 1914, Gordon's mood lightened as the orchestra struck up the strains of a dance tune. She never missed a step.

On embarkation, Gordon reflected how sad it was "to leave dear old Europe." She cheered, "but we'll return." [21] Earlier that year in Rome she had written in her diary that she made a point of tossing coins over her shoulder into the Trevi Fountain, as did other hopeful tourists. Of course, Gordon would be back.

Gordon and Tom

When the *Olympic* docked in the harbor of New York at 8:30 A.M. on September 23, 1914, a bright and hopeful future welcomed Gordon Conway. The United States was far from the battlefront, the economy looked good, a score of intimates was eager to renew old friendships, and the horizon sparkled with opportunities for talented young women. The arrival day not only mirrored behavior of the past, but forecast the lifestyle of Gordon Conway in the two decades to come. The day's packed schedule was typical of Gordon's crowded hours and a social calendar that would compete with a demanding career exactly one year later. However, the social activities also provided the context for most of Conway's business connections. Because Gordon's personality and principles cannot be separated from filial duties, this milieu will serve as a backdrop for a cameo profile of the mother and daughter team.

On that September day, Gordon and Tommie Conway bade farewell to a host of new acquaintances, retrieved their trunks from Customs at noon, and hugged friends waiting at the gangplank. They went to the Waldorf, then to the Marie Antoinette for a bite to eat, then for a spin in "the machine" of Dallas friends also disembarking in New York. The bunch

dropped by the Ritz for a cocktail, then rushed back to the hotel to change. Dressing for the evening was de rigueur. Dinner on the Ritz Roof Garden flowed into dancing on the Amsterdam Roof until 2:30 A.M., when the night-owl crew proceeded to Jack's for bacon and eggs. Gordon and Tom arrived home at four in the morning. Their habits varied little until the calm of Gordon's retirement to Mount Sion in 1937.

Gordon had been reared as a New Woman by Tommie Conway, herself a New Woman, in the company of two dozen or so of the same. Gordon and Tom fanned out into intersecting clusters of New Women and men from the East Coast, Western European capitals, and Dallas. This group acknowledged the duo as avant-garde social and cultural leaders. The striking Conways appeared more like college roommates than like mother and daughter. Gordon's former school chums thought the women resembled sisters, though one observer added that Gordon was a mother to her mother. A friend wrote that no two people could have been closer. Another agreed that the two were inseparable and that she never remembered seeing a more "devoted pair than Gordon and her mother." [22] Gordon's diaries testified to the close relationship and to a near-adoration of her mother. Forming the habit early in Gordon's life, the two women operated as a tight-knit team, an alliance that intensified after John Conway died in 1906 when Gordon was barely eleven years old. A cousin explained that "the responsibility Gordon felt for 'Aunt Tom'. . . [stemmed] from her father's request that she take care of her mother." [23] It was not a case, however, of a weak and withdrawn person who needed the help of a strong and aggressive personality. Both women were determined individuals, self-directed, strong-willed, intelligent, engaging, and attractive. In the complex and complicated relationship, Gordon was the partner who was endlessly

accommodating. Her personal identity was inextrica-
bly intertwined with that of Tommie Conway, whose
life in turn was defined by Gordon's talent, resourcefulness, and eventual fame.

Gordon's Dallas schoolmates admitted that "her
mother was at her elbow all the time." [24] They relayed
rumors that circulated after Gordon's wedding in December 1920 that Tommie Conway walked her daughter down the aisle like a father who gives the bride
away. On reaching the altar, however, she did not retreat the customary few steps, but stepped forward as
would a maid of honor, only inches from the bride.
Building on the same theme, British stage buddies recalled a popular tune, "And Her Mother Came Too,"
that could have been written about the pair. These
English friends reported that this song involved London stage colleagues of Gordon's. Dion Titheradge
and Ivor Novello wrote the music inspired by the legendary inseparability between star Elsie Janis and her
mother. In dedication to his own ever present mother,
Jack Buchanan changed the "her" to "his" in what became for the popular actor a lifelong signature piece
that first was introduced in a scene entitled "Too Much
Mother" in a 1921 André Charlot revue in London.[25]

Family and friends confirmed the opinions of early
observers that there had been "too much mother" all
of Gordon's life. It was a time, however, when maternal supervision and chaperon companionship were
expected and prevalent well into an offspring's adult-
hood. For example, ambitious stage mothers of movie
stars like Ginger Rogers and entertainers like Gypsy
Rose Lee were generally accepted as normal, along
with zealous mothers of such famous heroes as General Douglas MacArthur. Certainly, this controlling
element in their relationship played a crucial role in
Gordon's life—especially in her seven-year marriage
and the stress that accompanied her twenty-two-year
commercial art career. To maintain the close tie, Tom-

mie Conway even sacrificed a second marriage to longtime beau Tom Camp—a man Gordon adored and
considered a surrogate father. For years he argued that
Gordon deserved a life of her own. A showdown occurred after Gordon's wedding in December 1920.
When Tommie Conway refused yet another proposal
of marriage and moved in with the newlyweds, Tom
Camp married another Dallas woman. Some recalled
Tommie being surprised and quite upset that she had
misjudged Camp's willingness to continue the court-
ship as before.

Remembrances and anecdotes from a network of
informants shed light on the formidable female pair,
as does international press coverage of the women
who were at home anywhere and mixed with assorted
persons from poor painters to powerful presidents.
Among dozens of reports, four stories stand out.
Friends pointed out the period of Gordon's haphazard
schooling at the National Cathedral School when
extracurricular activities were arranged by Tommie
Conway, then in residence in Washington, D.C., during semester courses. Gordon and her dormitory mates
joined Conway friends, like Mary Borah, the wife of
Senator William Borah, on outings around the capital,
such as a cruise on the Potomac aboard the *Sequoia,* the
presidential yacht of chief-executive William Howard
Taft. Having become friends with the Taft family at
East Coast resorts, Gordon was fond of dancing with
son Charlie Taft, whom she affectionately called "the
kid of the White House." [26] Another typical tale was a
1913 press report in Rome that credited "an American
girl" with inaugurating a new series of intricate steps
at tango teas held in the Excelsior Hotel.[27] As Tommie Conway told it, she and friends cheered from
nearby tables and spectators swarmed to the corridors,
as Gordon and a variety of Italian boyfriends demonstrated the thirty-eight tango steps she had perfected.
Friends also verified 1914 news reports that just be-

fore the two sailed on the *Olympic,* Dallas sojourners helplessly witnessed the Scotland Yard arrest of Gordon and Tom while they rearranged trunks in their London hotel room during the wee hours of the morning. Amid gales of Conway laughter, the espionage charges of signaling to a German U-boat were quickly dropped, and the misadventure was happily lampooned by the press. Finally, friends remembered news coverage that surfaced in the late 1920s on doings that involved a wreck on the Riviera. With their usual aplomb, the women rescued their driver, who had panicked when the car lurched past a curve on the Grande Corniche Road and loomed over a precipice. The chauffeur remarked that the pair never lost their poise, pulled him from the wreckage, soothed his nerves, gathered their belongings, and hailed a ride to Cannes in time to arrive promptly at some social affair.

As background to the career of Gordon Conway, the informal interchange of visual information between mother and daughter influenced the designer's modus operandi. A friend recalled that "Mrs. Conway was very artistic. Gordon evidently got her talent from her mother."[28] Indeed, lifelong habits of consulting each other on every detail—be it the length of curls across a forehead, floral designs in needlepoint, or white asparagus for dinner—were a form of communication between Gordon and Tom that carried over into the designer's professional life. In the creative process, each woman supported and energized the other. Tommie Conway usually accompanied Gordon on her peripatetic design commissions. When they were required to be apart, Gordon called, cabled, and wrote at every turn of fortune—when the costumes at a dress parade went well and when they did not, when colors matched and when they did not. Tommie Conway could not have been more interested in her daughter's chores: every button, bow, and bangle deserved concern and every seam and seam-

stress received comment. The two women cared passionately about color, form, line, composition, and texture, no matter what the venue. As with the visual treats that the Conway pair conjured for their private pleasure, together, they conferred on Gordon's consciously constructed visual creations for the public eye on page, stage, and screen. These creations reflected the artistic and social changes that occurred between the world wars, each as surely progressive as initiatives, referenda, recalls, and voting rights for women.

Gordon's metamorphosis into a working woman did not change the duo's treatment of money. In Cleburne, for example, at the end of the previous century, Tommie Conway had insisted that a portion of John Conway's property—the family home, for example—be put in her name. Gordon's records reveal detailed accounts, ranging from the repayment of a twenty-five-cent bus fare borrowed from Heyworth Campbell, to bridge losses of $2.40, to a loan repayment of one thousand francs to Bobbie Appleton for racing bets. Accountings of Monte Carlo winnings and the settlement of a loan from her mother for a Steinway piano were included, along with Gordon's commercial art fees and dealings related to the ownership of securities and property.[29] Gordon acted as the financial guardian and family bookkeeper. She inherited both her father's business acumen and her mother's determination to be a woman of property and independent means. Acquaintances marveled at Gordon and Tom's business sense, even after they suffered losses during the Depression. Through the years, the Conway women sought and received plenty of advice from men about financial matters, but in the final analysis, the two women made their own decisions. One observer speculated that the male-sounding names "Gordon" and "Tom" helped the women when negotiating financial affairs—at least on paper. Similar to pseudonyms appropriated by many

New Women professionals of the era, the male names may have imbued their demeanor with confidence and imparted a subtle authority among business colleagues.

Tommie Conway reinforced certain attributes in her daughter, like dependability. Gordon was reliable, almost to a fault. She rarely was late, placing promptness high on her list of essential virtues. If an associate was late, Gordon knew it would cause havoc in her daily schedule. Likewise, she felt that it was bad manners to spoil other people's days by making them wait. Though Gordon was quite flexible in personal things, she was a perfectionist in her work, always reaching for the highest standards. Her mother had sensed long before that Gordon was good at a great many things and that she easily won recognition. Though Gordon had an understated presence that belied a driving ambition, friends agreed that she seemed marked for fame and destined for achievement. Gordon's ambivalence toward thrusting herself into the public spotlight was counterbalanced by Tommie Conway, who always stood in the wings, urging her on.

As to their set of values, Gordon and Tom shared the overarching principles of the Ten Commandments. Both believed in faith and hope. Gordon, especially, possessed a devout faith in God as represented by the Episcopal and Anglican communion. As to minor vices, Gordon was guilty of chain-smoking, considered at the time as immoral by some. Bawdy jokes within a certain range of taste were welcomed. Though indiscretions may have occurred now and then, neither woman was known to be loose with sexual favors. Flirtations certainly abounded, but were acceptable only to a point. The behavior reflected a pattern typical of many a New Woman's intimate life, in which there was lots of talk about sexual freedom but limited activity. Drinking cocktails, of course, was part of the Conway world but more from a standpoint of their group's social habits than their own. The women schooled themselves in the right wines and mixes to serve. The ritual of drinking, combined with the ambiance in which cocktails were served, was the appealing factor. Some associates confided that Gordon's two daily cocktails escalated through the years, especially during bouts with cancer when she overindulged to fight the pain. Tommie Conway, however, flatly disapproved of her daughter imbibing. Curiously, Tommie, who could out-party the whole Conway cast of characters, rarely took a drink herself. She had been known to strike a pose in the middle of the dining room table and sip champagne from her tiny slipper, but such a drinking jest was rare. Intoxication was a way of losing control, and Tommie Conway knew it.

People were important to both Gordon and Tom. Keeping in touch with friends was a value that took much of the Conways' time. Since trust was a major bond between the two, their loyalty to each other spilled over into fierce loyalties to friends. The Conway pair were not self-righteous, welcoming all sorts of human combinations from legally wedded couples to same-sex couplings among their male friends. They were less accepting of men with mistresses, not so much because of moral judgment as from skepticism about a woman who would settle for this second-rate status. In addition, the Conway world was an adult world, which included people with a mutual reverence for pets. Gordon and Tom looked on their animals as if they were offspring, especially their cats, some of which were elevated to near sacred status. Indeed, children played a peripheral role in the women's lives, with the exception of Gordon's many godchildren.

In the Conway pas de deux, similarities between the two surfaced, like an American belief in possibilities. Gordon especially possessed a ferocious optimism about the world. A subtle competition existed among their set as to staying well-informed on international affairs and political issues, as well as keeping up-to-date on what was "in" and "out" in the social and cultural arena. They debated many topics, but the talk rarely translated into active advocacy, so the two women's actions were basically apolitical.

Entertainment was a big part of living for the pair, from the arts to card games. Gordon, in particular, enjoyed sports. One reason for her appreciation for athletics, resort life, the beach, and gardening was her love of the outdoors. The effect of climatic conditions on her life cannot be overstated. She craved the sun and warm weather, which gave her energy and a feeling of well-being. In addition, both women cherished tradition and heritage, and depended on the role of civilization to set standards; yet they honored the idea of progress—a careful progress, that is. Design played an enormous part in the Conways' thoughts and actions, for both believed that life was better if things looked good and functioned properly, from hairstyles and skirts to pillows, drawer pulls, and buildings. This affinity for the possibilities inherent in design was reinforced by a belief in the American Dream, which to them comprised the goods and services in the advertisements that Gordon was commissioned to illustrate.

For all their avowals about liking the same things, Gordon and Tom were quite different people underneath. Their modi operandi in applying the values they shared was vastly dissimilar. Though both were charming and engaging, energetic and enthusiastic, each embodied these qualities in her own way. One observer viewed the difference as analogous to law-enforcement officers dressed in the same uniform while playing the roles of "good cop" and "bad cop." Though Gordon was loathe to admit the strain, the contentious side of Tommie's personality took a toll

on her through the years. Yet she staunchly defended and praised her mother, always making excuses and amends. On occasion, Gordon even severed relationships due to Tom's ire. A childhood friend of Gordon's once angered Mrs. Conway when she innocently described Tommie's youth as "growing up in her mother's boarding house in Cleburne." The friend considered the story as complimentary: that she came from such humble beginnings was remarkable given Mrs. Conway's chic and sophisticated ways. The friend soon received a "loving letter from Gordon" expressing regret that the two had best not see each other again.[30] Mrs. Conway's wrath also resulted in the firing of dependable housekeepers. These dismissals caused the designer countless delays and inconveniences because she then performed the household duties herself, while searching for replacements willing to work under such conditions. Indeed, whereas Gordon was congenial and cheerful, her mother could turn irritable and petulant. Whereas Gordon was patient and generous, her mother could be demanding and selfish. While Gordon was amiable and conciliatory, her mother could become arbitrary and stubborn. While Gordon was understated, her mother was intense and high-strung. However, except for a few skirmishes with friends and wrangling with household help, the two women actually worked as a productive team. Like the double side of the lead character in Bertolt Brecht's *The Good Woman of Setzuan,* each played a vital role in the other's life.

Gordon and Tom certainly looked nothing alike, a happenstance commented on frequently by those who knew them best. Throughout her lifetime Gordon never felt she measured up to her mother's good looks and sense of presence. She could wow passersby in self-designed gowns, attract raves from couturiers, and inspire press coverage as the ultimate in chic, but

Pastel portrait of Tommie Johnson Conway by Porter Woodruff, Paris, 1922.

she never felt equal to her mother's style. From an early age images of women influenced Gordon, like her Valentine present from Tommie Conway in 1907. The gift book, *A Dream of Fair Women,* featured illustrations by one of Gordon's and Tom's favorite artists, Harrison Fisher. His images portrayed an ideal of beauty possessed by Tommie, a feminine ideal of classical, curvaceous, and lyrical beauty with a small bone structure that Gordon knew she lacked. At the turn of the century, the popularity of the Fisher images was in sharp contrast to Gordon's tall, svelte, streamlined, and elongated look. During her youth she snipped out her face from a mass of snapshots in the family scrapbooks. The surgery on the albums did not cease until the female image represented by her own face and figure came in style with the New Woman of *Vogue* and *Vanity Fair* and the silhouette to follow of the flapper in the 1920s.

The Harrison Fisher representations, beloved by the Conway women as well as by thousands of other turn-of-the-century readers, have been labeled the "Beautiful Charmer." Fisher's images competed for public popularity with a variety of images like the famous "Gibson Girl" by Charles Dana Gibson, alternately called the "American Girl" and the "Outdoors Girl." The images also vied for attention with other early twentieth-century images like Howard Chandler Christy's "Debutante," "Western Girl," and Christy's "The American Girl." This unprecedented cacophony of contrasting female images included J. Alden Weir's "New England Woman" intellectual, Lou Rogers's "Suffragist," Harry W. McVickar's "The Evolution of Woman," A. E. Foringer's "Red Cross Nurse," and later, John Held's "Flappers."[31] Of course, a major

contender in the visual contest was the "New Woman" image of the Condé Nast publications—images that Gordon Conway both resembled and portrayed.

This explosion of female images issued from the technological and social changes brought on by the mass-media phenomenon early in the century. This cultural revolution was underway when Gordon and Tom stood on the deck of the *Olympic* as the ocean liner slipped into its berth in the harbor of New York on that September morning in 1914. Inspired and challenged by the fray, the nineteen-year-old Gordon Conway welcomed the new opportunities open in the fields of print, stage, and film media. She played a major role in shaping and reflecting image making in the United States and Western Europe. Cheering Gordon on, Tommie Conway was, as always, standing at her daughter's side.

CHAPTER TWO

THE SOUL OF VERSATILITY

Dear Garden

During the fall of 1915, Gordon was properly initiated into the Condé Nast publishing world by Heyworth Campbell. Campbell, essential to Gordon's career, was a pioneer in the development of commercial art. He did much to legitimize the new profession during the early modern period. His main strengths were a thorough knowledge of the burgeoning field of commercial graphic design, insight into creating a public image, contact with a network of top people in the print media, and the drive to make use of these assets. Campbell served as Nast's first art director (1909–1927), and later worked for other publications, including Nast rival *Harper's Bazaar* (spelled *Bazar* in the early years). A popular and respected leader in the new profession, he was passionate about the role of commercial art in modern society. An indefatigable advocate, Campbell argued that the commercial artist had an obligation to educate the mass public. He wanted people to know that aesthetic standards and quality art were involved. He worked tirelessly, often at his own expense or for a nominal fee, making speeches and giving lessons to an astonishing number of art and business organizations across the nation, such as the American Institute of Graphic Arts, the Advertising Club of New York, the Art Directors Club of New York, and the New York School of Applied Design for Women.[1] For the new field to impact society, he preached the efficacy of

working in groups, which was especially important for freelance artists like Gordon. Though Gordon would follow much of Campbell's advice, she avoided this practice that had advanced many male careers. Her lack of formal participation in the network of professional associations was a major reason that Gordon's reputation as an artist slipped from acclaim to anonymity after her retirement. Unlike many other artists, she never encouraged a support system that would perpetuate her design legacy.

Heyworth Campbell included Gordon in the inner circle of the clockwork operation at *Vogue* and the jovial menagerie at *Vanity Fair.* The two offices sported a fraternal air and swank trimmings, thanks to the decorating talents of Clarisse Coudert Nast—the chic Mrs. Condé Nast herself, who banished all trace of office furniture austerity. Contrasting sharply with other "usually dingy" editorial surroundings, the Nast operation established a long record of stylish decor. Jacques Barzun remembered the publishing company in the 1920s when, as an undergraduate at Columbia College, he was asked to contribute several pieces to *Vanity Fair,* then located in the Graybar Building on Lexington. He recalled that the office was "furnished in dazzling art deco style, unlike almost any earlier magazine editorial premises."[2]

In such a stunning setting Gordon felt right at home. The atmosphere also proved amusing. An accomplished magician, *Vanity Fair* editor Frank

Crowninshield entertained with magic tricks, displayed photographs of the Denishawn dancers with his staff's names scratched over the captions, and telegraphed outrageous messages to friends under unlikely signatures. Editors Dorothy Parker and Robert Benchley tacked quirky advertisements that were clipped from mortuary trade journals to the walls. Heyworth Campbell offered his own size "thimbles" full of gin as special treats to staff and freelance contributors alike, a habit that continued during Prohibition. Tucked between the jokes and jest, though, was the work of a serious and creative staff.

Each Friday Heyworth Campbell hosted an open house for a large assemblage of aspiring illustrators and designers loaded with portfolios for him to review. The competition was keen, according to Eduardo Benito, the French artist and magazine cover illustrator whose New York commissions commanded as much as one thousand dollars per drawing. During the teens Condé Nast imported Continental talent to augment the covers by his American team of George Wolf Plank, Helen Dryden, Claire Avery, Frank X. Leyendecker, and E. M. A. Steinmetz. The European artists, whom the Nast staff called "Beau Brummells" and "Knights of the Bracelet," included Benito, Georges Lepape, Georges Barbier, Paul Iribe, Charles Martin, André Marty, and Pierre Brissaud.[3] Nast's competition also vied for artists famous for their colorful covers. *Harper's Bazaar,* for instance, negotiated contracts over the years with Erté, beginning in 1916, for his stunning cover drawings. Gordon Conway held her own in this company.

The congenial atmosphere at the Nast office was the backdrop for a deep rapport that developed between Gordon Conway and Heyworth Campbell, who also became a friend of Gordon's mother. Recalling Campbell's winning way with people, Frank Crownin-

shield's first secretary found him "quite charming and very attractive."[4] Within weeks Campbell became Gordon's mentor, adviser, and close friend. "Dear Garden," he began letters of advice.[5] She returned the banter by labeling him a "Douglas Fairbanks double."[6] When the three met for cocktails, Tommie Conway was christened "Mrs. McChesney," a name inspired by the title role of a hit play that season.[7] Tommie looked and acted like Emma McChesney, the quintessential New Woman whom the Nast publications vowed to inform, instruct, entertain, and, to a certain extent, create. Tommie Conway was as much an aspirant to the ranks of New Womanhood as her daughter, if not more so.

A survey of three years of Campbell's advice and affectionate chastisements provides insight into Gordon's professional development: "If you are going to make a substantial success and real money . . . you will have to get more character in your work and develop a more professional quality." Though he discouraged her from taking a formal art school course, he urged her to master "the elementary stages. . . . [and give] more careful attention to the mere mechanical business of rendering." Over the months he praised Gordon's originality, promptness, and productivity, but cautioned: "It is not merely a matter of turning out these drawings by the yard. . . . Experience and practice is not all that is necessary; you must make your preliminary drawings more careful. . . . Not because your figures are incorrect in proportion or detail, but to eliminate the suggestion of effort that so materially detracts from the charm of your finished drawings."[8] Gordon soon credited Campbell with the inspiration that made her figures appear to slide effortlessly from her fingers onto the page.

Providing a custom-made education, Heyworth Campbell acted as a professor, with the urbane landscape of Condé Nast's magazines as the campus and his office as the classroom. Campbell and the staff at the two Condé Nast magazines were busily creating a public personality for the young discovery by tagging Gordon "the artist who draws by ear"—the persona of an unschooled artist that she would appropriate throughout her career. Yet Campbell knew she needed help with the technical aspects of editorial and advertising illustration and design. He recommended a few "Life and Antique" classes at the Art Students League and directed her to such private tutors as Margaret Bull and Arthur Finley. Campbell wrote that "Miss Lucile Lloyd, a mural painter, is taking a few pupils at the Van Dyke Studios." Urging his protégée to use his name when phoning for an appointment, Campbell explained that "she does not attempt to teach so called commercial, fashion or poster art but can I believe give one the fundamental art training that is really an essential in the successful development of any of these branches of the graphic arts."[9]

Campbell's mention of commercial, fashion, and poster art as branches of the graphic arts is important, for it sets the cultural stage for Gordon's career. During the early twentieth century, with the rise of mass printing methods and the fields of advertising and public relations, commercial graphic art developed its own cadre of artists different from the high-culture art salons of the past. Many "fine" artists took commercial orders in an effort to scrape by financially but rarely dignified the work by considering it a worthwhile job. Artists like Man Ray admitted to using earnings from fashion photography to subsidize experimental studio art. Whether a rebel Modernist painter, a representational studio artist, or a high-powered connoisseur, most maintained an attitude of disdain toward commercial art. In an Evelyn Waugh novel about the period, the narrator, a British artist working in

Paris during the 1920s, protests that the art students ignore the Louvre and "quite simply want to earn their living doing advertisements for *Vogue* and decorating night clubs."[10]

Over the centuries artists had worked for pay, but they usually were sponsored by the church, the state, wealthy families, or royalty. Many of these clients believed art to be a high calling, like religion or philosophy. Indeed, most elevated artistic expression to the status of "fine art." With the industrial revolution and rise of democratic movements, a wider range of sponsorship developed. The patrons who had sponsored individual artists and their salons were replaced by a combination of middle-class customers, institutions, and, perhaps most important, businesses that were more commercially driven than the previous patrons. These new commercial clients often were accused of having a shallow appreciation of art. In reaction, cultural enclaves elevated the fine artist to a more exalted status. The artist was "no longer a craftsman, no longer a servant, he is now a priest," according to aestheticians like Friedrich W. J. von Schelling and Friedrich von Schiller and nineteenth-century poets like Samuel Taylor Coleridge, Percy Bysshe Shelley, and John Keats.[11] In the tradition of Romanticism, the concepts of "art for art's sake" (*l'art pour l'art*) and "the artist as deity" were not to be tarnished by commercial transactions with clients.

Of the fine arts, architecture or architectural design was the only profession in which the importance of the relationship between the artist and the client was acknowledged and valued. This relationship closely resembled the collaboration between commercial artist and client. In both cases, artist and client frequently joined forces and formed informal partnerships that contributed to many modern design movements. Within the visual arts establishment, drawing was essential. Yet the profession of illustrator, though respectable, lingered in the shadows like a stepchild. Also, graphic art, long a respected component of the fine arts, became suspect when commissioned by clients who sold things and made a profit. The medium itself was not at issue, only the motive behind the commission and the money that the job represented. To fine art elitists, the profession of commercial art raised the issue of the origin of ideas and inspiration. The problem for fine artists was that commercial artists did not insist on their own ideas, nor did they claim that their work resulted from a divine vision. The ideas and inspiration for the commercial artist often originated in the client's pocketbook.

Though many high-culture authorities looked askance at the materialism and crassness of commercial art practitioners, certain art movements of the late nineteenth and early twentieth centuries honored the democratic potential of the graphic arts for a mass audience. Many gave these forms of expression equal billing with easel painting and sculpture. Both the British and American Arts and Crafts movements set the stage for elevating the applied arts to the rank of the fine arts, though their disdain for the machine and for industrial mass production often appeared inconsistent with this support of the applied arts. Movements that began during Gordon's youth and those soon to be born lent new support to the applied arts, including commercial graphic art. Joining forces with science, technology, and democratic social theory at the turn of the century, the major initiatives in design and illustrative art achieved an astonishing influence that continues to this day.

The study of the Modern Movement in design and illustrative art is loosely united today under the broad umbrella of art history. Modern design, however, should be considered separately from Modernism in the fine arts. The history of design is more closely aligned with that of architecture and engineering. During Gordon Conway's early years in America and abroad, she witnessed revolutionary changes in modern design that deserve mention. (Further exploration of design history can be found in Part Two.) A kaleidoscope of movements produced an unprecedented interchange of new shapes, forms, textures, colors, ideas, and inspiration that not only influenced Conway's career but changed the way the world looked at itself. Among such influences were Belgian and other Continental Art Nouveau initiatives, the organic forms of Spain's Antoni Gaudi, the Orientalism craze, and the innovations in the British Isles through *The Studio* publication and the artwork of Aubrey Beardsley and Scottish designer Charles Rennie Mackintosh. Part of the whirlwind in design issued from the Russian writings and theories of *Mir Isskustva* ("The World of Art"), theories that evolved into the design initiatives of Diaghilev and the Ballets Russes. There were design efforts from Sweden and other Scandinavian countries, such as the Svenska Slöjdföreningen, as well as the Vienna Sezession and the Dutch de Stijl. The efforts in Germany produced the Jugendstil, the Deutscher Werkbund, the Bauhaus school, and ultimately the International style. Other parts of the revolution included movements like French Art Moderne, the Italian Futurists, and the American "Form Follows Function" aesthetic, evolving from the organic design theories of Louis Sullivan and Frank Lloyd Wright, as well as from the later Streamline style and Industrial Modern. Strands from these movements intersected with major artistic and technological initiatives highlighted in the 1925 Exposition Internationale des Arts Décoratifs et Industriels Modernes, which became the inspiration for the popularized term "Art Deco." This landmark event of twentieth-century design took place during the time Gordon Conway lived and worked in Paris.

In spite of monumental design accomplishments, the individual commercial artist still faced an uphill battle for acceptance within the fine arts establishment. Top fees and public enthusiasm, though, eased the discomfort over whether or not the work was defined as high art. Complications existed too within the field itself, with commercial artists and clients alike. During Conway's era, much of the work was considered "throwaway" art by publishers, advertisers, stage and film producers, and the artists themselves. Some commercial artists did not care whether their work was labeled art, because the skill was only a means to an end, such as the assurance of a comfortable living or the education of a mass audience. Viewing their work as that of journalists, some illustrators and cartoonists left work at newspapers and magazines, where the once-used drawings often were tossed into the trash can. They accepted the ephemeral nature of the work and would have expressed curiosity that historians, curators, and collectors of today would expect it to be preserved. Designers of theater and film costumes shared the same attitude toward their work, but their designs were even less likely to be preserved because many artists did not sign their names. Costume designers often viewed their work as a collaborative effort: together, they were part of a community of artists creating a work of art for the stage or screen. Continuing the tradition today, some costume designers feel so strongly about the shared expression that they refuse to add their signatures as a matter of principle.[12]

Forming the habit early on, Gordon quickly retrieved her drawings from print media clients after graphic reproduction. She agreed with the concept that costume design was a collaborative effort but signed her drawings nevertheless. She added her signature not only for identification but to indicate that the work was art. Heyworth Campbell had convinced her of that.

Smart Setback, a novel about the 1920s that was highly touted by publisher Alfred A. Knopf, reflects the ambivalent status of commercial art and provides biographical insight into Conway's world of design and New Woman status. The author, Wood Kahler, modeled the book's female protagonist on his friend Gordon Conway. He explores two themes related to her life: the celebration of modern design and woman's search for identity through creative work. Kahler creates atmosphere in the novel by describing architectural, interior, fashion, and advertising design; he declares skyscrapers "the first and finest contribution America has made to the art of the ages." In a plot similar to that of a Philip Barry stage play, the book describes career options in the 1920s for intelligent and capable society women longing to escape from the boredom of household chores or an unimaginative job. The heroine discards years of guilt caused by family accusations that her love of smart clothes is "wicked." She becomes a New Woman who designs clothes and opens a distinctive dress shop near Fifth Avenue. She acknowledges her lack of business experience but explains that she is a hard worker and has fashion contacts all over the world: "I know the famous Felix Kraus in Vienna. And Main Bocher in Paris. And in London, Gordon Conway, an artist in more ways than one." As though the words came straight from Conway herself, Kahler's character proclaims that "it doesn't matter so much whether you're making a dress or painting a picture. Just so long as you are creating." The book reflects the culture's ambivalent opinion of fashion drawing when the heroine apologizes for registering in a fashion design school:

Proof page with Heyworth Campbell's birthday greeting to Conway, 1915.

"Of course I know it isn't art." Defending the heroine's action, the painter-writer hero exclaims "Why not? It's more art than the stuff society portrait-painters do."[13] The retort could have issued from Heyworth Campbell.

Until Gordon was established, Campbell was close at hand, ever helpful. As she ascended to fame, he remained an encouraging friend: "I am terribly proud of you. . . . your consistent application is admirable. . . . Eventually the signature of Gordon Conway will create more of a stir than the mention of LePape [*sic*], Plank or the Kaiser."[14] She would recall throughout her life that the attention of Heyworth Campbell had provided a unique entrée into the commercial art world that would bind her to a career. Under his tutelage Gordon Conway blossomed into a professional artist.

A Noted Silhouette and Poster Artist

Gordon's first appointment with Heyworth Campbell lasted the entire morning on that September day in 1915. The occasion would be remembered for a lifetime, the story told again and again. Campbell showed Gordon and Tommie Conway many original drawings destined for publication. In her usual dry, terse style, Gordon recorded the events of the day in a few simple declarative sentences: "He advised me about my work and I met Miss Avery an artist." With the respect appropriately reserved for one of the most distinguished of *Vogue* cover artists, she added, "Mr. Campbell phoned Helen Dryden about me."[15] The symbolic importance of these few words cannot be overestimated. Indeed, these low-key, matter-of-fact comments belie the lasting significance of the event in Gordon Conway's life.

On October 30, 1915, Heyworth informed Gordon he intended to publish the pen-and-ink sketch "Girl with a Harp," though this inaugural piece did not appear until the February 15, 1917, issue of *Vogue*. (As was the custom of many art directors, the publication of a purchased sketch could be delayed due to space, design, layout issues, caption text, or financial restraints.) Gordon later joked that her first illustration commission was no bigger than a dime. Her jest reflected her talent as a raconteur, an affinity shared by her mother. Over the years Tommie Conway embellished stories to friends who relished each and every

tale, especially about Gordon's career. The story of Campbell's first purchase highlighted details of the celebration that ensued among Gordon's high life friends. The custom—uniting the celebratory act with the creation of a Conway mythology—gave psychological support to the young woman artist, a practice that continued until Gordon's marriage and revived after her divorce. Also, these celebrants—sophisticated cheerleaders from the worlds of Wall Street and Fifth Avenue—frequently opened doors to future jobs. This special drawing was heralded on December 18, 1915, at Gordon's twenty-first birthday party, which was held at the Lenori Apartments, where she and Tommie Conway lived. Heyworth Campbell surprised Gordon with a proof page of the illustration along with a ten-dollar gold piece that she treasured until her death. This proof page was cleverly personalized by the art director into a greeting card that read "Birthday Greetings to Miss Conway," and was signed with Campbell's well-known signature initials HC in a circle.

Drawing in Harper's Bazar *illustrating a women's information request column, a regular feature in the magazine, 1917.*

Bright Bits
from
"The Royal
Vagabond"
Sketched by
Gordon Conway

"Do you think I am going to let a little thing like
a kingdom stand between me and a girl like you?"

Shivering Janku and a cold, cold queen.
HER MAJESTY (—7°): What are you
talking about?
JANKU: S-sir? I mean Ma'am?

"Horrible Harold" show-
ing how a Frenchman would
sing "The Flowers That
Bloom in the Spring, tra-la."

Dainty baggage (Dorothy Dickson) evading
uniformed attendant (Carl Hyson).

"Marcel, if you keep
on hollering at me like
that I'll get so unstrung
that—well, I'll kick h——
out of you, that's all."

Fly-stepper on
furlough from
the nursery.

Demonstrating that the flowers that
bloom on the wall, tra-la, are not neces-
sarily wall-flowers in the technical sense.

Proof page, Judge, *1919.*

Actually, Gordon's first published illustration appeared in *Vanity Fair* on June 1, 1916. That year also witnessed her art in *Vogue* and a smattering of advertisements that triggered more festive evenings. Though her first works of art sold to Campbell were black-and-white illustrations and line drawings, from the beginning Gordon produced lively silhouettes. It was her work in this genre that first garnered national attention. She soon won acclaim for her striking color posters and billboards for the New York stage. As Campbell predicted, Gordon's career spiraled upward. Just weeks after the first submissions were sold to Campbell, her sketches were accepted at *Harper's Bazaar* and published in 1916.[16] Gordon's dependability and promptness soon became a legend at the Hearst publication when she came to the magazine's rescue after Porter Woodruff failed to meet a dead-

line. In gratitude, Henry B. Sell gave Gordon three original Erté drawings from the Hearst company's collection. *Harper's Bazaar* also competed for the New Woman as consumer. Through the years the magazine shaped and reflected the image right along with the Nast publications. Graced by a Conway drawing during 1917, a popular column for New Women in *Harper's Bazaar* carried readers' inquiries about new roles for women as well as clothes, etiquette, and entertaining. Throughout the teens, editors Henry Sell and "Miss Steinmetz" purchased her illustrations on a fairly regular basis until Gordon's departure for Europe as a newlywed.

Increasing her output during the New York period, between 1915 and late 1920 Conway worked for such distinguished publications as *Judge, Theatre Magazine,* and the *New York Times.* The most distinctive

Silhouettes for Theatre *magazine, May 1919, include images of Dorothy Dickson and the Dolly sisters.*

and popular work that she did before moving to Europe, however, was done for *Vanity Fair* between 1918 and mid-1919. Color covers in January and August 1918, combined with monthly pages of parodies, continued to garner praise in the years ahead. Both kinds of expression, the stage jobs and the covers and print parodies, involved editorial illustrations and advertising art that featured silhouettes, line drawings, caricatures, page decorations, croquis, fashion sketches, and color illustrations for magazine and program covers and for posters and billboards. For almost all of the assignments Gordon depicted trim, slim, and lively New Women—women itching to escape the page. These bodies take on a life of their own. Some popular favorites displayed her feel for wry images and parodies of the New Women. She became so busy she occasionally hired a student to do lettering. She executed

all the drawings herself, however, without benefit of an assistant or an apprentice, at a time when many art salons employed assistants. This practice would eventually take its toll on her health.

During her New York period, Gordon executed advertising commissions for a variety of clients that provided consumer goods and services ranging from automobiles to shoes, from watches to candy. These jobs required an enormous amount of work because she created clusters of figures for several series of advertisements. A case in point is the 1919–1920 nationwide advertising campaign mounted by the National City Company to attract women securities customers. Besides theater posters and billboards, this was Gordon's most ambitious and popular advertising achievement. Twenty different posters and window cards graced display areas and storefronts across the nation.

The posters depicted women with new freedom, visibility, and agility, like a figure skater who should "keep off of 'thin ice'" in your investments." Gordon's posters also presented women in traditional female roles in the process of being altered, such as consumers being urged to "Select your securities as you would your furs or gowns, with careful regard for value, quality, price and satisfaction." One poster portrayed a woman spinning yarn by the fireplace while considering: "Old-fashioned thrift is never out of date. Invest your savings in income yielding securities."[17]

These advertisements for National City attracted news coverage. During the teens, when large-scale mass advertising was new, journalists began reporting visual treats for the public. One such article highlighted the work with headlines that accompanied a Conway silhouette: "Beguiling Sparkle in New Window Cards."[18] The caption added that Gordon's posters "have a Voguish swish that sells the securities. . . . It becomes difficult to refrain from shopping for bonds, short term notes, and preferred stocks when casting an eye at the current window cards." The Gordon Conway power to persuade was still at work in 1923 when the company utilized the silhouettes again in a new advertising campaign. As part of their public relations effort the company also gave permission in the early 1920s for a nationwide reading campaign promoting books for men that displayed a famous Conway silhouette in five thousand bookstores across the nation. Though thrilled with the public reception, Gordon was most honored when her artwork was used in 1920 as a teaching aide in lecture classes at the Metropolitan Museum of Art.

Gordon's advertising art was closely aligned with magazine illustration. These two expressions within print media rarely are separated in the minds of the general public who are bombarded daily by thousands of images. These two categories of commercial art rarely are analyzed. There is a subtle difference, however, in the intent and tone of the final products. Moreover, a philosophical difference often separates editorial illustrators from advertising artists. In sum, editorial illustration informs and narrates, while advertising illustration promises and persuades. A fine line divides the two, but the distinction is essential in understanding the role of the commercial artist, for whom the goal of the client is paramount. Indeed, the purpose of the client determines the artist's direction. Not all illustrators are comfortable with both approaches. Over the years, some book illustrators have agreed with fine art advocates and eschewed advertising jobs. In Gordon's editorial illustrations, she worked like a journalist with a sketching pen and a reporter with a camera. Providing information, enlightenment, and entertainment, this art accompanied feature articles, stories, and books, as well as drama reviews in newspapers and magazines. By contrast, in her advertising illustrations, Gordon worked like a barker with a brush, appealing to consumers with her art. The advertisements motivated the viewer to act a certain way or to buy something right away. She created these images to persuade, to make an appeal, to raise expectations, to effect change, to construct dreams, and to create fantasies.

Gordon felt she had to work in both arenas. The client was more important to her than any philosophical considerations regarding the evils of advertising, which seemed minimal at the time. Moreover, with increasing living expenses for Gordon and her mother, fees became essential, and financial security took a higher priority than the moral certitude she would have gained by refusing commissions on philosophical grounds. Gordon agreed with Heyworth Campbell and genuinely believed that advertising was not only good for the economy and the country, but valuable in the daily lives of individual citizens, especially women.

A Freelance Artist

A cross section of Gordon's career activities during her New York period provides insight into the daily routine of her life as a commercial artist. As a freelance artist—and a woman artist at that—she found herself in daily pursuit of opportunities for financial and professional success. She worked through referrals and direct contact. With letters of introduction in hand, Gordon and her mother called on potential magazine and stage clients. Her endeavors produced a wealth of confirmed job offers mixed with what she discovered to be hazards of the trade—rejections, delays, and proposals that never materialized. Exploring leads took the same amount of time and energy whether they were productive or not. Being both a loner and a perfectionist, Gordon insisted on working by herself when she could have hired an assistant to ease the workload. On occasion she did sign with advertising services like Stormbergs and Malcolm Strauss. Difficulty in collecting her fees from Strauss and from a cabaret performer proved distracting and an inefficient use of her time and led Gordon to seek legal advice. These payment problems caused her to institute a policy requiring a portion of her fee to be paid up front.

An example of Gordon's modus operandi and her commitment to her freelance status was a diary entry in mid-October 1919: "I sketched all the morning. . . . Mother and I went to see Miss Peyser, the editor of *Everyland* magazine who called me to come and see her about some work. Then we went to see Mr. Kron at Binger & Company who sent for me. He offered me a position with his firm under contract and to name my own price. It's a remarkable place all in blue and silver, the kind you see in the movies, but I couldn't work there." [19] Gordon's versatility, originality, dependability, and alertness for potential business attracted offers of full-time staff positions with publishers and assorted enterprises alike, but she remained self-employed and acted as her own agent.

One of the keys to Gordon's success was a distinctive style in the presentation of a certain kind of female image. The works that defined her reputation portrayed chic, svelte, streamlined, sophisticated, and agile women—New Women images showcased in *Vogue, Vanity Fair,* and *Harper's Bazaar.* This style was not the usual fare for certain magazines and deep down she knew it. Nevertheless, she approached *Collier's Weekly* and *Woman's Home Companion,* but was not surprised when she was turned down. Whether on paper, on stage, or in person, Gordon carefully developed her style like a commodity for the consumer market—a product that a large segment of the public liked and came to expect. While collaborating with clients, Gordon maintained this unique style and still captured the essence of the project she was hired to illustrate, be it a short story, magazine cover, stage play, or consumer product. She quickly absorbed instructions from editors, whizzed through manuscripts, sketched at rehearsals, reviewed promotional copy, and studied garments to be advertised. She was capable of changing styles in a flash—as quickly as a photographer changes a lens—yet she rarely changed styles just to get a job or to please a client. (It was true that toward the end of her career, when illness halted her film work, Gordon did experiment with current styles in an attempt to regain magazine illustration commissions.) All her drawings, however, were not populated with these signature New Women. She altered her style when the job inspired it, as with her illustrations for

VANITY FAIR

Cover, Vanity Fair, *August 1918. This young woman, who is a Zina-like character (see Image One in Part Two), drums up enlistments for World War I.*

Wood Kahler's writing. Wanting to produce a different image for her friend's fiction, Gordon created bold, thick, and heavy blocklike figures of female and male images that she felt conveyed the characters in his stories.

This analysis of Gordon Conway's professional methods of production would be incomplete without a discussion of her peripheral career and social activities that stimulated income, increased public visibility, continued her education, and affected her success. These marginal functions were nurtured and expanded through public relations, networking, customer entertainment, quasi-official and nontraditional methods of communication, and the invention of a marketable public persona similar to a product image. Often judged as superficial busywork, these social activities are essential in a design profession linked to an entertainment industry that is fertilized by

celebrity and fame. Gordon marshaled social opportunities into contacts that led to clients, commissions, and notoriety. She was a pioneer in public relations and image building for women, with a special skill for celebrity development as well as self-promotion. Alternately energizing and interfering with her work habits, the hectic and time-consuming chores produced both a positive and a negative impact on her career and ultimately triggered health problems that forced her into an early retirement.

Between mid-1915 and late 1920, Gordon was busy plying her trade and maintaining social relationships with a large network of friends and colleagues in New York, the East Coast, and Dallas. Presenting a composite of experiences and a collection of random business-related activities is instructive in analyzing the artist's freelance approach that brought her professional success and public popularity. For example,

Drawing of Dorothy Dickson, 1919–1920. This drawing is similar to an oil painting that Gordon Conway gave to Dickson. The painting was later stolen from an exhibition in New York.

Gordon joined Dorothy Parker and Thorne Smith for tea at Sherry's and afterward for dinner at the Algonquin Hotel to discuss their magazine assignments. She proceeded to appointments concerning lingerie and candy advertisements, which were squeezed in between planning sessions over lunch and cocktails with Condé Nast, Frank Crowninshield, Heyworth Campbell, and Dorothy Parker. One meeting involved Gordon's *Vanity Fair* covers and page parodies poking fun at World War I debutante-volunteers and the foibles of New York high society. Her own experience and informal case-study approach to such social events informed these parodies.

There were times when she struggled to make deadlines that led nowhere. Two projects that Gordon had counted on apparently never developed beyond the proposal stage: she was invited by Houghton Mifflin Company to create a jacket cover for Rafael Sabatini's *Scaramouche* and was asked by theater colleague Sanford E. Stanton, press director for the Selwyn brothers, to illustrate his book on jazz.

Other business-related activities included a trip by Gordon and Tom to view a French poster exhibition in the converted stable of sculptor Gertrude Vanderbilt Whitney in Greenwich Village. Gordon made herself available to help actress Margaret Lawrence with her personal wardrobe. Gordon listened to her hairdresser as he often whispered the name of a prospective advertising client. She picked up letters of recommendation from Ned Wayburn and had tea with Eleanor Gates about silhouettes for a children's book. She frequently stopped by the advertising department at Condé Nast publishing for assignments. Any venue attracted Gordon, along with Tommie, such as the Coney Island show, featuring Mlle Dazie, a popular entertainer she had dressed in a distinctive garb. Between cast parties and photographer's sittings, she read scripts, worked up budgets, and made sketches for Broadway shows that never were staged. She delivered sketches to *La France* and taxied to a shop to work on the window display. Gordon and Tommie sometimes supped with Ethel Wodehouse before P. G. Wodehouse–Guy Bolton–Jerome Kern smash-hit musical comedies, like *Oh, Lady! Lady!!* These suppers often followed rehearsals at a number of Broadway theaters, including the Princess Theatre, where she sketched performers both for black-and-white editorial illustrations and for color posters.

Gordon met with reporters about the theft of her picture of Dorothy Dickson that had been cut from its frame in the lobby of the Alhambra Theatre by inebriated Columbia College football fans. Among dozens of drawings of Dickson, the image was one of Gordon's few oil paintings and had been a special gift to her friend. Gordon joined Porter Woodruff at the library for research on historic dress. These two friends visited exhibitions at the Art Students League and the National Academy of Design, and then proceeded to a tea dance. In the latest stylish attire, Gordon, Tommie, and a covey of intimates trekked to the Paramount lot at Fort Lee, where the women performed as bit players in two movies. Though nothing

This photograph of Gordon Conway by Maurice Goldberg is similar to Goldberg's photograph of Conway featured in "The Seven Vanities of Vanity Fair,*" December 1918.*

came of this adventure, Gordon and Tom were aware that the discovery of unknown talent in such silent films was possible. Gordon was available, of course, for film design work, but the two women hoped for acting jobs as well. When no movie offers surfaced, the group celebrated their performances anyway, over cocktails following the New York screening of the films. Gordon waited hours in the Conways' apartment for the director to pick up the cover design for the *Woman's Press* of the YWCA. A reporter interviewed Gordon over drinks for a feature story in a Texas newspaper. She sat for a fellow sketch artist to complete a pastel portrait that her mother had commissioned. She rushed to Madame Marie Apel's studio for a critique of some experimental artwork she had finished. Typical of her crowded schedule, Gordon completed Red Cross posters, painted scenery, and collaborated with a friend in constructing a stage model that required working long past midnight. Ever sensitive to the needs of charity and following Heyworth Campbell's example, Gordon found time to contribute sketches to causes as varied as the French Wounded Emergency Fund, an Allied Charity Ball, the Manhattanville Day and Night Nursery, and the Babies' Ward of the Post Graduate Hospital.

Gordon's resourcefulness and tenacity soon were rewarded. In December 1918, she was honored as one of "The Seven Vanities of *Vanity Fair:* Portraits of a Few of Our Most Revered and Redoubtable Staff Artists." The picture captions applauded the artistic flair of these seven staff women who entertained a growing Condé Nast readership and captured the spirit of the times. The cultural and social authority of *Vanity Fair* was growing, and the magazine had become a sort of secular Bible, especially to Gordon's associates. The magazine's tribute page featured illustrator Helen Dryden, known since 1912 for her stunning

covers of *Vogue,* and Myrtle Held, then a volunteer canteen worker serving American soldiers in France. Photographed in a variety of New Woman looks, three artists were garbed in idiosyncratic trouser outfits: humorist and satirist Thelma Cudlipp, Dada rebel Clara Tice, and Ethel McClellan Plummer, called the magazine's dean "sketchifier." Well-known characters in the Village, both Tice and Plummer shared the title that year as "the uncrowned queen of Greenwich Village." The sixth honoree was occasional Conway collaborator, British-born Anne Harriet Fish (Mrs. Walter Sefton) known simply as "Fish" to colleagues and admirers.[20]

The caption for the seventh image acknowledged that "Gordon Conway is the latest addition—and one of the most welcomed—to *Vanity Fair*'s family circle. Like Miss Dryden and Miss Plummer, Miss Conway is the soul of versatility, and not only paints and illustrates, but designs costumes and scenery for musical comedies as well."[21] Indeed, Gordon was as successful in her stage work as she was in her magazine and advertising work.

Versatility and Vision

Gordon's stage work dated back to 1916 with her silhouettes for exhibition dancers and performers in cabaret. Like the contact with Heyworth Campbell, her first cabaret account grew out of Gordon and Tom's social orbit in the fall of 1915. Gordon often swirled around the dance floor with exhibition dancers at the Hotel Plaza Grill. Inspiring much applause were her dances with Basil Durant, a partner she tagged "the best tango in New York."[22] Like young men with whom Gordon had waltzed from Dallas to the Danube, Durant was typical of expert ballroom dancers employed by restaurants, clubs, and hotels to facilitate good times among hesitant initiates of café society. Influenced by the Vernon and Irene Castle dance craze, Durant was poised to launch a stage career, and several restaurant-entertainment managers were ready to sponsor him. Gordon was available to help both with silhouettes for cabaret brochures, menu cards, wine list covers, table tents, newspaper advertisements, posters, and other promotional graphics. When Margaret Hawkesworth joined Durant, the two performed at popular venues, including the Century Grove roof garden cabaret of the Century Theatre, the Paradise Club, and the Palace Vaudeville Theatre. In addition, Gordon costumed popular cabaret performer Maurice, who commissioned her services again for his cabaret and nightclub work during the 1920s in Paris.

Cabaret also introduced Gordon to stage legend Ned Wayburn, a multitalented and prodigious worker who collaborated with many Broadway producers. He staged productions for Ziegfeld's theater and roof garden cabaret. Gordon created promotional graphics for Wayburn, and with Florenz Ziegfeld's approval, she costumed scenes for the *Ziegfeld Midnight Frolic* productions on the roof garden of his New Amsterdam Theatre. (Wayburn also ordered her designs for legitimate theater productions, like the Lew Fields production of *Back Again* starring the Dolly Sisters.) Wayburn remained one of Gordon's stalwart clients, even after her move to Europe. Also commissioning cabaret work was supporter and friend Dorothy Dickson, along with her husband and dance partner, Carl Hyson. Inspired by the Castle-dance phenomenon, the couple became the rage of the café society scene, which, in turn, led to Broadway triumphs for Dickson. Gordon costumed and created posters and promotional graphics for the Hysons' performances at a variety of cabaret venues, including the swank Palais Royal.

Gordon loved cabaret. An authority on the genre, she had been storing images and rhythms in her head since youth. In Paris, before the Great War, this teenage cosmopolite had exclaimed that the Olympia tableaux were "the most shocking I've ever seen."[23] Gordon realized that she had become an amateur critic of cabaret performances when experienced viewers such as Tommie Conway and her beau Tom Camp quickly agreed with her reaction of shock. Certainly, during Gordon's early years of attendance, cabaret was beginning to be appreciated by segments of the theater-going public. Reflecting the symbolic move from basement joint to roof garden, the once suspect entertainment ascended to popular acceptance among café society and aspiring urbanites. In the teens respectable middle-class New Women and New Men rose from supper show tables to enter the spotlight on the dance floor. These talented amateurs joined the professional dancers, who probably had been amateur performers themselves only months before.

In this intimate stage genre, the space for stage and that for audience merged. Audience participation was expected. This vehicle of entertainment became more personal and was more intimately involved with the audience than a standard theater production. A theater separates the audience by the distance and elevation of the stage, as well as by years of professional stage tradition and ritual. Loosely defined, cabaret is a revue entertainment in an intimate setting that includes food and drink. This type of revue generally is presented in "editions," that change once or twice a year. A central theme ties the acts together, but rarely is there a story line as in musical comedy. The costumes and sets become so dominant that they are viewed as performers themselves, as opposed to costumes that simply characterize individual roles played by actors and actresses. Cabaret has a maddening number of names. Countless hybrids and transatlantic cross-fertilizations make definitions complicated. The nuances in definition usually are associated with style of presentation or city of origin, as in the Berlin cabaret and Paris music hall. Gordon worked for all sorts of revue productions on both sides of the Atlantic, but to avoid confusion, the term "cabaret" will be used for all of them in this study.

After 1921, cabaret showcased not only Gordon's graphic art, but hundreds of her most exotic and erotic costumes as well. For editions in London and Paris, she again collaborated with Hyson, designed for the Tomson Twins, and worked with two cabaret greats of the period, Léon Volterra and Percy Athos. Her cabaret costuming and graphic art attracted some commissions for the legitimate stage, although most theater jobs actually grew out of her print-media work. For example, her jazzy silhouettes and lively line drawings landed Gordon her first legitimate theater job in late 1917, when the *New York Times* ran her editorial interpretation of *Behind a Watteau Picture* by the Greenwich Village Players. The newspaper and other publications published Gordon's editorial illustrations

over the next two years, including ones for *The Maid of France,* Frank Craven in *Going Up,* Alice Brady in *Forever After,* Helen Hayes in *Dear Brutus,* Henry Miller in *Molière,* and productions featuring World War I hero Lieutenant Gitz Rice. These editorial illustrations quickly led to commercial-theater advertising jobs, along with costume design and several scenery design assignments. Interestingly, a major commission emerged from a drawing rejected by Heyworth Campbell. Producer E. Ray Goetz transformed the artwork into a poster for the December 1917 opening of *Words and Music.* Directed by Leon Errol with Marion Davies in the cast, this musical revue at the Fulton Theatre was coproduced by Raymond Hitchcock, a longtime supporter along with Goetz of Gordon's stage work.

The interaction between the magazine and advertising illustration worlds and that of the stage should not be underestimated in evaluating the Gordon Conway oeuvre. The proper presentation of the design was essential to Gordon. Her aesthetic instinct emphasized the finished product; the attention to detail down to the last red-tipped fingernail is evident in almost every drawing. She shared this interest in the total picture with other costume designers who were trained as artists and illustrators and who drew the whole figure, like Barbier, Lepape, and Erté. However, another practice in costume design uses the drawing as only a device, to create a final product. This method features sketchy impressions of garments, with the bodies barely penciled in and often without the head and limbs. Such renderings usually display fabric swatches pinned to the page, a procedure Gordon frequently used herself, even when she delineated the exact textural detail in the sketch. These intricacies—required in her advertising jobs—account for extra hours of work.

Encouraged by producers Raymond Hitchcock and E. Ray Goetz, Gordon applied a total design concept to the 1917 production of *Words and Music.* Though the revue was short-lived, the assignment was an auspicious beginning for the twenty-three-year-old woman. As in most stage productions of the era, other designers, shops, costumiers, and artisans floated in and out of the process and received program credit for such accoutrements of dress as shoes, hats, tights, and stockings. Gordon's first effort at an integrated design package involved only a small number of costumes and sets for specific scenes. Selecting certain motifs and colors, she repeated the images in the program and posters. This kind of control over an overall design scheme was a goal Gordon worked toward throughout her career. This practice allowed her to transpose script themes into visual motifs that could be repeated in two- and three-dimensional forms. In Gordon's imagination, this creative concept did not differ greatly from her illustrative mise-en-scènes on the printed page—the pictorial tableaux and vignettes for magazines, with women ensconced in glamorous, luxurious, and exotic settings.

To Gordon, a total design concept required a wide range of responsibilities, whether the stage production was comedy, tragedy, farce, melodrama, or musical play. The initiatives included illustration and graphic design, coupled with three-dimensional art like costumes, scenery, lobby decoration, and publicity window display. Such a package combined both advertising and editorial illustration, as with artwork accompanying press coverage and drama reviews. The advertising element might include any or all of the following: program covers and page decoration, sheet-music covers, handbills, brochures, flyers, table tents, window cards, newspaper advertisements, eight-sheet posters, and twenty-four-sheet billboards. In addition to providing the actual artwork, Gordon oversaw the execution of the designs. Though rarely acknowledged, this impulse for a total design concept is related to the vision of architects, landscape architects, interior decorators, and urban planners. Acknowledged even less is a similar impulse found in the art of the couturier. The vision for a total look springs from the same creative source, and Gordon Conway knew it.

As *Vanity Fair* had recognized, Gordon Conway was a versatile artist. She shared this attribute with other designers who experimented in a variety of arenas, including modern staging. Here were men—and mostly men they were—who could build stage sets, design dresses, plan office spaces, illustrate books, reshape display counters, advertise shoes, construct buildings, decorate ocean liners, and design textiles. In contrast, today's design world compartmentalizes creative expression, and versatility is discouraged. In fact, the legacy of Gordon Conway has suffered because of her versatility. With the benefit of hindsight, recent observers have attempted to explain the obscurity of her record, speculating that her professional reputation might still be intact if she had not "spread herself too thin." [24] Rather than pay tribute to Gordon's all-encompassing vision, these advocates of specialization pointed to their perception of a lack of focus and expertise in one specialty. The variety of genres also made it more difficult to identify and define Gordon's accomplishments.

The Gordon Conway oeuvre should be viewed within the broader context of design history. During the first two decades of the twentieth century, versatility was a key ingredient in the innovation and experimentation of modern design movements that aspired to rearrange and reshape the visible world. In the teens, inspiration for Gordon's outlook and work habits came from both sides of the Atlantic. She kept up with these multifarious developments through books, photography, exhibitions, and press coverage. Yet she found herself on the fringe of various design systems, which for the most part were led by male architects and engineers. She neither competed within these orbits nor participated in their politics of fame and success. Gordon knew a few design leaders and fellow neophytes, but a vast number she did not know. Some pioneers were a generation older and already recognized, while others, like herself, were starting out. A brief overview of her network of colleagues addresses inevitable questions about Gordon's schooling, apprenticeships, and professional circles. A look through the lens of these transatlantic forces gives insight into her career.

Gordon absorbed ideas and experiences from two vantage points: Europe before and after World War I, and New York during and after the war. Both stood as backdrop to her work in the 1920s and 1930s. First, the design revolution that produced the new European stagecraft influenced the adolescent Gordon before the war began. Even though she did not know them personally during her career, she was inspired in her youth by the likes of Edward Gordon Craig, Percy Anderson, and the battery of international talents working for the Ballets Russes, such as avant-garde designers Alexandre Benois, Léon Bakst, Sonia Delaunay, and Natalia Goncharova, to name a few. Gordon thrilled to their productions, but she was not part of the milieu of Serge Diaghilev or Max Reinhardt. Although she must have been conscious of the contributions of her contemporaries, Conway's archives lead one to assume that she was not acquainted with English and Continental designers her own age like Dolly Tree, Charles Gesmar, Ernst Dryden, and Doris Zinkeisen.[25]

The ideas of Parisian couture also influenced Gordon before the war when she and her mother were customers of Jacques Doucet, Worth, Madame Jeanne Paquin, and Paul Poiret. She later collaborated with these four houses during the 1920s, along with the ateliers of Edward Molyneux and Jean Patou. Gordon's role of artistic interpreter of couture collections for women's magazines brought her into close touch with these designers and their artisans. This job required more originality than mere fashion rendering, and can be compared to the creative fashion photography of such notables as Edward Steichen, Baron Adolphe de Meyer, Horst P. Horst, Baron George Hoyningen-Huené, and Cecil Beaton. Also in Paris in the 1920s, she met Georges Barbier and Christian "Bébé" Bérard. In London during the 1930s, she collaborated with Serge Chermayeff and the budding Norman Hartnell. In addition, during her final year in British film, she hired the talented young Margaret Furse as an assistant.

The prewar initiatives of Paul Poiret especially influenced Gordon. Along with theater design, Poiret championed a total design concept for life itself—a philosophy that led to the Atelier Martine addition to his couture house in 1911. This decorating studio was inspired by the famous Wiener Werkstätte, founded in Vienna in 1903 by such architectural giants as Josef Hoffmann. With a natural bent toward design as a whole, Poiret claimed his mission was to "costume whole environments."[26] Though engaging different levels of social theory, Poiret's ideas were not too different from the tenets of Walter Gropius and members of the Bauhaus movement, who proclaimed that "the complete building is the ultimate aim of all the visual arts."[27]

During and after World War I in New York, Gordon witnessed firsthand the early innovations in staging and costuming called the New Stagecraft or the New Movement. The effort testified to the universal vision and versatility of set and costume luminaries Robert Edmond Jones and Joseph Urban. Both men were also illustrators and interior decorators, and Urban was a gifted architect as well. No evidence, however, has surfaced that Gordon knew Jones or Urban, or for that matter, Adolphe Appia, Lee Simonson, or Aline Bernstein—one of the few female professional designers of the period. Nor did she know rising design notables her own age like Norman Bel Geddes, Charles LeMaire, Hugh Willoughby, Alice O'Neil, Travis Banton, and Jo Mielziner. Exceptions were actor-designer Rollo Peters, industrial designer Raymond Loewy, and fellow illustrator Helen Dryden. Though not a designer per se, Eva Le Gallienne influenced Gordon through her versatility and vision of the theater.

In the relatively small arena of New York theater, print media, fashion, and advertising, Gordon witnessed a visual revolution that transformed American theater and altered the stage of everyday life, including department store display, modern household furnishings, and advertising layout. The American innovators gathered inspiration from Vienna to Glasgow, Belgium to Darmstadt, and St. Petersburg to Weimar. Men like Urban, Peters, and Loewy were born near these European design centers that influenced their work in the United States. Other designers absorbed ideas not only from Europe but also from Japan through study, travel, and personal interchange. They recast the ideas from abroad and broadcast the new vision across the country. These ideas intersected with native expression like that of the Chicago-based initiatives of Louis Sullivan and Frank Lloyd Wright, who in turn had incorporated ideas from British theorists John Ruskin and William Morris and advocates of Japonisme. (See further information in Part Two.)

Though they operated in separate spheres, Gordon shared a philosophical outlook with avant-garde couturière Sonia Delaunay, who began a European career in 1905 after leaving her native Russia. Along with her husband's avant-garde art, Delaunay's versatility and originality were celebrated by Modernist artists in Paris. She originated new design concepts for the theater, as well as for the female silhouette. Delaunay believed that liberated forms, shapes, and colors helped women participate "in a new society and proclaim their independent spirit." Though she, like fellow Modernists, would not find her vision of the modern woman the same as the New Woman portrayed by Gordon Conway, the looks were rooted in a similar philosophy. Delaunay marshaled the forces of "art, fashion and life into a single bold partnership . . . clothes were at last to be given the power and self-assurance of paintings."[28] Indeed, early in the twentieth century, costume and fashion design were linked to the larger mission of art and design. Gordon was a witness to it all and agreed with modern design leaders that "nothing need be ugly."[29] She trusted her own instincts and experience. She absorbed the revolution in the way things looked and vowed to do her part to revitalize the visual world around her. The stage was no exception.

THREE FOR TEA

Anatomy of a Stage Design Career

During Gordon's New York period, more than forty-five stage productions, exclusive of cabaret, showcased her art. Though some were small or single orders, the quantity reveals the variety of her connections with producers, directors, stage managers, publicists, and actresses. Gordon preferred a coordinated effort—a total design concept—from the standpoint of time and energy as well as creative inspiration. The need for fee payments and job strategy dictated that she accept jobs on short notice, whether just before an opening or well into a run. Besides her modest effort for *Words and Music,* only one production in New York involved a total design concept: *The Charm School* in 1920. During her New York period, this play was Gordon's most accomplished stage offering, featuring costumes, program cover and page decorations, posters, and promotional graphics. Such a concept should not be confused with uncoordinated orders for a single show—commissioned by various staff and consisting of unrelated graphics and assorted costumes for different scenes. There were times when staff was unaware of her other work for the same show—such as an order by the lead actress for a Conway gown. Assignments for different clients associated with the same show meant a haphazard, segregated approach. Examples included such uncoordinated efforts as Gordon's costuming and graphics for *Hitchy-Koo II of*

1918, for which she met individually with both Irene Bordoni and Raymond Hitchcock. For *Wedding Bells,* one of the ten best plays of the 1919–1920 season, Gordon worked with Selwyn publicist Sanford E. Stanton on posters, while in a separate sphere she created costumes for the star Margaret Lawrence. (The actress also had commissioned clothes for her personal wardrobe the previous year when Gordon sketched her for *Tea for Three* posters.) In terms of today's stage job designations, Gordon would be thought of as a costume designer, image maker, production artist, publicity photographer, casting consultant, and personnel troubleshooter all rolled into one. Her ability to create an integrated design package, which first was inspired by her study of the script, later would blossom during the 1920s and early 1930s on the Continental stage and screen.

An overview of Gordon's work method for *The Charm School* provides insight into the career of a costume and graphic designer. It also reflects the Broadway milieu of 1920—the same year that welcomed two major cultural and political changes: women's suffrage and Prohibition. The New York season between August 1920 and June 1921 witnessed 157 new productions and has been labeled a comedy year, the natural aftermath to the armistice. Opening on August 2, *The Charm School* was produced and directed by Robert Milton. He also coauthored the script in collaboration with Alice Duer Miller, who adapted the three-act play from her own popular book. The comedy featured musical interludes by Jerome Kern and a cast of seventeen, including Sam B. Hardy and James Gleason, who would appear thirteen years later in British films dressed by Gordon.

Ten months before the opening, Gordon recorded that she was studying *The Charm School,* which "Mr. Milton is turning into a play and has asked me to do the costumes and posters for it."[1] Milton's advance notice pleased Gordon because she liked being part of the creative process from the beginning. The plot centered on a young automobile salesman who inherited a girls' school, hired bachelor friends as professors, and insisted "charm" be taught to the aspiring New Women. Mayhem and romance collided on the stage. Gordon designed all the costumes and graphics around a central theme of lighthearted, supple images that were inspired by the sprightly schoolgirls in the play. Print-media illustrations included billboards, posters, handbills, and the cover and page decorations of the program. In March she attended meetings with her sketchpad. Rehearsals began at the Longacre Theatre. She met Milton at the Migel shop, known for its famous silks, for fabric selection. She then went to Franklin Simons & Company, the department store constructing her designs for the eleven actresses in the show. She raced back and forth to fittings and rehearsals, which melded into more conferences with her sketchpad for costume corrections and staging ideas. These efforts flowed into more fittings, rehearsals, a change of theater, and the dress parade. In the midst of a flurry of telegrams and flowers, a gala send-off was staged by Tommie Conway and friends at a preopening dinner at the Algonquin Hotel. Gordon's illustrations were a smash, from her tiny sketches of the slender schoolgirls that edged the program pages to the giant graphic classmates that enlivened the billboards across the Gotham skyline she so adored. Her costumes also caused a stir when the smartly dressed and gymsuited young bodies sashayed

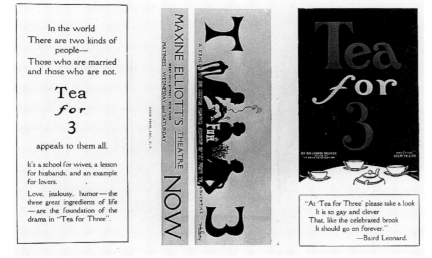

Program for Tea for Three, *1918.*

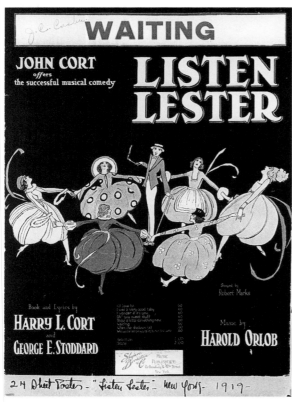

across the Bijou stage. Looking like one of the sophisticated soubrettes that she had dressed, Gordon attended the premiere and was gratified to see her total design ideas come to life on stage.

The play's modest run of eighty-eight performances typified a dilemma faced by Gordon and fellow designers. She had learned in 1917 that a failure—or even a moderately successful show—was a hazard of the trade. Obscure productions do detract from a designer's record, according to Ann Sheffield, a present-day woman costume and set designer, who spoke about this kind of "bad luck."[2]

The 1918 productions of *Listen Lester* and *Tea for Three* offered Gordon the opportunity to expand her talent for an overall design scheme in the field of graphic and illustrative art. Her silhouettes and sketches graced newspaper advertisements, fancy table tents, brochure handouts, posters, billboards, and program graphics. Though it is difficult to imagine given today's blizzard of print paper, these coordinated ephemera—stunning promotional and editorial graphics—caused quite a stir. For example, to celebrate the opening of a new theater in 1918, Gordon executed a clever and distinctive program cover to be used for all the productions at a single theater. She prepared as well a matching brochure of unique moveable parts that highlighted a fancy folding technique of intersecting colors and forms. Praising these unusual graphics was an article in the October 2 *New York Telegraph* with the headline: "Beautiful Playhouse Highly Praised by Magazine and Newspaper Men." The news article announced the formal opening of the new Selwyn Theatre on 42nd Street west of Broadway, and the premiere of *Information Please!,* written by and starring Jane Cowl. This same striking turquoise and peach cover with page illustrations graced the program seven weeks later when Jane Cowl opened in *The Crowded Hour,* written and staged by Edgar Selwyn. Though Gordon worked with friend and colleague Cowl, the graphic art was ordered by Sanford E. Stanton, press executive for Selwyn and Company and ardent Gordon Conway supporter who acted as a mentor for her stage work in the manner of Heyworth Campbell. This identical cover with page designs heralded subsequent programs for Selwyn productions as late as 1922. To the stage devotee today, a program seems ordinary and is taken for granted, but on October 2, 1918, the newspaper explained the novelty: "The audience to-night is going to experience another pleasant sensation in the make-up of the theatre program. Instead of the usual offering a simple eight-page leaflet containing sketches by Gordon Conway will be distributed."[3]

An examination of the fee that Gordon received from the Selwyn management provides insight into the pay scale of stage graphics and offers the opportunity for an interesting comparison to fees paid by magazines and consumer advertisers in the teens. In

Sheet music cover for Listen Lester, *1918. Dancers circle with agility and verve, typical of Conway's portrayal of movement.*

PHONE 47 BRYANT

SELWYN THEATRE
42ⁿᵈ STREET WEST OF BROADWAY

UNDER THE DIRECTION OF
SELWYN & COMPANY

Cover for Selwyn Theatre program, used by Selwyn and Co. for productions at this theater between 1918 and 1922.

the fall of 1918, Gordon was paid $150 for the Selwyn Theatre color program cover with matching pages, including the coordinated folded brochure. Six months before, she was paid $100 for a *Vanity Fair* color cover, and $50 to $60 per page of black-and-white line-drawing parodies that ran as a series for eighteen months. The Condé Nast cover payment of $100 was not bad, since the *Vanity Fair* salary scale in May 1919 included $100 a week to managing editor Robert Benchley and $25 a week to Robert E. Sherwood as drama reviewer. Early in 1916 at the beginning of Gordon's career, *Vogue* paid her $36 for three silhou-

ettes, and in April, *Harper's Bazaar* paid $80 for two black-and-white illustrations. In early 1917 she donated a World War I poster that raised $100 during a benefit auction; the amount greatly pleased both Gordon and the charity. That May, Neiman-Marcus paid Gordon a total of $294 for sixty-eight separate clusters of croquis. This figure included a $20 payment for a panel of sixteen "waists" published in a half-page advertisement in a Dallas newspaper. As part of six separate commissions for an advertising campaign that same fall, Franklin Motor Car paid $22.50 for three color illustrations. In December 1917, Gordon received $45 for two costumes and one poster for *Words and Music.* Exactly one year later, *Judge* paid Gordon $70 for one page of seven silhouettes.[4] In the final entry to her 1918 diary, Gordon revealed: "I made $1,844.50 on my sketches—I hope to do lots better in 1919."[5] Though her income during the teens was supplemented by Tommie Conway's real estate and securities investments, Gordon still needed more work to support herself and her mother in their upscale style of living. She strove harder to compete in the marketplace of commercial art—an experience that proved invaluable during the Depression when art fees were the two women's sole source of income.

During the teens, New York theater clients sometimes sought Gordon's advice on costumes and sets on an informal basis, a favor she was willing to grant. In this case, her name did not appear in the program credits even when Gordon furnished graphic art for the production. She did receive credit, by way of her signature, for all of her many theatrical posters and billboards. Gordon's first major stage advertising account in 1917 started a minor craze and developed a following for the striking posters and billboards. She transposed the sheer wizardry of movement, which was popular in her lively silhouettes and illustrations, to multiple sheets of color graphics. Early in the century, posters and billboards were themselves a form of public entertainment with active spectators—a phenomenon difficult to imagine in today's avalanche of advertisements. Gordon's notable graphics advertised such popular shows as *Good Morning, Judge; Toby's Bow;* and *Nighty-Night* at the Princess Theatre. Decorating the skyline of New York, the billboards stood out like giant portraits of some of the most famous personages of the Great White Way. Among an impressive array of luminaries were Lenore Ulric in *Tiger Rose,* Irene Bordoni in *Sleeping Partners* and *As You*

Neiman-Marcus Co

The Store of Individual Shops

—Good morning! Weather fair. One year ago today on corresponding Wednesday the weather was cloudy. Temperature was 46 degrees above zero.

For the Women of Dallas Who Are Watching for the Early Spring Skirts We Feature Today 100 Novelty Skirts

—of Jersey
—of Crepe de Chine
—of Cascadieu
—of Taffeta
—of Rajah

Some are in the solid colors, striking the newest Spring notes in the vivid greens, the striped effects, the vivid color contrasts. Wide or flaring models—narrow or crushed belts.
$16.50 to $32.50.

In the Undergarmentry the Special Sale of L'Ervelle Undergarmentry Is Pleasing Thousands

Patron after patron has commented on the winsomness and the freshness of the garments—the exceptional quality of the Crepe de Chine—the difference of the silhouette.
—Camisoles specially priced at
95c—$1.45—$1.95—$2.25
—Teddy Bears specially priced at
$1.95—$2.75—$2.95
—Gowns specially priced at
$3.95—$4.37—$4.95—$5.95
—*In every instance comparison is in favor of these lovely, fresh, winsome L'Ervelle Undergarmentry. Come down the first thing this morning to see for yourself.*

Just a Word About the Newer Spring Blouses

—Like the illustration of White Georgette with the tiny tucks, the laces, the new neck line and the adorable sleeves—this Blouse may be worn for either afternoon affairs or for shopping.
$25
—Other Blouses delineating the cubist effects, the contrasted shades, fashioned of Georgette, are priced
$13.50 Upward to $25.

(Top) *Conway drawing believed by her family to have been done for Neiman-Marcus.*

Graphic designs and advertisements in Dallas in 1917 for Neiman-Marcus department store and a local real estate firm, and a program cover for a fashion show benefitting the Dallas chapter of the French Wounded Emergency Fund.

Silhouette of Dorothy Dickson, ca. 1918–1919.

Were, McKay Morris in *Aphrodite,* and George M. Cohan in *A Prince There Was.* Two posters especially prized by Gordon featured Minnie Maddern Fiske in *Mis' Nelly of N'Orleans* and *Wake Up, Jonathan!*

Gordon created popular images for dance duo Dorothy Dickson and Carl Hyson in theater productions such as *The Royal Vagabond.* Her graphics of the pair in Jerome Kern's *Rock-A-Bye Baby* soon were pasted over much of Brooklyn. These posters and billboards caused such a stir that friends collected Gordon for a caravan spree across the Brooklyn Bridge so they could photograph the gathering of spectators. In a mass of bold colors, the artwork portrayed alert bodies with precise movements. A leitmotif of Gordon's style was motion, agility, and energetic gesturing that symbolized a new freedom of the body, especially for the New Woman. With vigor and vitality, Gordon's figures were not cast in a set form like the static poses presented by certain illustrators of the day. Gordon's pen inspired the lines to perform, evok-

ing printed statues that could not stand still. Even in the most restrained vignettes, Gordon's illustrated bodies were itching to move, if only with a flick of a finger or twist of a toe. These lively images reflected Gordon's appreciation of the impact of motion pictures upon the depictions of the human form. The spry figures captured Gordon's sense of how her own body worked, especially her supple frame that moved with equal ease on the sports field and the dance floor. They testified also to her knowledge of anatomy.

Fifty years later, Dorothy Dickson remembered her own lithe and limber figure as caught by Gordon's brushlike frozen gestures in movie frames. In addition to posters and billboards, Gordon captured Dorothy's subtle grace and lyrical movements in illustrations and silhouettes for the *New York Times* and the *New York Tribune,* as well as on the pages of *Judge* and *Theatre Magazine.* Joining Dorothy in these silhouettes were Gordon's images of other dancers who all but dance off the page, with the tantalizing steps of the Dolly sisters, the gliding turns of Irene Castle, and the balanced pirouettes of Anna Pavlova. By late spring of 1918 Dickson was so impressed with Gordon's style that the actress cornered Condé Nast at one of his famous Park Avenue soirées to insist that the publisher introduce the pair. The meeting of the two young women at *Vanity Fair* launched a lifelong friendship and a seventeen-year collaboration on two continents.[6]

While most of Gordon's posters and billboards displayed color and captured motion, a few caught the nuance of a production by creating a subtle mood and tone. One such twenty-four-sheet billboard featuring Bertha Kalich so impressed Famous Players–Lasky film studio that they ordered a comparable advertisement for their "upcoming screened production of *Everywoman.*"[7] A 1919 issue of the *Poster* praised the work: "Perhaps the most interesting poster of the theatrical season, from the point of view of art, was that for Mme Kalich's play, *The Riddle: Woman* . . . done against a dark background, in a futuristic maze of violet, green and black." The image of Bertha Kalich "was virtually a portrait of the sinuous, dreamy woman of the play—accentuating her mystery, her passion, and her allure. Very hazily done, in dark moody colors that suited the theme of Scandinavian intrigue, it was an excellent indication of the play. Withal, it was of utmost simplicity in the drawing, a fact which served to emphasize its force."[8]

Gordon was eager to be part of the American theater's coming of age. She especially was drawn to comedy and musical theater. Encouraged by frequent client and manager F. Ray Comstock, she championed the Princess Theatre innovations with friends P. G. Wodehouse and Guy Bolton, who worked with Jerome Kern and other composers in developing the American musical comedy. She created striking drawings for early examples of this genre on Broadway, like the posters and billboards for the 1918 and 1919 productions of *Oh, Lady! Lady!!, Oh, My Dear!,* and *The Rose of China.* She also created posters and graphics for Guy Bolton's comedies produced by Comstock and Morris Gest, like *The Five Million* staged by Robert Milton, and *Adam and Eva,* which was selected as one of the best plays of the 1919–1920 season. During her European career, Gordon continued to welcome Bolton's scripts which were always full of charm and wit. Long after their Princess Theatre collaboration in New York during the teens, Wodehouse and Bolton explained their insistence on having a plot for these intimate musicals: the musical comedy book, lyrics, and music were "integrated in a fashion then unknown, the lyrics fitting into the story and either advancing the action or highlighting a character."[9] Jerome Kern likewise stressed that "musical numbers should carry the action of the play and should be rep-

resentative of the personalities of the characters who sing them."[10]

In American drama history, the period during and after World War I is remembered for the flowering of new theatrical concepts and technical innovations by such groups as the Washington Square Players, the Provincetown Players, and the Theatre Guild. Coinciding with these changes were the first full-length plays of Eugene O'Neill, the 1920–1921 Pulitzer Prize–winning plays *Beyond the Horizon* and *The Emperor*

Portion of a poster for Oh, Lady! Lady!!, *1918, one of the famous Princess Theatre musical comedy productions by Jerome Kern, P. G. Wodehouse, and Guy Bolton, and produced by F. Ray Comstock.*

Photograph of Dorothy Dickson perched on the fender of a Delage she purchased from Blake Ozias, New York City, 1920.

Jones, which the awestruck Gordon praised as unique. Though not part of this central core of activity, Gordon and her colleagues in popular comedy and musical theater were influenced by the ideas and issues. As she began her European career in 1921, these trends were beginning to coalesce with centuries-old British and Continental stage practices that in turn were invigorated by Broadway transplants to London's West End.

Political ferment influenced Gordon's stage work as well. She listened to debates among friends active in the Actors' Equity strike and in the founding of the Theatre Guild, whose landmark production of *John Ferguson* she attended in August 1919. She attended lectures and volunteered her services for their benefits. Though the innovations did not affect Gordon's stage commissions for advertising and editorial illustration, the issues did encompass costuming problems. As a consequence of the strike settlement, not only

did performers win the right to contract for positions, but the profession of costume design attained a new status. The terms required that management furnish costumes for the actors and actresses, who until 1919 had dressed themselves at their own expense except in the rare case of the superstar. Gordon Conway felt optimistic about the new horizons open to costume and set designers. The lure of the theater itself attracted her to stage work—the creative challenge of production, the camaraderie of collaboration, and the excitement of performance were the magnets. Gordon always had been stagestruck.

La Voiture Chic

In October 1919, the *New York American* reported that "Gordon Conway is not only furnishing all of the theaters with posters, but selling a French automobile, the DeLage, which is the latest triumph in the French

Photograph of Gordon Conway, now Mrs. Blake Ozias, descending from a Delage in Paris, published in Vanity Fair, *October 1921.*

automobile circles."[11] The project held personal significance for the young artist. During an appointment at the Delage showroom in March 1920 Gordon met her future husband, Blake Ozias, the New York representative in charge of expanding the American market for the highly touted motorcar. Ozias was dissatisfied with an advertisement originally aimed at the French market—a beautiful drawing he had commissioned by noted French artist Georges Barbier. The composition was taboo in marketing circles because Barbier's figures hid most of the automobile detail. Gordon Conway quickly solved her client's problem. As was her custom with product advertising, she placed the car, its features in full detail, in the foreground. Entitled "La Voiture Chic," the striking advertisement ran in upscale magazines like *Town and Country* and *Country Life*. Gordon also introduced Ozias to rising star Dorothy Dickson, who purchased a Delage and appeared in clever photographs for a celebrity promotional campaign that brought public visibility to both the manufacturer and the actress.

Blake Ozias was smitten with Gordon Conway. He admired both her persuasive pen and her sparkling personality. In her Delage advertisement, Gordon drew a chic redheaded model—a figure that seemed stolen straight from the artist's own mirror. The drawing proved prophetic, for Blake romanced Gordon in an identical Delage, and the two were married nine months later. Due to her celebrity status, a corresponding image of Gordon stepping out of a Delage in Paris later appeared in *Vanity Fair*. Reporting Gordon's wedding and the couple's move to Europe, the photograph held the same promise as her advertisement. Both images portrayed the chic New Woman pursuing an independent, glamorous, and cosmopolitan style of life.

Blake Ozias was different from Gordon's café society beaus, but the pair had much in common nonetheless. The couple discovered that they both had been born in December, were interested in the graphic arts, and had relished life in Europe before World War I. Aspirations to the good life, both culturally and materially, would be common threads in their relationship. While living on the Continent, Blake became so affected by a personal aesthetic conversion experience that he opened offices as a printseller and publisher on his return to New York. In September 1914 he issued *A Catalogue of the Highest Grade Prints* from museums and private collectors in England and France. Ozias explained that the two countries possessed "an atmosphere vibrant with art." [12] In the book's introduction, he confessed that as a child he had not been surrounded by art, but in 1912 he was given a reproduction of a fine painting that deeply changed his life. Thinking that others might respond similarly, he offered such enlightened fare through the mail. He laced biographies with short critical pieces on such artists as Whistler, Inness, Rembrandt, Corot, and Lillian Genth. The choices for reproduction included monotones, photographs, photogravure, carbon prints, facsimile prints, and monoprints. His effort might be described as a museum-by-mail or an educational extension service, one aimed at citizens unable to travel to Europe and who feared these treasures would be destroyed by the war. Ozias combined two successful national print-media tools for his educational venture. Though the Ozias effort was totally unrelated and on a much smaller scale, one model was the mail-order catalogue craze heralded both by Richard Warren Sears and his Montgomery Ward competitors. The other model represented the goal espoused by Condé Nast, who believed in educating a select readership in taste, style, and "culture" through high-quality mass publications. Seeing himself as an educational popularizer, Ozias subsequently published a how-to book

instructing women to be self-confident and knowledgeable hostesses when serving French, German, and Italian wines. Blake firmly believed that: "Wine drinking is an art. . . . [and contributes] to gracious living." [13] He especially prided himself on instructing women—like the two Conway women—on how to live the good life, one that ranged from appreciating great literature to driving fine automobiles. Blake's natural talent for teaching had been reinforced by his parents, who had taught, and by his experience as an instructor in 1899 in a one-room brick schoolhouse north of Lewisburg, Ohio.

Gordon and Blake soon discovered that they were both inveterate Francophiles. He loved French cuisine, wine, art, and literature. She loved French cuisine, wine, design, and Parisian haute couture. They both loved the French language. Blake was fluent. After all, according to a family history, he was Vaudois, a name given to members of an early Christian sect that survived in the Alpine region of France, claimed religious independence long before the Reformation, and later merged with the French Huguenots. Blake's father, Ezra John Ozias, called "E.J.," descended from Jean Ozias, later named John, who emigrated to America in 1753. After Ohio became a state in 1803, the family settled on "Congress Lands" and became pioneer leaders in Preble County. [14]

Gordon and Blake found they were both Anglophiles as well. His love of England stemmed from one line in his family's lineage, as did Gordon's, with her British-Welsh legacy tracing back to the Conwy [sic] Castle ancestors in Wales. After they married, the couple explored the Yorkshire roots of Blake's mother, Leora Wheatley, whose family had later settled in Medina, Ohio. When Blake's parents visited the couple after Gordon and Blake moved to England, the foursome toured Blake's maternal ancestral sites, especially Flatby Moor in Yorkshire, the farm where Leora Wheatley Ozias's father had grown up. They trekked to family environs near York, to Kilt Hammerton where Great-Great-Grandfather Wheatley was buried. This interest in genealogy remained a common bond between Blake and Gordon.

Though Blake's family traveled to sites of family ancestry, Ohio remained their most powerful magnet. Most Ozias men and women lived only miles apart in Preble County. Considering Blake's peripatetic wanderings, countless urban abodes, and cosmopolitan ways, no stronger contrast in lifestyle can be cited than the four lines carved in granite under his father's name on the family gravestone: "LIVED HIS ENTIRE LIFE IN THIS COMMUNITY AS A TEACHER, FARMER, BUSINESS MAN, AND NEIGHBOR." The priorities and practices of the Ozias women also reveal a set of values that may have shaped, consciously or not, Blake's expectations of Gordon as a woman and a wife. The women in Blake's family tended to express their independence in roles that were self-sacrificing and public service oriented. For instance, Blake's aunt Dr. Mary Ozias Cromer was a distinguished medical doctor in Greenville, Ohio. His sister-in-law was a nurse who happily joined forces with Blake's wealthy civil engineer brother in Columbus civic work. Another role model extolled as a woman of steadfast community service was Blake's mother. After graduating from a Lebanon, Ohio, university, she taught many years in the Lewisburg public schools and at the Sunday school of the United Brethren Church and was a faithful member of several women's clubs. On that same sturdy granite stone, marking five Ozias graves in Ohio, her inscription resonates: "AN INSPIRATION TO HER FAMILY." [15] Intelligent, industrious, solid, and dutiful, Leora Ozias was the kind of woman who was glad to do her own housework and who searched for apparel bargains in the Sears catalogue. These women did not mirror, nor did they aspire to, the New Woman dancing till dawn on cabaret floors in urban capitals or the New Woman silhouette on the pages of *Vogue* and *Vanity Fair*.

In spite of Blake's support for women's independence, he was ambivalent about the demands placed upon the marriage by Gordon's career as a commercial artist and costume designer—endless appointments, multiple deadlines, countless rounds of fittings, incessant social engagements, and the relentless pressure of the marketplace.

For Gordon Conway, the imperatives of marriage, family, friends, health, finances, and especially her mother's happiness usually took priority over professional or artistic concerns. For two decades Gordon subsumed her career in an arena of personal demands, rather than the other way around. The one exception, however, may have resulted from Heyworth Campbell's advice and a string of successes in the teens. In March 1918, two years before Gordon met Blake, she hesitantly informed Campbell of her wedding engagement to a naval aviation student pilot she had known for three months. She worried that Campbell was "quite peeved. . . . [because] marriage interferes with art." [16] Though she had been affianced since early January to Yonkers native Stanley McCormack, who was training at M.I.T. in Boston, the engagement was not announced in New York and Texas papers until the day after she shared the news with Campbell. She broke the engagement the following August just after her *Vanity Fair* cover and monthly page appeared, while designing posters for five stage productions and preparing for two major design projects for the fall season at the Selwyn Theatre.

Gordon often hovered on the threshold of romance. Friends remembered countless beaus and a dozen proposals from Dallas to Europe and back again to New York. Two admiring beaus, enamored by her charm and entertained by her sense of humor during finishing school days in Lausanne, caricatured Gordon's flair and panache on paper. They surprised her with these drawings, along with declarations of affection and inquiries about marital plans.

An experience with another student would not be so amusing, when a captivated suitor in 1913 became so distraught over repeated refusals to his marriage proposal that he attempted suicide. Deeply grieved by the pain of the handsome young count from Brazil, Gordon—joined by her mother—stayed in close communication during the recovery period and remained his friend for life. Other disappointed boyfriends, like Wood Kahler, found that they too could count on her to be a constant friend. The same loyalty would greet their future wives.

From the time she was an adolescent Gordon never lacked for sweethearts. One or two dates per day became the norm, but most of the time the dates were in the company of a cadre that always included her mother. Beaus were considered friends who periodically dipped in and out of Gordon's world as romantic interests, like aspiring poet Brevard Connor, a World War I veteran and Dallas family friend residing at the Yale Club. Curiously, just weeks before meeting Blake in 1920, she confessed, "I am mad about Brevard." Gordon and Brevard dressed up like babies for costume parties at Freddie Duncan's art studio, dined at Polly's in the Village, danced after the theater till 2:00 A.M. at Rector's, and celebrated till 4:30 A.M. at the Greenwich Village costume balls. He dedicated a series of poems to his special "Daisy" and showered Gordon with flowers, candy, bottles of gin, and stacks of sheet music for her new Steinway grand piano. Among a maze of acquaintances the young couple would steal precious moments alone to indulge their legendary "deep talks." [17] Friends agreed that over the years the two had an on-again, off-again romance. During the spring of 1920, the glow was extinguished again when she became preoccupied with five more young suitors, and Brevard gravitated to a male lover.

That same spring, Gordon and Tommie Conway boarded the train for a two-month stay in Dallas. Though no business commissions were sought, the trip provided scads of parties, lots of dates, shopping sprees, the sale of the Ross Avenue house, and a June wedding of a friend in Paris, Texas, where Gordon's Aunt Olliewood Leake lived. After five years as the star bridesmaid, this time Gordon willingly caught the bouquet. Among her friends who married that year, two married men twice their age, a happenstance that may have influenced Gordon's openness to dating an older Blake Ozias. On her return to New York, and in the midst of ambitious assignments in July, Gordon realized that Blake was accelerating his attention. All of a sudden, this romance was different from the rest. She found herself in a Delage on long drives to polo games at the Meadow Brook Club, to aviation races at "Mitchel Field" on Long Island, and through Central Park in the moonlight. Gordon signaled the shift by a sudden change of nomenclature in her diary. After years of labeling the automobile "a machine," she switched to "the chassis" and "the coupe." [18] His name then changed from Mr. Ozias to Blake Ozias, and then to Blake. He proposed on September 12, and Gordon accepted.

How very odd, Dallas friends whispered, that he was not at all like men they knew, with a regular job and a steady income. Decades later, Dorothy Dickson recalled the similar opinion among their New York show business crowd: "he was certainly nice enough, but different." [19] Having heard that Blake issued from recently arrived, rural Greek immigrant stock, Dallas-ites worried that his background would be a problem, given Gordon's blue-blooded Virginia heritage coupled with her Texas money and cosmopolitan New Woman habits. A few hinted that Gordon's mother passed around the tidbits of doubt, garnished with recollections of aristocratic Italian beaus who became World War I heroes and were still in touch with her daughter. Gordon was oblivious, though, and no one could remember a complaint, not one disparaging remark from her about Blake or his family. By several reports, Tommie Conway's opinions were quite another story. Blake was no Idlewild Club bachelor, nor had he attended an Ivy League college, and though he pronounced words correctly from a French menu and appeared financially secure, he was not from moneyed stock, with stylish tastes and reared with social privilege.

Surprisingly, dancing was an issue. The rage for ballroom dancing at that time cannot be overstated—a parallel, perhaps, to the current craze for jogging and aerobics. Though the couple went dancing during their seven years together, other table guests or exhibition dancers raced to Gordon's side. In one evening out with Blake, she might dance with twenty different partners who were only too glad to locate a woman who was light on her feet and had a sparkling personality. The worst charge leveled at Blake, however, was that he wasn't any fun. While two mutual friends staunchly defended Blake's subtle sense of humor, a battery of voices testified that at parties and out dancing Blake seemed grim and grave. To Gordon's friends, he was "just the sort" to recommend Shakespeare and embrace T. S. Eliot's *The Waste Land*.[20]

It was true that Blake did not resemble Gordon's other beaus or the boyfriends and husbands of her friends or her mother's escorts. Observers felt that Blake seemed older than the new husbands who were twice the age of two of her newly wed friends, and he certainly acted older than Tommie Conway. When Gordon met Blake at the Delage showroom, she was twenty-six and he was thirty-nine years old. Along with good manners and courtesy, a certain mellowness and gentleness characterized Blake. He offered a protective and solicitous demeanor that appealed to Gordon and may have reminded her of her father. John Conway had been sixteen years older than her mother, and he still loomed large in Gordon's life, even though he had died when she was just eleven. Gordon gave her mother a special gift every December on her parents' anniversary date, and her diaries honored John Conway's December birthday, along with her memories of his reverence for the family home of Mount Sion in Virginia. Perhaps Gordon longed for the same mature and nurturing male attention she had experienced when her father was alive. As her December wedding date approached, Gordon would write in her diary, "I am divinely happy."[21]

Tea for Three

One of Gordon's most original graphic design projects for the theater had touted the 1918 hit comedy *Tea for Three*. Little did the artist know that the title would describe her life from the September engagement in 1920 until the divorce in 1927. Two weeks after they were affianced, Blake moved Gordon and Tommie Conway into separate quarters of his home at 65 West Ninth Street in Greenwich Village. The three-story townhouse provided a charming studio for Gordon and was situated a couple of blocks from where the two women had lived during earlier sojourns and conveniently near to the burgeoning Whitney art gallery and Wanamaker's department store. The three walked to the Greenwich Village Theatre and Provincetown Playhouse, as well as to the "goofy clubs" like the Pirate's Den and other nightspots that especially entertained the women. These three people living under one roof strove to make the arrangement work. For example, one thing that had attracted Gordon to Blake was his consideration and kindness to her but, more especially, to her mother. That fall Blake showered them both with attention and affection, not to mention daily surprises of flowers, chocolates, and books, to which he added French lace handkerchiefs, French kid gloves, and French perfume. This ritual of gift giving was a highly structured form of communication among the women and their clan, and Blake knew it. No matter how small or inexpensive the present, Blake learned that this social custom was part of the women's definition of good manners and the good life. The argument that such exchanges are inherently superficial and materialistic belies the ingrained social code that perpetuates the tradition. This type of social gesture was exploited by merchandising strategists in the growing consumer market, especially among women consumers.

Though Gordon and Tom's lifelong habit of dining out at all hours did not cease, the three dined more often at home with regularly scheduled meals prepared by Blake with the aid of his newly hired Japanese butler and the butler's wife. Gordon and Blake set up family belongings recently shipped from Texas, painted furniture discovered in out-of-the-way shops, brightened the house decor, and arranged masses of floral bouquets. As the fall lengthened, Gordon rejoiced in her diary about the couple's long strolls alone, which often included their shooting of home movies "around the neighborhood" in the Village. They explored its curious alleyways and Washington Square, where branches of green and golden leaves rustled

overhead. These blissful moments were recorded with contentment and joy as the wedding day grew near. One observer suspected a sense of relief in Gordon's demeanor—relief from the competitive and demanding schedule of her work. Intimates agreed that never before had Gordon seemed so happy.

Gordon and Blake established a salon made up of his small cadre of intellectual friends, mutual friend Wood Kahler, and a few disconcerted members of the Conway circle who bounced in and out on occasion. In this engaging but understated salon they avoided political talk except for discussions of women's rights and Prohibition. It differed from the salon installed by Mabel Dodge, whose high-profile soirées were held just one block over on Fifth Avenue and had made recent history. The couple hosted teas, cocktails, home-movie presentations, luncheons, and dinners. All were accented by conversations that slipped in and out of French and considered literature, drama, art, design, and world history. After the Oziases' departure for Europe in early 1921, Kahler recalled the salon and urged the couple's return to New York "so our little group of Serious Thinkers can have a means for expressing our aesthetic demeanors." [22]

Other members who shared Kahler's interest in reconstituting the salon were Blake's friends, English writer Richard Le Gallienne and Raymond Loewy, who was to make a major impact on American design as an industrial designer. Kahler also wanted Blake as the editor of *Arts and Decoration* magazine, a publication that represented the group's abiding interest in design, including a philosophical approach to the role of good design in everyday life. Loewy joined Blake in admiring the elegantly designed and crafted Delage automobile, different models of which whisked the friends to polo matches and aviation races on Long Island. Indeed, Loewy, a Paris native and World War I hero, took seriously the importance of visual effects in life: during the war he had decorated his trench with remnants from battle-scarred houses, geraniums, and pages from *Vanity Fair*. After moving to New York, Loewy worked as a fashion illustrator for both *Vogue* and *Harper's Bazaar*. Gordon and Blake identified with Loewy's goal "to improve things people live with from the moment they wake up till they go to bed."[23] These fellow design enthusiasts signaled a new approach to the age-old preoccupation with beauty. They joined other theorists and practitioners who found new moorings in democratic principles, science, technology, and consumerism, and who eschewed the roles that religion, royalty, and rich families had played in art and design. The goal involved an almost messianic hope and a utopian ideal. Their new secular ideology advocated good design to lift all classes of citizens out of the ugly, the mundane, and the tedious in life.

Almost immediately that autumn, Gordon placed her career on hold—forsaking numerous business opportunities—in order to concentrate on her impending marriage. Posters and advertisements for Delage were exceptions, as was a drawing that illustrated Blake's article in *Arts and Decoration*. Gordon would not ignore, of course, the Dickson-Hyson dance team, so costumes and posters emerged for their September 22 opening at the Palais Royal. That summer the Hyson couple repeated a year-old plea that Gordon become Carl's dancing partner. After all, more stage and screen offers surfaced for Dorothy, who frequently was tapped for single performances in the legitimate theater. Six decades later Dorothy Dickson laughed as she remembered "racing in the Delage" from her musical stage shows to the Hysons' midnight cabaret performances. Gordon considered the partnership, but she doubted that exhibition dancing would mix well with an already demanding commercial art career. Moreover, she had demurred because the romance with Ozias was brewing. For his part, Blake tried hard

to accommodate Gordon's career in show business and the print media and attempted to become part of her social circle. Dorothy and Carl were favorites of Blake's, especially Dorothy. The four celebrated each other's birthday festivities like Dorothy's July 26 gala, Carl's November bash, and Blake's party in early December. Gordon's 27th-year soirée was hosted by the Hysons at the swank Palais Royal, just a week after Gordon and Blake's December wedding.

During that fall, at Dorothy Dickson's insistence, Gordon donned her most stylish attire to appear with her friend in a Famous Players' film production. Accommodating as ever, Blake brought sandwiches so the cast could enjoy an urban picnic. For Gordon, the relationship was off to a grand start. She even hinted to one journalist that she might forsake the feminist practice of using her maiden name and switch to her married name in her professional work. Gordon was so caught up in wedding festivities and the life she and Blake were planning that her career lagged behind in second place. There was a tie for first place: Gordon, Tommie, and Blake probably were not aware of a subtle jockeying for position, perhaps even competition, but an ever so slight change in the focus of Gordon's attention occurred. Two people had to share Gordon, a dilemma the three had not anticipated. Since John Conway's death fourteen years earlier—with the exception of Heyworth Campbell's influence and to some extent that of Sanford Stanton of the Selwyn organization—Blake was the only male whose presence affected decisions about Gordon's daily life. To the regret of most friends, Tommie's suitor Tom Camp was not to have his way. New priorities were surfacing, schedules were changing, and the timing of activities shifted. There was a new agenda, and Blake was in charge. For instance, he orchestrated the evening salon, whereupon subjects turned from Broadway hits and the people, places, and things in upscale maga-

Wedding announcement photograph of Gordon Conway that appeared in newspapers in New York City and in selected Texas cities, 1920.

zines to the weightier topics he preferred, such as the works of Zola and Ibsen. Tommie Conway sensed a slower tempo to the talk, perceived longer sentences, noticed less laughter, observed fewer drinks, and witnessed less dancing. Now the guests left before midnight. The usual mirth and zest were gone, and entertainment as she knew it sank into dreariness. In addition, though a prenuptial agreement regarding Gordon and Blake's finances was in progress, Tommie probably was skeptical. One thing Tommie Conway did not mistake—she was no longer the center of attention. Nothing appeared on the surface, and though Gordon seemed impervious to any fissure, the arrangement brought subtle disruptions into the lives of Gordon and Tom and Blake.

On the night before the wedding, Blake wrote Gordon a letter she later described as "the most beautiful letter I've ever had."[24] "My Beloved," he began, "We are to be married tomorrow and in conforming to the established law of the church we shall, in taking our vows, repeat the ancient formulas set down for us." He spoke of the historic and symbolic meaning of the ceremony but added that it would be "no more than mockery were it not for the love we have for each other. . . . Then let me here take my vows without the prompting of the priest—let me take them just for joy in my love for you and in this priceless possession of your love."[25] At high noon on December 11, 1920, Gordon Conway became Mrs. Blake Ozias at nearby Grace Episcopal Church on Broadway. The private ceremony was officiated by the Reverend Charles Lewis Slattery in the 1846 gothic-revival landmark church with its marble spire that stood as a special beacon to Gordon. The best man was artist Rea Irvin, who later served as the first art director for the *New Yorker.* Besides Tommie Conway, the service was attended only by three Conway intimates, who all served as witnesses. Though the Ozias family could not come, sixty guests descended from all directions to celebrate the occasion in the couple's Greenwich Village home. Years later, a guest recalled the scrumptious wedding brunch, accented by wine and masses of flowers, and heralded by telegrams, gifts, and scores of good wishes.

Originally, Gordon and Blake had made reservations to sail on the *Olympic* on December 29. They canceled. Leaving on Tommie Conway's birthday was not Gordon's idea of a happy birthday present. As the postponed date approached, Gordon became more hesitant, even morose. Determined to send the couple off on a happy honeymoon cruise, her mother composed a special message the night before the couple sailed. Following Tommie's wishes, Blake delivered the letter as the RMS *Aquitania* pulled out of the slip on the afternoon of February 3, 1921. "My Darling Child," the letter began, "I have just told you good night for the second time." Tommie Conway confessed, "I do so want you to be happy and have a good time. If you will stop and think every time that you worry about me, that is what I don't want you to [do] and it would make me unhappy if I knew it. Just make up your mind that we will have to be separated for awhile." She begged Gordon not to worry about her, for Blake "won't like me if you are unhappy about me." She reminded Gordon that "he has been very smart and patient with us both." [26]

On the first day out, amid the usual shipboard fanfare she always relished, Gordon confessed in her diary, "I certainly hated to leave My Darling—felt as if I just couldn't." On the second day, still distressed, she wrote, "Blake was lovely to me, as he always is." Well into the cruise, Gordon was joined by her new husband and a host of new friends in toasts "always to the health of my Precious Mother." After the newlyweds watched a glorious sunset from the top deck, Gordon seemed cheered, for it was a "wonderful day." However, she betrayed a deeper feeling: "I miss my Darling Mother, though." The luxury liner knifed through beautiful waters, and the couple visited with scores of interesting passengers. Gordon discovered on board Bobbie and Katharine Appleton, lifelong friends from previous Long Island holidays whom Gordon and Tom later visited at their homes in East Hampton, Paris, and on the French Riviera. Most of the time, though, the lively and spirited Gordon sat in a deck chair writing long letters to her mother. The highlight of the crossing turned out to be not the usual dance numbers, horse racing bets, and deck promenades, but a flood of wireless messages she received from New York. The couple settled into the exquisite Claridge Hotel in London, and Blake arranged for a week full of theater outings, but a stack of letters and cables was the pinnacle of Gordon's honeymoon. The habitually happy, energetic, talented, independent Gordon—this twenty-seven-year-old cosmopolitan gypsy—summed it up: "Quite homesick." [27]

CHAPTER FOUR

CHANNEL CROSSINGS

Enter Mr. Fing

In his wedding-eve love letter Blake made another pledge to Gordon. Acknowledging their dual careers, he wrote: "I shall try to achieve the ambition that I know you share with me and shall try to help you to achieve your ambitions."[1] The ambition of Gordon and Blake differed from the ambition of those whose sole aim was fame and fortune. Their goal was to have money to maintain a creative lifestyle—a lifestyle focusing on the arts, entertainment, and quality material goods, often called "the good life" by contemporary journalists and upscale consumers. By moving to Europe with her husband, Gordon closed the door to a growing New York clientele and lucrative fees. She and her mother, however, received good income from their stock market and real estate investments, a condition that lasted until the Depression, when the artist assumed the role of sole breadwinner. Though both women were perceived as big spenders, they kept up with accounts, anticipated shortages, repaid obligations, and were shrewd consumers of convenience and luxury items. By comparison, Blake's finances appeared erratic and mysterious. Though he was quite intelligent and basically responsible, cautious, and certainly capable of holding down a midlevel management job, Blake possessed a curious restlessness that led to peculiar business entanglements. Not by nature a risk taker, Blake was an uneasy entrepreneur. Even

loyal friends grieved that he possessed poor business judgment. With a prenuptial agreement between Gordon and Blake to hold moneys separately, the ups and downs of Blake's business dealings did not materially affect Gordon and Tom's finances. Gordon's financial records indicate that Blake did repay some of the loans he regularly borrowed from the two women. Regardless, money problems eventually helped corrode the relationship, not so much because of lack of funds as because their attitudes toward financial matters clashed. He was prone to financial surprises, and she was open, direct, and resourceful in her financial dealings.

In the spring of 1921 Gordon stood at the threshold of international recognition, but from February to May, her innate drive and determination lay dormant. Those who knew Gordon's professional and social pace argued that she deserved a sabbatical or at least a vacation to enjoy her new marital status. She cherished married life, liked Blake's friends, and performed as a model helpmate, mending his clothes and accompanying him on dozens of business-related social functions. As for Blake's financial ventures, however, no sooner had they arrived in London than Gordon experienced uncertainty and frustration about his business dealings, just as she had done a short while before in New York. During the brief period between their wedding and the Atlantic crossing, Blake had abruptly announced a new job with a publishing firm. This same uneasiness revisited Gordon in London

*Photograph by Janet Jevons of Mr. Fing and
Gordon Conway, London, ca. 1922–1924.*

when a disagreement suddenly arose with a partner and a lawsuit ensued. Blake won the case, but hurriedly took on two new partners she knew nothing about, hardly dissipating her distress over the venture.

As to her own profession, Gordon made all the correct career-building moves, and Blake kept his wedding-eve pledge to help her achieve her ambitions. They took William Wood, installed by Condé Nast at British *Vogue,* to lunch along with a portfolio of thirty-five pages of her drawings. They talked with art agents and carried Bobbie Appleton's letters to friends in the advertising business. Broadway colleagues like Ned Wayburn had supplied her with letters to London stage moguls that she delivered to Charles B. Cochran, Albert de Courville, Joe L. Sacks, and Alfred Butt. She completed her résumé with complementary publicity photographs taken at Hugh Cecil's studio. Unknown to her, Blake had first introduced Gordon's work to the photographer, who immediately offered help with London stage and print-media connections. She was so pleased with the picture proofs that she rushed them off to Tommie Conway, now moved from the Greenwich Village house to the Plaza Hotel in New York. Over the next months, Gordon returned the favor by commissioning Cecil to photograph scores of her cabaret costumes.

During that spring, the tempo of Gordon's step slowed, and the pace of her work lagged. The vivacious and spirited young woman known for her pizzazz and panache lapsed into a string of nagging illnesses, back problems, and ennui. Blake's attentiveness comforted her, but among the gifts, flowers, and design books he brought her, the highlight each day remained the cables and letters from "my precious Mother." [2]

One occurrence in mid-March, however, enlivened Gordon and was reported in a flurry of letters to Tommie Conway: the discovery of a feline foundling. At the time Gordon and Blake had moved from the Claridge Hotel into a less expensive furnished flat. This relocation established a pattern of inconvenient moves for Gordon that mushroomed over the next six years. The couple ate out most of the time, frequently at one regular spot, the Chantecler [*sic*] in Soho. The restaurant would become a sentimental landmark for the couple because it was where they found "Mr. Fing." Over the years the tale of the cat's discovery was embellished on both sides of the Atlantic. The story of Mr. Fing went like this: On that fateful day in March, a jet black cat with the instincts of a performer in his blood spotted Gordon seated with her husband at a secluded table for two. Peering intently at the stylish American redhead, the alley cat targeted the hip sash of Gordon's navy blue and white polka-dot dress. He leapt resolutely from a nearby window sill and landed

Photograph (London, 1921) by Hugh Cecil of Gordon Conway as the quintessential Jazz Age flapper.

gracefully in Gordon's lap, where he nestled throughout the luncheon. The coup was complete: Gordon was conquered and the restaurateur vanquished. Only negotiations remained. Blake paid one guinea. Fing could come back for visits.

The cat became an integral part of Gordon's public image as well as a cherished companion in her personal life for the next thirteen years. Originally called "Bily" [sic], this jet-black feline assumed the role of a potentate over all the pets she later adopted. Gordon insisted that he was a Persian cat and christened him with the new name of Mr. Fing. Though certainly less bizarre, Gordon's invention of the cat's public persona predated by ten years Josephine Baker's adoption of a pet leopard as a publicity ploy in Paris. Mr. Fing graduated into true celebrity. He added a unique touch to Gordon's already distinctive public persona that coupled a red-haired unschooled artist with a so-

phisticated New Woman. The pairing of the cat and artist was just the kind of staged jollity that Frank Crowninshield would have both encouraged and spoofed in *Vanity Fair.* Attending Mr. Fing's occasional press conferences, the amused British press covered Fing's doings, such as first-class transatlantic travel, in such magazines as the *Tatler, Eve: The Lady's Pictorial,* the *Sketch,* the *Bystander,* and the *Illustrated Sporting and Dramatic News.*

With a renewed zest for life, Gordon revealed in her diary that it was Blake who insisted that she carry the cat home. Mr. Fing settled down with Gordon and Blake in yet another flat, where, only doors away, he would be joined by his new friend, Tommie Conway. Though no prior mention was made of her mother joining the pair, a diary entry in April reported that Tommie had reserved a stateroom on the next ocean liner. Whether Tommie Conway decided, or Gordon

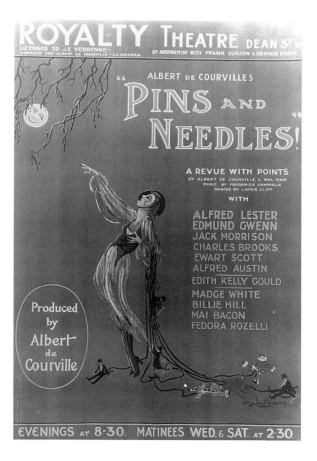

requested, or Blake deemed it wise for Gordon's mother to join the couple, no one seems to know. Tommie Conway put her business in order and sailed the last day of April on the SS *Nieuw Amsterdam.* Blake's reaction is not known, but new horizons opened for Gordon. It was now tea for three again, or four counting Mr. Fing, but the seating chart would change.

All of a sudden Gordon purchased more art supplies. Stage work picked up. Poster and costume commissions issued from Charles B. Cochran for the revue *League of Notions,* which Gordon remembered as John Murray Anderson's *Greenwich Village Follies.* Albert de Courville assigned Gordon posters as well as costumes and sets for a dance number and two scenes in his revue *Pins and Needles.* The Ozias-Conway triumvirate cheered the June arrival of the Hysons. The trio attended the gala tea for Dorothy and Carl hosted by Charles B. Cochran at the Ritz Hotel. Cochran introduced the dancing pair to the press and to stage luminaries as the new stars who were imported to revitalize his production of *London, Paris, and New York.* Cochran arranged box seats for the revue and treated the group to dinner and dancing at the Savoy Hotel after the show. Following the Hysons' successful July 4 opening at the London Pavilion, Gordon's posters created a fanfare over their new presence in the show. Rehearsals, meetings, and fittings filled her days once again. Gordon, Blake, and Tommie attended the annual Theatrical Garden Party, where Gordon ran into friends and colleagues, including Jennie and Rosie Dolly who, billed as the Dolly Sisters, stole the spotlight that spring in *League of Notions,* their first international success. The sisters set up times to discuss costumes and personal wardrobes. London associates soon reported that Gordon's posters of the Dollys were pasted "all around town." One of Gordon's posters of

Dorothy Dickson was reproduced in a mid-September issue of the *Sketch,* the first major news piece about her work in Europe. Gordon was indeed back on track.

During August 1921 the group celebrated the selection of Dorothy Dickson for the title role in the London production of *Sally,* the Ziegfeld hit by Guy Bolton with music by Jerome Kern and Victor Herbert. Though Gordon, Blake, and Tommie moved to Paris that same August because of another Ozias business venture, Dickson insisted that Gordon design some of her costumes. Gordon crisscrossed the English Channel for fittings of her designs at B. J. Simmons and Company Limited costumiers and for conferences with Dorothy and the couturière Lucile, who also provided dresses for Dickson. When the show premiered that fall at the Winter Garden Theatre, the role of Sally catapulted Dorothy Dickson to instant fame.

The three applauded Carl Hyson as well in his new stage efforts in London. He pioneered early productions of cabaret—an entertainment that would gain great popularity in London by 1924. Hyson staged a new edition of his *Folies de Montmartre* at the Queen's Hall Roof. Soon to follow were his productions at Rector's Club, which were entitled *Palais Cabaret,* and also the shows, *Rectors One O'Clock Revue.* Soon to follow was Hyson's most celebrated show, *The Midnight Follies* at the Hotel Metropole. These editions featured costumes, small props, and graphics designed by Gordon. The Hyson shows introduced producer Percy Athos to her talent, which led to exclusive work for the *New Princes' Frivolities.* These legendary Athos productions showcased some of Gordon's most original designs during the golden era of London cabaret.

From Auteuil to Bushey Grange

Between 1921 and 1927 Gordon's commissions multiplied in Great Britain and on the Continent. The assignments required countless trips back and forth on boats and trains across the English Channel between London and Paris. In fact, the sight of Gordon Conway on board a Channel steamer prefigured the 1933 motion picture *Channel Crossing* and the actresses she dressed for their roles as fashionable young professional women on their way to the Continent. When Gordon was not commuting to meetings, fittings, rehearsals, and performances, she forwarded art by airmail, a recent advance that greatly accelerated her work orders. Knowing Gordon's compulsion for prompt delivery, friends and colleagues joked that even the sketches had sprouted wings.

After their move in August 1921, the Ozias-Conway family settled quickly into Parisian life and gravitated toward the company of the English-speaking café society. Though Gordon and Blake spoke French, Tommie Conway and many of their other friends did not. At the end of the year, in search of a permanent residence, Gordon and Blake leased a home in Auteuil, and Tommie established residence at the Hotel d'Iéna. To Gordon, the charm of their new abode reminded her of their joyous townhouse days in Greenwich Village. While putting the rooms in order, she admitted to "working like Miss Lulu Bett," a reference to the house-drudge and title role of a recent Broadway hit.[3] Thinking the move a permanent stay, friends filled the house with flowers and housewarming presents. Every corner was banked with violets, tulips, and mimosa Gordon had arranged. Five men in Blake's office thrilled Gordon with fifty luxuriant branches of mauve and white lilacs as a special New Year's Day treat. She mused that the blossoms were a perfect way to welcome 1922. Gordon began to feel that her family of three had settled for a while between New Year's and Lent. On a cold and rainy evening before an open fire during that year's Mardi Gras festivities, Gordon wrote of her contentment in her diary. Expressing love for Blake, she confided that they had "stayed home together which I like most to do."[4] Blake often added love notes in the diary margin, especially on the eleventh of each month in honor of their December 11 wedding date. One entry typical of his devotion read, "Gordon Dear. . . my love for you grows with the days!"[5]

Friends and colleagues visited their new house, including frequent house guest Inez Gibbs Hayward, a Dallas beauty recently married to future stage and film impresario Leland Hayward. Another Dallas friend who called on them was Margaret Page Elliott, whose husband was a career army captain stationed in Paris after World War I. Wood Kahler, now retired from Wall Street and living in Europe, was in Paris seeking publishers and inspiration for his new career as a novelist.

Costume design, Channel Crossing, *1933.*

Also living in Paris and joined by his longtime companion George Sebastian, Porter Woodruff illustrated for *Vogue* and freelanced for some of the same London magazines that featured Gordon's work, including the *Tatler* and *Eve*. Woodruff was completing an oil portrait of Gordon as a belated wedding present for the couple. Over the next several years he delineated Gordon's silhouette for *Eve*'s popular "Butterfly" column featuring well-dressed Continental luminaries. Though he was a popular and well-paid illustrator and portraitist, Woodruff aspired to be a studio artist. Just as she supported Kahler's writing career, Gordon encouraged Woodruff's ambitions. (For familial, personal, and financial reasons she herself did not have the freedom or the opportunity to

shift to a career in the fine arts.) When Woodruff was honored with a one-man show in London in June 1923, she applauded. He attained the status of a serious artist of the Maghreb landscape when he and Sebastian later moved to Northern Africa.

Porter Woodruff was also painting a portrait of Margaret Elliott, who remembered the friends close to Gordon and Tommie, especially Woodruff, with affection. One Elliott story about the Conway-Ozias retinue was typical of the legendary Jazz Age world. She recalled a madcap evening when Woodruff grew too "tipsy" to tour the Paris nightspots, so the friends folded his body into a bathtub and poured the remaining Champagne over his limp frame, leaving him to lie undisturbed until their return six hours later.

Such shenanigans became the norm. As the decade plunged forward, the two women and their band of cosmopolites attracted even more Continentals, British natives, American expatriates, and of course, Texans on extended stays. In the beginning Blake appeared to enjoy the intersecting circles of glamorous gadabouts. He entered into the festivities during the first two years of marriage but gradually found excuses to be absent, whether the parties took place in Paris or London.

With new business projects in Paris, London, and parts beyond, Blake established an office on the Rue de Chabrol to manage newly acquired work for a stove manufacturer. Continuing a practice established during Blake's promotional campaigns for the Delage automobile, Gordon produced French-language posters and illustrations for Lawson stove advertisements. However, "Chez Lawson" was not as impressive as it sounded, according to Margaret Page Elliott, who confided that the office "was a dinky little place," not

at all what she expected based on Gordon and Tommie's usual regal surroundings.[6] Elliott worried that Blake's erratic business endeavors and Gordon's recent successes were beginning to erode the relationship. Elliott's account of Gordon's increasing reticence about her talent and professional life was later reinforced by others. Pointing out the sharp contrast in careers, friends observed that as Gordon's accomplishments grew more visible, Blake's efforts faded into the shadows. Taking a signal from Gordon as her professional reputation and personal popularity spiraled upward, her supporters toned down their usual praise in Blake's presence, though Tommie Conway never hesitated to raise the flag of jubilation.

As to Gordon's work environs, she operated from a variety of venues on both sides of the Channel. Her working conditions were subject to Blake's spur-of-the-moment moves. She was forever notifying clients of different addresses and telephone numbers, and locating new lithographers, photographers, seamstresses,

Oil portrait by Porter Woodruff of Gordon Conway, Paris, 1922.

fabric shops, and art supply stores. While seeking jobs in Paris, she worked doubly hard to keep up with the sporadic orders that arrived from London, like ones from Percy Athos, Charles B. Cochran, Robert Courtneidge, Albert de Courville, Dion Titheradge, Carl Hyson, and Dorothy Dickson, as well as from art director Peter Huskinson who purchased random drawings for the *Tatler,* the *Sketch,* and *Eve.* Gordon recorded in her diaries that clients telegraphed their orders. For example, Hyson, who expected immediate action, often sent urgent "Marconis" from London to Gordon in Paris.[7] With her usual efficiency Gordon responded with airmail deliveries of updated designs and new creations for his cabaret follies. After all, she had trained herself to meet deadlines in New York in the days when she bustled from one place to another with her mother. Yet her new milieu was different: the distance was greater, the workplace was more diverse, she barely knew the people, and the stakes were higher. Gordon no longer was the latest debutante discovery and youngest artist on the Condé Nast staff; she was competing with the finest, already established, and mostly male illustrators and designers in Europe. Though Blake kept his promise, assisting her with appointments and sharing house chores, he was strangely oblivious to her problems in setting up studio space and the need for continuity in her work. Gordon never complained, but Tommie Conway made a mental note of his indifference to her work requirements.

Gordon enlisted the help of friends and colleagues to set up meetings in an effort to establish stage and magazine connections in Paris and Europe during the fall of 1921 and early 1922. Gordon called on the Paris representative of *La France: An American Magazine* with a letter from her former New York client, the managing editor of the magazine. Blake's friend Georges Barbier charmed Gordon with talk of art possibilities over a glass of Dubonnet in his atelier. With the help of Pierre Duchart, a contact was made with the publisher Tolmer. (The "Tolmer" in Conway's diary probably refers to Paris printer and layout authority Alfred Tolmer.) Porter Woodruff introduced her to Marcel Astruc, with whom she discussed work options. With Woodruff acting as an intermediary, Gordon also attended a session at the "*Bon Ton* office" with Lucien Vogel, the distinguished publisher who employed fine artists as illustrators and showcased innovative techniques like *pochoir* in fashion, costume, and decorative arts publications. Gordon knew that acceptance by the legendary Vogel and his retinue was de rigueur in the world of fashion illustration and design in Paris. Prior to World War I, Vogel, along with his wife and her brothers, had created *La Gazette du Bon Ton,* a deluxe fashion journal revived in 1921 by Condé Nast. Also with Nast's help, Vogel had published an edition in the midst of the war that commemorated the 1915 Panama Pacific International Exposition in San Francisco, a venue that showcased the latest in Parisian haute couture. Vogel and his family's talents were crucial when Nast launched the French *Vogue* in 1920. Though never financially lucrative for the Nast empire, it reflected the very essence of haute couture chic and artistic merit through top-quality illustration and photography.

Curiously, nothing resulted from most of these appointments; Gordon ran into a polite reluctance. This innovative and hard-working female American freelance artist—married to an American businessman—encountered a closed shop in the elite publishing arena. Gordon Conway was not the only one, however. She joined a host of other commercial graphic artists, mostly male, from the United States living in Paris, who found work predominantly within the English-speaking enclaves of Europe. Gordon realized that

Costume designs for "Hat Number," Casino de Paris, Paris, ca. 1924–1925.

plenty of gifted artists who were French citizens vied for the same illustration jobs, not to mention the competition from such transplants as the Russian Erté, who had established permanent residence in France. The field was dominated by what the Condé Nast staff in New York labeled the "Beau Brummells," a cadre of French, European, and émigré male artists who were permanently rooted in Paris. After all, a hint lingered in the air that the Americans would stay in Europe just as long as it was inexpensive to live there and personal freedom flourished. Despite the United States' pivotal but late entrance into the Great War, the suspicion smoldered that at the slightest sign of trouble, the Yankees would race back across the Atlantic to the safety of another continent.

Undaunted by the vagaries of the print-media establishment, Gordon turned to theater and cabaret in Paris. She delivered Ned Wayburn's letter to the renowned Madame B. Rasimi at the Théâtre Ba-Ta-Clan. She sought out Léon Volterra, an astute businessman with an engaging personality who had owned the Casino de Paris since 1917. Financing the reopening of a revue at the Folies Bergère just after the Battle of the Marne, Volterra had emerged as a giant in Parisian entertainment. This contact led to future Conway assignments at the Casino de Paris, the chief rival to the Folies Bergère. Gordon's tenacious groundwork also paid off two years later with a total design concept project that was commissioned by Tommie and Jack Tomson, the British-born brother dance team. In Paris, the Tomson Twins produced editions of their *Midnight Follies* at the Club Daunou, which was located at number seven Rue Daunou near the Place de l'Opéra and across from Ciro's restaurant, one of Gordon's favorite haunts and an important venue for informal business contacts.

Gordon also cultivated contacts in the consumer and entertainment business who were interested in public visibility, such as the owners and managers of restaurants such as Ciro's that featured dancers and musicians. Her status as a young American artist and the quintessential New Woman had preceded Gordon to Paris through word-of-mouth and in the American and British press. A number of Continentals were impressed with Gordon as a personality, along with her talent and affinity for image building and newsmaking. Ciro's restaurant was ripe for this kind of clientele to supplement the occasional visits of its most famous guests—the Prince of Wales and his entourage. The very essence of café society, these connections of mutual interest usually were unofficial, with an unspoken understanding between the parties to promote each other, as well as to introduce interesting people who ought to know each other anyway. Such was the case with Gordon, Ciro's, and Calouste Gulbenkian in the spring of 1922.

Ciro's management arranged a lunchtime introduction between the young artist, her stylish mother, and Calouste Gulbenkian, the oil-rich Armenian acknowledged by the press as the wealthiest man in the world in the 1920s. The financial tycoon had established headquarters in Lisbon but frequently visited other European capitals where members of his family maintained homes. Though Gordon eventually became lifelong friends with his wife, daughter, son-in-law, and daughter-in-law, the patriarch was the first in the family to discover her charm and pizzazz. He showered Gordon and Tommie Conway with attention, sending twelve dozen roses in one sweep as a token of esteem. In April Gulbenkian hosted a farewell soirée for Gordon. Guests were startled to learn that the dinner-dance at Ciro's was a going-away party, since Gordon and Blake had made no secret of the fact that they were enchanted to be residents of the City of Light. No sooner had Gordon put the Auteuil house in order and followed up on business appointments than Blake abruptly announced a move back to England.

When considering Gordon's attempt to maintain a full-scale domestic life along with a career, the distraction of relocating, even with the help of a household employee, should not be overlooked. For instance, during four of their seven years of marriage, Gordon endured twelve such moves in Paris alone. The earlier meanderings of Gordon and Tom from one luxury hotel to another deluxe apartment paled in comparison to Blake's pattern of job and house relocations. The moves required more time and energy than would a proverbial starving artist unpacking a small satchel of belongings in a garret. A home was one thing and the studio another. In addition to arranging art supplies for a home studio, Gordon's days were filled with washing crystal, polishing silver, pressing linens, and hanging clothes in closets. These household chores coordinated easily with Gordon's work on advertisements for Lawson stove, as well as graphics for Blake's next venture, the Dura automobile, but she found it difficult to handle large-scale projects, experiment with her art, and expand her clientele at a makeshift home studio. Gordon aspired to two full-time jobs: as a professional commercial artist and as a wife and homemaker. Unlike Woodruff and most of her male colleagues, married or not, Gordon found her focus to be split in half.

Within weeks of the Gulbenkian party, the Ozias-Conway trio traveled back across the Channel. During the late spring of 1922, they hunted houses in twenty rural locations before agreeing on the country estate of Bushey Grange in Hertfordshire about thirty miles north of London. The terms of the lease are

Bushey Grange, 1922–1923. Gordon Conway holding Mr. Fing next to her cheek in a "field of wild daisies," perhaps awaiting Dorothy Dickson's visits, which often included the actress's high kicks and cartwheels.

unknown, but the three were in and out of the manor house over a period of two years. To Gordon it was an idyllic spot.

Across the Ocean and Back Again to Bushey Grange

Between their two summer sojourns at Bushey Grange, Gordon, Blake, and Tommie returned to the United States for an extended visit that combined business with a holiday. On December 27, 1922, they embarked on the RMS *Majestic,* the world's largest ocean liner, in its inaugural year of operation. Mr. Fing was

the toast of the voyage. He garnered attention at charity auctions, at shipboard horse races, during cocktail hour, and promenading on the deck. "A good start on the new year, I hope to continue," Gordon recorded in her diary[8]—a remark occasioned by the $625 raised in a charity auction on New Year's Day from her two sketches of Ruth Draper and Wilhelm Backhaus, who donated entertainment services for the British and American Seamen's Institutions. She rendered eight more for sale the next day, showed other work at tea time on the third, and was singled out with passenger applause as the ship's "note of thanks."[9]

On the eastbound voyage in February, Gordon donated more artwork "for the cause" on the RMS

Gordon Conway near the Oziases' home and studio in Chelsea (London), ca. 1922–1923, between residences at Bushey Grange.

Berengaria.[10] Sketches of passengers Gladys Cooper and the Dolly Sisters yielded $250 for the seamen's charities at an auction arranged by Harry Green while on the cruise. Gordon also provided special showings of previously produced posters and drawings of the Dolly Sisters, presenting one to the sisters on the spot after their performance with Edward Dolly and Jack Haskell, a producer of *Sally* and *The Cabaret Girl.* That Gordon traveled with her artwork and supplies is a point worth mentioning. Lugging a trunk filled with a repertoire of posters, graphic reproductions, and original drawings, as well as press books—even during those days of ready luggage handling—took planning, time, and effort that she was willing to de-

vote to her career. This urban nomad was used to living out of trunks and producing on demand.

During their trip to New York and Ohio, Gordon did hint, however, at the stress of creating artwork in gypsy environs, opulent though they may have been. Working on trains, in New York hotel rooms, and in Broadway managers' offices, Gordon sighed that she was working "Certainly under difficulties," as she struggled with a deadline for artwork for *Lady Butterfly* ordered by Ned Wayburn and Oliver Morosco at the Globe Theatre.[11] The day before she sailed back to Europe, she delivered Wayburn's posters and graphics and was paid in English pounds; on January 19, 1923 Gordon recorded payment of £110.10 for her

Photograph of Gordon Conway on the deck of the Berengaria, *1923.*

illustrations. Also before the ship sailed she rushed to Brooklyn with sketches for "Shadowland" and kept appointments with past accounts.

Gordon's business activities in New York were interwoven with duties involving Tommie Conway. Gordon nursed her mother through another illness and helped the sick but determined woman depart for a visit to Texas. She also rummaged through Manhattan Storage, selecting furniture headed for Europe. The New York stay was highlighted by dancing at the Plantation Club in Harlem and eleven stage productions, not counting cabaret numbers and three Wayburn shows. Plays included the acclaimed *Rain,* which she tagged "the best show in town," and *Seventh Heaven,* which she thought mediocre but which starred Helen Menken who friends insisted was Gordon's double.[12] The holiday in the United States also included a train trip to Ohio, where Blake visited his family, and a business stopover in Pittsburgh for the Lawson stove people.

Before she left New York in early 1923, Gordon realized she had crowded one event on top of the other. She rationalized, though, that most were related to maintaining business contacts in Manhattan through a show business and café society network. Being a loyal café society member—like membership in the informal fraternity of the Algonquin Roundtable to which New York friends belonged—was as demanding and time-consuming as any official dues-paying association membership or, for that matter, a regular job, like those of Gordon's friends in Dallas and of relatives in Tidewater Virginia.

Back in Europe and England, Gordon and Blake eventually gravitated to Bushey Grange. The summer of 1923 almost replicated the one the year before except, as Gordon recorded in her diary, without the severe rains. Carl Hyson, Dorothy Dickson, and their young daughter, "Little Dot," frequently visited Bushey Grange along with scores of other guests. During that summer, Gordon and Carl happily conspired over sketches, fabrics, and cost estimates with Madame Perot, who executed Gordon's sketches for Carl's cabaret follies. Designing all the costumes for the two 1923 editions of *The Midnight Follies* at the Hotel Metropole, Gordon featured a special duo creation entitled "China Love" that dressed both Carl Hyson and his dance partner Vera Lennox. She arranged for actresses to wear her popular cabaret jockey costumes to the annual Theatrical Garden Party, advising the women to be available to the press. Photographs did appear in prestigious publications, including one in the *Tatler* on July 4, 1923. This photograph, however, betrays a discrepancy often apparent when a costume sketch is compared to the constructed garment in a photograph. The real costume on the real female body is a far cry from the well-tailored ensemble on the tall bone-thin figure in Gordon's renderings. Except for Dorothy Dickson, her daughter Dorothy Hyson, and a few others, the comparison of the rendering with the finished product is all too often disappointing, because Gordon's costumes look ill-fitting, and the models look pudgy. She would face this problem more acutely during her motion picture work and learned to adapt the image-marketing methods of Hollywood stills photography that hid fabric wrinkles and women's weight.

Conversations at Bushey Grange turned to Dorothy Dickson's stage career, including her 1922 role in Jerome Kern's *The Cabaret Girl,* coauthored by P. G. Wodehouse. Gordon had designed a costume and poster for the play at Dorothy's request, though Dolly Tree was commissioned to dress the show. The theme—and very title of the show—presaged British acceptance of cabaret as a respectable stage genre and symbolized its popularity. In tandem with the Hyson pair and later Percy Athos, Gordon played a major role in cabaret production during the ascendancy and reign of the golden age of London cabaret.

Bushey Grange had been the venue the previous summer for work Gordon hoped to continue, like her poster commissions. She took pride in winning honorable mention in the Loomas poster competition at Barker's during 1922. Her movie posters and billboards covered much of London. Future American film executive Walter Wanger hired Gordon to advertise four films with seven different posters. Her fees ranged from the regular price per poster of ten pounds and ten shillings to fifteen pounds and fifteen shillings for one labeled "Mrs. Nanook" for the silent-film classic, *Nanook of the North.* Other highly touted posters promoted *Foolish Wives, A Bill of Divorcement,* and images of Marion Davies and Lyn Harding as the stars of *When Knighthood Was in Flower.* Invited by Wanger to the private screenings at The New Gallery Cinema, Gordon requested she be permitted to bring Blake as her guest, as well as his parents, who were visiting the couple at Bushey Grange.

The Ozias-Conway trio continued the practice of hosting dozens of house guests, parties, and picnics. Another floating salon was installed. As in Dallas, New York, and Paris, the groups seemed composed of single people, even when they were married and arrived together. Friends from prewar days in Lausanne, especially the young men from "The Villa" school, seemed to locate Gordon and her crew wherever her residence happened to be. The crowds dined, took tea, drank cocktails, smoked, sang, danced, and played tennis and croquet. Most of all they conversed. On occasion the entertainment consisted of readings, like Lewis Galantière's rendition in French of Anatole France's *La Vie en Fleur,* published in 1922. Both summers of 1922 and 1923 featured the pastimes of charades, "21," Russian bank, Mah-Jongg, Ouija board, and "spiritual seances."[13] Though a cook was hired for meals, duties began to smother Gordon as she marketed, cleaned, gardened, and attempted to sketch. Exasperated, Gordon finally admitted in her diary the difficulty of trying to paint in a house full of people. Nevertheless, she relished the pleasant days in the country. The hours sailed by as she arranged "ten different kinds of flowers" to fill the house with massive sprays.[14] She renewed the herb garden and meandered with a peaceful herd of sheep grazing in a glade nearby. She skipped with Mr. Fing through the blanket of daisies warmed by a hazy sun.

During those halcyon days, however, one event on September 12, 1923, left a tear in the fabric of the Ozias couple's relationship and signaled the beginning of the end for the marriage. Very few indications of domestic problems had surfaced in Gordon's diaries and letters. There were, of course, a few remarks about Blake not paying his hotel and restaurant checks, and leaving Tommie Conway with the bills, but those complaints were isolated and seemed without rancor or judgment. Blake may have felt, however, that if there were entertainment charges other than his own, he should not have to pay for the traveling circus that always seemed to be on hand. Prior to this incident in the fall, the few hints of trouble in Gordon's diary actually emanate more from what was not recorded (her habit of praising Blake, so obvious in the beginning stage, stops abruptly). The event was only obscurely alluded to and remained a guarded secret and a sadness she chose not to share with anyone. Uncharacteristically, the usually cheerful Gordon lamented, "I feel so unhappy and he has hurt me so," adding that she felt "more miserable than anyone will ever know." She confessed, "My heart is broken." This sadness eclipsed the happy times of two summers in the Hertfordshire countryside. Indeed, on that Tuesday she spent "the most unhappy night of my married life." [15] From this date on Blake no longer reaped the blessing of "my sweet kind Blake." [16] The loving references to "my precious Blake" disappeared from the diary. Like the diary references to Blake when they fell in love during the summer of 1920, the change of nomenclature in Gordon's writing was telling. Blake was identified on the pages only as "B.O." from the fall of 1923 until well after the divorce.

From Mulberry Walk to Montparnasse

Living five months here and five months there, the couple's nomadic existence expanded beyond the peregrinations of earlier months. One stop along the way turned out to be a charming "corner house" at 22 Mulberry Walk in Chelsea that contained a studio with tall windows and long ribbons of precious light. Ever eager to notify clients of her whereabouts, she informed Henry Sell back in New York at *Harper's Bazaar* about

the new quarters. He shared her delight in return: "Mulberry Walk, Chelsea! What a sound that has, and I presume it is just as nice as it sounds." [17] To Gordon it was.

In addition to portraits of Mr. Fing, the sun-filled atelier welcomed another installment of two types of autobiographical drawings begun in New York in 1920, explored further in Part Two. However, these images of introspection taper off after one special December 1923 drawing. This arresting and uncharacteristic drawing entitled "Madame La Vie" pictures a redheaded woman removing her young and pretty face framed with red hair as though it were a mask. Beneath the mask is an old and wrinkled face, a face that frightens the male companion. Created soon after the September 1923 diary entry revealing Blake's unkindness to her, the sketch is significant both biographically and symbolically. (The illustration "Madame La Vie" and the author's interpretation appear in Part Two.) This landmark image signaled a sudden change in Gordon's life, for she immediately shifted her priorities and started an intense search for work. Though Peter Huskinson purchased the sketch in December 1923, he did not publish it in the *Tatler* until 1926.

Beginning in late 1923, Gordon eagerly sought commissions. Leading a full-speed search, in July 1924 she reported that she was "busy trying to see people. . . . trying to sell sketches." She approached producer Julian Wylie at the London Hippodrome, but nothing materialized from the meeting. She hurriedly followed up on potential clients suggested by Dion Titheradge; he plied her with letters of recommendation to stage notables "Mr. Bryan at Daly's" and André Charlot, who would seek out her designs in the years to come. [18] In the meantime, Gordon, Blake, Tommie, and Mr. Fing moved again.

A 1923 illustration subsequently published with headlines "Over the River," Paris Times, February 26, 1925. Also labeled "The Blues," this drawing illustrated an article observing that Gordon Conway "sure can get that Blues feeling into her posters."

A random selection of jobs in London during this period included posters for Odette Myrtil in two separate shows and designs resulting from dinner meetings with Alice Brady, in town for her movie opening and seeking Gordon's help with a personal wardrobe. Gordon sold four fashion illustrations to *Eve* for six pounds and six shillings; one drawing to the *Sketch* for four pounds and four shillings; and ten costume designs to Rector's for sixteen pounds. She sold a poster that featured an African-American jazz theme for ten pounds and ten shillings to Oddenino's Imperial Restaurant; the poster probably promoted their new cabaret acts. Two separate orders that turned into misadventures involved the Dolly Sisters and Peggy O'Neil. Though Gordon welcomed such high-profile clients, she took pause after the cavalier attitude of the performers who misplaced or lost her sketches.

In the midst of this hectic work and social schedule in both London and Paris, Gordon struggled to find time for one of the things she really loved— her continuing art education. Also realizing that such education was crucial to a successful career, she tried to fit in art classes with artists she admired like Bernard Adams. His wife, in turn, commissioned Gordon to design some of her costumes for the London stage. Gordon herself tutored students seeking commercial art and costume design instruction during the summer of 1923 at Bushey Grange; she received one pound and ten shillings for one month of lessons from each of a small number of pupils. The art influences on the Gordon Conway oeuvre came from a wide variety of sources and cannot be limited to any one style or proponent. The libraries of the Louvre and the British Museum stand out as the most frequent sites for Gordon's research visits, which often were shared with Porter Woodruff. Other colleagues with whom she shared exhibitions, workshops, and camaraderie included sculptor Seymour Fox, caricaturist Edmundo "Mundo" Searle, and illustrator and future film costume and set designer Reynaldo Luza.

The European capitals offered a wealth of exhibitions at museums and commercial art galleries. Among Gordon's favorites were the Tate Gallery, the Royal Academy, and the Leicester Galleries in London, along with the Salon des Tuileries, the Grand Palais, the Guimet Museum, the Léonce Rosenberg Galleries, and the Salon des Indépendants in Paris. Japanese and other Oriental art attracted attention, as did "the moderns," as Gordon labeled the Modernists. One display in Paris in November 1921 led Gordon to exclaim that the work of Spanish artist Federico Beltrán-Massés "gives me a lot of inspiration."[19] Gordon exposed herself to an astonishing amount of visual expression, ranging from the works of Max Beerbohm, Paul Manship, Jacob Epstein, Jean Paul Forain, Amedeo Modigliani, Paul Gauguin, Kees Roovers, and Kapp the caricaturist, to that of theater design legend Edward Gordon Craig. Especially significant were three theater art exhibitions she attended between 1921 and 1924 at the Victoria and Albert Museum that included Ballets Russes designers and an important Léon Bakst one-man show. Gordon studied too in her own library, replete with art, design, and theater books and portfolios of reproductions given to her by Blake and her mother. Also those European cities themselves were a kind of open-air museum, from the Chelsea flower show to the graphics of the London underground, and from the markets of Paris to the crowds in the Place Vendôme. Indeed, every day and every place educated Gordon's eye.

CHAPTER FIVE

THAT RED HEAD GAL

A Dallas Daughter in Drury Lane

Encore critic Geoffrey Moore claimed that cabaret at its best was "representative revue."[1] The advisers to Francis Towle's 1922 "supper entertainment" at the Hotel Metropole included revue impresarios George Grossmith, J. A. E. Malone, and André Charlot, who found producing a revue in a standard theater less complicated than bothering with the logistics of a restaurant not built for theatrical performance. In stage parlance, the revue often is lumped together with other popular musical genres. The definition and history of cabaret, revue, and musical comedy are complicated by traditional legitimate stage practices and by legal regulation terminology, not to mention the confusion with music hall, variety, vaudeville, burlesque, and countless hybrids.

Great Britain has had a long record of revue that should be distinguished from revue in France, its birthplace, and in the United States. Originally an "end of the year review," this stage presentation was composed of "a succession of scenes in dialogue and song representing such incidents or individuals as have preoccupied the public . . . during the course of the year." One strain developed into the nineteenth- and twentieth-century "spectacular revue" of the Parisian music hall, which is a "series of tableaux produced with a lavish display of scenery and costumes." The British revue includes satiric presentations in "songs, sketches, burlesques, [and] monologues" of

current social, cultural, economic, and political events loosely woven together without a story line or book. Recognized as a seminal figure in British revue is James Robertson Planché, who produced and wrote on all phases of theater, including scenic and costume design, in the first half of the nineteenth century. In 1825 he produced "the first attempt in this country [England] to introduce that class of entertainment so popular in Paris called Revue."[2] At the turn of the century, following the restrictions of Victorian society, the Edwardian period "provided a fertile soil in which to re-sow the seeds of French revue, which itself had been enjoying a notable revival across the Channel."[3] Revue has been associated with chorus girls in exotic costumes singing and dancing around scenic decorations, but the size of the cast and degree of lavishness divided productions into two separate and competing camps, the spectacular and the intimate revue. Gordon Conway worked in both arenas.

Pleased with Gordon's work for his 1921–1922 revues, Charles B. Cochran commissioned Gordon in April 1923 to dress an entire scene and create posters for his new revue, *Dover Street to Dixie,* at the London Pavilion Theatre. (The hit of Cochran's revue was "The Plantation Revue," which featured an African-American cast starring the incomparable Florence Mills, who had mesmerized audiences around the world.) Gordon conferred with Cochran in London on five occasions and, true to her rapid pace, delivered the sketches eleven days later before returning

Photograph of Gordon Conway and Dorothy Dickson visiting a Paris market, 1925.

to Paris. She would not see the show, however, until July 31 on a return trip to London.

On June 26, 1924, Dion Titheradge engaged Gordon for his revue *The Odd Spot,* starring Binnie Hale with music by Geoffrey Gwyther and Gordon's former New York client Gitz Rice. She delivered a batch of drawings on July 4, worked at the dress parade, and "corrected costumes" at two dress rehearsals, but missed the opening on July 30 at the Vaudeville Theatre because Blake had to return to Paris that day. Finding Titheradge pleasant and responsible to work for, she wrote, "He's a peach," when he helped her acquire jobs following her renewed determination to expand her career.[4] Titheradge commissioned costumes in November 1925 for *Tricks,* a revue he authored and produced. So fond was Gordon of these costumes that she adapted several for her own wardrobe. Besides good press for the production costumes, the personal *Tricks* dresses elicited raves on the Continent and on board the *Homeric* during a January 1926 voyage to New York. *Tricks* premiered at London's Apollo Theatre on December 22, 1925. It was another opening that Gordon missed.

Gordon also worked with Dion Titheradge on his musical comedies. He had engaged her for costumes and graphics in the summer of 1924 for "a comedy with music in three acts," entitled *Patricia,* that showcased Dorothy Dickson in the title role. As in her New York career, Gordon welcomed musical comedy to her stage repertoire abroad along with revue and cabaret. Playcraft, Limited, under Titheradge, Gwyther, and Leslie Henson, along with the management of His Majesty's Theatre, George Grossmith and J. A. E. Malone, was determined to combat American domination of West End musical productions. The publicity stressed an "All-British musical comedy" featuring London's original "Sally" and "Cabaret Girl," in an ambitious appeal to loyal British subjects in defense against the Yankee stage invasion.[5] The show featured a new twist in the story line, a detective story about stolen plans for a wireless television. Composer Gwyther, with authors Denis Mackail, Arthur Stanley, and Austin Melford, created the musical, which opened at His Majesty's Theatre in the fall of 1924, following a smash tryout at the Palace Theatre in Manchester.

When Dorothy Dickson visited Paris earlier that spring for the opening of the Club Daunou's *Midnight Follies,* she asked Gordon's opinion of the *Patricia* script and urged her participation. During this Paris trip, and one in 1925 to the Oziases' summer place in Le Vésinet, the press covered the two colleagues' shopping trip to the Paris market. Over the next three years other publicity pictures were arranged for the two women, like a spate of November 1925 publicity photographs of Gordon hand-decorating Dickson's *Peter Pan* shirt for this Christmas production. Pictures of Gordon appeared with feature stories and news releases in the Paris editions of the *New York Herald* and the *New York Times,* as well as shots in the *Tatler,* the *Graphic,* the *Sketch,* the *Sphere,* and the *Mirror.* These images convinced Gordon that her usual svelte frame was gathering unwanted pounds as she turned thirty years of age. She launched a liquid diet of "café-simple and perrier water."[6] The diet proved a monumental task considering that Gordon's habits were geared to multiple daily repasts, like lunch at Ciro's, tea at Armenonville, cocktails at the New York Bar, dinner at Le Boeuf sur le Toit, and midnight libations at Florence's and Bricktop's.

Patricia was one of Gordon's most ambitious commissions. She dressed Dickson in a wide range of frocks, from a cotton apron to an evening gown of multilayered chiffon encrusted with rainbow-colored crystal and gold beads, wrapped in a striking cloak of cyclamen pink lined with deep fuchsia, and encircled with fur. The deep V-necked gray-blue bodice swirled into shaded tiers from turquoise to chartreuse green. The signature piece of the musical comedy, however, turned out to be an oyster white house dress splashed with flame red dots and accented by matching red buttons marching right down the front opening from neck to knee. It was topped with a snappy rickrack-trimmed royal blue apron, replete with pockets holding garden gloves and clippers. The image of the brightly dressed "Patricia" with nimble feet appeared on posters and billboards that stopped passersby in London streets. The larger-than-life Dickson danced with a double chorus line of her own shadows in silhouette. Though Gordon reversed the dress colors in the poster to a flame red background, the snappy cotton house dress became a costume legend. She labored equally for the entire cast, letting her imagination soar for the Fancy Dress Ball scene. Though the production itself was only moderately successful, Gordon Conway's costumes garnered popular and critical acclaim.

Correspondence about *Patricia* from August and the early fall of 1924 serves as a window onto the costume design world of the era, and offers insight into Gordon's professional relationships and modus operandi in preparing for the scheduled opening on October 31. For instance, Titheradge telegraphed Gordon in Paris that plans had changed again: the number of costumes had to be reduced to twelve costumes at two guineas per sketch. He closed with an urgent plea for her to come to London. Plans changed yet again, and the number eventually rose to eighty-five designs. He wrote on October 10 that the show was "going amazingly well," but he needed designs for four more fancy costumes for the girls in Act 3 and "four more tennis frocks and two afternoon frocks for the girls." He continued: "I want Dorothy to wear different dresses in Acts 2 & 3 and an evening cloak in Act 3. Could you send some really brilliant designs for these (Dot's dresses I mean) by return of post?" He apologized for his businesslike letter but added "you know how my life is. . . . We all miss you very much."[7] Twelve days later and only nine days before the opening, he left an urgent letter for Gordon's London arrival with "Mr. Adams at the Little Theatre," because Titheradge had to make an urgent trip concerning the preview in Blackpool. He instructed Gordon to get in touch instantly with "Miss Idare and Archie Nathan," for "I need five more fancy dresses. . . . [and] fancy costumes for Max Rivers. . . . something Spanish, a Valentino costume wouldn't be bad, but the colors mustn't be violent otherwise they'll make Dot's frock look washy. . . . go ahead and work as fast as you usually do. . . . Don't get panicky but do your best."[8]

During a November 1925 London stay, Gordon was asked by producer William Mollison, whom she called "Jim," and Herbert Clayton to design costumes for *Mercenary Mary,* starring former client Peggy O'Neil, at the London Hippodrome. Gordon was in good company, acting as the London counterpart to noted costume designer Hugh Willoughby, who had dressed the original Broadway show, though no record exists that they met. While costumier Idare et Compagnie was given program credit, Gordon was not. Nevertheless, she proudly took friends to see her creations on August 14, 1926. The highly popular production elicited editorial concern from English cultural arbiters: one review called it a dance-mad and "furiously jazzed" Broadway musical comedy.[9] Another Broadway musical comedy hit at the London Hippodrome, *Sunny,* also credited Idare et Compagnie for the costumes with no program mention of Gordon. With music by Jerome Kern and book and lyrics by Otto Harbach and Oscar Hammerstein II, *Sunny* opened in London on October 7, 1926, and starred Binnie Hale and Jack Buchanan. The musical comedy wound up featuring only one of Gordon's costumes—a clown costume for the chorus. Though she marked the costume sketch for the Tiller Girls, the program and publicity relabeled that famous dance troupe as the "Sunny Girls."

Gordon's work for *Tip-Toes* had begun on July 26, 1926, when Dorothy Dickson wired about her new title role in the George and Ira Gershwin Broadway hit. As was her custom, especially for Dorothy, Gordon began sketching right away. She departed two days later for London, staying alternately with Dorothy Dickson, with Rita Gulbenkian Essayan and husband Kev, or with Tommie Conway and Mr. Fing, who periodically joined Gordon during work in London. She and Blake made occasional contact, but he seemed to fade farther into the background. Anyway, he always seemed to be traveling on business to Lyon, Leipzig, or Manchester. She conferred with management at the Winter Garden Theatre in Drury Lane where the show opened on August 31, 1926. She en-

joyed work with Laddie Cliff, who played one of the two brothers to Dorothy Dickson's "Tip-Toes" Kaye. Gordon was pleased to be working on a show written by Guy Bolton, her transatlantic colleague, who co-authored the book with Fred Thompson.

Gordon enjoyed reconnecting with friends and colleagues like Bolton, who were working and traveling in Europe. During the mid-1920s in Paris, a curious incident involved a telegram and song from an American in Paris who had been inspired by the *New York Herald* article about her artwork. The signature read Irving Berlin. (She had met the songwriter through a friend, occasional actress and frequent bride "Bunty" Burton, at her rollicking New York shindigs during the teens.) Gordon found the message mysterious but amusing. The sender stated: "being also an artist myself I feel that I have a right to address you without a formal introduction as I believe the chief function of art is to break down all false barriers." His song was entitled "My Amber Lady," and the lyrics he penned were dedicated to Gordon, who was "some limber baby."[10] News of an Irving Berlin song in her honor spread like radio waves. The title was translated by friends and reporters into "That Red Head Gal," a song title already coined by two American songwriters. Since the appropriated title captured Gordon's flair and panache, "that red head gal" name stuck and to this day remains a part of the Gordon Conway legend.[11] The telegram with lyrics may have originated with Berlin, but probably was a practical joke, which was typical of Gordon's friends, like Frank Crowninshield and his absurd wires. Another suspect was Dorothy Parker, who was visiting Paris around that time and who partied to the wee hours with Gordon's crew. Another welcome visitor to Paris and possible prankster was friend and New York stage notable Ray Comstock. However, the jest probably was the work

Photographs of Gordon Conway's Paris studio appeared in selected English-language newspapers in Paris in 1924 and 1925. These pictures may be by the photographer "Bonney" who is credited with another photograph of Conway's studio that appeared in the Paris Times Sunday Pictorial Section.

of Wood Kahler, who had attended those same "Bunty" parties and adored Irving Berlin tunes. He had written for the *New York Herald* in Paris (which he called the "Paris Herald") articles about Gordon and once referred to Gordon in a letter as his "amber lady." For Gordon, these friends triggered fond memories of her career beginnings during World War I, the *Vanity Fair* drama review skirmishes between Dorothy Parker and Condé Nast, grand ole Gotham before Prohibition, and the Broadway musical comedies at the Princess Theatre that were highlighted by Gordon's collaboration with Comstock, Wodehouse, and Bolton.

During Gordon's 1926 work on the musical comedy *Tip-Toes,* complications arose involving Dorothy Dickson's costumes at LaRue Limited costumiers. Though the August 16 tryout at Glasgow's Alhambra Theatre was a hit, Gordon's job was a nightmare from the performance in Glasgow onward: "Dot's evening dress was so badly made that she wore one of mine in one act." [12] The next day, Gordon scurried about Glasgow "shopping for Dot" before returning to London to settle the costume imbroglio.

"Working very hard," began the late August diary entries. [13] In preparation for Dorothy's return from Scotland for the London *Tip-Toes* opening, Gordon moved out of the Dickson flat. On August 29 she moved into the home of Rita Gulbenkian Essayan, a compatriot in the crisis who furnished her limousine and ran errands for Gordon. On the 30th she became distraught on arriving early at LaRue to find that the costumier "had none of Dot's dresses ready to fit." [14] She worried at the "dress rehearsal, which was terrible . . . [and] worked all afternoon over those dresses." [15] She did not eat, having forgotten a luncheon meeting with her most important magazine account, Peter Huskinson of the *Tatler.* She wrote: "sketched till 3:00 A.M. . . . started sketching at 7:00 A.M. . . . [and]

worked hard all day with those dresses of Dot's." [16] On August 31, she scribbled: "terribly tired and nervous." [17] Like an ending to a 1920s musical comedy—voilà!—she reported the show a "Huge Success." [18] Instead of flowers she and Tommie Conway gave French lingerie to their favorite star. After a supper party in their honor, Gordon celebrated late with the cast. Not only was the production a success, but Gordon's costumes attracted accolades, as in the September 1, 1926, issue of *Eve,* with its full page of Gordon's five "original designs for the entrancing dresses" for *Tip-Toes.* The magazine called the two-dresses-in-one a "surprise! . . . curtain" because the skirt could be raised and lowered by pulley-cords. [19] This unique Conway garment consisted of a short white chiffon frock hidden underneath a white taffeta lace-trimmed ball gown.

Complimenting Gordon after the *Tip-Toes* opening, Madame Stella Nathan added that she and son Archie Nathan had one regret about the show: "I'm afraid you forgot about us!" On behalf of their firm, which had been "Court and Theatrical Costumiers and Fancy Dress Makers" since 1790, she urged: "if you have any other Productions a little later on, don't forget to come to see us." She concluded: "do also congratulate Miss Dorothy Dickson for me on her great success. . . . she is a little marvel." [20]

Remembering Dorothy Dickson and her costumes fifty-eight years later, an ardent Dickson fan, Michael Bolloten, referred to his extensive Dickson archive, which he had set up in New South Wales, Australia. He described nearly every garment that graced the star in every production save one. Bolloten, who stood in "endless queues" to view the dress rehearsals of his "GODDESS," described "Gordon Conway's masterpiece" in Act 1 of *Tip-Toes.* The gown was "the vividest chartreuse dotted with silver sequined discs. . . . [with] deep square-décolletage, capacious sleeves from under arms and narrowing to the wrists." Adorning Dickson was an "endless diamond-necklace," and "the skirt's myriad panels of fringe 'danced' as she (RAVISH-INGLY!) danced to 'That Certain Feeling.'" Bolloten was equally enthusiastic about Dickson's costumes in the 1927 London production of the Rodgers and Hart musical comedy *Peggy-Ann*. He explained that he had always "*raved* over 'Peggy Ann,' Act I." He recalled the scene built around "Where's That Rainbow," a song Bolloten still played on dinner-dance circuits in Australia. His enthusiasm increased as he remembered Dickson's high kick, then "step-by-step she became à la RADIANT Sunflower!—bolero! Slit skirt! Aigretted toque! even a 'heaven-high' parasol . . . all in this yellow!" As a man after Gordon's own heart, Bolloten described the kind of detail that took so much of the designer's time—a special touch of trim on that bright yellow ensemble with the diagonal bands of black and silver.[21]

For *Peggy-Ann* during 1927, Gordon collaborated almost exclusively with Beth Miller of Chez Beth, someone who understood and appreciated Gordon's drive for perfection. At times, however, she was required to work with the costumiers with long-established theatrical business contacts. Gordon's working relationship and rapport with Beth Miller lasted till the end of the decade. (She would have a similar rapport with Jill Casson, costumier for her last stage production in 1934.) Gordon made sure Chez Beth also executed costumes for *Confetti,* the first film she dressed.

Meeting frequently at the Ivy for lunch conferences, Gordon worked concurrently with Jim Mollison, Herbert Clayton, and Jack Waller on *Princess Charming,* called "A Romance with Music," which was soon to open at the Palace Theatre. On August 26, 1927, the three men introduced Gordon to Folies Bergère star Alice Delysia, whom Charles B.

Cochran had promoted as the French revue queen of London. After dozens of meetings, fittings, and refittings, the costumes, especially the court dress for Delysia, were complete, as were all the dresses for Eileen Redcott that Gordon had Elspeth Fox-Pitt execute. Gordon was again in good company, as Delysia's other dresses were designed by couturière Jeanne Lanvin. After the September 16 dress rehearsal of *Princess Charming,* Gordon complained that Mercia & Company "had not made one of my designs correct."[22] In her drive toward perfection, she suffered frustration and pain when her vision was not matched by her colleagues. Gordon drove herself mercilessly to produce—a compulsion that foreshadowed the exhausting pace of her 1930s film work.

An Original Fashion Design by Gordon Conway

As commissions for the stage increased, so did print-media work, requiring a great deal of Gordon's time until the end of 1930, when graphic work was eclipsed by celluloid art. Jobs had included illustrations for Wood Kahler's fiction such as his April 27, 1924, story in the magazine section of the Paris edition of the *Chicago Tribune,* as well as poster work for the Red Cross. Besides the fashion and cosmetic advertisements, her advertising accounts included cigarettes, liquor, and a motor boat engine. She worked on posters for the Dura automobile and produced a trade magazine cover spotlighting the car. This advertising job arose unexpectedly in early September 1924 during *Patricia* poster work. Urged by Blake, this commission surfaced as abruptly as Blake's April announcement of his new position as the European sales representative for the American cars Dura and Studebaker.

In October 1924, Gordon accepted a challenging

Tear sheet of illustration for Wood Kahler's article, Paris edition of the Chicago Tribune, *April 27, 1924.*

two-year assignment with *La Donna: Revue Italienne d'Art et de Modes,* published by Periodici Mondadori on the Via della Maddalena in Milan. Whether she had contacted the publishing company on the Oziases' business trip to Italy in May is not certain. She had learned about their new editorial policy through a friend who recommended her, Vittorio Podrecca, the director of Teatro dei Piccoli, a children's theater in Rome. Editor Fantini's letters explained that Mondadori had recently purchased the twenty-year-old women's magazine and intended to make it "the most modern and the most elegant of the Italian fashion magazines, in the style of *Vogue, Harper's Bazar* [and] *Femina.* . . . reserved mostly for style." The original magazine had been limited in its coverage of fashion, because "it was primarily a magazine of artistic and literary variety dedicated to the woman." The publishers wished to showcase Gordon's "elegance of style . . . [and] rare fantasy" in four-color and black-and-white illustrations. The editor reported that an agreement had been reached with the most renowned high fashion houses in Paris and London to support the magazine's new information service. Gordon was free

to select the couture models for interpretation, but each sketch would require explanatory notes worked out with their Paris representative. Gordon agreed to six hundred lire a month for four monthly pages, with a minimum of three designs per page. The assignment soon doubled to 1,200 lire a month for twenty sketches, including individual sketches and clusters presented in a vignette form. In response to Gordon's request, the magazine agreed to publish her artwork unedited, and to return the sketches after publication.[23]

For *La Donna* Gordon created a different female image. These models showed a hint of dimple and curve; of course they were not fat, but more muscular and shapely than the wafer-thin figures for other clients. This new sculptured look surely was conscious, and may have been influenced by American sculptor Seymour Fox, now located in a new studio and preparing for an exhibition in Paris. She and Fox attended sketching and life classes in Paris together, and made visits "to the Barbizon."[24] Other influences on both artists must have emanated from the 1925 Paris Exposition Internationale des Arts Décoratifs et Industriels

The love of form is so noticeable in French Society that "Le style c'est l'homme" epitomises the outlook as completely as it did in the 18th century

Sketches and designs by Gordon Conway

This attractive beige frock is given distinction by the frills of blue and white check which trim the neck and sleeves

What Paris says:—

By "UNE PHILOSOPHE"

Tear sheet of Eve, *March 18, 1925. Gordon Conway's sketch illustrates an article reflecting her view about the positive influence of Parisian couture on many New Women.*

Modernes, a treasury of design exploding with new forms, colors, and ideas. As work for *La Donna* carried Gordon further into the haute couture world, she focused predominantly on Edward Molyneux. Yet she also interpreted the collections of Paul Poiret, Madame Jeanne Paquin, Jean Patou, Madame Madeleine Vionnet, Madame Jeanne Lanvin, Madame Jenny, Charlotte, and Chantal. Gordon's mother liked the new silhouettes as much as *La Donna*'s editor on receiving the sketches. Tommie Conway mailed notes to friends on magazine tear sheets about her own preference for these shapelier women.

For the female image in advertisements and magazines of the Great Eight consortium, Gordon stuck to the slim-lined figures that were her trademark. On January 26, 1925, Peter Huskinson offered a major commission to Gordon, who then maintained a studio at 230 Boulevard Raspail in Montparnasse. He wrote from the *Tatler* that "Porter Woodruff has disappeared into the blue, and therefore I am wondering if you would like to do the sketches for the fashion page as well as the odd pages you are sending me." Never afraid of urgent deadlines, which he stressed were February 3 and 17, Gordon accepted immediately. The magazine announced that each issue would contain a full color page entitled "An Original Fashion Design by Gordon Conway." The job entailed two sketches of dresses and one sketch of a hat or ac-

cessory every fortnight. He also responded to Gordon's recent design proposal, assuring her that this new assignment could include "your first idea of giving a complete costume in detail, hat, shoes, accessories, etc. which was very effective." [25] Thus she devised the "original" concept, which later evolved into a popular four-color page vignette that informed and delighted style-conscious Continental women from late in the decade to the end of 1930.

Gordon's "original" works for the *Tatler, Eve,* and *La Donna* were works of Gordon's imagination, in contrast to fashion advertising illustration. The drawings were not replicas or photographic renderings of a couturier's talent. Georges Lepape described the difference in a November 6, 1936, outline for a proposed design portfolio entitled *Fashion Drawing* that was based on classes he taught between 1924 and 1938 at the Paris campus of the New York School of Fine and Applied Art. He delineated two different kinds of fashion drawing. The first category was: "Commercial drawing, practical, very factual, no interpretation or stylization that would distort the original. . . . for mass-circulation magazines with a wide readership, for periodicals and daily papers." The second category, which he stated served class fashion publications like *Vogue,* Lepape divided into two segments:

A. Realistic drawing, but very stylized, bold and sumptuous, reflecting a life of elegance and luxury in an appropriate setting.

B. Free drawing, also very stylized but in which fantasy, imagination and composition are tied in with the luxury and elegance of a novel and picturesque setting. Here the artist is no longer interpreting a model, he is creating and inventing everything.

Gordon Conway operated in each of these arenas, and would agree with Lepape that the artist had an advantage over the fashion photographer, since the artist "may, through his interpretation, impose fashion. . . . by creating and inventing, he can force fashion to follow in the furrow ploughed by his own imagination and Art."[26]

Gordon's commercial fashion drawing—though less introspective and personal than her unpublished early drawings—served as an autobiographical record, with vignettes based on scenes in her flat at Bryanston Court and inserts of her mother's and friends' monograms on handbags and blouses. Red hair, as usual, crowned those tall, svelte frames, and the graceful and agile figures energized the page. Gordon's print assignments reflected her creation of character for stage and screen; she delineated roles in real life as in a stage setting. Gordon translated her New Woman silhouette for thousands of readers by creating the character on paper, like characters in the scripts, novels, and short stories she studied. With a nod to the mode in Paris, a subtle new female image had emerged—a confident image with an understated look, a no-nonsense approach to style, and an American touch of practicality. Gordon designed for active women, women who actually moved—women who danced, drove, skied, swam, pushed, pulled, stooped, reached, and ran. These New Women differed from the women in the frozen tableaux of the fashion drawings in *La Gazette du Bon Ton,* women who seemed anchored in place without muscles and moving limbs. She created ensembles for women like herself—an energetic businesswoman who liked to be comfortably clad as well as smartly dressed.

Gordon had an American knack for putting things together, for organizing and making clothes work for the busy life of a professional woman or active volunteer. Her knowledge of fabric and cut, coupled with the assemblage of wardrobe, was Gordon's special touch. She coordinated a look that carried a woman from work to leisure and back again. Because of her own experience, she believed that well-assembled attire helped organize a woman's life. The *Tatler, Eve,* and *La Donna* drawings featured her idea of a New Woman with a new life, dressed with a flair from head to toe in a streamlined environment of her own making. As with her favorite stage commissions, Gordon could design the settings as well as the costumes and present a vision of how life ought to be lived. On her *Eve* black-and-white fashion pages, Gordon sneaked in another Yankee strategy. Tapping the same market as Condé Nast's *Vogue* pattern company, Gordon, a knowledgeable seamstress, offered do-it-yourself designs for Continental readers. The "En Suite" page of the November 26, 1924, *Eve* featured an unusual tunic among three other sketches with sewing instructions in the captions. An identical tunic showed up on Gordon herself in a photograph of her studio, shot for 1925 articles in the Paris edition of the *New York Herald* and for the *Paris Times Sunday Pictorial Section.*

Recognizing Gordon's ability as both an illustrator and an original fashion designer, a journalist wrote in March 1924 that she was "one of the most cleverest [*sic*] American designers in the French capital. . . . Almost any artist can illustrate fashions, but very few can create new ones in the manner of the famous 'Redhead Gal.'"[27]

A Picture-Postcard from the Palais de Justice

The year 1927 garnered rave reviews for the smartly dressed *Peggy-Ann* and for the dazzling costumes in the movie *Confetti* that launched Gordon's career in British film. The praise would be bittersweet, for it coincided with Gordon and Blake's divorce in Paris. After Gordon's return from the United States the year

Gordon Conway and Bobbie Appleton at the races, Longchamps, Paris, ca. 1925; two photographs of Conway in Cannes, 1928.

before, the last remnants of the Ozias partnership had drifted into nothingness. Mentally, emotionally, and physically, Gordon and Blake ceased to be a pair. At one time Gordon believed that she and Blake and her mother could be three happy companions. Now there were two, and the equation would never again change.

The first of three extended trips to the French Riviera between 1927 and the spring of 1928 took place in early January, when Gordon and her mother traveled to Cannes on a pleasure trip sprinkled with commercial art business. They relished the Carnival parades, fireworks, and soirées of the pre-Lenten celebration. Gordon, who rarely began a diary entry without a weather comment and loved mild climates and bright sunshine, soaked up the sunny and cloudless blue

skies, gentle warm breezes, and fragrance of orange, lemon, and pink laurel trees. Blake drove Gordon and her mother to the coast, but after an overnight stay, he returned to Lyon. The women stayed at the Grand Hotel until March 19 attending the races and gambling at the casino. Gordon, lucky in cards and games, multiplied her winnings starting off with the thousand francs Blake had given her for Christmas plus another thousand francs lent by Bobbie Appleton.

The Cannes visit was another installment of get-togethers over the past six years with Katharine and Bobbie Appleton. The couple followed the international racing circuit in Europe with their string of race horses and polo ponies, all the while entertaining friends at their Riviera home and apartment suite in

Paris. The Oziases and Tommie Conway often joined the Appletons at Longchamps, Le Tremblay, Enghien, Auteuil, and St. Cloud. These venues attracted news reporters who snapped pictures of the racing set like the picture of Gordon and Bobbie Appleton at the Grand Criterium at Longchamps ca. fall 1925. Since renewing contact with the Appletons on the *Aquitania* in early 1921, Gordon had created a series of designs for the couple, such as annual Christmas cards, invitations, and graphics for the Riding Club of East Hampton. Especially supportive of Gordon's career, Bobbie Appleton introduced her to potential clients. The Cannes visit was no exception.

During the holiday Gordon worked on color covers and regular fashion pages for *Eve,* corresponded with Quentin Tod in London about costumes for a new revue featuring his choreographed ballet scenes, and shipped *Peggy-Ann* designs and "Savoy sketches" to Chez Beth. Following standard business practice, she scouted new commissions in the Cannes environs amid Carnival festivities, betting at the races, gambling at the casino, sunbathing on the beach, motoring along the Corniche, and dancing till dawn at Ambassadeurs and Cirque Nautique Club. She viewed collections at the Riviera shops of Molyneux and Poiret, received a sketching job from Ambassadeurs, met with Baron St. Marc and an editor, "Mr. Martin," about illustrations and fashion comment for *La Saison de Cannes,* and secured an order for two color magazine covers from Erskine Gwynne for his *Boulevardier* in Paris.

During this two-and-a-half-month stay, Blake's name was mentioned in her diary only once: on his departure the first day. The record reveals few letters and no wires or calls. A little less than a month after her return to Paris, Gordon recorded a meeting with attorney André Gadd concerning divorce proceedings. Just like that, the divorce was announced in her diary.

The couple wrote to Uncle Fitzhugh at Mount Sion that it was an amicable parting. Very few warnings of domestic problems had surfaced in Gordon's diaries and letters. Since that night in September 1923, things had been different between the husband and wife. Blake's subsequent remarriage to Nina Matar in September 1927, after the divorce, raises the question of whether some sort of impropriety was involved. Friends recalled that Nina Matar once had been considered both Gordon and Tommie's close friend. Though rumors abounded, Gordon's diary provided no evidence pointing to an extramarital affair. As with Blake's third marriage to Blanche Aldine several years later, close friends conjectured, but they simply did not know the details of the breakup.

In 1927, Gordon was a young-acting and ambitious thirty-three years old, Blake was a stodgy and melancholy forty-six years old, and Tommie was a determined and energetic fifty-seven years old. The three had aged at a different pace. Their energy levels had shifted since that promising time in New York in 1920. There can be no doubt that initially Gordon and Blake had been very much in love from that first meeting over a Delage advertisement in March 1920. Most of her friends felt Gordon continued to love Blake until the summer day she died in 1956. During World War II he visited Mount Sion, both with and without Nina, while living in Washington, D.C., where he served as executive director of the War Production Board's Division of Information. He kept in touch when he accepted a post with the United Nations Relief and Rehabilitation Administration (UNRRA) in London several years later. Blake, considered by many friends to be old before his time, ironically, outlived both Gordon and Tommie Conway, dying six weeks short of his eighty-sixth birthday in Hartford, Connecticut, "after a long and severe illness" on October 19, 1967.[28]

Although to this day there is unanimous agreement

De Life and de Ladies de Luxe

Impressions by GORDON CONWAY

Stroll along the Croisette.
Salutations.
Tugging at flu-flu.
Insistant photographers.
Cocktails at the Cercle.
Chat with the Baron.

Dash to the boudoir.
Quick change.
Meeting with Bobbie.
Dry Martinies.
Gift of the Emerald.
Lunch at the Grand
New Hispano.
Drive to Mandelieu.
Colors of the jockeys.
Indifference to the races.
Desire of being seen.

Return in the Hispano.
Tea on the yacht.
Cocktails at the Majestic.
Dash to the Carlton.
Conversational coiffeur.
Quick change.
Latest Worth models.
Orchids on the shoulder.
Sixteen bracelets.

12.30 P.M.

3.30 P.M.

9.30 P.M.

Late arrival.
Glare of the hostess.
Introductions.
Cocktails au Bar.
Gala aux Ambassadeurs.
Dull captain on the right.
Poor dancer.
Tight shoes.
Kick from the coktail.
Exhilarating syncop-
ation of Billy Arnold.
Fireworks and champa-
gne.
Unexpected glimpse of
one's ex-husband.
Nudge from the neigh-
bor.
Exit from the gala.
Stumble up the stairs.

Entrance au baccara.
Loosing the chemise.
Clashing the chock.
Champagne au bar.
Cutting of the cards.
Banque that ran.
Pile of mauve plaques.
Bacon and eggs.
A last night-cap.
Daylight approching.
Return in a taxi.
Adieu to the comte.
Tumble into bed.........
Till to-morrow.

GORDON CONWAY.

Tear sheet of illustrations published in La Saison de Cannes, *1927. Note autobiographical sketches and "impressions" by Gordon Conway.*

on the couple's early devotion, the liaison is a curious match for friends to ponder. Margaret Page Elliott, recalling the 1920s in Paris with Gordon and Blake, stated that she "was not impressed with him at all." She regretted not making herself more available; she should have made time to "pal around" when Gordon reached out for a sympathetic ear but was involved with her husband's military and diplomatic responsi-bilities in Europe. Another Dallas contemporary speculated that Tommie probably would have preferred Gordon to be the wife of one of her Continental pre–World War I sweethearts, a Prince Colonna–type, or one of the Idlewild Club bachelors, or a younger Bobbie Appleton sort. Dallas friends agreed that Blake was not what they had expected for Gordon. "Not her equal, really" was the consensus, especially when she could have married any beau from the banks of the Trinity to the Thames, the Seine, the Tiber, and back again to the Hudson and Rappahannock.[29] As Dorothy Dickson averred, their café society set and theater crowd felt he was different, nice enough, certainly, but different.

Blake was different too, most likely, from what Gordon had anticipated. From that painful September 1923 night, the couple's attitudes silently clashed. The way money was spent, for example, seemed an annoyance, though they maintained separate accounts as she and her mother had long done. The undercurrent was always present that Blake had not met his share of the expenses. Gordon and Tom's cast of characters doubled between 1924 and 1927, producing more options for the social gadflies. At the beginning of the marriage, Gordon stayed home with Blake if he declined to go out. However, not one to languish at home week after week, she gradually joined the group alone, explaining in 1925 and 1926 that "Blake wouldn't go."[30]

The voyage to the United States on the *Majestic* was disrupted when grippe prevented Tommie Conway from sailing on January 6, 1926. Because Gordon would not leave her mother, Blake sailed alone. The two women later embarked on the *Homeric* and cruised into the harbor of New York on January 20. The mild evening delighted Gordon, as did the "gorgeous silhouette of the skyscrapers outlined only by lights [on the] lovely moonlight night." She arrived in time for another Ozias family visit to Lewisburg, which seemed to go quite well. Ohio friends dropped by, and they went on walks and listened to the radio, and Gordon tatted with "Mommie" Ozias. She also accompanied Blake on business trips to Toledo for the Dura and to New York for the Studebaker. During her three-month trip, Gordon filled graphic art

commissions for Ned Wayburn's *The Maiden Voyage,* including work on his "American Indian scene." Traveling southwest by rail on the "Sunshine Special," Gordon and Tommie found the usual gala festivities in Dallas and in Paris, Texas, where her *Tricks* dresses stood out among the crowd. The abundance of news coverage was highlighted by a *Dallas Times Herald* feature article that included photographs and reports of Gordon's exciting life and career on the Continent.[31]

The Texas visit was cut short by new assignments in New York, coupled with career-related activities like the new productions of *Tip-Toes* and *Sunny,* meetings "with Juliette at *The New Yorker,*" an International Exhibition of Stage Designs, a special theatrical evening with Richard Le Gallienne's daughter Eva in her own production of Ibsen's *The Master Builder,* and attendance at *Petrushka* and *Skyscrapers* with "very modern" sets and costumes by Robert Edmund Jones.[32]

The magnetism of New York revelry during Prohibition also counted as a factor in Gordon's decision to lengthen her stay in the United States. Gordon took Charleston lessons at Ned Wayburn's studio and soon would instruct Continental friends, who like herself had been mesmerized by Josephine Baker's introduction of the dance in Paris four months before. She practiced the steps at penthouse parties, the Cotton Club, Texas Guinan's, and the Mayfair Club in the Crystal Room at the Ritz. More than ever before, the sophisticates of café society were closely knit, more visible, available, and in touch. The encounters seemed like reunions with everyone Gordon had ever known from Dallas to New York to Europe. Bursting with excitement, she "saw everybody I know. . . . [and] every theatrical person one ever heard of." From February 5, when Blake sailed on the *Olympic*'s eastbound crossing, the couple did not see each other for two and a half months, not until Gordon, Tom, and Mr. Fing arrived in Paris on April 17. The couple rarely wrote, cabled, or called each other. There was one message, however, from Blake on March 30. The cable arrived at the Plaza Hotel while Gordon was at the Madison Hotel, attending a "snappy party" stocked with what American friends tagged "re-enforcements" that would sustain the crowd until 7:00 A.M. No need to rush back, Blake cabled.[33] Perhaps the cable had a twist of accusatory sarcasm, commenting on her activities and extended stay. Perhaps not: the message might have made a direct statement, the kind Gordon liked, without indirection or biting nuance. Blake, after all, was moving to another new business address and had moved the couple into yet another residence, this one in Passy, which marked the twelfth move over the past four years in Paris alone.

The New York visit and ocean crossings did not rekindle nostalgic reminders of happier days, when Gordon was charmed by Blake's maturity, protectiveness, and kindness, and of their shared love of books and the arts. Though she continued to read three books a week, the couple no longer curled up in front of the fire together, contentedly reading and conversing. Times she treasured when he read entire books out loud to her, such as *Main Street* by Sinclair Lewis and Oscar Wilde's play *Salomé* in the original French, had vanished.

As the two separated in the spring of 1927, Blake attempted to reconcile. But someone else now read out loud to her, and someone else shared the most celebrated peacetime event of the 1920s with Gordon. She had met up with the "Mon Capitaine" of her diary—an Englishman in demanding and passionate pursuit since their first acquaintance in Cannes earlier that year. (According to Conway records, "Mon Capitaine" was probably Captain Neville De Brath.) An astonishing number of communiqués arrived at her Paris flat, two to three letters and cables a day, along with twice-a-week deliveries of enormous bouquets of orchids, iris, and violets. In late May he made another urgent trip to Paris to see Gordon. They strolled through the shady Bois de Boulogne and picnicked beneath her favorite trees. This ardent new friend read *Young Men in Love* by Michael Arlen out loud to Gordon. In the Bois at dusk on May 21, a historic bonus unexpectedly played itself out overhead when the couple heard cheers that Charles Lindbergh was descending toward Paris for the famous landing at Le Bourget Air Field. Tingling with excitement, they gathered in the Place de l'Opéra at dark. Swept into the madness of the revelry, the pair celebrated till dawn at Harry's New York Bar. A week later someone else whisked Gordon to the roof of the Plaza Athénée to witness the American hero and his "Spirit of St. Louis" soar across the skies of Paris. Missing the Lindbergh landing and public outpouring with Gordon must have been especially painful to Blake, for as a devotee of aviation he had taken her to many an air show and stunt exhibition. Days before, he had told her the divorce was a mistake. On the day of his reconciliation plea, emblematic of the broken bond, Gordon read alone to herself Ernest Hemingway's *The Sun Also Rises* in its entirety.

Blake Ozias was kind, gentle, and considerate, Gordon had reported early on. Yet the divorce papers submitted to the French Civil Tribunal at the Palais de Justice provide charges of the husband's insults and negative attitude toward the wife, making her life unbearable, intolerable, and untenable. According to the record, he threw her out of the domicile. The papers include a statement that through her lawyer Gordon had attempted to reconcile, but that Blake had refused with such verbal abuse to the attorney that she had dropped the proposal. Perhaps behind the scenes the couple agreed to an exaggerated claim to expedite divorce proceedings in France. No evidence points conclusively in either direction.

Remaining close friends with both Blake and Gordon, Wood Kahler noted Blake's ineffectiveness in business. He wrote Gordon after dining with Blake in Paris in 1929, one month after the stock market crash wrenched the American economy, that even before the crash things did not look bright financially: Blake's "business affairs . . . [are] at a very low ebb." Kahler added, "He is no businessman." [34] Dallas friends thought Blake's income a mystery. But Gordon had never been financially dependent on him. The couple signed a contract when they married that their property would be held separately, an arrangement that may have been questioned by Texans, since in the Lone Star State community property is the law. During the divorce proceedings, Gordon refused alimony. In 1927 Tommie Conway still had money.

In an attempt to sort out reasons for the breakup, Gordon's friends testify to two factors that conspired to drive the lovers apart. These factors strike at a deeper level than the laundry list of implied reasons, such as differences in age, height, money, and background, and an alleged affair with Nina Matar. The "second Mrs. Blake Ozias" seemed to be a symptom of the problem, not the cause, although any wayward affection may have triggered the actual divorce. Rumors abounded: the divorce occurred because Blake was older and shorter, or because of Blake's lack of business acumen, proper breeding, and a dynamic personality. These suspected causes might have been worked out if a solid bond had existed between the two at a deeper level. In sum, Gordon's professional success and personal popularity, coupled with her mother's omni-

presence, might have made Blake feel he was running a weak second. One observer who visited the three in Paris—a debonair youth born of "Old Dallas" ancestry who was a cousin to Tommie Conway's young friend Howard Hughes—offered insight into the relationship. He mused that "Blake was the perfect backdrop for Gordon's talents." [35] Indeed, in Gordon's shadow, Blake may have felt less than a stand-in's stand-in. His sense of inadequacy lurked in hidden corners, popping out to mock her in unexpected ways. A diminished ego seemed to strike out at Gordon at vulnerable times, as in a letter written a few years after the divorce. In an otherwise pleasant letter, one paragraph took a perverse turn. As though Blake blamed Gordon for her good fortune of having talent, ability, personality, vivacity, and charm, he inquired what it must be like to live with so many talents.

In vying for Gordon's love and attention, Blake probably felt powerless next to her mother. Dallas friends repeated that "Her mother was at her elbow all the time." [36] On June 2, 1927, Tommie Conway entertained twenty for cocktails late in the afternoon of Gordon and Blake's last hearing at the Palais de Justice, a hearing to submit the second and last divorce application. If any guest suspected the party honored the occasion of severance, there is no record. Blake attended Tommie's cocktail party at the Plaza Athénée, a gesture from all three that would signal friendly relations over the years. In a few days, Tommie received a curious postcard that pictured a complex of French governmental office buildings. The picture-postcard featured the judicial center of France, the Palais de Justice. Blake wrote only one sentence: "My Dear, I thought you would like to see the spot where your daughter and I met to end our marriage." [37]

CHAPTER SIX

POEMS OF CHIC

Two Good Companions

When Gordon Conway answered Dorothy Dickson's telegram about the *Tip-Toes* costume commission in July 1926, she closed the door to more than her studio. The June 1927 divorce from Blake came and went, and Gordon never missed a step. Keeping busy, after all, was the best way to forget the dashed expectations of their seven-year marriage. Certainly, a busy schedule was the best way to ignore Blake's quick remarriage to Nina. During that summer, Gordon and Tom began relocating to London, and Gordon accelerated contact with her British business connections.

In mid-July, Gordon joined Dorothy Dickson and Geoffrey Gwyther for a five-hour drive to the seacoast. Along the way, they stopped for a lunch conference with American producer Lew Fields and British producer Lee Ephraim and their wives in preparation for the *Peggy-Ann* tryouts at Southsea. Gordon rushed back to London for costume corrections at Chez Beth and for rehearsals at Daly's Theatre, long advertised as "The Premiere Musical Comedy Theatre of the World." On July 27 Gordon completed a poster of Dorothy Dickson in the afternoon, joined Ephraim in his box that evening, and later reported that "*Peggy-Ann* opened with splendor." [1] Not only was the show a success, but the dresses got good press. The Richard Rodgers and Lorenz Hart musical comedy, written by Herbert Fields and produced by his father Lew Fields, originally had opened on Broadway in late 1926 under the direction of Gordon's former client Robert Mil-

ton. It was yet another musical comedy with a Cinderella story line and a woman's name for the title. The show has been judged "a daring work for its day" because of its Freudian dream scenario and the innovation of costume and set changes made on stage for all to see. Another musical comedy convention was ignored when the entrance of the dancing girls was delayed, and "they were used functionally within the plot rather than as unrelated ornaments." [2] Dorothy Dickson danced the title role with her usual aplomb and precision, and, aided by the stunning costumes, made each scene sparkle. Movement in Gordon's garments flowed easily. Dickson remarked that of all the costume designers with whom she worked, Gordon provided the most functional clothes: "They were cut on the bias, you see, and allowed me a lot of freedom of movement." [3] From the audience, Dickson fan Michael Bolloten noticed that the skirts fell right back into place, hugging her body, even after high kicks and broad sweeping dance steps.

Answering requests for press interviews, Gordon made appointments with both Sasha and Lenare studios for publicity photographs, often taken with Mr. Fing. During late July and August, she received several design offers, including a costume assignment for Irene Vanbrugh and the sets and costumes for *Their Wife,* produced by a group that included actress Joan Antill. Years later Antill recalled that her fellow producers and cast felt confident of a hit—how could they miss with a "wicked comedy" brilliantly written by Frank Stayton? Presented at the Little Theatre, the

Drawings and film stills, Confetti, *1927. Note Annette Benson in silver lamé gown against a set designed by Conway, and conversing with Jack Buchanan and two supporting actresses also dressed by Gordon Conway.*

farce was directed by Nigel Playfair, who played the lead in a star-studded cast. According to Antill, it was "the wrong theater," and the play closed after a short run. Antill testified to the modish costumes by Gordon that were executed by Chez Beth, "a chic new shop in London."[4] Lauded as "very modern," the "smart gowns" were praised by the London press for the uneven hemlines and broad-brimmed felt hats "turned up in front and caught with a large paste buckle," along with splashy colors and trim such as Gordon's unusual bishop-style sleeves, appliquéd with zigzag strips of yellow and orange satin.[5]

In early August 1927 Gordon accepted a film assignment that changed her career and ultimately her life. Graham Cutts contracted for costumes for *Confetti,* which he directed for the First National–Pathé production company in England.

From late August until early October 1927, *Confetti* was shot on location in the balmy air of the

French Riviera at the Nice studio of Rex Ingram and his wife, actress Alice Terry. Gordon was as impressed with Ingram's talent as a sculptor as she was with the films he scripted, acted in, directed, and produced. The Ingrams, joined by their friend and star, Ivan Petrovich, discussed future collaboration with Gordon, who returned to the Riviera a few months later in anticipation of assignments at Ingram's studio. It was typical of Gordon's prompt and direct method of working that she stayed up most of the night studying *Sapho* by French novelist and playwright Alphonse Daudet. The next day she offered costuming and artistic recommendations for the proposed film adaptation. Though she would see the Ingrams socially in the months to come, to Gordon's regret, nothing materialized from the film meetings.

The shooting of *Confetti* showcased the restaged festivities of the Battle of the Flowers on the Côte d'Azur. The silent film extravaganza was the first movie

produced by the newly merged company of First National–Pathé. Gordon's stay at the Negresco Hotel was actually her second visit that year to the Riviera, where she had witnessed Carnival firsthand. The research value of the experience made Gordon an important resource for the production. Besides dressing the film, she bought props, worked with sets, and joined Reginald "Foggy" Fogwell in casting the film's crowd of revelers. The *Confetti* arrangement was a professional dream come true. Gordon knew she was capable of designing motion picture sets along with costumes and yearned to break into art direction in England. On December 16, 1927, she celebrated the private screening of *Confetti* at the Mayfair and was elated when her showy and lavish costumes garnered accolades. She recorded on Christmas Eve that "Mr. Balcon sent for me." Gordon judged the call from producer Michael Balcon at the end of the year as a sign of good luck. She was soon awarded a contract for a new film in 1928 based on her *Confetti* success.[6]

Observers have asked why Gordon did not work in American film. She had nibbles from East Coast studios and from Hollywood, but she never seriously considered Hollywood. She judged the "tinsel town" environment too risky. Friends and colleagues like Dorothy Parker and P. G. Wodehouse passed on horror stories warning of the industry's deceitful internal practices that destroyed the careers and the personal lives of certain artists. In the late 1920s and early 1930s Gordon believed in the cause of English filmmaker Michael Balcon, who espoused the creation of "indigenous film" that expressed British national character and themes, and that eschewed Hollywood imitations.[7] Though Gordon admired the best of Hollywood and certainly used the studios' wardrobe department system as a model for her department at Gaumont-British, she never limited herself to its products.

Confetti offered the creative interchange she craved in a professional environment free of internal political machinations and crass profit motives. She delighted in the cast of characters both on and off camera, many of whom were friends and professionals she could trust. She loved the work with director Cutts, cameraman Roy Overbaugh, original scenario author Douglas Furber, and stars like Jack Buchanan, Annette Benson, and Robin Irvine. Also, Gordon advocated shooting on location—real places and events as background for the movie. The atmosphere was as pleasant as it was creative, with Tommie Conway's fried chicken suppers for the cast and staff on the terrace of the Cuttses' villa, swimming in the Mediterranean, and dining and dancing at Biffi's, the Grand Blue, Ambassadeurs, and the Perroquet. Professionally, the experience foreshadowed the fulfilling work and conviviality on such

films as *The Good Companions,* directed by Victor Saville, one of Gordon's favorite directors. Unfortunately, not all the films she dressed would be as rewarding.

To Elstree and Islington

Gordon launched her film career in 1927 during a period of euphoria and great expectation in the British motion picture industry. A new determination emerged to combat Hollywood's domination of celluloid entertainment that had smothered British initiatives. According to British film historian Rachael Low, "There was a depression in British film production between the years 1924 and 1927."[8] Film authority Ernest Lindgren stated that "During the First World War, America had acquired an unassailable supremacy in the world market. . . . By 1925 it was estimated that 95 percent of screen time was given over to American films. . . . American distributors were entrenching themselves even more firmly in an already impregnable position by the practices of mass salesmanship known as blind booking and block booking."[9] The sales strategy required exhibitors to book an entire series of six to ten American-made movies in order to exhibit one outstanding or popular "super" film. Calls for protective legislation resulted in the passage of the first Cinematograph Films Act in 1927. Popularly known as the "Quota Act," the legislation attempted to curtail block booking and "imposed on both renter and exhibitor the obligation to acquire and show . . . a minimum proportion, or quota, of British films in respect to the foreign films acquired and exhibited."[10]

Regardless of the merits of the legislation and the argument that the act encouraged inferior films labeled "quota quickies," the act resulted in a rise of British feature film production and exhibition. The increase provided creative production professionals like Gordon Conway with an opportunity to showcase their talent. Film luminaries Michael Powell and Michael Relph both have acknowledged the experience that was gained through their "quota quickie" work as young filmmakers.[11] From a mere 26 feature films produced in 1926, the number rose to 190 in 1934—the year that Gordon's last four films were released. Regardless of the merit of the films, or which company produced what film, Gordon created exemplary work that was commissioned by talented producers, directors, and actresses. Many of Conway's costumes are now lost to screen viewers, however, because the production as a whole has not been valued; most of these films are rarely exhibited, and others have not been preserved. A few are not even listed in major film references.

Though industry setbacks occurred, immense changes during these years helped the British film business. In addition to the production delays caused by the sound revolution, Hollywood imports began to shrink after the 1929 Depression in the United States. The explosion of sound production that revolutionized the industry was not recognized at first as a boon in England. Popularly acknowledged as the first sound production, *The Jazz Singer* premiered in New York on October 6, 1927, but did not reach London until September 27, 1928. Gordon's first experience with a "talkie" was *The Terror,* which she viewed in London on October 30, 1928. (In her diary, she distinguished sound productions from silent films, calling them "talkies" well into 1930.) Other film innovations, however, raised her hopes higher. Viewing a color motion picture on November 23, 1928, she became enthralled with recent color developments, the technical advancements of which she had followed for years. Unfortunately, Gordon's career ended before her talent and passion for color could be applied to the screen medium.

Although Gordon harbored no illusions about the uneven quality of British film in the late 1920s, she was excited about the revitalization and innovation taking place in the industry. Rachael Low observed that before the final passage of the Quota Act in the House of Commons in November 1927, "there was a great deal of movement in the industry, growth and reorganization of the companies already in existence and the formation of new ones with new financial alignments. . . . There was a more confident search for capital, sometimes over-confident. The new type of company required big names on their Boards and on their staffs, and in their efforts to expand British production quickly many of them imported foreign talent, much of it from Germany." Summarizing the beginning period of Gordon's involvement in British film, Low reported "a number of wild, grandiose schemes, and by the end of the decade when sound production caused a further upheaval there were signs of trouble and a number of new groups were already in difficulties." Low concluded that "The twenties ended with the bustle of company formation, much of it involving grand schemes and impressive financial arrangements but little actual production. . . . Studios were hastily built or acquired and described enthusiastically as the new British Hollywood."[12] Gordon vowed to be part of this cinematic revolution.

During late 1927 and throughout 1928, Gordon's world was filled with film appointments and proposals. Phone calls came in from new investors. Gordon was sent scripts to read and was invited to submit costume proposals. Businessmen with no film experience joined seasoned filmmakers in hosting cocktail hours full of motion picture deals. Restaurant customers—men huddled in deep strategy film speculation—waved her over to join their tables for movie talk. Over the weeks British Filmcraft producer George

Banfield "rang up," sent scripts, and arrived one day unannounced at her flat with her friend "Prince George of Russia," a Russian Revolution émigré now working as a London interior decorator. One film executive sent his own studio car to pick up her sketches. Though she did only a modicum of work for B.I.P. (British International Pictures) through the years, some directors associated with the company stayed in contact until she left England in 1936. There were calls about proposals from Harry Lachman, for instance, before he went to Hollywood. Also, there were subsequent meetings with producers Reginald "Foggy" Fogwell and Mansfield Markham, as well as with British Lion representatives. Gordon returned these overtures with her own kind of promotional and public relations initiative—like a party on Thanksgiving Day, a date usually reserved for personal friends. In her diary, Gordon recorded that her flat was crowded on the American holiday with visitors who were "all film men."[13]

Gordon was being rushed. Experienced filmmakers and amateur film people alike suddenly cared how screen performers were dressed. For months Gordon had been preaching the importance of "better-dressed British pictures." The filmmakers knew, as she knew, that she was just the one to do the job. She found herself on a roller coaster of opportunity at two studios. Though both were quite a distance from her flat, she endured the inconvenience and hassle because she wanted and needed the work. Either the studio sent a car or friends obliged with back-and-forth automobile rides during this propitious period. Gordon completed assignments within days, rushed to Gainsborough studios in Islington, then to First National–Pathé studios in Elstree, and back again to Islington.

On January 6, 1928, Gordon also found herself an informal ambassador for the British film industry when she contracted for *God's Clay,* a new film for First National–Pathé directed by Cutts. According to Low, the influx of foreign stars and technicians who aided the new studio output were mostly "Continental visitors to a large extent replacing the Americans of earlier years."[14] Gordon was assigned to leading lady Anny Ondra, a Czechoslovakian star popular with the German and Austrian film public. Gordon treated her to luncheons at the Park Lane and Kettner's, escorted her on shopping trips, and personally supervised every phase of her fittings. Australian actress Trilby Clark visited Gordon's flat for a costume sketch display accompanied by cocktails. So taken was Clark with Gordon's style that several days later she purchased garments from Gordon's personal wardrobe. Other women were attracted to the artist's clothes, like the secretary to Graham Cutts who brought a friend to buy pieces from the two Conway women's out-of-season wardrobes. Foreshadowing assignments with other film companies, the combined work of costume design and public relations paid off. Gordon judged that her career was spiraling upward when she made the news, viewed rushes at Elstree on January 31, 1928, and was told that her dresses were "a success for *God's Clay.*"[15] Then, all of a sudden, to her dismay, one studio job ended. *God's Clay* would be her last film for First National–Pathé, which became caught up in yet another business upheaval and was soon to be taken over by Warner Brothers studio.

On January 11, 1928, Gordon began working in Islington on a Gainsborough production entitled *A South Sea Bubble,*[16] directed by T. Hayes Hunter. Shot on location in Colombo, Sri Lanka, and along the Algerian coast, the film starred Ivor Novello, Benita Hume, and Annette Benson. Though the popular cast promised a large audience among British moviegoers, lukewarm reviews appeared, including one in *Variety* after the premiere at the London Hippodrome. The trade show screening on July 23, 1928, merited a similar critique in Gordon's diary when she congratulated herself that the "dresses [were] not so bad." She agreed with the critics that the movie was "not so good." [17]

The distinction between the success of film costuming and the lack of critical acclaim for the production itself should be taken into account when evaluating Gordon's film projects. This distinction is especially significant when the films no longer exist or when Gordon did not receive screen credit for the costumes commissioned by actresses on an individual basis. (Gordon had received private commissions from stage actresses since the teens in New York.)

On April 27, 1928, Annette Benson called Gordon for costumes for the British Lion production of the Edgar Wallace thriller *The Ringer,* a wildly popular play adapted frequently for other entertainment media. One *Variety* review judged Benson's performance as "outstanding" and pointed out that the stage hit had been translated into most languages and currently was being presented at two hundred theaters in Germany alone. In mid-July Benson returned to Gordon for costumes for *Sir or Madam,* directed by German director Carl Boese, another British film industry effort combining English and German talent. Though it was shot at B.I.P. in Elstree, Arthur Clavering produced the film for Warner Brothers as their first quota movie under the name of Foremost Productions. Well before the October trade show, the costumes garnered full-page coverage in the August 23 *Kinematograph Weekly.* [18]

Film actresses continued to engage Gordon during 1929. For instance, Heather Thatcher on September 6 requested designs for *Express Love* directed by Sascha Geneen. Gordon was proud to have Thatcher display her costumes because of her flair for modeling haute couture. That same fall, Edna Best came for cocktails several times to discuss costumes for *Sleeping Partners,* photographed by German cameraman Karl Freund and produced by Geneen's company, Sageen. It was adapted and directed by Sascha Geneen and Seymour Hicks, who, with Lyn Harding, played one of the two male leads. This French bedroom farce had been written in 1916 by Sacha Guitry and had a history of numerous stage and screen adaptations. Gordon's familiarity with the story dated back to her theater poster assignment for the 1918 Broadway production at the behest of star Irene Bordoni. Gordon's costumes for *Sleeping Partners* demonstrated yet again that film dressing can be appreciated even when the entire production draws critical disdain. Judging the film "stagey" with limited sets and action, *Variety* nevertheless praised the costumes: "Although it looks anything but a million dollars, it's about the first British film in which the femme lead, Edna Best, dresses well and carries clothes Swanson fashion." [19]

To Gainsborough and Gaumont-British

Gordon was encouraged on September 29, 1928, when Chandos "Shan" Balcon, older brother to studio head Michael Balcon, called from Islington with a new film assignment, *The Return of the Rat,* the third in the popular *Rat* film series. She felt comfortable with the production staff since she had developed a rapport with director Graham Cutts and cameraman Roy Overbaugh. After studying the script, she watched *The Triumph of the Rat,* the 1926 film also starring Ivor Novello and Isabel Jeans. Gordon already was familiar with the original 1924 play and 1925 film about the romantic underworld life in Paris popularly known as "Apache." The screenplay was another episode continuing the original story of the very popular stage

Drawing and film stills, The Return of the Rat, *1929,*
"Cabaret" chorus number. (Bottom left) Isabel Jeans and Ivor
Novello at costume ball with the "Cabaret" chorus in the back-
ground. (Above) For the same scene, note Gordon Conway with
director Graham Cutts, inspecting hand-painted designs on arms
and legs of chorus girls.

play *The Rat,* which had been coauthored by Novello
and Constance Collier under the male pseudonym of
David L'Estrange. After weeks of worry, on April 29,
Gordon expressed satisfaction with *The Return of the
Rat,* "which turned out to be a very good film." [20] Her
judgment was reinforced by the critics after the trade
show for the synchronized sound production that
screened at the Tivoli on July 19, 1929.

Besides creating costume renderings for the film,
Gordon sought estimates and arranged fittings with a
variety of costumiers. As with her work on *Confetti,*
she went beyond standard costume design practices, helping to cast mannequins and extras for the
"racetrack," "ballroom," "white coffin," and "cabaret"
scenes. Throughout the fall Gordon met with the two
Balcon brothers, Cutts, Overbaugh, general manager
Harold Boxall, and art director Alan McNab. This
crew met both at the studio and over cocktails with
Tommie Conway at the Conways' Bryanston Court
flat. During the filming, the *Evening Standard* film
critic pointed out that: "The dresses worn by British
film actresses have often been criticized by cinema-

goers. . . . [Graham Cutts] is determined that this re-proach shall not be levelled against his cast. He has engaged as dress-designer Miss Gordon Conway, who has designed frocks for many stage productions in London and New York."[21] Quoted in several articles, Gordon explained that her responsibility as designer was "not to suit the whims and fancies of the star," but to portray the character she gleaned from the script in consultation with the director and writers. Conferences with the cameraman and art director too were necessary because lighting and color values must be considered: "I must know what the backgrounds are—if my dresses will blend. . . . One never ceases learning; every day I have to correct myself."[22]

She also worked closely with publicity manager W. J. "Bill" O'Bryen. Known for clever promotional schemes, he peppered news releases with costume tid-bits, as well as four stories on Gordon herself—like her Conwy [sic] ancestral roots in Wales and her re-cently acquired eighteenth-century manor house in-herited from English forebears who settled in colonial Virginia. The releases included her views on autono-mous film wardrobe departments and on women in executive positions in film production. Indeed, *The Return of the Rat* attracted a myriad of press reports, including one on Gordon's decoration of the cabaret girls, a dance troupe once trained by André Char-lot. Gordon's sparkly and spangled costumes were tantalizingly brief on the female torsos, but were decked high with massive fanlike headpieces. Describ-ing the effect, the *Film Weekly* reported that the girls "had breast plates of black sequin and tight-fitting trunks of the same material . . . headdresses consisted of a black sequin skull cap surmounted by an enor-mous plume of black and white feathers." The most original costuming, however, according to the publi-cation, was the "fantastic pattern painted on their bare necks, arms and legs with black greasepaint fixed with gum arabic." The *Tatler* carried Gordon's picture with Cutts as he inspected the leg designs on the dancers.[23] Handbrushed daily by Gordon and McNab into scrolls of arabesques, these body designs proved to be the pièce de résistance for the press and the public alike.

Dress designs for Isabel Jeans as the vamp and for Mabel Poulton as the wronged woman received news coverage too. Gordon made sure that she dressed the supporting cast properly, thus adding to the accuracy, charm, and overall effectiveness of the film. She spent hours selecting in-house garments at costumiers, as well as purchasing accessories like parasols, handbags, and shoes at department stores and from Caledonian market vendors. She sifted through scores of cos-tumes for guests in the masquerade scene. With 150 extras acting as the crowd at the Longchamps races, the assignment was enormous, especially without the help of aides and shoppers who assisted her counter-part in America, the Hollywood wardrobe executive. Gordon explained to journalists visiting the set that the extras must be "costumed in the smartest Paris fashions. . . . [and] why she gave this girl a picture hat and that one an uneven hemline." She stressed that Cutts and Overbaugh approved every performer's cos-tume, such as morning coats and silk hats for the men escorting the women in spring attire at the races. As in previous interviews and in articles she wrote about film costuming, Gordon seized the platform for her crusade for "better-dressed British pictures." The British press enthusiastically reported Gordon's ideas: "I hope to see every studio with its own designer and dressmaking staff as they have in Hollywood. . . . When I have designed a frock and want it made, as soon as I mention that it is for film purposes every dressmaker at once puts up the prices to two or three times their real value." She urged that "It would pay studios over and over again to make their own dresses and keep a stock and alter and use again."[24]

Between August 1927, when Chez Beth executed designs for *Confetti,* and her final costuming job for *Wild Boy,* released in May 1934, Gordon worked with a plethora of couturiers, costumiers, dressmakers, seamstresses, tailors, lingerie and undergarment specialists, shoemakers, and milliners. (These designers and businesses' names are listed in the "Catalogue Raisonné: A Reference Guide to the Artwork and Career of Gordon Conway," which appears at the end of this study.) Gordon's modus operandi is worth noting because little scholarship exists on the day-to-day duties of costume designers and artisans who execute the ideas. Remarkably, Gordon was one of the early few who regularly received screen credit and publicity coverage. Though stage programs usually provided such notice, commercial costumiers rarely received screen credits or print-media recognition. Eclipsing the analysis of the arduous costuming process, most commentary—whether books, articles, or exhibition catalogues—spotlights beautiful stars displaying elegant garments in glittering settings, with supporting text that underscores the glamour. Hollywood had encouraged this fantasy approach since the early years of moviemaking. Dressing a film was romanticized by both studio publicity and fan magazines as frothy and fun, ignoring the long hours of tedious and frustrating work that required years of training and subtle skills of diplomacy.

In Gordon's case, a producer or director contacted her, rather than an art director arranging the collaboration, as had been the practice with many production teams. After conferring on a production budget, she negotiated with couturiers, costumiers, artisans, and department stores about the fees and execution of her designs. Appointments followed at these venues away from the studio for measurements, fabric and accessory selection, pattern approval, draping, and fittings—all of which she supervised. Additional fittings were required too because of production changes or corrections to ill-constructed garments. Gordon's connections with legendary British theater costumiers, now engaged in film work, expanded to include dealings with new shops springing up all over London. Designing both period costumes and modern-day clothes for forty-seven films, Gordon worked with an astonishing number of businesses including Worth, Molyneux, B. J. Simmons, Nathan's, Berman's, Paul Caret, Chez Beth, and the young Norman Hartnell. She shopped for incidental items like hose, gloves, and costume jewelry at such department stores as Harrods and Selfridges in addition to department stores that specialized in "modern dresses" for stage and screen. Gordon, joined by a number of these costumiers, felt a responsibility to inform as well as entertain female moviegoers. Many women based even the most limited wardrobe on Gordon's screen clothes, a practice that paralleled the impact of Hollywood designers on the American fashion industry.

During Gordon's six-year film career, the movie that garnered the most press coverage for her costumes was *High Treason,* directed by Maurice Elvey in 1929. Shan Balcon called on April 8, and she met with Elvey two days later. With her usual prompt response and indefatigable effort, she delivered dozens of sleek futuristic designs on April 12. Expressing relief, Gordon reported that "Everybody was crazy about my sketches."[25] During the massive publicity campaign, moviegoers agreed with the media's enthusiasm for Gordon's "fashions of the future."[26] Women especially relished the possibility of such functional yet fashionable garb. Considered an early science fiction triumph, this British movie was inspired by *Metropo-*

lis, the 1926 German-made futuristic film classic. Produced both as a silent film and as the first talkie for Gaumont-British, *High Treason*'s scenario was adapted by L'Estrange Fawcett from a play by Noel Pemberton Billing, a prominent Member of Parliament. The all-star cast included Benita Hume, Jameson Thomas, and Humberston Wright. After a private showing of the sound production on August 8 at the Marble Arch Pavilion, Gordon judged the film "very good and the dresses looked well."[27] Considering the exuberant public praise for her Modernistic, innovative, and functional attire, her film career seemed right on track.

Gave Mother an Awful Scare

Gordon jotted a diary entry on New Year's Eve that she "drank out the old year and in the new" and commented that "1929 has been quiet and slow."[28] The remark was a curious statement when considering the notoriety issuing from the respected and popular films *The Return of the Rat* and *High Treason*—visibility that was coupled with praise even for her work on discredited quota films. Her assignments for the *Tatler* and *Eve* drew ever increasing attention. Gordon's color covers for the weekly magazine *Eve* numbered at least thirty; this artwork continued in demand, even after July 1929, when the magazine was reconstituted as *Britannia and Eve.* Three years before, editor Peter Huskinson had agreed to Gordon's proposal for a regular full-color page of original designs in the *Tatler,* but none were published until 1929. Gordon's first installment of these original ensembles appeared in the March 13 issue and garnered wide public acclaim. In addition, starting in September 1928, C. D. Notley of Harrods commissioned scores of fashion croquis. These advertisement illustrations mushroomed during 1929 and 1930 to include at least seven other retail accounts: Selfridges, Debenham & Freebody, Dickins & Jones, Gorringes, Marshall & Snellgrove, Swan & Edgar furs, and Gooch's hats.

At the close of 1929, Gordon's record of films was not a bad count for a freelance designer when she is compared to her Hollywood counterparts who rarely accepted stage or print commissions while on contract to a studio. The film costume historian Elizabeth Leese explained in her seminal study *Costume Design in the Movies* that "It was unusual for a studio to allow any of their department heads to divide their loyalties."[29] No design exclusivity was required of Gordon until her mid-1931 to 1933 contracts with the holding company that controlled both Gainsborough and Gaumont-British studios. In 1929, Gordon was determined to keep the magazine and advertising accounts, because film work in England had not developed as she had been assured it would in 1927—especially her dream of heading an autonomous wardrobe department. Not only had print been a staple of Gordon's profession, but its social environment offered a pleasing one-on-one relationship between the illustrator and the editor or art director, which was backed up by a traditional code of manners and ethics. In Gordon's experience, the print world provided stability and geniality without the caprice and machinations that seemed rife within the movie world, an environment often clouded by personal idiosyncrasy, greed, and egocentricity.

Not only did Gordon Conway's counterparts in Hollywood devote full time to film, but their creative efforts were supported by staffs. Adrian, for example, was reported to have supervised 150 employees at Metro-Goldwyn-Mayer, a number that frequently expanded during special films. When Samuel Goldwyn contracted Chanel in 1931, her Paris assistant in Hollywood relied on one hundred new assistants hired by the studio. Yet Gordon carried out most of her film work with only four helpers. She did not secure a full-time assistant until May 1932. Of course Gordon had access to the best talent from retail businesses in London, such as the Worth family, British and French couturiers since 1858; L. & H. Nathan, theatrical and court costumiers since 1790; and B. J. Simmons and Co. Theatrical Costumiers, established in 1857. However, the total control and centralized work space enjoyed by most Hollywood wardrobe executives were missing in Gordon's movie work. Her creativity was interrupted by frequent trips to scattered geographical sites. Required to spend far too much time in coordination, she found her work was unavoidably time-consuming, disjointed, exhausting, and debilitating. Actresses and executives alike sometimes kept her waiting at various locations for hours, or they missed appointments altogether. Though Gordon argued for a different organizational and logistical setup, the hectic scurrying about continued at the studios.

In the fall of 1929 Gordon reported to friends how exhausted she was. Not yet under an annual contract to a studio, she nevertheless struggled to change conditions, but she was ignored. Her busy social schedule did not help matters. On November 11, Gordon was on her way with Wood Kahler to a cocktail party given by British *Vogue* editor Madge Garland, when she suffered an attack of what she thought was food poisoning from oysters at Scott's. She returned to her flat in excruciating pain. The next three days were filled with doctors, around-the-clock nurses, and solicitous friends waiting in the drawing room with flowers, candy, cigarettes, and books. She confessed, "I suffered agonies of all agonies. . . . Dr. Creighton says I've had a heart attack." However, the almost thirty-five-year-old Gordon did not record any fears regarding her future health. She worried only about her mother's reaction: "I gave Mother an awful scare."[30] Gordon dragged through work assignments at home and languidly received well-wishers. She pulled herself out of bed on November 27 for the private screening of Heather Thatcher's *Express Love* at the Regal Theatre. The consensus of well-wishers stationed at the flat was that a trip to Paris would do the trick for such an overworked designer. On December 5, luggage was loaded onto the Golden Arrow train for France. Dozens of parties, cabaret visits, and couture fittings were arranged. Gordon's friends and Tommie, though, were busier than Gordon herself. Uncharacteristically listless and subdued, she begged off on most occasions, attending only two of several parties celebrating her thirty-fifth birthday. Gordon described how bad she felt and saw her doctor at the American hospital who prescribed "nerve medicine." She pursued illustration work between bouts of illness. However, when offered commissions by Erskine Gwynne and Mark Real for magazine work in Paris, she reported that "they offered me work there, which *maybe* I'll do."[31] This diary entry was a first for Gordon, never known to turn down a commission.

When Gordon, her mother, and Dr. Tom Creighton returned on the Golden Arrow just before Christmas 1929, she attempted to insert new and relaxing recreational activities into her daily routine. Gordon played golf at Sunningdale and Swinley golf clubs. (She enjoyed seeing the Prince of Wales tee off and dine and dance at these two clubs near his favorite retreat of Fort Belvedere in Berkshire.) On weekends, friends like Ursula Jeans joined Gordon there, or at Addington, Stoke Poges, and Ranelagh, where they played eighteen holes before lunch and another eighteen after lunch. Determined to improve her score,

Gordon took lessons during the week at the golf school in Regent's Park. With friends at first solicitous of her health problems, Gordon's schedule showed promise of adapting to her weakened state. Soon, however, the old work habits and social demands crept back into her life. With only two weeks' grace, she accelerated her activities on January 18, which by a weird coincidence was the day that the Gainsborough studio was destroyed by fire. On that day she raced to the Empire to view *Hallelujah,* an acclaimed film with an African-American cast that she judged "one of the best productions I've ever seen."[32] Gordon's relaxation agenda shifted into a demanding duty as she hurried to the Chelsea Flower Show and "point-to-point races at Old Surrey and Burstow."[33] Days and nights found Gordon dashing from restaurant to club, including the latest "very smart" nightspot called The Not and to Nash's, a new London club she had joined. Between golf sessions, Gordon coached Ursula Jeans for an American part in a new stage play. Drew Pearson came for cocktails to bring greetings from fellow journalist and Gordon's friend Harold Horan in Paris. Parties abounded, like those given by Ethel and Leonora Wodehouse. There was also Graham Cutts's birthday party she would not miss. Gordon made two nightclub visits at the request of Carl Hyson, who wanted to confer with her on his shows at the So-So and at the Bat. With regret, she dismissed the jobs as a "wash-out." Sadly, Carl had fallen on hard times, according to a former associate. Decades later, composer and cabaret pianist Ian Grant explained that Hyson was saddled with serious gambling debts, often asking him and fellow performers to wait for their salary until after the next greyhound race.[34]

Gordon's pace quickened with attendance at stage shows and films in an effort to develop business contacts. She had no new film work in 1930 and was disappointed that a theater costuming job with Charles Laughton and Gillian Lind did not work out. There were, however, costume sessions with Mabel Poulton, appointments at the Dorland Advertising Agency, and meetings to discuss television programming with Roger Eckersley at the British Broadcasting Corporation. Gordon reported business conferences such as the one when "a London designer asked me to go into the interior decorating business with him."[35] Regard for her talent for interior design was partly fueled by her stunning stage set designs and by the popular backgrounds she placed through the years in her graphics for the *Tatler* and *Eve.* One *Eve* cover featured Gordon's own Art Moderne red chair in her flat. A sketch for a Harrods advertisement featured her Bryanston Court fireplace wall. Gordon granted favors that required time and energy, such as devising a chart of colors and textures for a friend's Rolls Royce and giving advice on house and office interiors. She designed a single costume for a revival of *The Maid of the Mountains,* but Gordon now judged this once popular British production that she had illustrated during her New York period as "boring and old-fashioned."[36] She worked on a poster for Merivale Press and attended the couture showings of both Madeleine Vionnet and Jeanne Lanvin. Gordon attended the usual cultural functions related to the arts and to fashion, including events hosted by such notables as the Duchesses of Westminster and Rutland, the private exhibition of Cecil Beaton's work, and the "conversation pictures" at the home of Philip Sassoon.[37] A highlight of her activities in 1930 was official seating at the inaugural dinner-dance honoring industrial artists—an event hosted by Herbert Morgan at the Café Royal. She welcomed this career recognition at a time of ill health and financial restraint.

New Hemlines go to Smart Lengths

THE irregular hem is the outstanding fashion-note of new Model Gowns, as shown at Harrods. It is a style-device that lends itself to a host of graceful treatments—scarcely two alike. Witness the three charming modes pictured, and note the fabrics—they are particularly important.

'MEDINA' The bustle effect that so many French designers sponsor is subtly suggested in this beautifully moulded gown of Moiré. Painted draperies fall almost to the floor at the right—at the left the line is short and simple. *14 Gns*

'LAURETTE' Fan-shaped flares, cleverly introduced at front, sides and centre back give the new silhouette to an enchanting gown in Ninon. Diamanté embroideries star the slenderly moulded bodice. *16 Gns*

'L'ELEGANTE' Deep decolletage is supremely smart—as in this gown of sapphire Ring Velvet. The drooping cape effect is echoed by the dipping flares, which fall almost to the floor. *14 Gns*

Salon for Model Gowns, First Floor.

HARRODS

HARRODS LTD   LONDON SW1

Autobiographical illustration of Conway's flat, seen in Harrods advertisement section in The Tatler, *October 3, 1928.*

Nine Men and Me

Stage work reemerged in Gordon's life. On May 8, 1930, she signed a contract for *Charlot's Masquerade,* an André Charlot revue presented at the new Cambridge Theatre. The assignment began early that spring when choreographer Quentin Tod invited Gordon to create a collection of costumes and one stage set for his ballet. The two friends discussed the project further while attending an exhibition of Ballets Russes designs in late March. Quentin Tod's ballet vignettes—starring Anton Dolin and Dora Vadimova—soon were incorporated into the revue production. Besides Charlot and Tod, Gordon conferred with Bertie Alexander Meyer—the executive lessee of the Cambridge—and the stage manager, the book author, the lyricist, and the composers, as well as board members from British Celanese Limited. While working with Charlot's production staff, Gordon noticed, once again, that the field was dominated by male talent. She underscored in her diary that the

conferences often numbered "*nine men and me.*"[38]

The Cambridge Theatre was the second of six theaters built in London in 1930, and embodied a different perception of visual space in England. The new building sheds light on Gordon's philosophical approach to design, the status of modern design theories in Britain, and the need for stage producers to confront the competition of the motion picture palaces. The Cambridge management produced a lavish souvenir brochure acknowledging that the public was enjoying the luxury and comfort of many new cinema houses and should be "entitled to expect more commodious and up-to-date Theatres." The building was easily accessible to the public, since it stood at the conjunction of seven streets known for centuries as the Seven Dials. The auditorium seated 1,200 people and offered the latest conveniences from lighted ashtrays to carpet. The streamlined steel-framed and concrete construction was the creation of Wimperis, Simpson & Guthrie. Members of the noted firm, along with interior designer Serge Chermayeff, were "ruled by the principles of functionalism. . . . to let fitness of purpose decide the final forms and colours."[39] Indeed, the Cambridge architecture caused quite a stir. One article extolled the "austere simplicity of broad unfretted [sic] surfaces and sweeping curves," and praised the designers who have learned from "Continental experiments. . . . [but who have not been] seduced by modernity for modernity's sake."[40] The *Tatler* critic summarized most opinions that the structure "ensures that the last word in theatreland has been spoken."[41]

Gordon met with the revue's set and costume designer, Serge Chermayeff; as a consequence of the collaboration, he and his wife became lifelong friends of Gordon and Tom. Chermayeff inspired Gordon with his interior design, lighting, furniture, and especially his bold and streamlined stylized dancing figures in gold and silver at the Cambridge. The theater brochure called attention to Chermayeff's sense of the whole design, the "harmony of feeling. . . . long sweeping lines of construction. . . . [with no] disturbing and useless ornament." Chermayeff illustrated the graphic publications for the theater, following a set of ideas through in every detail. His cover of the revue playbill, similar to the souvenir booklet, featured an industrial motif of interlocking gears as part of a drive mechanism. A stunning design, many thought, but others found the cover peculiar and unrelated to the themes of the musical revue. Indeed, Chermayeff had repeated the circular motifs of the building scheme, from the entrance-vestibule floor "suggesting the vortex of movement from this point" in history in the evolution of societal development.[42] This overall design initiative of Chermayeff was just the kind of work that Gordon aspired to professionally, whether it was labeled art direction or production design. She had absorbed design theories and practices from various modern movements during the early years of the design revolution and long before the influential 1925 Paris Exposition. Gordon understood that Chermayeff's graphic design issued from the overarching plan of the Cambridge itself. For instance, an idea presented in the theater booklet discussed the trend of progressive "mechanized development" as expressed in the design scheme. This idea was similar to one she herself had articulated only a year before during press releases and interviews about her futuristic and functional costumes for the science fiction film *High Treason*.

For many British citizens between the world wars, the encounter with modern design was a jolting visual experience that produced either enormous praise or bitter disdain. (These reactions seem strange to today's observer, surrounded by landscapes saturated with modern forms.) Some diverse reactions to functionalism are revealed in the landmark book *The Long Week-End: A Social History of Great Britain, 1918–1939*. The authors, Robert Graves and Alan Hodge, pointed out that "the word functionalism was first heard in 1930, applied to the sugar cube architecture style imported from Germany." The term also applied to manufactured goods, but in the authors' judgment, the "functionally designed objects were usually ugly in shape." Interestingly, from the standpoint of Gordon's work, the term "functionalism" was appropriated to describe fashion in the 1930s and often was coupled with the adjective "amusing." This new combination of words, according to the authors, now replaced the outdated terms "the Victorian *chic* and the Edwardian 'smart.'"[43] Expanding on the impact of the Cambridge architecture, the *Play Pictorial* praised the "Designers and Builders of this Prodigy of Entertainment. . . . Its interior construction, its scheme of decoration is unlike anything seen in London up to the present. . . . for a moment it takes one's breath away because of its strangeness to the eye. . . . one realizes that here is a thing of beauty, a house of luxury, a veritable Temple of Art . . . [and] Palace of Drama."[44]

Besides Gordon and Chermayeff, *Charlot's Masquerade* gathered a cluster of design talent for the revue's string of sketches called "little playlets", with set and costume designers A. E. Barbosa, Phyllis Dolton, Philip Gough, Charles Judd, and the design team of Marc Henri and Laverdet. Executing both modern dress and period costume designs were a variety of costumiers including Alias, LaRue, Morris Angel, and Patricia Orwin. For the ballet costumes, André Charlot hand delivered Gordon's designs to the atelier J. Muelle in Paris to execute the Louis XVI–style costumes for "Snowdrop and the Seven Brothers." Though some of Gordon's late-eighteenth-century-

Costume design probably for Charlot's Masquerade, London, 1930.

style designs are not marked with the title of this revue, they probably are the ballet offerings, judging from the resemblance to the press pictures of the show. For the "Snowdrop and the Seven Brothers" costume and set renderings, Gordon and Tod studied Louis XVI dress and decor at the Victoria and Albert Museum with the help of James Laver of the museum staff, a respected scholar of costume and culture.

Gordon's work seemed like two separate productions, with other artistic staff weaving in and out in a haphazard fashion, attempting to give some unity to the show. Initially Gordon was involved in a limited capacity with the costumes and sets for Tod's ballets. In July, however, the management asked her to assist with casting, a role she gladly accepted. Though it was a short nineteen days till the dress parade, Charlot himself requested costuming for the finale involving thirty-five costumes, which she quickly produced. Management also asked for costume designs for the opening scene and, for the last scene of the first act,

"Skating Shoes," the roller rink attire that featured high-laced boots, turbans, and costumes with white fox–cuffed sleeves. The *Tatler* judged: "The skating dresses designed by Gordon Conway are very fascinating; the coats have small basques which are held in position by narrow belts caught with buckles. Beatrice Lillie's is of an exquisite pink-red begonia shade, while those of the chorus are of white lined with red, with the result that there is a lovely sheen, indeed they suggest snow on which the sun is setting."[45] Gordon's circular skirt construction for Lillie allowed the comedienne to sing and dance on roller skates while taking comic spills with an understated burlesque agility. The *Star* critic A. E. Wilson marveled that the revue "fully matches the beauty of its architectural setting. . . . and in colouring, grouping, lighting and staging it has an artistic charm and taste not always to be found in revue."[46]

Charlot, Meyer, and a synthetic fabric company developed a clever promotional scheme in which Gordon played a major role. The show's costumes were constructed from Celanese synthetic fabrics of taffeta, satin, crepe, suede, and locknit. Gordon's opening gala gown of her own design was Celanese georgette and was made by the dressmaker Marguerite on the recommendation of new colleague and friend Teddie Holstius, advertising manager for Celanese. Holstius urged Gordon to consider design work for the firm. Executives had been impressed by her guidance during the company's recent dress parade at the New Century Club and by her window displays of their fabrics, as well as by her costumes for *Charlot's Masquerade.*

The revue playbill featured a full-page Celanese advertisement reflecting the milieu in which Gordon and her costume colleagues worked: "It's a great thing. . . . even for Celanese which is used by the most famous couturiers, worn by the smartest women . . . to have been chosen from all the fabrics of the world to dress Charlot's Masquerade which opens this—the world's most modern theatre. Yet, when one thinks of it, this choice was inevitable. . . . for the theatre is fashion's mirror and the mirror of fashion must perforce reflect. . . . CELANESE."[47]

Pointing to this interaction between theater costumes and commercial dress interests, a Birmingham journalist emphasized that "*Charlot's Masquerade* is *revue à la mode.*" Following the August tryout premier, the critic regretted that the playbill did not credit the designer's name because "the dresses are of the loveliest form and colour, and worn to perfection." Praising "the beauty of its costumes," the critic pointed out that the revue's "greatest distinction is in its ballets, like 'The Masque of the Red Death,' a medieval *danse macabre* from a story by Edgar Allan Poe, and 'Snowdrop and the Seven Brothers,' which is a fairy tale that seems like an exquisite pastoral by Antoine Watteau realized in terms of dance."[48]

Gordon stayed long enough in Birmingham to review the costumes and sets. She also attended the Celanese-hosted opening night party at the Queen's Hotel. She then hurried back to London by train with Celanese representatives; this trip provided time to discuss the promotion of the fabric.

After the September 4 opening in London, the *Tatler* ran a portrait of Gordon, a full-length photograph in a long dinner gown of her own design. It was one of at least six photographs by Janet Jevons that appeared in periodicals touting the revue throughout England. Linking stage costuming and fashion once again, the caption observed that "the bright revue . . . owes much of its success, as far as scenery and dressing are concerned, to the genius of Miss Gordon Conway, the famous dress designer. . . . Miss Conway not only knows how to dress other people, but dresses herself with a distinction and chic which are rare, even in these days of good dressing."[49]

Most critics liked Charlot's revue, and audiences seemed quite pleased, but much to Gordon's chagrin this miniature extravaganza ended after a modest run. Gordon was puzzled and frustrated. Last-minute assignments, no matter how praiseworthy, were taking a toll on her health. Although she accepted future revue work, she yearned to be in charge of a totally integrated production with an overall design scheme. Commenting on the status of revue in general in 1930, Sheridan Morley remarked that the "small-scale Charlot revues [had] been the great success story of the West End in the Twenties." Therefore, he expected the same success for the lavish inaugural show of *Charlot's Masquerade* at the Cambridge. Morley reminded his readers that the first Charlot revue of 1924, with much the same talent, had partially broken the American dominance of the musical stage in both London and New York and had at last made British performers like Beatrice Lillie, Gertrude Lawrence, and Jack Buchanan stars on Broadway. However, in 1930 Morley lamented, "For some unfathomable reason, people didn't want to see revues anymore."[50] British impresario Charles B. Cochran offered an analysis of the situation: "The process of unification is the most important element in revue today. It is not enough to pitchfork on to the stage a series of sketches, songs and dances. There must be design and form, balance and rhythm, and the best way to achieve these objects is to . . . bank on one man's inspiration and ability to carry out his ideas."[51] Gordon would have agreed with her former client, but she would have pressed for *one woman*'s inspiration—for Gordon Conway's inspiration and the ability to carry out her own ideas in an integrated, well-planned, and unified manner.

Dressing in Poems of Chic

On November 4, 1930, Gordon received what she thought would be a major career advance—an opportunity to execute a total design concept. André Charlot invited her to design the costumes, sets, and promotional graphics for his new production of *Wonder Bar*. Based on the Berlin hit about Continental night life, the British production changed from the fictional location of Berlin to a cabaret in Vienna because of the political unrest in Germany. The musical play starred Dorothy Dickson as Liane, a society matron smitten by cabaret life, Danish matinee idol Carl Brisson as the gigolo Harry, and a supporting cast of seventy-five including Elsie Randolph and Gwen Farrar.

During an interview decades later, Dorothy Dickson remembered the excitement, glamour, and originality of the production, but she recounted an unpleasant experience that had affected her for a lifetime. This remembrance provides an insight into the era's political upheaval. On a trip to Berlin to see the original production, Dickson became fearful and insisted that she return to England, for she "felt the decadence of the Nazi regime" that was taking hold in Germany.[52]

Gordon first immersed herself in work for a major poster, which soon became the program and sheet-music cover as well. On November 12 she spent ten hours on the poster alone, promptly delivering it to Charlot, who "liked it immensely."[53] The days were filled with costume renderings and set designs for the Savoy Theatre, which was to be transformed into a cabaret setting that melded the stage and audience space. Several *Wonder Bar* set drawings by Gordon illustrate cabaret vignettes that spread from the stage and orchestra pit into the stalls, thus drawing the au-

dience into the act. These set renderings are reminiscent of Gordon's jazz motif series of 1924, and they explode with the vitality, vivacity, and intimacy of the Continental night life she knew so well. Reflecting themes in the show, they burst with jazz and jokes, mimicry and martinis, bands and banter, smoke rings and song, and terpsichorean delights from tango to tap to ballroom dancing and Dickson's signature high kick. All of a sudden, though, Gordon discovered that someone else was receiving the credit for the staging in the playbill and publicity. Attention shifted to Basil Ionides, the interior decorator who had assisted with the redesign of the Savoy Theatre in 1929. As to Gordon's set designs, no record has emerged explaining the confusion. Typical of Gordon's cooperative spirit, she proceeded good-naturedly with the costuming and graphic designs.

Paralleling the design interaction between the Cambridge Theatre and the Charlot revue, the streamlined style of the Savoy Theatre lent itself beautifully to the staging and dressing of *Wonder Bar*. The structure had been built exclusively for Gilbert and Sullivan's light opera but was completely remodeled in 1929. The Savoy was what a theater architectural authority has called "an Art Deco delight . . . [with its] silver splendour" that was created to blend with the stainless steel façade of the reconstructed Savoy Hotel next door.[54] *Country Life* claimed that in London "the new Savoy Theatre is the first really outstanding example of modern decoration applied to a public place on a commercial basis."[55]

During the planning, Dorothy Dickson, Elsie Randolph, and Gwen Farrar often dropped by Gordon's flat for dress conferences and cocktail hours. Dickson remembered the long white satin gown and matching evening coat trimmed with white fox collar, cuffs, and hem that allowed her to glide across the stage and stalls. This celebrated white satin ensemble was high-lighted in the *Sketch* along with a clever costume invented by Gordon—"a Venetian blind" dress with pulley ribbons that lowered and raised the skirt, presenting alternately a demure old-world matron or an experimental New Woman. Among the press notices, one review in particular must have cheered Gordon. In a Christmas Eve review, the discriminating "Trinculo" of the *Tatler* found *Wonder Bar* at first novel and intriguing, but said that the absence of boundaries between the stage and stalls grew distracting, making the audience feel like spectators at a lacrosse match. The glimmer of a plot was all too often hampered by the rationing of dialogue and popping of champagne corks. The critic acknowledged, however, that "Miss Dickson looks, and dances, enchantingly. . . . [and] Miss Gordon Conway's dresses, to the male eye, are poems of chic." [56]

The following April, Gordon created more posters, including one for Dickson. She worked nineteen hours over two days on one for Carl Brisson; though he was a star she found intolerably conceited, he was charmed by this graphic. The musical play ran successfully in the West End and moved on to venues like the Empire Theatre in Kingston-upon-Thames. This show has undergone several adaptations to stage, film, and television since the original German version. Al Jolson played in the 1931 Broadway version and was joined by other megastars for the spectacular produced by Warner Brothers–First National studio in 1934. Unfortunately, Gordon was not given the opportunity to design for these adaptations: the Broadway costumes were designed by Yetta Kiviette and Charles LeMaire, while Hollywood designer Orry-Kelly created the film costumes. No record has surfaced that these costume designers were familiar with Gordon's exemplary designs.

Though the show was successful in London, Gordon wrote on January 7, 1931, that she made repeated trips to André Charlot's office "trying to get my money." [57] A stage historian sheds light on the situation: "Charlot's liabilities were said to be £60,000 by the Official Receiver in 1931." [58] She could not afford to live without payment, so she quickly moved on to other opportunities. On May 4 Gordon had scheduled a luncheon meeting at the Café Anglais with revue producer Archibald de Bear, Bertie Meyer, and film art director and stage set designer Clifford Pember. Two days later she delivered sketches to the Cambridge for the new show *The Sign of the Seven Dials.* In addition to the usual meetings with management, she supervised fittings at Worth, Idare, and Laddie Limited and scurried around looking for "costumes for Miss Pollock." The opening on June 2, though, inspired only a cool "pretty good" in her diary. Four days later she registered regret that the show closed. [59]

During the spring of 1931, Gordon's career and promotional activities intertwined, as usual, with her private life, which often produced commissions. From her earlier days in London, when visits to the Grafton Gallery became a habit, she found art exhibitions fruitful, like a special spring showing of Persian art. Most influential was her April 1 visit to an exhibition by Modernist sculptor Jacob Epstein at the Leicester Galleries. Over the past year, her writer-friends Denis Mackail, Teddie Holstius, and Wood Kahler had books published which called for the usual Conway celebrations. Gordon's attendance with Tommie Conway at Eugene O'Neill's *Strange Interlude*—it began at 6:00 P.M., had a short dinner break, and continued until 11:00 P.M.—inspired the reaction "simply brilliant." [60] Among a score of stage productions she relished Noël Coward's *Cavalcade* and the

Liquor advertisement, The Sketch, *September 16, 1931.*

latest presentation from the Théâtre de la Chauve-Souris, which she especially enjoyed because she could mingle with the performers at Bertie Meyer's cast party. Earlier that January she mentioned a meeting at Gainsborough studio with one of her favorite movie people, Shan Balcon. Though other film people conferred with her that spring, the season had filled with appointments with three advertising agency representatives, attendance at couture showings, liquor advertising assignments for Burt Lytel, and covers for Mr. Beaumont at the *Bystander.*

With skeptical reserve, Gordon traveled on June 29 to Gainsborough offices, where Shan Balcon asked her to dress films for both Gainsborough and Gaumont-British. The two studios were linked in business ownership as well as by the production management of Shan Balcon's younger brother Michael. Upon signing a contract with Gaumont-British, Gordon threw herself into work with renewed enthusiasm for film design, convinced this move was the direction her career should take. Her professional goals had been revealed three years before in one of three articles she authored during that short-lived euphoric period in the British film industry. Seeing her career

as a steady progression, she wrote in the April 18, 1928, issue of *Picture Show* that "dress designing for the films is perhaps the most interesting of all other forms of dress designing."[61] Gordon called her beginning as a poster artist "excellent training, for it develops a sense of line and colour, and helps one to realize the truth of the old maxim that it is the simplest things that gain the most striking effect." Going from designing theatrical posters to dressing a stage production "was a perfectly natural and logical step," as was moving from stage design into film. Viewing costume design within the larger framework of design itself, Gordon sounded as though she was philosophizing about modern architecture or industrial and product design when she wrote that "excessive elaboration defeats its own ends." Her costume work in film, she concluded, "served to strengthen my conviction that the most telling and striking effects are usually secured by carefully studied simplicity."[62] To Gordon, the principles of design were the same whether applied to a building or a costume. In the years to come, she would have much opportunity to exercise those principles.

CHAPTER SEVEN

DRESSING THE TALKIES

The Story's the Thing

Gordon explored design arguments in an article entitled "Dressing the Talkies" for the *Film Weekly.* Like a modern architect arguing that design begins with the function of a structure, Gordon emphasized that "the story's the thing," quite apart from the performer's personality, the marketing value, or other distractions. "I try my best by means of line and drapery and materials, to express that story in terms of clothes. . . . it is my theory that clothes can and do tell the story and express its spirit." Gordon expanded on her career goals: "I have not, as yet, done the art direction for a film, but I must plead guilty to having a few ideas on the subject, some of which I have tried out on my own London flat." On the value of costuming in production, she lamented: "I can't understand how it is that so few people amongst makers of movies take it . . . seriously."[1] In an article she wrote for the *Bioscope,* Gordon complained that financial department heads protested her dress costs until she confronted the men with the celluloid evidence. Movie film, she argued, "underlines every conceivable defect in the material or finish of a frock. . . . Fortunately, the general recognition of the designer's status is spreading." Gordon pointed out that in addition to creating costumes to tell the story, film dressing set fashion styles around the world—a happenstance that challenged the preeminence of Parisian haute couture. From a marketing standpoint alone, moviemakers would benefit from good design, since multitudes of female picturegoers admitted that fashion was a primary reason for attending the cinema. Indeed, fashion sold film tickets. "The best producers," observed Gordon, were beginning to show an "increasing recognition of the importance of the dress-designer."[2]

Expanding upon these trade-journal remarks, Gordon stressed the "difference between the colour as seen by the eye and as seen on the screen." She called attention to new color systems like the "panchromatic films," and pointed out that even films shot in black and white required the management of color. In addition to studying film rushes, Gordon analyzed her color drawings using a small eye-glass implement of sapphire glass that transposed color into various shades of blacks, grays, and whites providing a contrast of hue, value, and texture. She noted that light blue and "a weird yellow" produced a better "white" on the screen than white itself, which often caused "halation," a distracting halo image. Gordon concluded that the designer's responsibility was "to see that the frock does not quarrel in colour or in line with the sets."[3]

Broaching another topic, Gordon yearned for the day when actresses would avoid exaggerated outfits like the "wired ruffle" made famous by film idol Greta Garbo. She argued that a costume influences the way an actress feels about a role, thus affecting the performance. Pleading for the "appropriateness of clothes,"

Photograph by Janet Jevons of Gordon Conway, London, ca. 1926. This image appeared in several periodicals including a special edition of The Bioscope, *1929.*

of Windsor comes out swinging for Paris." Though designers today still use "the silver screen as their runway," more attention is paid to "the self-effacing work of letting the character's clothes speak for the character, rather than the costume designer forcing a 'fashion statement.'" Speaking of her mode of working, whether she designs from scratch or "shops" the character in the stores, Mirojnick points out that "long before she thinks of the clothes, she's consumed with the story." She must know "what's in the character's closet before you're ready to dress the character for the role."[5]

Though Mirojnick's ideas resemble Gordon's, there is a crucial distinction regarding the present-day motion picture milieu. In many screen stories of Gordon's era, writers, directors, and producers conceived female characters as the personification of chic abundance. They delineated scores of sophisticated New Women dressed à la mode in cosmopolitan scenes. Since the dream was fabricated by the film industry and espoused by manufacturers, retailers, editors, advertisers, and consumers, clothes for that kind of woman's role did indeed hang in the movie "character's closet." Gordon was capable of providing both a fashion statement and a character's true image, an image made possible by what has been described by Mirojnick as "the inner game of costume."[6]

The first film under Gordon's 1931 contract, *Sunshine Susie,* was directed by Victor Saville. Gordon's costuming helped to tell the story of a spunky bank secretary, though it was not a screen style show like many of that era from Hollywood. A viewing of the film today raises questions regarding the plausibility of the lead's frequent wardrobe changes and the appropriateness of a stenographer all dolled up in a long fur-trimmed red satin dinner gown with a matching evening coat. However, the New Woman aspirations

Gordon described a film scene of an actress decked out in an evening gown of "flowered chiffon with flamboyant jewellery [*sic*] when dining with a lot of unshaven men in a mining camp." Many filmmakers and publicists exploited such "exotic creations," knowing that costuming contributes to a box office hit, but she reminded readers that "simplicity of line is the safe rule" for effective film dressing.[4]

Sixty years later, views similar to those of Gordon Conway were expressed by a renowned contemporary film costume designer. The costume designer for *Wall Street* and *Fatal Attraction,* Ellen Mirojnick, observed: "In the 1930's, Hollywood designers dressed stars in distinctive new fashions for an unsophisticated audience. Today, the goal of costume is to disappear into the director's vision: the art direction, character development and structure of the film." Mirojnick provided an interesting analogy: "Grand Hollywood names battled the Paris couturiers like Chanel, Schiaparelli and Dior for the title of fashion dictator. They always went a full 15 rounds. In this corner, we have Joan Crawford glittering in Adrian's sequined, satin shoulders; in the opposite corner, the Duchess

of this office girl—determined to become an affluent private secretary—were true to the script.

Gordon launched into this film work with gusto on July 1, 1931. Appointments began with the star, the popular Berlin singer Renate Müller. Müller had been hailed for the title role of the ambitious young working woman in the stage and screen productions, originally entitled *Die Privatsekretärin.* The film resulted from a coproduction and distribution agreement between the Gaumont-British and Gainsborough holding company and Universam Film Aktien Gesellschaft (UFA), a studio near Potsdam. On December 7 Gordon celebrated the premiere with Tommie Conway and two beaus at the Capitol Theatre in the Haymarket, followed by a gala supper given by Gainsborough at the Kit-Kat Club. *Variety* judged this pioneering British musical "probably the best box-office picture which has yet come out of the English studios." Calling Saville's direction "reminiscent of Lubitsch," the review added that the film "rates as much better entertainment than the average American talker. . . . Twenty more like it every year and the English studios will have those world markets knocking on the door." As to the contributions of Gordon and her art direction colleagues, the "settings and everything are well over English standard."[7] Gordon worked simultaneously on *Sunshine Susie* and *Michael and Mary,* also directed by Saville for Gainsborough, a film based on a British story and current West End hit by A. A. Milne. The studio atmosphere was sprinkled with cautious new hopes for a rejuvenated film industry.

From July 1931 onward, Gordon met regularly with Saville, film actresses, department store staff, and costumiers. She met with studio officials, some of whom, like Herman Fellner, had recently emigrated from Germany. The executive she seemed to confer with most frequently was Shan Balcon. For instance, he set

up and accompanied her to screenings of the original German version of *Sunshine Susie,* as well as to rushes from *Michael and Mary* and *Lord Babs.* Gordon was often asked to represent the studios at promotional film trade functions. On November 20, Gordon and Shan Balcon dined with Tommie Conway at Bryanston Court before representing the studios at a trade show starring Greta Garbo and Clark Gable. Over the months Shan drove Gordon home after late fittings and long shooting sessions, which often flowed into cocktails or supper at the flat. Though this courteous gesture was performed on occasion by brother Michael Balcon and by other members of his production team, it was Shan who was Gordon's mentor in the studio system.

Friendly exchanges of this kind also occurred with British Lion executive Bryan Edgar Wallace, who drove Gordon home from the Beaconsfield studio where his father, mystery writer Edgar Wallace, filmed adaptations of his books and plays. Rachael Low explained that the 1931 arrangement with Michael Balcon was for him "to produce a series of joint Gainsborough–British Lion films which would be made at Beaconsfield" by experienced directors and technicians from both studios.[8] In a growing atmosphere of expansion, optimism, and camaraderie, Gordon dressed two Wallace mystery films, *The Frightened Lady* and *White Face.* Unfortunately, following Wallace's unexpected death in Hollywood in 1932, the once promising agreement dissolved. The last coproduction Gordon costumed at Beaconsfield was not a British thriller at all, but an adaptation of a German cinema hit. Entitled *There Goes the Bride,* this popular film was the vehicle for Gordon's first designs for rising young star Jessie Matthews.

So hectic was October that Gordon neglected to record in her diary details of the *Michael and Mary*

Costume design for Nora Swinburne in White Face, *1932, later featured in a film still.*

premiere. She missed the Gordon Selfridge election night party on the 27th, but did report that "the National Government was elected by a huge majority."[9] She was quite busy costuming *Lord Babs,* directed by Walter Forde. Just as Edna Best and Elizabeth Allan had felt welcome at Bryanston Court through the years, so would the actresses from *Lord Babs.* By meeting them in her flat, Gordon made costume collaboration with colleagues convenient and convivial. The magnitude of this service was reinforced late that fall when Gordon and Tom slipped out of a highly touted concert by the "14-year-old violinist Yehudi Menuhin" in order to receive Cathleen Nesbitt for tea during work on *The Frightened Lady.*[10] These courteous gestures were appreciated by most colleagues, and friendly expressions of gratitude flowed back to Gordon from production staff and actresses alike. Anne Grey, whom Gordon was dressing for *The Faithful Heart,* surprised Gordon with a birthday gift corsage, a mass of orchids she wore throughout that mid-December. Outside the purview of film costuming and public relations for the studio that fall, Gordon set up displays of sketches, accompanied by high tea, for clients like New York theater luminary John Murray Anderson and the *Bystander* editor.

On November 25, Gordon wrote that she and Tommie attended the Edgar Wallace stage thriller *The Case of the Frightened Lady* a second time, because "we're doing it as a film."[11] Gordon's use of "we" is significant. Unlike many assignments of this quintessential freelance artist, this job seemed to tightly link Gordon to the films and production staff by a feeling of loyalty and shared goals. Not even at *Vogue* and *Vanity Fair,* where Gordon felt part of the Condé Nast publishing family, did she use the pronoun "we." Her exclusive film contract made her part of a community of artists and technicians.

Throughout that fall, Gordon confessed to "feeling rotten [and] so tired."[12] She even struggled to attend events like the American dinner at the Savoy Hotel on Thanksgiving. Uncharacteristically, she fell asleep now and then during stage performances and films. Yet the hectic pace continued. On November 4 she joined eight men to judge the finals for studio scholarships for twelve young actresses. Since her attitude on the value of female leadership in the arts and entertainment industry is well-documented, Gordon no doubt made a plea for production opportunities beyond acting for the women. Indeed, she would see to it the following year that winners were rewarded with a smattering of training from the production side of moviemaking, with a special focus on costume design, public relations, and publicity. A parallel project for training young men in production, however, received priority attention at the studio. After all, the training had long been one of Michael Balcon's chief projects. The clusters of talent that the producer encouraged have been called "Balcon's bright young men" and "Mr. Balcon's Academy for Young Gentlemen."[13] This early apprenticeship program trained twenty-four men in all facets of motion picture production from cinematography and editing to publicity and—relevant to Gordon's interest—art direction.

As the months rolled into 1932, it fell to Gordon, as the only woman executive, to be in charge of the female winners. She could not bear to see the young women let down. After interviews, she joined the twelve for lunch at Punch's, and later met each at Marshall and Snellgrove "for a new wardrobe." Gordon escorted the young women around the studios, treated them to tea in her flat, demonstrated sketching, answered questions, addressed their problems, and listened to their hopes and dreams. Even before 1931 had come to a close, an exhausted Gordon scratched her

schedule into what looked more like a business calendar than a diary. These diary entries reflect daily work demands soon to double, a routine that would ultimately incapacitate Gordon and blight a brilliant career:

Thursday, December 3, 1931: ". . . Met Miss Chrystall and shopped with her—12:30 at Marshall's—3:00 Hartnell's with her—4:00 at Worth's—5:00 at Paul Caret's. . ."

Friday, December 4, 1931: ". . . 9:30 to the studio— met her at Worth's at 12:00—2:00 met Belle Chrystall at Daphne's—at 2:45 took her to Paul Caret's—3:45 to Norman Hartnell's—met Cathleen Nesbitt and went with her to Caret's at 5:00 . . ."[14]

On December 31 Gordon "talked business" over lunch with studio business manager Harold Boxall and production assistant Shan Balcon. To what extent she emphasized her dilemma is not known. Gordon would not have mentioned her ill health, and she probably felt guilty about complaining of overwork. Male executives were pushed to the limit too, but the men always wound up with assistants, or found staff to carry out their instructions. One boon that seems to have resulted from her New Year's Eve conference was the hiring of special assistants. A search for biographical information on them, however, has led to naught. Gordon's "Miss Prescott" began work the following May. Joining the effort to boost productivity would be "Miss Taylor" and "Miss Watts." Later in 1932 Gordon welcomed sketch artist Joyce Murchie and aide Betty Claire, affectionately called "B.C." in Gordon's records. The distinguished costume designer Margaret Furse worked for Gordon during the early years of Furse's career at Gaumont-British.[15] These young women became loyal members of Gordon's circle who would spend as many as ten hours a day by her side, exerting energies on behalf of the feature films Gordon dressed between mid-1932 and the end of 1933.

Reflecting on Gordon's work situation during an interview, director Michael Powell acknowledged Michael Balcon's well-known modus operandi of a close-knit production team. Balcon fostered creativity and cooperative harmony among his mostly male staff. These men felt free to express opinions and try out innovative measures on their own—as long as they stayed within the budget, that is. Powell doubted, however, that Michael Balcon would have understood the pressures that a sensitive perfectionist like Gordon Conway experienced. He added that "Mick would not have been sympathetic" with a woman of Gordon's background, who was determined to have it all—a rewarding career and public popularity along with a network of friends in tandem with a life of taste and style that demanded its own overarching design scheme and subtle intricacies of manners and ritual.[16]

During 1931 Michael Balcon faced his own set of pressures. As he explained in his autobiography, Balcon forged ahead with the first Gainsborough talkie on the heels of rebuilding the Islington studio after its destruction by fire during a remodeling job to install sound equipment. He also worked toward increased production at Gaumont-British, which was in the throes of a massive building campaign at the Shepherd's Bush studios in Lime Grove. Balcon experienced "five years of grinding work, every hour of the day occupied and often large portions of the night as well, with no respite even over weekends" for himself and the entire staff, in an effort to meet the studios' combined goal of twenty films a year.[17] As his career moved toward its most acclaimed period at Ealing Studios, Balcon recalled his resolve during the Gaumont-British foray to make only one film at a

time. Gordon would have understood that resolve. Although she juggled piecemeal projects with aplomb, she preferred concentrated effort that exhausted all design possibilities while striving for the finest quality of production.

Studio complications connected with corporate ownership surfaced about this time and ultimately led to Balcon's resignation in 1936, the year that Gordon returned to the United States. The interference with internal production by board members and majority stockholders C. M. Woolf and the Ostrer brothers during the early 1930s began to undermine Balcon and his production team. These owners urged Balcon to hire foreign stars in pursuit of world markets. Balcon listed other pressures that arose from national crises in 1931: "Recession and depression culminated in Britain going off the Gold Standard, the resignation of the Labour Government, and the formation of the so-called National Government coalition under Ramsay MacDonald." A few days after the premiere of *Sunshine Susie,* Michael Balcon suffered a nervous breakdown that required a six-month recovery.[18] Because of his own stressful experience, Balcon probably was not fully aware of Gordon's difficulties with an intolerable workload, limited budgetary allotments, inefficient wardrobe department procedures, and declining health.

Another Hectic Day

On New Year's Day of 1932 Gordon escorted Anne Grey to fittings with couturier Paul Caret for her sophisticated attire in *The Faithful Heart,* directed by Victor Saville. They had appointments as well at Marshall and Snellgrove, who furnished patterns for Gordon's designs and arranged a special showing of new fabrics for upcoming film assignments. Shopping with Mabel Terry-Lewis followed sessions with Edna Best, whose dual role as mother and daughter in the film required special attention to Southampton-pub and working-class dress spanning twenty-five years.

For the next assignment Gordon studied Edgar Wallace's book *White Face,* to be directed by T. Hayes Hunter and filmed at Beaconsfield. Nora Swinburne and other female stars came to Gordon's flat for costume measurements and tea at the end of January. In early February Gordon commenced designs for *Jack's the Boy,* a comedy-with-music directed by Walter Forde, based on a story by Jack Hulbert and Douglas Furber. One authority felt it reflected the methods of "that brilliant French director" René Clair. Following the late June trade show, *Variety* proclaimed that the company had "never made a better picture. . . . a crackerjack picture for the home market."[19] The original material, with lots of rollicking knockabout English humor about London bobbies and Scotland Yard, was welcomed by Michael Balcon, who led the campaign for "indigenous" British themes throughout his career. This cause of Balcon's provides insight into Gordon's film work. Strategies were needed to expand Britain's motion picture market, but Hollywood retreads were no way to lure audiences. Though coproduction with German companies showed promise, questions persisted about appropriating Continental themes for British film. Films rooted in English tradition were too few; borrowing from alien cultures for the sheer purpose of selling movies produced sterile, insincere, and artificial products. Balcon once said, "We shall become international by being national." Gordon would agree that a people had its own story to tell with its own characters and characteristics, a point driven home in Balcon's later triumphs at Ealing studio.[20]

Jack's the Boy starred Jack Hulbert and his wife Cicely Courtneidge, a popular slapstick comedienne whom Gordon later dressed in three more productions. Arriving at the Hulbert-Courtneidge home for scheduled conferences, Gordon often found Courtneidge busy, asleep, or out, thus requiring annoying return trips. It was a hazard of the film trade that actresses like Courtneidge, Jean Colin, and others skipped appointments without notification, thus leaving Gordon waiting at scattered venues all over London. Even the tardiness of a good friend like Edna Best was irritating. During the May filming of *Marry Me,* Renate Müller often was late, forgot, or refused to fulfill engagements, a behavior Gordon had come to expect during work on *Sunshine Susie.* Gordon would agree, of course, with Michael Balcon when he expressed sadness over the 1937 suicide of blonde and bubbly Müller, feeling the actress had been forced to appear in the media as a model Aryan woman for Nazi propaganda. However, in 1932 Renate Müller's habits caused thoughtless delays for film and costume colleagues. To Gordon, keeping appointments and being on time were not just good manners but sacrosanct practices.

Gordon was assigned to dress supporting actress Polly Ward, and she reported that she "took her all over London trying to find dresses for her in *Jack's the Boy.*" In just a week she repeated the task at twice the pace when Polly Ward was replaced by Winifred Shotter. To meet the deadline, Gordon brought two seamstresses from Marshall and Snellgrove to the studio, where they quickly fitted outfits so the film could commence shooting. These exceptions now seemed to be the norm, causing her to label this February 11 "another hectic day." In the midst of snowstorms and contest girls, she had to cut short a meeting with Dorothy Dickson, who had made a special trip to see her. Gordon raced back to central London for afternoon appointments, with the last fitting ending at 7:00 P.M. A beau had invited himself to dinner, and her mother had made plans for bridge, so the three supped hurriedly and rushed to the game. As friends shuffled the cards, Gordon slumped in a chair as a spectator; she later added a subdued diary entry of "I watched." [21]

Four days later, after revising designs for *Jack's the Boy,* Gordon studied patterns, searched for new fabrics, and attended conferences at the studio. She "rang up Mother and found she was ill." A doctor was present along with a neighbor, but Gordon tore home to confer with another doctor she had summoned. The medical reports agreed: the illness was a routine "stomach upset . . . nothing serious." Nevertheless, she stayed until 5:00 P.M., when she had to meet Shotter for a fitting. Gordon had two important functions to attend that night in addition to the premiere of *Lord Babs.* Nonetheless, she recorded "I didn't go to any, naturally." [22]

Tommie's upset was part of intermittent bad health she had experienced since the previous fall. Though the two women usually employed household help, Gordon always found time to prepare food trays, play backgammon, massage her back, read books aloud, sketch in her sickroom, and take her for Dr. Creighton's "picquer" treatments. In a rare admission of irritation concerning her mother, Gordon confessed she felt like "a trained nurse." [23] As the English spring unfolded the blossoms and leafy branches that she treasured, Gordon was drowning in duties and pleasures alike. Long on the brink of overload from a full career and a busy social calendar, she had been saved by her own sense of balance and timing. Gordon's conscious attempt to contain and design her life was becoming a burden. For the first time in thirty-seven years, her

determination to live a creative life—to make art out of life—seemed to waver.

Film Stars Who Never Act

On March 22 Gordon and her mother hosted a cocktail party before the trade show of *The Frightened Lady.* A week later Gordon began designs for *Love on Wheels.* On Saturday, April 2, after a long day of fittings, she escorted lead Leonora Corbett to a meeting with Michael and Shan Balcon, director Victor Saville, scenarist and lyricist Douglas Furber, and dance arranger and lead Jack Hulbert. The next evening Corbett dined at Bryanston Court, and more supporting actresses were scheduled for fittings at Selfridges. The workload caused Gordon to miss the April 27 trade show of *The Faithful Heart. Love on Wheels* was full of British humor and performed by an English cast, but the scenario was another German adaptation. The home market cheered the movie, but reaction in the international market was mixed. Following the July 27 trade show, *Variety* felt it could have been a "knockout hit" in the United States with its fine cast along with "first-rate directing, the application of what we know as modern German camera shots of an impressionistic order, and practically everything in the way of present day mechanics." [24] The critic felt that singing and dancing opportunities were allowed to drag, even in obvious scenes such as the sheet music and piano departments, chorus girls' advertising tableaux, and cabaret rehearsals.

Helping with an April 1 press luncheon, Gordon dressed Corbett for publicity aimed at the female moviegoer, an ever increasing consumer of film products who relished the song-and-dance shenanigans of buying and selling at Selfridges department store where the movie was filmed. For the first time in Gordon's film career, the 1932 motion picture provided an opportunity to dress mannequins, though the film was certainly more modest in scale than Hollywood fashion classics. (Gordon may have been influenced by the commercial draw of fashion in American films like *The Dressmaker from Paris,* a 1924 Paramount film dressed by Travis Banton.) For *Love on Wheels* Gordon expanded her collaboration with department stores like Galeries Lafayette and resumed work with the London ateliers of Molyneux and Worth. The ultimate consumer herself, Gordon repeated shopping rounds that spring, making sure she and Tommie Conway were dressed à la mode, often in fashions she had helped to create.

Despite the difficulties of working with some film people, Gordon liked the process of collaboration and the sense of community such productions inspired. She announced that "our film started" on April 5. After a Sunday "take" at Selfridges, she and Tommie Conway treated team favorites Leonora Corbett, Shan Balcon, and Victor Saville to cocktails and supper. Alec Saville and William Thiele escorted her on fun evenings such as Victor Saville's May 2 party celebrating yet another screening. She lunched with Harold Boxall, T. L. Rich, and Shan on May 9, when "we draped the artists' models" and checked countless costume effects for *Love on Wheels.* The close interaction among members of the movie team generated a special kind of energy and creative spirit. Gordon's community of personal friends also generated a certain kind of psychological support, so she frequently included the group in between appointments. Rita Gulbenkian Essayan offered her car for a quick visit when Gordon dashed to Berman's to oversee fittings of waitresses' costumes. Other friends stood by as she searched for shoes and "stockings for the artists' mod-

els." She paused only to insist that her actresses show up for lingerie and underwear selection so that she could control those telltale screen bulges. Once she persuaded a beau waiting at the studio to run to Swerlings for hats, while she fitted gloves at a nearby shop for chorus girls in an advertising routine.[25]

Gordon also took friends to the seasonal haute couture collections of the designers with whom she collaborated, such as Norman Hartnell. One of Paul Caret's showings, however, caused a problem when an unauthorized design of Gordon's appeared on the runway. The staff protested that they knew Gordon was scheduled to attend the showing, so would not have featured the gown if it had been their intention to take credit for the design. An April 7 letter of apology explained, "We are very distressed about the satin and lace teagown, and wish to offer you our most sincere apologies. Princess loved the design, and asked Mme José to enquire at the time you were thinking of ordering it from us whether you would object to our reproducing it." Paul Caret, in turn, requested help from Gordon on an unpaid Gainsborough bill of forty pounds for "the pink dress and the green taffeta frock."[26]

Gordon proceeded with her usual social activities, such as the visits of American diplomats, who flocked to the flat; she, in turn, attended functions at the United States embassy. She also celebrated the weddings of friends like Cyril Grixoni and may have pondered what a future held without marriage. She resumed the habit of registering her own wedding anniversary in her diary, adding the number of years she and Blake would have been married.

Gordon's deep conversations with Teddie Holstius during lunches at the Royal Air Force Club remained a must on her calendar, and their discussions often turned to their favorite world figure, the Prince of

Wales (soon to become King Edward VIII and then the Duke of Windsor). Gordon hung on every word when Teddie described his private talks with the prince on visits with him at Fort Belvedere. This dialogue between Gordon and Teddie continued for two decades. For instance, Teddie wrote to Gordon at Mount Sion years later, expressing his continuing disappointment with the Prince of Wales and his dashed hopes after the monarch's abdication in late 1936 and subsequent marriage to Wallis Simpson.

Authorities on the Duke and Duchess of Windsor claim that the first visit to Fort Belvedere by Wallis and Ernest Simpson occurred in January 1932. The Prince of Wales's visits to Bryanston Court, where the Simpsons rented a flat only steps away from Gordon's, soon became legend among residents, who were fascinated by the new romance between the prince and Mrs. Simpson, as was the foreign press. Gordon and Tom had been smitten by the young royal since the 1920s, when the prince sat only tables away at Ciro's in Paris and at the Embassy Clubs in both Paris and London. They celebrated his June 23 birthday even after they returned to the United States, and would recall hall conversations and pleasantries exchanged as the future king held the elevator door for them at Bryanston Court. Gordon appreciated the prince's interest in the British motion picture industry, as well as his own amateur filmmaking that was featured in the Gaumont-British documentary *The Prince of Wales,* presented at a gala screening in June 1933. She kept track of his royal tours to the film studios. Concerned about industrial exports, the prince believed that "Trade follows the film." [27]

The proximity of the Simpson residence adds a curious twist to the Gordon Conway story. Sharing identical flats on the same floor and surrounded by the trappings of high style that welcomed London notables nightly, an observer might expect Gordon and Wallis Warfield Simpson to be friends. Only six months apart in age, the two Americans both placed a high value on the sophisticated tastes of the beau monde, including Parisian haute couture. Both women had skillfully appropriated strategies from consumerism, café society, and the entertainment media that helped to democratize the glittering lifestyles and dress of the aristocracy. The women's objectives differed, however, and so their worlds rarely intersected.

The new building construction at Gaumont-British often interfered with Gordon's duties, so she worked on assignments at the Gainsborough lot until the summer of 1932. On May 18 the *Daily Film Renter* reported: "Miss Gordon Conway, who has been responsible for the dressing of Gainsborough pictures, will continue to act as dress designer for both studios." [28] During May and June she viewed two motion pictures in their original German in preparation for dressing the musical *Marry Me,* directed by Austrian-born filmmaker William Thiele, and the comedy-with-music *There Goes the Bride,* directed by Albert de Courville with songs by Noel Gay. From May until December, Gordon made no diary entries, only sketchy business notations in pocket calendars that revealed countless appointments compressed into tiny time slots. This accelerated record reflected a film company in flux. Indeed, Gordon would agree with cinema authorities that "the year of decisive change was 1932" at Gaumont-British. [29]

Gordon began work on *Rome Express* with a lunch meeting on May 10 with Shan Balcon and a conference with Culley Forde, the wife and gifted assistant of director Walter Forde. This first film produced at the newly rebuilt Gaumont-British facility at Shepherd's Bush featured an all-star cast and was recognized overnight as a British film classic. A pivotal noon meeting took place with Michael Balcon on July 7. Gordon was assigned a car and driver to make transportation between the two studios of Gaumont-British and Gainsborough, the costumiers, and the department stores more efficient. Other topics discussed at the July 7 meeting may have included permission for Gordon to design stage costumes for Alice Delysia in the C. B. Cochran London production of Jerome Kern's *The Cat and the Fiddle* (called by Sheridan Morley "the only real smash hit" of the West End musicals in 1932[30]). However, well before the meeting Gordon had started Delysia's designs.

Gordon and Michael Balcon must have discussed finances for costuming, salaries, and increasing wardrobe staff in addition to Miss Prescott. Three days before Gordon met with Balcon, the *Financial News* had announced that "Miss Gordon Conway, who designed the futuristic costumes for 'High Treason,' and has since been responsible for the dressing of Gainsborough Pictures, will continue to act as Dress Designer to both Studios under the new scheme. There is also a scheme in preparation for the employment of the most expert fitters in the country for constant work under Miss Conway's direction."[31] This report, alluding to the new schemes, typified press coverage over the next fourteen months about Gordon's position and expanded costume initiatives at the studios. Describing the new wardrobe setup, one such article headlined Gordon as one of the "Film Stars Who Never Act: Women with Big Jobs in British Studios."[32]

A Woman Prophet of Film Fashions

During the late afternoon of June 29, 1932, Gordon attended a Gaumont-British party. The reopening of the Shepherd's Bush facility in Lime Grove attracted world attention. Pioneering efforts in British film had begun at the studio in 1914 and in 1927 had been spurred on by a previous Gaumont-British expansion. With a total production record of 126 films, a current laboratory output of two million feet of film a week, and a projected capacity of forty pictures a year, the company seemed destined to be the hub for a Hollywood on the Thames. An elaborate thirty-three-page brochure commemorating the new opening reveals much about the physical plant, located in an urban setting in London. The brochure also provides insight into the company's policy—or lack of policy—on costume design, and reveals the paucity of female executives in the film industry. The brochure lists a board of directors of nine men and a thirty-two-member "combined executive" with only one woman. Assigned the title of "Dress Designer" in a long column, Gordon's name appears next to last, just above that of publicity manager.[33] The closest nod to wardrobe recognition in the brochure is a shot of the makeup room. Even if major costume work was to continue at Gainsborough, it seemed strange to neglect facilities at Gaumont-British. The oversight reflected management's priorities, a position contradicting press releases extolling new wardrobe initiatives under Gordon's leadership.

Since costume designers often work under art directors, Gordon's modus operandi in relation to film art direction is worth noting because she collaborated directly with producers, directors, cameramen, business managers, and publicity managers. Her practice differed from Michael Powell's experience as a director. During a 1984 interview, he praised Gordon's artwork while sorting through dozens of her drawings and apologized for not remembering appointments recorded in her diaries and schedule books during work on *The Fire Raisers, The Night of the Party,* and *Red Ensign.* He doubted he knew her, because wardrobe personnel worked under the art director. Powell insisted she must have worked under Alfred Junge, "an extraordinarily talented art director" who had recently settled in England.[34]

The same reluctant attitude toward the role of costuming is reflected in Michael Balcon's autobiography, which covers half a century of work showcasing 350 films. The reverence bestowed on art direction to the exclusion of costume design is telling: by default, costuming was relegated to the periphery of production. Balcon proudly described work with celebrated art directors, including Junge from Germany and Oscar F. Werndorff from Austria, along with former Shepherd's Bush apprentices like longtime team member Michael Relph. He neglected wardrobe collaboration, except for one anecdote involving a costume designer. He joked that noted designer and friend Margaret "Maggie" Furse teased him about firing her at Gaumont-British during a period of austerity. Balcon wrote that "ungallant as it appears, I have to confess that I do not remember her then."[35] Limited collaboration with art directors is corroborated in Gordon's diaries and scheduling books; she only occasionally detailed work with Junge, but kept his phone numbers near at hand, just as she did for Andrew L. Mazzei, Alexander Vetchinsky, and Werndorff. Alan McNab and Norman Arnold turn out to be the art directors with whom she established a close working relationship and friendship.

Even actresses dressed by Gordon in dozens of chic and distinctive gowns do not recall her work, reflecting contemporary attitudes about costume designers as only one notch above publicity staff. Exceptions are Dorothy Dickson and Dorothy Hyson, now Lady Quayle, who reminisced during conversations over a five-year period about Gordon's flair and originality. Both women fervently recounted colors, fabrics, detailing, accessories, wearability, function, and appropriateness of Gordon's costumes. During interviews five decades after their work with Gordon, actresses like Evelyn Laye, Jane Baxter, Nora Swinburne, Elena Sylva, Heather Thatcher, Constance Cummings, Elizabeth Allan, and Ellen Pollock did not remember her. Most, however, did appreciate the look that Gordon had given them years ago.[36]

The low status of costuming in late 1920s and early 1930s British film—in contrast to the vast wardrobe domains of Hollywood—is paralleled by a dearth of historical evaluation. Even the thorough Rachael Low rarely mentions costume design in her monumental history of British film. The index to her 1920s volume features design as it refers to art direction, with little attention to costuming and no reference to Gordon's designs of the late 1920s. In the volume covering 1929–1939, few references appear in the index on clothes, costume, couture, design, dress, fashion, frocks, gowns, or wardrobe, though Low's film inventory supplement correctly identifies nineteen of Gordon's film credits. Referring to the early 1930s, Low observes that "more attention was given to costume design, not only for historical films which now became popular, but with contemporary contributions from several fashionable couturiers." In a brief entry Rachael Low mentions that costumes in 1935 were "not hired from an anonymous theatrical costumier as was more often the case at Elstree."[37] Yet no mention is made of apparel designed by Gordon that was executed at costumiers, department stores, and couture houses.

Film writings from the late 1920s and early 1930s offer little explanation about costuming objectives and wardrobe executive responsibilities. Costume design seemed tacked on as an appendage to production, instead of being an integral part of the entire effort. The lack of historical data reflects the attitude of the period toward costume design. Thus it may be asked, where did the profession of costume design belong in the overall scheme of things, and where did female executives like Gordon fit into the structural hierarchy of management?

Two 1933 reference books published in London offer insight into Gordon's motion picture milieu. *The World Film Encyclopaedia: A Universal Screen Guide* offers a curious set of priorities in the table of contents. Essays on production, subsumed under the section "How Films Are Made," introduce nine topics ranging from scenario to casting to editing to cinema management, but with no reference to the wardrobe department. Oscar F. Werndorff's essay on art direction in the "How Films Are Made" section uses the word "dress" only once, and only in reference to period films. A separate piece on costuming restricts the topic to fashion alone and is tucked between an essay on makeup and one on film censors. This essay, entitled "Secrets of Screen Fashion," by a female novelist in Hollywood, ignores the role of wardrobe in creating character and telling a story, and is directed at women as consumers. The author explains: "The film as an arbiter of fashion is a new force in women's lives. . . . The stars of the screen serve as models for women all over the world. . . . The screen can and does serve as an admirable fashion guide for every woman." The essay on makeup by Max Factor, also separate from the production commentary, reinforces the appeal to consumerism. This film encyclopedia features no wardrobe department photographs, but exploits costume creativity nevertheless with scenes of glamorous stars lounging in alluring attire in swank settings.[38]

The other 1933 publication, *THE PICTUREGOER'S*

Who's Who and Encyclopaedia of the Screen To-day, includes many essays on British production, but also excludes comment on British film costume. It jumps to Hollywood for wardrobe department data with a piece about Adrian. In the section on directing, Victor Saville does at least include costuming but with no mention of Gordon by name. She would agree with Saville: "In collaboration with our designer, a dress chart is made for every scene, and dresses designed according to the mood of the scene, in conjunction with the cameraman and art director, whose business it is to see that the colours of the dresses are suitably blended with the lighting." An article on Germany's UFA properties department acknowledges storage for costumes and accessories, along with saddles, swords, and handcuffs, as well as a tailors' workshop for repairs. The encyclopedia includes nine identical photographs from the Gaumont-British commemorative brochure, but the only wardrobe scenes are of three MGM dressmakers in Hollywood. Photographs of actresses dressed to the nines appear throughout but, as in the other encyclopedia, leave costume designers uncredited in the captions.[39]

If film costume designers received little in the way of recognition within the predominantly male management hierarchy, they were nevertheless popular with the viewing public and instrumental in forging a link between the movies and consumer practices. Gordon's experience in promoting and advertising consumer items and stage productions helped film promotion. As an illustrator she knew the way an image should be presented to appeal to the dreams and aspirations of the consumer. In sessions that could last three hours, she worked closely with the photographer to create stills of her costumes in an effort to compete with glitzy Hollywood publicity stills used in selling the mystique of the New Woman. Gordon not only sold motion picture tickets with her costuming, but she also hoped to tie in to the marketplace with the sale of costume copies, patterns, fabrics, and accessories, in the manner of Macy's 1932 sales of over 500,000 copies of an Adrian gown designed for Joan Crawford in MGM's *Letty Lynton.* Reinforcing the interaction between film studios and retail sales, an article in *Fortune* during the mid-1930s claimed that 1,400 stores sold copies of movie dresses—dresses copied by manufacturers from Hollywood stills, which, in turn, were used in advertising campaigns when the films were released.[40]

In England during 1932 and 1933, however, the cross-fertilization between film production and retail sales was not fully developed. Nevertheless, heavy one-inch headlines hailed Gordon as "A WOMAN PROPHET OF FILM FASHIONS" in an article in the *Sunday Referee* announcing her "New Post in British Films: First Studio Dress Department." The journalist speculated that it was not "far-fetched" for Gordon to dream up an outfit one day, "and next spring, perhaps, you and I will be wearing it." Quoting Gordon: "Parisian dress designers are beginning to copy what they see on the screen. . . . very often we are a jump ahead of the fashion houses."[41] Confirming these expectations of Gordon's new department was *Pearson's Weekly:* "Time was when Paris dictated the fashions. . . . [now] British films are taking the lead. From the studios at Shepherd's Bush are being evolved fashions in advance of anything which can be created in Paris."[42]

Elizabeth Leese, a noted authority on film costume history, points out that it was 1948 before wardrobe departments were recognized by the Academy of Motion Picture Arts and Sciences, and it was 1964 before costume was honored by the British Academy of Film and Television Arts.[43] In contrast, the profession of art direction has received "Oscars" since the beginning of the Academy Awards in 1927—the same year that Gordon began work in cinema and began expressing her philosophy of delineating character by costume and her aspiration toward art direction in order to create the total look for a film.

Engineering the Moment

On the day after Gordon attended the 1932 Fourth of July celebration at the United States embassy, she welcomed American actress Esther Ralston and longtime British friend Heather Thatcher to tea for a discussion of *After the Ball,* a motion picture filmed back-to-back with *Rome Express* during Ralston's stage appearances in England. The talk included plans for *It's a Boy* that would highlight the svelte Thatcher and Wendy Barrie in stunning and sleek attire against a handsome streamlined setting. Directed by Milton Rosmer, *After the Ball* was a tuneful cosmopolitan comedy built around a masked ball that showcased League of Nations diplomats in Geneva. The film required a great deal of Gordon's time with Ralston at the London Palladium, Marie Burke at the Alhambra Music Hall, and Jean Adrienne at the studio.

Next came a wardrobe for the first woman allowed on board a British battleship, played by Jessie Matthews in *The Midshipmaid.* Directed by Albert de Courville with music by Noel Gay, the comedy was adapted from the Ian Hay play and was John Mills's first motion picture. More sessions emerged with Matthews and Kathleen Harrison for *The Man from Toronto,* which highlighted styles for the lead, a chic young urban sophisticate. The comedy-with-music was directed by Sinclair Hill and shot on location in Amberley. In the *Observer,* C. A. Lejeune observed:

"The Sussex lanes and meadows in this one are so attractive. . . . The British productions are taking us at our word, and turning out films of the English country-side . . ."[44] The film also gave Gordon the opportunity to feature provincial garb from an obscure hamlet, clothing that delineated the roles of older female characters who spearheaded an Arts and Crafts movement revival in rural England. Though her costuming was not mentioned, Gordon helped create the characters that *Variety* praised when the film premiered the following year: "The way it is done makes for exceptionally good comedy. Many of the scenes are bucolic and there is a cast of minor characters doing type bits with such excellence as characterized Hollywood productions for many years. . . . [The] production throughout [is] well up to the best standard."[45]

On August 6, 1932, Gordon and Tommie Conway presented bouquets of orchids backstage at the Palace Theatre to Delysia, donned in Gordon's costumes for

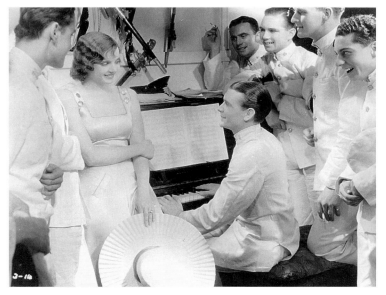

Drawing and film still of a costume designed for Jessie Matthews in The Midshipmaid, *1932, with John Mills (at the piano) in his first film role. Jessie Matthews remembered in an interview with her biographer, Michael Thornton, that "Gordon designed for me the most stunning pair of satin cocktail pyjamas. In the original design, they were meant to be worn with a leotard, but Albert de Courville (director) . . . insisted that I wear them without the leotard. When I came to look at the dailies of one scene with John Mills, I insisted they re-shoot it. I said 'For God's sake, you can see my nipples!' De Courville just laughed and said, 'Great. That will raise the grosses.' That was how they thought." (Quote from Michael Thornton's letter to author, August 8, 1996.)*

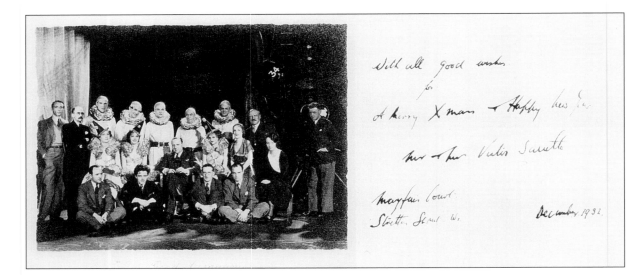

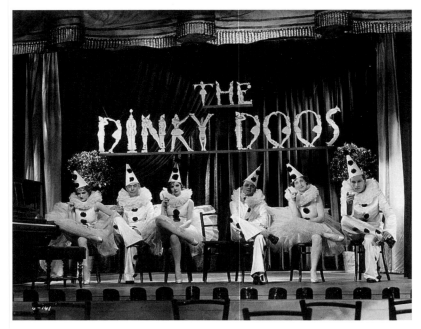

Christmas card for director Victor Saville and wife featuring the cast and production team for The Good Companions, *1933, and film still from which it was made. Also note still of the film's troupe of touring performers, or the "concert party," called "The Dinky Doos."*

the opening of *The Cat and the Fiddle.* Gordon then threw herself into dressing Joan Wyndham for *The Lucky Number,* a screen comedy originally entitled *Five and Six,* directed by Anthony Asquith and filmed partly in Hertfordshire not far from a spot close to Gordon's heart, the sylvan setting of Bushey Grange now razed for development. She then traveled south by rail for a weeklong stay at the Selsdon Park Hotel during more studio filming on location near Sanderstead. On her return she met with Morris Angel and Mr. Marks of Marks and Spencer, and scavenged for wardrobe paraphernalia at the Berwick Street Market. Her scrambled days intensified as she viewed rushes of *The Midshipmaid* on September 17 and hurried to the Film Guild and the BBC. She made sure not to miss an October 5 screening of *Marry Me,* and kept appointments at Film House, where she usually conferred with Harold Boxall. Another film assignment that fall, the acclaimed *I Was a Spy,* triggered memories of Gordon and Tom's evacuation from Europe in 1914—memories that made her take pause as the Nazis gained power in Germany. Working again with Victor Saville, Gordon dressed Madeleine Carroll as the heroine in the touching true story of a patriotic Belgian nurse during World War I.[46]

Saville scheduled a special conference at noon on October 7 to discuss *The Good Companions,* though costume preliminaries had begun full force in mid-September. Gordon took pride in dressing the screen adaptation of the literary and stage classic by J. B. Priestley. For this quintessential British story, appointments mushroomed with Jessie Matthews and the costars. Sessions included Olive Sloane, called affectionately "Miss Olive" by Gordon and a frequent guest at Bryanston Court. The film inspired the same camaraderie off the set as on. Among Gordon's treasured keepsakes would be 1932 Christmas cards with cast photographs and personal notes from the Savilles and from Jessie and Sonnie Hale. Covering the film's shooting at Shepherd's Bush, on October 19 the *Era* noted Gordon "taking an eyeful" of a "music emporium" scene that featured a popular-song publisher accepting tunes by Inigo Jollifant, played by John Gielgud in his first screen role. The camera close-up of sheet music from *Jack's the Boy* and *Marry Me* led the journalist to note the studio's "shrewd advertising" and clever marketing strategy.[47]

The autumn found Gordon also meeting with Peter Arno, whose cartoons paralleled Wood Kahler's high society satires; indeed, the critics had tagged Kahler "the Peter Arno of novelists."[48] Evenings at the flat included cocktails and supper for guests like Shan Balcon and Quentin Tod, two friends she could count on as responsible colleagues and good company. She partied with illustrator Reynaldo Luza and dined with Lewis Galantière, old friends who reminisced about their electric days in Paris during the 1920s before the Depression.

Illnesses soon doubled. In mid-October Gordon rose from a sickbed under the care of two doctors to discuss outfits over lunch with Cicely Courtneidge playing the dual role of mother and daughter in *Soldiers of the King.* The delight of this assignment centered on teenage Dorothy Hyson in her first film role. It triggered Gordon's memory of the year before, when she had cheered Hyson's budding glamour on her birthday. Gordon wistfully confessed that "Little Dot is little no longer."[49] Years later, Hyson, now Lady Quayle, remembered director Maurice Elvey as "a dear, very genial, easy-to-get-along-with, likeable person. . . . [and] so was Victor Saville who was very liked and very pleasant," and responsible for her role. Saville had spied the sixteen-year-old with her mother, Dorothy Dickson, at a cocktail party in the

Costume design for Dorothy Hyson featured with Anthony Bushell in a film still, Soldiers of the King, *1933.*

home of Edna Best and Herbert Marshall. He inquired on the spot: "Will you let Little Dot do a film test?" She recalled that "the best scene for me . . . [that] everybody remembered" was with Anthony Bushell, squeezed into a boatlike contraption "on a little tank in the studio. . . . Three men on a platform waved willow branches tied to a stick over us" and made the water ripple. "I wore a great big organdy hat. . . . The sunlight went through this marvelous organdy hat and gave me a wonderful halo. . . . it was Gordon who engineered this moment."[50] There she was, Dorothy Hyson, lying back in a punt on the river Cam, all decked out in a long powder blue organdy gown with a matching picture hat casting fluttering shadows across her luminous face, being romanced by Bushell while floating beneath shimmering branches in the twilight.

Women Who Make British Films

Out of the fourteen feature films released by Gaumont-British in 1932, Gordon's eleven motion pictures received, on the whole, box office success and favorable critiques in Great Britain, with mixed reviews in New York. On October 19 she attended a special screening of *There Goes the Bride,* the story of an heiress running away from a prearranged marriage. The next week *Variety* wrote that it was a "corking good picture for the English market, with odds on its succeeding as a good musical programmer abroad." The review recognized the film's technical accomplishments: "art direction [is] miles ahead of the imitation clover stuff they used to do here. Photography [is] swell, with a lot of imagination and good lighting."[51] New York *Variety* reported that the film was "superior in appearances and studio carpentry."[52] Indeed, the sleek set for Owen Nares's apartment was the essence

of simplicity of line espoused by the advocates of modern design. Just as streamlined as the setting and with a striking tailored understatement was Gordon's design in "soft honeycomb woollen" for Jessie Matthews, an ensemble that created quite a stir with the female public. A sketch of this practical four-piece traveling outfit in graduated shades of ivory, beige, toast, and cocoa was reproduced in *Weldon's Ladies Journal,* promoting the ensemble's pattern for sale.[53]

The headlines on *After the Ball* in the November 27 *Sunday Chronicle* read "Dazzling Luxury and Polish." Calling it "a brilliant new British spectacle. . . . [and] another screen success which has brought joy to many people," the article raved about the film starring Basil Rathbone at the New Gallery Cinema. The critic added: "One of the real stars of this production is Gordon Conway, the fashion expert who gowns all Gaumont-British films. The fashions in this production impressed even me, and vast libraries could be filled with what I do not know about fashions."[54]

The most successful Gaumont-British film released in 1932, both critically and financially, was *Rome Express,* a mystery drama set on board a Paris train to Rome. Premiering at the Tivoli Theatre, *Rome Express* garnered accolades, as in *Variety* on November 20: "One of the best pictures made in this country, and, all things considered, one of the best feature pictures ever made anywhere. . . . No Hollywood all-star aggregation could have done better. The technique is Continental. . . . no detail is lacking." Even with the expense of bringing Conrad Veidt from Germany, the critic speculated that the film was produced for "well under $150,000 [though] in Hollywood it would have cost about double that sum. . . . Properly exploited, [it] should be a tremendous success in America."[55] It was. When the film was screened in New York on February 24, 1933, *Variety* raved, "probably the best

British film shown over here to date. . . . [It is] rather a combination of *Grand Hotel* and *Shanghai Express,* nevertheless it is original in conception and execution." The critic judged that "From a European standpoint it's the best example of tempo and action that's been accomplished. From an American view it is in the Hollywood vein but needs about 10 minutes trimming."[56] In December 1933, the *New York Times* included *Rome Express* in its "Fifty Red Ribbon Films," an honorable mention category accompanying the selection of the world's ten best films. Out of 125 foreign films, *Rome Express* and *The Good Companions* were two of five British pictures selected from a total of 479 films reviewed in the newspaper.[57]

In a November 20, 1932, critique for the *Observer* in London, C. A. Lejeune reflected on *Rome Express.* She wrote that the reopening of Gaumont-British studios the preceding summer "threw out a confident challenge to the world. . . . For the first time in the history of British films we have a production that can be judged by international and not by British standards, and can present its case in a form as efficient and persuasive as Hollywood's own." She described "the three cardinal sins of British production . . . [as] bad lighting, bad photography, and slow tempo" and concluded that *Rome Express* overcomes these weaknesses and that "judged by any standard of entertainment . . . is a first-class job." Now that their production departments work well together and have superior technical standards in "lighting, photography, recording, and sets . . . [Gaumont-British] must concentrate on the stories, acting, direction, and dialogue." Not one word, however, was written by Lejeune about the effective and role-defining costumes. Following the practice of male-dominated art departments, the critic's mention of "sets" no doubt was intended to include the wardrobe department.[58]

Whereas C. A. (Caroline) Lejeune intended her reviews for both men and women moviegoers, much of the news coverage on Gordon's film costuming was written for the women's sections of newspapers and magazines. A typical title appropriated for such coverage was: "Moderns to Follow," a column in *Modern Weekly* that touted Gordon's career.[59] The journalists who wrote these articles were mostly professional working women gathering news on New Women like themselves and many of their readers. One major article by Vere Denning, appearing in the April 1933 *Modern Woman,* analyzed female opportunities in the film industry. Judging Gordon one of the most successful "picture dressers in England," the columnist observed that she not only worked magic with the appearance of actresses but was an "attractive woman" herself. Denning featured Mary Field, director of nature shorts and editor at British Instructional Films, and Sybil Sutherland, publicity manager at B.I.P. Also included was Culley Forde, assistant director to husband Walter Forde for *Jack's the Boy* and *Rome Express.* Pointing out Culley Forde's "tact" and twelve years of film experience, Denning speculated that "she would probably be making films independently by now, but . . . finds it more satisfactory to be her husband's right hand than to blossom out on her own."[60]

Entitled "The Women Who Help to Make British Films," Vere Denning's essay observed: "For many years it was considered that the only possible opening for women in the film industry was as actresses, and even nowadays it is the exception rather than the rule to find women holding responsible executive" positions. She argued that filmmaking was the "young, vital, brilliant child of British industry, . . . and, like any other precocious infant, needs the peculiar genius of women as well as that of men in its upbringing." Denning averred that too often "the cry goes up . . . that women are unfitted for a career." Women were accused unjustly of an inability to live "in separate, watertight compartments," a male technique permitting work and private life from interfering with each other. "Only in times of great stress does a man carry the worries of his business hours into his private life." The columnist worried that "women are as yet far too apt to let the problems of the working day become their dinner companions and bedfellows." Her words would later prove to have been prophetic for Gordon: "Ultimately, this worrying over details leads to a physical and mental collapse."[61]

Noting that Gordon was "responsible for the clothes of every actress, from the principals to the crowd players," Denning emphasized that "she has just finished work on a cast of five hundred for *Waltz Time.*" The magnitude of the job inspired the columnist to close the essay with a quote by Gordon: "The work needs endless patience, boundless enthusiasm, a feeling for colour and line, and an imperturbable temper in the face of four irate dressmakers, five maddened film directors, six infuriated wardrobe mistresses and a hundred temperamental actresses."[62]

Fittings and Flowers

The *Waltz Time* project of late 1932 was taxing but brought Gordon the satisfaction of interpreting elaborate nineteenth-century Viennese attire for the screen. She collaborated closely with director William Thiele and producer Herman Fellner on this version of Johann Strauss's *Die Fledermaus* that the studio claimed was the first full opera on the screen. Gordon was interviewed on the set by the *Star,* which extolled the period costumes on December 3 as "MAGNIFICENT GOWNS" with headlines that proclaimed "Evelyn Laye's

Luck in Film of an Opera." The author judged that every woman "will envy the actress her six beautiful frocks. . . . Miss Conway has also supervised all the clothes for nearly 200 men and women who take part in a ballroom scene, as well as a number of extremely pretty dresses for Gina Malo."[63]

The year 1932 showcased hundreds of popular images that held great promise for Gordon's motion picture future. However, the images extracted a price. Up and down with ailments that fall, Gordon often had to sketch in bed, but she submitted designs in her usual prompt manner. The instant a doctor left instructions she could be up for an hour or so, she scheduled fittings in her flat and supervised chores over the phone or through her assistants. Just as Gordon began to feel she held an edge on the onslaught of work, mid-December arrived, and she was down again with a fever. From bed on December 14, she "wrote two letters to Chan and Mr. Samuel at the studio and my fever went up over two degrees!"[64]

The reason for her distress has not surfaced, but a landmark meeting with the two executives took place at the studio on the morning of December 20. Though Gordon would dress eighteen more films for the studio, from that day on the sense of community she felt with members of the production team vanished from her diary. Perhaps it stemmed from general problems endemic at the studio such as budget cuts, vying for funds, policy decisions, and dashed expectations. She progressed mechanically through a litany of duties, but the spirit was gone. Special screenings no longer inspired celebrations at Bryanston Court. Trade shows would come and go with little fanfare. Her diary handwriting style changed, and the pronouns "we" and "our" disappeared from her work vocabulary, except when referring to her loyal staff, with whom she spent more time on both a social and professional level. Actresses continued to flood the flat on business and for parties, along with selected actors, directors, and writers, but no record exists of executive team visits to Bryanston Court after that fateful meeting in December.

Considering this development in Gordon's career from 1915 forward is puzzling, for she was a keeper of relationships no matter how difficult. She juggled prickly personalities and never participated in intra-studio squabbles. A balanced person who was flexible during negotiation, she was innately conciliatory and understanding of people's feelings. Gordon over-looked shortcomings in others and treasured friend-ships above all else save the filial devotion to her mother. Of course, she always stood her ground about design principles and quality standards, whether for a studio contract or a freelance job, but her policy was one of firm courtesy that usually produced an amicable compromise.

The evidence from Gordon's documents and doz-ens of interviews has uncovered little explanation about this apparent misunderstanding between Gor-don Conway and Gaumont-British. One cause might have been three motion pictures she did not dress but could have—films she may have felt she should have dressed. Gaumont-British's universally acclaimed *Ever-green,* which propelled Jessie Matthews to interna-tional stardom in 1934, often is assumed to have been dressed by Gordon, but Berleo is credited for the cos-tumes. The studio decision to engage another designer for *Evergreen*—when Gordon had created so many original frocks for Matthews and worked so well with Victor Saville—could have caused a rift. Also released in April 1934, *Princess Charming* starred Gordon's friend Evelyn Laye and credited her colleague Norman Hartnell for the costumes; the film was an adaptation of the musical play for which Gordon had contributed

designs for Alice Delysia back in 1926. Also inviting speculation is the lack of credit for Gordon's contri-butions to another international Gaumont-British hit, *Jew Süss.* The German director Lothar Mendes, his as-sistant Graham Cutts, and actor Dennis Hoey con-ferred with Gordon several times in September 1933. She did research at the British Museum for this period film about the eighteenth-century German court, but the film carried a credit line for Herbert Norris alone as a "costume and period adviser."

Information that may be related to the situation emerged from Gaumont-British in November 1932, including memos and letters in the Michael Balcon Collection at the British Film Institute Library and Information Services. A misunderstanding developed over competitive bids between the studio and the his-torical and theatrical costumiers, B. J. Simmons and Company, who very much wanted to dress the stu-dio's period pictures, especially *Waltz Time.* One point stressed by both sides was that Simmons had "exe-cuted all Miss Evelyn Laye's dresses for every produc-tion in which she had appeared." According to one internal studio memo, producer Herman Fellner gave the costume house an opportunity to lower the bid for Laye's clothes to meet the prices of Maison Arthur by lowering the bid from £443.13 to £375 and finally to £325. The memo writer stated that this move was contrary to studio policy and that giving Simmons "two opportunities of adjusting their estimates to that of another competitor . . . is not our way of doing business. Whether Mr. Fellner adopted this course in order to satisfy Miss Evelyn Laye I do not know, but it does appear that B. J. Simmons & Co. are attempt-ing to use every possible string they can pull." Ac-cording to a B. J. Simmons letter, "the Technical Di-rector and Miss Gordon Conway were both in favour of our costuming the rest." Studio records report that

"They did not obtain the order for the remainder of the costumes because apparently at this stage Miss Gordon Conway realized what was happening and discussed the matter with Mr. Samuel on the question of price," and the job for the additional clothes went to the lowest bidder, Morris Angel. The documents do not record a misunderstanding between Gordon and the studio, but do point to a potential for misunderstanding.[65]

The only clue about the Gaumont-British situation rests with Gordon's subsequent correspondence from Teddie Holstius. In 1936, when his negotiations for a Hollywood script contract took an unexpected negative turn that debilitated Holstius for months, he exclaimed to Gordon: "We both know quite a lot about that!" He wrote of a British studio offer too but took pause when he remembered how Gordon was overworked and underpaid at Gaumont-British. He coined a phrase to describe his hectic work pace: working like "Gordon at Gaumont," with "never a minute or a meal."[66] Perhaps that 11:00 meeting on the morning of December 20, 1932, dealt, after all, with the same old problems that had surfaced before: long hours, limited staff, and inadequate funds budgeted for costuming and salary, along with excessive expectations and guarded gratitude. When these problems were compounded by an inefficient organizational structure for the wardrobe department, the evidence points to costuming's low priority for management.

Friends witnessed Gordon's recurring illnesses. They ached to see her wilt before their eyes. Along with a message to "stay in bed you naughty wicked bad girl!" was the insistence from Val and Teddie Holstius that she relax at their Wadebridge place in Cornwall over Boxing Day.[67] Among gifts of ten Decca records and a Gramophone, the couple sent "two dozen gorgeous pink roses." Masses of bouquets arrived from friends and staff, flooding the flat during

Photograph of Gordon Conway with outstretched arms among friends at a "Baby Party," in London, published in The Sketch, *July 20, 1932.*

Gordon's relapses that continued through the two Conway women's birthdays, their wedding anniversary dates, Christmas Eve and Christmas Day, Boxing Day, and New Year's Eve and New Year's Day. Three dozen pink roses here, two dozen pink roses there—all mingled with sprays of lilac blossoms, jardinières of chrysanthemums, pots of green leafy plants, and corsages of orchids.[68]

Gordon was December's child, and the month renewed the spark in her life. Since the previous May she had neglected regular diary entries, loading the pages with patches of business appointments. However, on the 11th she returned to her diary reflection: "married 11 years ago today." She described Tommie Conway's surprise cocktail-supper for thirty friends celebrating Gordon's thirty-eighth year. Doré Gulbenkian's own birthday party on the 21st honored the doubly festive theme of Tommie's anniversary. Gordon attended Evelyn Laye's cocktail party on the 24th, just before the two Conway women's Christmas Eve soirée back at the flat. On that day before Christmas, Gordon shopped at Albert and Johnson's and Galeries Lafayette and, though weak, joined Tommie Conway to finish party favors and decorations for their yuletide trees and dinner table. At the day's start, though, Gordon made sure she taxied to the studio and delivered by hand her "presents to all four women in wardrobe."[69]

On Christmas Day she and her mother enjoyed a "family party from 1:00 to 7:00" at Alice and Percy Lawson-Johnstons' home. With a sense of contentment and abiding filial consideration, she wrote that "Mother got some beautiful gifts—a very happy Christmas." Though Gordon was too weak for the Boxing Day trip to Cornwall, she went to the "Empire and Carlton" on December 27, conspired on an Embassy Club birthday treat for her mother on the 29th, and "met Heather at the theatre" on New Year's Eve. She welcomed 1933 with a modicum of sleep and a marathon of bridge games before Dorothy Dickson and Geoffrey Gwyther arrived for tea on New Year's Day.[70] There is no doubt that Gordon had been disappointed and discouraged, if not downright hurt, by events at the studio in mid-December. However, she had regained psychological momentum bolstered by her community of friends and by the team of bright young women, helped along by the glitter of shop windows, rattle of wrappings, sparkle of laden trees, tunes from the Steinway keyboard, tangy bites of chocolates, and the many-hued pinks of those sweet-smelling roses.

CHAPTER EIGHT

AN ARTIST IN CLOTH

Women of Wit and Weight

Using her truncated name for Shepherd's Bush, on January 2 the artist scrawled "Bush" across the page as she would on most 1933 diary pages. The abruptness seemed to have an impersonal edge to it, not at all like Gordon Conway. Her days flew by like motion picture images racing on a high speed setting. She "worked at home" repeatedly over the next ten months, and the Bryanston Court flat became more than ever an office away from the office.[1] Gordon began consultations right away with director Sinclair Hill and singer Violet Loraine for her first film role in *Britannia of Billingsgate.* Much to Gordon's liking the film featured genuine shots of Billingsgate Market and shots taken behind the scenes at Shepherd's Bush, where Gaumont-British studio was located. This West End adaptation continued a musical comedy story trend of working women who advance to affluence and notoriety, with "Vi" Loraine in the role of a fish-and-chips café owner making it big in the movies. Emblems of the actress's success included an elegant wardrobe conceived by Gordon. The next month Gordon dressed *Orders Is Orders,* another West End adaptation about bold women and moviemaking. It starred comedienne Charlotte Greenwood, with whom Gordon conferred at the Berkeley Hotel and at the Drury Lane Theatre, where Greenwood also was performing as a musical comedy stage star. Directed by Walter Forde, with the aid of his capable wife Culley Forde, the screenplay

focused on an assertive female assistant to a Hollywood director, coincidentally reminiscent of the Fordes' own professional partnership. The story revolved around a fictional Hollywood film company that unleashed a whirl of mayhem while shooting scenes at a British army barracks. Gordon was not mentioned by name, but the New York review in *Variety* complimented "the satirizing on American film manners and methods. . . . [with twin] burlesque-checkered suits. . . . [on the] stellar duo" of American stars Charlotte Greenwood and James Gleason.[2]

Gordon's costuming continued for Cicely Courtneidge in the role of a go-getting journalist trying to scoop a story from a rival male reporter in *Falling for You.* Gordon consulted with Courtneidge long distance in February and early March during filming on location in St. Moritz; she often refused evening engagements to wait for the calls. Quentin Tod introduced stage dancer Tamara Desni to Gordon during lunch at Bryanston Court. In her first film appearance, Desni's figure skating routines on screen are a showpiece of grace, especially in Gordon's choice of attire. In contrast, Cicely Courtneidge careens and leaps about in modish garb that ends up in a state of disarray. These opposing screen images present two kinds of well-dressed New Women.

Among the devotees of 1930s British film many English viewers love the harebrained antics of Cicely Courtneidge. However, admirers would not deny that she had a chubby figure, as did "Vi" Loraine,

Costume design for The Night of the Party, *1934, later featured in a film still. However talented as actresses, a number of women dressed by Gordon Conway had different sized and shaped frames from the bone-thin figures in Conway's renderings.*

Charlotte Greenwood, and even weightier supporting actresses dressed by Gordon, like Margaret Yarde in *The Man from Toronto,* Eva Moore in *Just Smith,* and Jane Millican in *The Night of the Party.* These talented actresses long have been appreciated for their ability to entertain, and they deserved the proper dressing they received from Gordon Conway. Indeed, the motion pictures and film stills of comediennes dressed by Gordon still have the power to amuse, recalling these women's sense of fun and knack for producing laughter. The photography often betrays the bulk and bulges of their bodies, in sharp contrast to Gordon's wafer-thin images on paper. The comparison can be disorienting, because the viewer loses an understanding of both the actress and the character role, asking: Is Gordon Conway's sketch drawn for the script character or for the actress hired for the part? Is the character's role best defined by the original drawing or by photographs of the final product?

An argument could be made that Gordon conceived the characters in these slim shapes after studying the scripts and conferring with the director. Gordon must have regretted that she no longer worked with casting, for she could not select the actress corre-

sponding to the body type in her head. The fact remains, though, that Gordon drew slender figures for actresses who turned out to be overweight performers. Observers familiar with her wafer-thin silhouettes often raise the question about the discrepancy between Gordon's figures and the weight of the actresses in the film stills. They suggest that the heavier actresses do not show off the gowns in the same manner as clotheshorse wisps like Constance Cummings and Dorothy Dickson in *Channel Crossing,* Dorothy Hyson in *The Ghoul* and *Turkey Time,* Jane Baxter in *The Constant Nymph* and *The Night of the Party,* and Anne Grey in *Just Smith* and *The Fire Raisers.* Since this book focuses on the images of the New Woman in the artwork of Gordon Conway, the heavy images cannot be ignored. The actresses, both as women and as fictional characters, were for the most part New Women who believed in suffrage, property rights, and employment opportunities, as well as the right to be fat and dress à la mode like any other size New Woman. These broader silhouettes were acceptable and respectable to British filmmakers and moviegoers, but were not permitted by most image-obsessed film executives in the United States. Hollywood producers dreamed of remaking the American woman as they sold millions of cinema tickets to aspirants determined to look like beanpole mannequins. The goal of the Hollywood moguls is a mass-media parallel to Condé Nast's elite publications reflecting his ambition for American middle- to upper-class women readers. The linking of the two goals, however, would have been anathema to Condé Nast and his editors, because most haute couture devotees felt screen fashion was tacky, gimmicky, and provocative. By Hollywood standards, not only were images of fat actresses taboo but the pleasingly plump silhouette was discouraged as well. The British industry and viewing public, however, accepted plump images of women such as Yvonne Arnaud in *A Cuckoo in the Nest,* Mary Clare in *The Constant Nymph,* and Carol Goodner in *Just Smith* and *The Fire Raisers*—all dressed by Gordon. Other actresses she dressed were not fat yet not paper-doll thin either—rather similar to Gordon's own weight and shape. (Though once slim, Gordon, by age thirty-eight, had added weight that eventually produced a matronly look. By 1933, however, her sense of style and flair were legend, regardless of her size.) Historically, thinness has been both praised and scorned for years. The bone-thin female silhouette was introduced in Western Europe and the United States in the teens, celebrated in the 1920s, and marketed in the 1930s, and this idealized silhouette continues to dominate popular entertainment and consumer culture.

Describing Cicely Courtneidge "as extremely funny . . . [and] a much-loved aunty figure to British audiences," Rachael Low avers that she "accentuated her size and ungainliness." The linkage of size and gesture marks another difference between Gordon's drawings and the photographic image. With a special affinity for the presentation of the body, Gordon Conway created figures that display a certain soigné look—an image with a dignified demeanor, subtle poses, and understated gestures that radiate poise and grace. Cicely Courtneidge's horseplay conveyed the opposite, with only hints of her acrobatic training: outlandish posture, awkward poses, and excessive gestures, with her clothes worn catawampus for effect. Gordon dressed other comediennes, however, who did not depend on burlesque and low comedy movements for chuckles and smiles, such as Charlotte Greenwood, who amused audiences with high kicks and grand sweeping gestures. Her exaggerated movements showed a disciplined restraint that kept her clothes in place. Greenwood possessed a fashionable look due to timing and controlled motion—movement without abrupt angles and disruptive gestures—in much the same manner as Rosalind Russell, another tall American actress playing comedy roles and known for her sense of style.[3]

The gestures and high kicks of Charlotte Greenwood, in turn, differed from those of Dorothy Dickson, whose nuance of movement and signature kick had the lyrical grace of ballet and ballroom dancing. Such subtleties accented her roles as the romantic heroine in sophisticated musical comedies and allowed her attire to remain in place no matter what the timing or the stride. Even an impromptu cartwheel of Miss Dickson's during a Bushey Grange weekend in the 1920s showed off a tastefully circling skirt. Once described as "the drift of thistledown," Dickson personified Gordon's lithe and supple image, with a refined form and subtle carriage that showed Gordon's glamorous gowns to their best effect.[4]

Those Nifty English Gals

After dining with friends at the Dorchester Hotel on January 19, Gordon attended the trade show of *The Man from Toronto,* which attracted welcome press cov-

Costume design and film still for Jessie Matthews, The Man from Toronto, *1933. Jessie Matthews, forty years after this film, emphasized to biographer Michael Thornton that Gordon Conway "had genius, there is no question about it." Matthews's favorite costume in the film was this "full-length organza dress with puff sleeves that Gordon made for me for the fete scene. It was breathtakingly delicate, and the essence of femininity. With that one costume, she captured my youth. Whenever I look at that scene, or the stills of myself in that dress, I feel the deepest sense of gratitude to her." (Quote from Michael Thornton's letter to author, August 8, 1996.)*

erage: "thanks to clever people like Doris Zinkeisen and Gordon Conway films are beginning to influence fashion."[5] Around this time, other British motion picture companies were beginning to garner recognition for their production wardrobes. Though notable work had been created earlier, little has been written about the unsung heroes of British film costuming prior to 1933. These sporadic efforts by early designers had been dependent on the whims of directors or producers and often went unheralded amid the ongoing blizzard of Hollywood screen fashion. Gordon would be the first to admit that professional costume designers in Britain had created outstanding film costuming over the years. Three women who first excelled in stage design deserve acknowledgment for their little-known contributions. Parisian Marcelle de Saint-Martin dressed films in 1921 for the British studio of Famous Players–Lasky at Islington. Dolly Tree, be-

fore her MGM triumph in Hollywood, dressed such British films as the acclaimed 1923 *Woman to Woman.* In 1926, Doris Zinkeisen dressed the actors, including Dorothy Gish, for Herbert Wilcox's first production of *Nell Gwynne.* Anna Neagle explained that her husband, producer Wilcox, hired Zinkeisen because her distinguished stage work made him realize his films could be more effective with proper costuming.

On the last evening of January 1933, Gordon invited Heather Thatcher to dine in order to go over ideas for *It's a Boy,* which resulted in weekly sessions at Worth. Thatcher played the role of a touted novelist whose life is complicated by the male pseudonym her publisher insists that she use. In a subplot Thatcher's New Woman character struggled with unwelcome anonymity while her book received notoriety in the press. *Variety* called it "one of the biggest successes ever turned out in England."[6]

On February 28, a special performance of *The Good Companions* ushered in a historic British film event when King George V and Queen Mary viewed a motion picture in public for the first time. A week before this charity matinee at the New Victoria cinema house, Gordon attended studio celebrations for the film that garnered international attention. *Variety* felt "this unusual picture. . . . does the film trade good, creating prestige for the industry. . . . Characterizations are outstanding, rating higher than any previous British picture. . . . [and] its essential Englishness might give it novelty appeal."[7]

Though C. A. Lejeune's review in the *Observer* neglected to mention Gordon's costuming as part of the superb characterization, it must have pleased Gordon and been music to the ears of Michael Balcon with his dream of indigenous British film. Building on her praise for *Rome Express* the December before, Lejeune proclaimed: "We have waited over twenty years for 'The Good Companions.' We have watched the British producers trying to copy the film manner of Hollywood. We have watched them trying to copy the film manner of Berlin. We had almost given up hope of seeing them strike out for themselves a national manner in filmmaking—an English manner, with the characteristic slow, packed development of the best English art—a picaresque manner, which has always been, in writing, painting, drama, and music, the English heritage." The film "shows us faces that we recognize, and places that we have lived in, and circumstances that move us with the incalculable emotion of everyday. . . . A good story, a wise director, a grand technical staff, a first-rate cast, and a sympathetic producer have combined to make 'The Good Companions' the first real British film that this country has turned out. We want more films of this kind, dozens more."[8]

In March Gordon had a follow-up lunch meeting with assistant director Bryan Wallace about *Orders Is Orders* and conferred with director T. Hayes Hunter about *The Ghoul,* a horror film starring box office favorite Boris Karloff. She set about designing a modest wardrobe for Kathleen Harrison, who played a savvy personal maid to Dorothy Hyson, for whom Gordon designed long chic evening clothes. A shift in story line must have occurred, however, for Gordon switched to short tailored outfits for Hyson. The film historian William K. Everson so admired the film that he preserved a copy from the original print to be viewed by motion picture scholars.[9] In agreement about the quality was Dorothy Hyson, who "was really impressed" during a later viewing. She admits, however, that in 1933 at "the first night . . . [I] thought it was so awful." Hyson fondly remembered Boris Karloff as "such a darling man . . . [and] very gentle. . . . [and being] carried by Ralph Richardson through flames." The then Prince of Wales was keen on British films, Hyson recalled, so the cast was thrilled when "he wanted to have a look . . . [at] a frightening scene . . . [during] his day at the studio. I was shut up in this room . . . and he [Karloff] lumbered all around . . . and they kept saying 'run and scream.' And I screamed and screamed, I screamed for real . . . [when] chased by Boris Karloff . . . [who] had me by a four poster bed strangling me."[10]

Young Dot's new film career was of great interest to Gordon and Tommie Conway, who joined Dorothy Dickson's dinner party on March 13 prior to the premiere of *Soldiers of the King.* Determined not to miss the occasion, Gordon had left her sickbed, from which she had supervised yet another series of fittings. The illness was part of a string of relapses early in the year. She recorded that she had "worked in bed" in between appointments for massages prescribed by Dr. Wilkinson.[11] The doctors thought excursions would be restful, like Sundays in Bray-on-Thames and an April visit to Frinton-on-Sea. Just as Gordon was unwinding in the sun, one Brighton trip ended because she had to take care of an ill Tommie Conway and Mr. Fing.

In early April Gordon worked four days straight on World War I nurse attire and Belgian dress for Madeleine Carroll in *I Was a Spy,* directed by Victor Saville. *Variety* in New York explained that the story was based on the memoirs of Marthe Cnockaert McKenna, played by Carroll, who is "a find. . . . Her work in this film, commendable throughout, is landing Miss Carroll a chance over here with Fox which is importing her."[12] On Gordon's return from Frinton-on-Sea in mid-April, an opportunity arose to showcase fashionable modern dress for *Just Smith.* Based on a 1932 West End play by Frederick Lonsdale and directed by its star, Tom Walls, the stolen-necklace mystery was renamed at such a late date that the stage title "Never Come Back" is penciled in the corner of Gordon's drawings.

For almost six years Gordon had been pleading the cause of "better dressed British pictures." This dictum was intended not only for the British motion picture industry, but for the British press and public as well. The assemblage of women in *Just Smith* introduces a puzzling phenomenon in 1930s England: accusations that the home industry did not hire pretty actresses. Criticism was leveled by the British press and the public itself in serious reviews and popular commentary alike. Reflecting this attitude, Rachael Low comments on Alexander Korda's knack for finding "beautiful girls," explaining his intention "to remedy the absence of glamorous film actresses in the British studios."[13] Yet the film *Jack Ahoy,* dressed by Gordon, starred the gorgeous Nancy O'Neil and exotic Tamara Desni decked out in stunning attire—pretty women in Gor-

don's costume gems who were carefully photographed for stills under her supervision. After *Jack Ahoy*'s premiere in New York, a *Variety* review countered the usual pejorative British judgment: the "studios still bat 1,000 digging up those nifty English gals."[14]

The British press not only complained about the beauty quotient of local actresses not being up to Hollywood standards but also denigrated much of British productions in general. Protesting the negativism is a letter from an indignant reader in Australia published in 1933 by the *Sunday Referee:* "You Fleetstreet bozoes can form little idea as to the intense interest in pictures in Colonial corps where the only attraction is the little tin-can cinema; where there are not the hundred other amusements to be had as in London!" The irate writer remembered when "four men did a fifty-six-mile journey (each way) to Nkana to see . . . Phyllis Konstam! . . . Colonials *cannot* understand why the British Press is so brainlessly pudd'n'headed as to be continually slinging mud at the British film industry, and why British pictures are always received in the British Press with sneers."[15]

Some Hollywood producers agreed about the magnetism of British female stars, for they stole pretty English actresses to appear in their American screen hits. Women Gordon had dressed who were lured to Hollywood included the ethereal Madeleine Carroll, the beguiling Wendy Barrie, the attractive Benita Hume, the pretty Elizabeth Allan, and the chic Anne Grey. The perception in Great Britain that Hollywood actresses were more glamorous had more to do with the packaging of images by the studio than the actual looks of the women. Not that Hollywood actresses were not attractive, but they did not have a monopoly on female beauty. One key was the shrewd combination of costuming, makeup, poses, and lighting in publicity photography, reinforced by the persistent hype that the women were glamorous. Hollywood's packaging of actresses, regardless of nationality, was not the same old stage advertising ballyhoo. The packaging of seductive images sent messages to millions of women with dreams and aspirations. The products of Hollywood portrait and still photographers, according to one authority, "kept people believing in and striving for a better life. . . . They kept the dreams alive between films, let the public examine more closely the cut of Garbo's new gown, provided fashion plates and beauty hints, and suggested that perhaps if you were lucky, this could happen to you too." These photographers "had nothing to do with making movies but everything to do with the selling of the dream that movies meant. . . . They were not mirroring life but illusion; their subjects were not humans, but gods—of love, of allure, of luxury, perfection incarnate from the golden age of Hollywood glamour."[16] The artful and tantalizing stills of slim and modish actresses, put to use in Hollywood's vast advertising machinery, arrested and influenced attitudes all over the world, including the British Isles.

A Big Shot in Polka Dots

From April into the summer Gordon dressed a number of supporting contract actresses appearing in two to three movies at a time; a dozen females passed through the flat for her supervision. At the end of May, Gordon revealed that she was "in bed suffering agonies," a statement identical to one four years earlier when doctors diagnosed a heart attack.[17] Surrounded by two doctors, staff members, and her mother, she went through a series of examinations between costume appointments at the flat. The spell may have triggered a June 16 meeting at the studio with Harold Boxall, the first meeting that year with Gaumont-

British management. Perhaps the June meeting had more to do with studio news releases announcing the in-house dress department at Shepherd's Bush. Friends begged Gordon all spring to take care of herself. The messages on cards that came with tulips, iris, lupines, stock, peaches, and champagne that filled her bedroom became not only a symbol of concern but a warning as well. Overwork was endangering her health, scolded Teddie Holstius, urging her to follow the instructions of his friend Russell Wilkinson, a specialist on Gordon's case.

During one bout of sickness Gordon read in bed *Murder in the Channel,* which sparked her creative instincts for a film she was dressing called *Channel Crossing.* Linking a string of stories, the principal story revolved around a mature financier's securities fraud and his infatuation with his young secretary, who is affianced to a man her own age. Designs for the roles of chic New Women percolated in Gordon's head, transforming into attire for the ambitious working woman like the lead, who inspired one critic to write that as the secretary, "Miss Cummings gives one of her best performances" of her career.[18] The trend-setting clothes were appropriate for creating the characters of modern professional women, especially the stunning ensembles of two fashion models traveling on an English Channel steamer to Paris in the film. After consultations at Bryanston Court with lead Constance Cummings, Gordon arranged fittings at Jill Casson, where her designs for Dorothy Dickson were executed as well.

Though Gordon would miss the premiere during an October trip to Paris, most reviews were positive, even though few mentioned the costuming. On April 15, 1933, an exclusive feature on Gordon appeared in *Woman's Own* and included a close-up of Gordon. The piece showed insight into the work of costuming and called Gordon's post "a strenuous one" because she was "responsible for all the dresses designed for Gaumont-British. . . . [and must] be an expert on 'periods.' She must know every tiniest difference between the dresses worn in 1860 and those of 1880. She must not allow even a bow or ornament that was not thought of then. . . . The dress designer must also be a colour expert . . . [which is] different from having 'colour sense,' for some colours photograph well where others do not. . . . Most important of all she studies personality. And woe betide her if she does not dress up all the more important stars in such a way as to bring out their best points! . . . When we think of dress designing we are apt to dream of those shops that make court gowns. But here, in the studios, the dress designer is almost the most valuable worker in the place." The journalist pointed out: "She is usually a woman, and her post calls for many more qualities than you might expect. In the film studios the dress designer has much more to do than just design dresses." [19]

Headlines in a September 1933 article in the *Sunday Referee* created a fanfare over Gordon's "New Post in British Films: First Studio Dress Department." Journalist Nerina Shute averred: "So many women have asked me. . . . 'What can a woman do in a film studio.' . . . eager to find any sort of executive position at Shepherd's Bush, or Elstree, and I have answered vaguely 'Continuity girl—about four pounds a week.' But from now onwards . . . I shall be able to say to them: 'Why, of course, there are jobs going! Haven't you heard about Gordon Conway and the Shepherd's Bush dress department?'"[20] Placing Gordon's 1933 salary in perspective to that of other executives and the continuity girl, Gordon Conway's contract read: "£15 per week on account of the following fees: £85 in respect of each of the first ten pictures; £65 in respect of each of the next succeeding ten pictures; £50 in respect of each picture in excess of twenty." [21]

According to Rachael Low, around this time an assistant art director worked for the surprisingly low salary of seven pounds, ten shillings a week, "considerably less than most art directors." Low reports that as head of both Gainsborough and Gaumont-British studios, Michael Balcon made £10,000 a year.[22]

Nerina Shute described Gordon as a "big shot" with a manner of "self-possession" and a Marion Davies look-alike with her smile and "tired-looking kindness." Gordon was "the busiest person pretending not to be busy. We were driven, after half a dozen attempts at an interview in her private office, to the comparative security of an empty dressing room." The journalist quoted the optimistic Gordon: "To begin with . . . I shall only employ about thirty girls in my work room. Not including designers and assistants. But the thing will grow, it must grow, of course, and I hope to employ at least fifty before long. . . . Gaumont-British is the first studio in England to organize a special dress department. . . . It will be run entirely by women." [23]

An article entitled "Dressing Up the Stars" in *Picture Show* called Gaumont-British "the first studios in England to be equipped with a special dress department. . . . Now, about thirty women, not including designers or assistants, are employed exclusively in turning out costumes in the dressmaking workrooms. At the head of this new department is Miss Gordon Conway, who has made a wonderful reputation for herself as an artist in cloth." [24] The section entitled "Our British Studios" in another issue of *Picture Show* acknowledged Gordon "for the delightful creations worn by the feminine players, and in a twinkling of an eye [she] can visualize the dress that will accentuate their type, flatter their good points, and disguise any defect in their figures." [25] Published only nine days before her last meeting with Harold Boxall, the magazine ran a photograph of Gordon decked out in a smartly tailored polka-dot dress with a white fold-over tie, and a broad-brimmed white hat tilted ever so chicly to the right. With her long, slender, graceful fingers, she held a portfolio of drawings and flashed her famous smile. The image recalls another polka-dot dress in the British press, the one that had announced Gordon's arrival and new stage commissions in 1921.

As though summarizing Gordon's professional dreams, the *Sunday Referee*'s Nerina Shute had concluded in 1933 that this woman artist was at the pinnacle of success: "And now, after dressing stage shows, and film productions, and making herself a name in the fascinating world of vanity, Gordon Conway is at the head of a new department in British film."[26] Gordon must have grieved that her dream of heading an autonomous costume department with adequate work areas and a full staff of skilled personnel lived only a short while.

Of the Gordon Conway–dressed films premiering in 1933, five opened in June. Gordon readied herself for a whirlwind of activity, though the "very hot" weather would take its toll. Feeling sick, she missed one of her favorite British ceremonies, the Trooping of the Colours. Gordon took Tommie Conway as her guest to celebrate "the first night of *Waltz Time*" on June 12.[27] The good press coverage that had begun the previous December for her costumes in the Strauss operetta now gave way to mixed reviews of the completed production, but her costuming and visual effects still ranked high. Calling it a "lavishly-staged production," the *Daily Mirror* reminded readers that it was the first British talkie for Evelyn Laye, who "looks a perfect picture in the colourful picturesque gowns of the period."[28] The *New York Herald Tribune* called it a "beautifully mounted screen operetta. . . . with taste and handsome sets."[29] In two reviews in the *Observer,* C. A. Lejeune praised the "musical romance in a Viennese 'period' setting. . . . [with] pleasing patterns of melody and light. . . . [and] Continen-

tal elegance . . . [of] the German experts at Shepherd's Bush." Lamenting again the negative reception for British films in London houses, she complained: "I have very good reason to believe that it is a sound bit of work, despite the implication of the renters, who have followed the routine usually reserved for peculiarly bad pictures and neglected to give an advance showing to the Press."[30] In the meantime, *Variety* complimented the "gorgeous sets and costumes in keeping with the period," a welcome statement that must have relieved Gordon, considering the stiff competition from Alexander Korda's recent costume pictures.[31] For example, two months after *Waltz Time,* the trade show of Alexander Korda's *The Private Life of Henry VIII* showcased extravagant costumes designed by John Armstrong. Serving as the vehicle for Charles Laughton's Best Actor Academy Award, this landmark motion picture attracted the world's attention to other lavish period films produced by the newly immigrated Korda family and their team of talented Hungarian émigrés. International audiences, already fascinated by Hollywood historical dramas, now whirred with accolades for these British period films, for which art direction included elaborate adaptations of costumes from the past. All at once, British film meant historical spectacle. These extravaganzas, interestingly enough, have been labeled "costume pictures" and "women's pictures."[32]

Grounding her designs in historical research as well as in her own instincts about women's screen fashion preferences, Gordon welcomed the challenges of period costuming in films like *Waltz Time* and *Jew Süss,* just as she welcomed period design for the stage. For whatever reason, during her tenure Gaumont-British produced few costume pictures to showcase Gordon's talent.

The British motion picture industry was encouraged and challenged by the world success of Korda's films. A film authority noted that more than ever "Gaumont-British began aiming their films at the lucrative American market. There was also a kind of royal assent in the Prince of Wales' edict: 'Trade follows the film'; British films shown abroad, the argument went, would stimulate interest in other national products."[33] Explaining that "films played a large part in the Victorian revival" in fashion, Robert Graves and Alan Hodge observed, "For some years American film stars had set dress and hair fashions among British filmgoers. In 1934, for the first time, a British picture had a similar effect: 'The Private Life of Henry VIII' started the vogue of looped, slashed, and padded sleeves, and one of the hat-crazes of the year—the Tudor halo style. . . . [The clothes] were put on the market before the film was released, as part of its publicity campaign. . . . every shop now had to stock replicas of film-stars' hats and dresses and shoes. Upper-class women still looked to Paris for their fashions, but the working girl to Hollywood."[34] This book reflected female marketing strategies that Gordon had espoused for years and recalled the claim in *Woman's Own* that the film "dress designer has much more to do than just design dresses." Indeed, Gordon was convinced that local manufacturers and retailers of apparel, accessories, fabrics, notions, and patterns in the United Kingdom could be beneficiaries of her work.

More to Do Than Just Design Dresses

On June 13, 1933, Joyce Murchie and George Merritt picked up Gordon and her mother for the 8:45 P.M. trade show of *It's a Boy*. Two days later they attended the trade show of *Falling for You,* followed by *Britannia of Billingsgate* on the 29th. The motion picture that created the most excitement for Gordon personally was Gainsborough's *The Prince of Wales,* "a talking-film record of the life of His Royal Highness" that included the Prince's own 16mm film record of his travels released through Gaumont-British. The June 22 premiere at the New Victoria Cinema was followed by a gala cabaret with the best of British entertainment, including Charles B. Cochran's Young Ladies, and Cicely Courtneidge and the Welsh Guards. Between regular costume duties Gordon worked hard on arrangements for the swank affair. Although the Duchess of Westminster was chairman, with Viscountess Furness as deputy chairman, Gordon worked in concert with their committee stalwart and friend Betty Lawson-Johnston, "liaison officer" for the event. They met in the Ormond Lawson-Johnston home, at the Garter Club, and at Bryanston Court, for gatherings like Gordon's luncheon to cover last-minute details the day before the royal premiere.[35]

On that June 21, Gordon's mind also dwelt on a new assignment discussed at "Bush" that morning: *A Cuckoo in the Nest,* the famous Aldwych farce of 1925 adapted to the screen. The farces that followed became beloved theater classics throughout England. Working with Tom Walls, actor-director for all Aldwych stage and screen productions, Gordon conferred not only on *Cuckoo* but also on *Turkey Time,* a film version of the 1931 stage production.

The summer filled with friends, colleagues, and staff whose common link was their affection for Gordon and concern for her recurring bouts of illness. In early June old friends melded with new at a luncheon given by Joyce Murchie at her art studio and at Gordon's luncheon at Bryanston Court for Sybil Sutherland, publicity manager at B.I.P. studios. As public relations duties for *The Prince of Wales* premiere and cabaret subsided, Gordon renewed other ties: Ethel Wodehouse entertained at tea with the usual lively repartee, and Doré Gulbenkian hosted cocktail hours for intimates that included Rita Gulbenkian Essayan visiting from Paris. Also in town were Porter Woodruff and George Sebastian, who lifted Gordon's spirits during dinners at the Garter Club, the site as well of other pleasant evenings with Count Mario Grixoni.

However supportive these reunions were, Gordon remained consumed by work. She began dressing *Friday the Thirteenth* after a June 26 conference with Victor Saville. Design sessions and two fittings took place with Jessie Matthews on July 8, followed by appointments with Muriel Aked, Belle Chrystall, Leonora Corbett, Ursula Jeans, Mary Jerrold, and Martita Hunt. Packed with British talent and shots of London, the film linked a string of six stories on the order of *Rome Express* and *Channel Crossing.* One of her most accomplished efforts, Gordon's costumes were keyed to workaday citizens loaded on a city bus going about their everyday lives just before a near-fatal crash during a rainstorm on a busy London street. Recent viewings attest that the costuming achieved the purpose of delineating character, providing atmosphere, and advancing the screen story. Yet, half a century later, the film's dialogue author and actor, Emlyn Williams, remembered nothing distinctive about the costumes except that Jessie Matthews wore skimpy nondescript chorine outfits.[36] (Jessie Matthews played "Millie the Nonstop Variety Girl," the sweetheart of a professor played by Ralph Richardson in his first major screen part.) This costuming opinion was commonplace—even within the industry—that achieving the "ordinary" required no special effort. The "nondescript" clothes paid off: Two critics for *Variety* wrote in two separate reviews following a November 15 London showing that the "narrative is absorbing, and with the sensationally strong cast cannot fail to grip and sustain interest" and "Jessie Matthews, as the chorine, is best."[37] As a follow-up to *The Fire Raisers,* on July 8 Gordon began a series of lunch meetings at the Garter Club with producer-director-scenarist Michael Powell, his partner Jerome "Jerry" Jackson, and Carol Goodner to discuss two more films that would be released in February 1934, *Red Ensign* and *The Night of the Party.*

Remarks from a November 1984 interview with Michael Powell were expanded in Powell's 1986 autobiography, *A Life in Movies.* He described the three films he directed that were dressed by Gordon and his brief tenure at Gaumont-British. His comments on art director Alfred Junge help to assess the atmosphere, pressure, and stress of Gordon's work environment.

Powell's brief time at Gaumont-British coincided with Gordon's last months at the studio. His recollections are essential to understanding the period:

The year was 1933. In Germany, Hitler had become Chancellor of the Third Reich and writers, actors, directors and artists generally were in fear of their lives and careers. Those who could, got out to Paris or to London. For many of them London was only a stepping stone to New York and Hollywood. But some of the most talented preferred London and brought first-class technical experience with them. They joined Michael Balcon and the sleepy British film industry woke up when he announced a programme of twelve to fifteen British features a year. . . . Mickey Balcon had decided to run his studios by the Hollywood method, which meant nearly autonomous departments, with a head of department who reported directly to him.[38]

Powell explained:

It is not generally recognized by the public that the most genuinely creative member of a film unit, if the author of the original story and screenplay is excluded, is the art director. In the legitimate theatre, his creative authority is recognized and "costumes and decor by so-and-so" are given credit and importance [that] they should have; but in the film world the producer and director and cameraman are so full of themselves that it is not sufficiently acknowledged that the art director is the creator of those miraculous images up there on the big screen, and that besides being a painter and an architect, this miracle man has to be an engineer as well.[39]

Gordon could have added that she too was capable of engineering such film moments.

Powell expanded on art direction during Gordon's tenure:

Alfred Junge, the great German designer who knew more about making films than anybody in the building, was head of the art department, with half a dozen ordinary art directors and a dozen draughtsmen working under him. . . . [in] the building which resembled a four-storey car park. . . . How cramped this man, who had been trained at the UFA Studios at Neuebabelsberg, and in the big spaces of the exterior lot at Elstree, must find himself in this jigsaw puzzle of a studio, where sets had to be built in the carpenter's shop, then taken apart and put in big elevators, which took them up two or three floors to a stage where they were reassembled. . . . [It caused] a queue of chiefs of construction, master painters, master plasterers, and art directors. . . . It was a daring act to enter here without an appointment, and for social reasons. Alfred was a Prussian, a great disciplinarian as well as a great organizer. He hadn't a second to waste.[40]

Although Gordon's costume department was supposed to be autonomous and although evidence has not surfaced in her records to substantiate a conflict with Junge, Powell's observations about Junge and the hierarchical structure of the studio shed light on Gordon's status at Gaumont-British. In contrast to Junge's art department, she had a small staff who worked in limited quarters. Gordon too was "a great organizer"

without "a second to waste," but courtesy and congeniality prevailed in her interaction with assistants, sketch artists, and seamstresses. She was a perfectionist whose hard work set an example of strict standards among her staff. She could be demanding, but Gordon was no autocrat, nor did she approve of such dogmatic behavior among colleagues. Gordon Conway and Alfred Junge were both creative and productive employees, but their ways of doing things differed.

According to Powell's interview and autobiography, he and Junge did not like being associated with *The Night of the Party*—a film Gordon dressed. One studio producer complained: "It's a phony. A lot of worthless people gathered together, the men in black tie and women in evening dresses, like *Dear Brutus,* without J. M. Barrie." Junge personally avoided the project, but Powell reported that "we got good service from his underlings."[41] Whatever Gordon's opinion of the film, it was her responsibility to create the "evening dresses" for that society drama ridiculed by the other male staff. In spite of the studio's formal organizational structure and publicity hype, Gordon probably was considered one of the "underlings."

Poetic Sensitivities and Intuitive Intelligence

Gordon attended the openings of movies she dressed, including *Orders Is Orders* on July 22 and *The Ghoul* on the 24th. She simultaneously threw herself into work on *The Constant Nymph,* an ambitious adaptation of a story that had inspired numerous stage versions on both sides of the Atlantic and three major films before mid-century. On July 25 she met with director Basil Dean, Victoria Hopper (who took the role of Tessa Sanger), and Jane Baxter (who played the part of An-

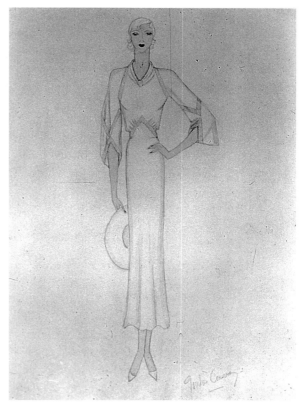

Production still of The Constant Nymph, *1933, with director Basil Dean on right, author Margaret Kennedy in center, and star Victoria Hopper on left; costume design for Leonora Corbett, also featured with Brian Aherne in a film still.*

tonia "Tony" Sanger). After one of her Sunday drawing marathons Gordon produced stunning styles for Leonora Corbett and Baxter and arranged for traditional Tyrolean dirndls for Hopper and Peggy Blythe. Though Gordon would miss the end-of-the-year trade show, *Nymph* garnered accolades from the public and the press alike, though it was criticized for bad sound. A devotee of both the novel and the stage production, Gordon was familiar with the sensitive story and was aware of its popularity.

An analysis of adaptations of the story gives insight into two decades of film criticism and the role of costume in creating fictional characters and atmosphere,

as well as film apparel in mass-media marketing. Based on a very popular 1924 novel by Margaret Kennedy, *The Constant Nymph* centers on a family called "Sanger's circus." [42] Upon the death of the father, an eccentric British-born expatriate composer and conductor, the relatives of their dead mother move the children from their idyllic Alpine retreat to the glittering world of London society and art patronage. The story focused on a teenage girl's love for one of her father's disciples, a married musician. They run off together just prior to the girl's untimely death in their Brussels hideaway. The daring theme was treated with sensitivity. The first stage production in 1926 starred

Edna Best as Tessa Sanger, the teenager infatuated with composer Lewis Dodd, a role introduced by Noël Coward but passed on to John Gielgud, who is associated with the part. Tessa finds herself at odds with her English cousin Florence Churchill, Dodd's wife. The first motion picture was a 1928 silent version produced by Basil Dean, who coauthored the stage and screen scenarios with Margaret Kennedy. In the 1933 screen version dressed by Gordon, Victoria Hopper played Tessa and Brian Aherne played Dodd, with Lyn Harding as Albert Sanger and Leonora Corbett as Florence. Ten years after Gordon's retirement from film design, a Hollywood adaptation featured Joan Fontaine in the role of Tessa, an Academy Award–nominated performance, with Charles Boyer as Dodd and Alexis Smith as Florence.

Reviewing Gordon's *Nymph* in April 1933, in New York, *Variety* proclaimed it

a high class motion picture. . . . and artistic. . . . [but] seems more likely to get good reviews rather than good grosses in America. Its poetic sensitivities and fine shadings are probably not assets on this side. . . . many Americans out in the maize country will be baffled to the point of annoyance. It is a poor comparison, but . . . [one] may be reminded of "Seventh Heaven." It's artistically along those lines, with imaginative lighting, camera angles and restrained storytelling that starts from the premise that those watching the images upon the screen have intuitive intelligence and don't have to have things spelled out. . . . Blonde and feminine Victoria Hopper . . . [and] Leonora Corbett . . . are both importable. There are several small parts excellently drawn.[43]

The 1933 British film showcases Gordon's talent, and once again the question arises as to why her superb costuming has garnered so little recognition. An interesting weakness of the film criticism during Gordon's era is the scant attention paid to costuming as a device for defining character. Literary criticism, by contrast, has long acknowledged the development of character in fiction by delineating dress.

In the novel *The Constant Nymph,* Margaret Kennedy uses the device of dress to illustrate the values and behavior of the characters, especially women. For example, when English cousin Florence first spies the Sanger daughters and their entourage in the Tyrol, she concludes that "there was no mistaking them. In their clothes or out, they attracted attention. Though dressed like peasants, they looked wilder than the wildest mountain people. . . . and so ragged!" In turn, the Sanger group judges Florence: "She was, to them, a strange type, from her neat gray travelling hat and veil to her comfortable, expensive low-heeled shoes. . . . [the] ease of her manners, the elegant commonsense of her dress." Dodd muses: "Her dress was admirably chosen to stand the exposure of such a day, being plain, cool, and of a soft cream colour which showed no dust. . . . He did not trace it to her clothes, but only knew that she looked as different as possible from the Sanger girls." One character observes that Florence "has style. Until you have more experience you cannot do better than to copy her. Later, I think, you should not dress quite so quietly. I shall take you to Paris in the autumn and have you dressed in the way I should wish." At the end of the novel Dodd and Tessa escape to the Continent on a Channel steamer: "She had put on, for this expedition, a new serge school-suit, very neat and brief, and she had a brown paper parcel by the way of luggage. . . . they found a sheltered place where they could watch the great, rattling crane which heaved up endless loads of luggage and plunged them into the hold. Tessa thought of all the clothes in all those boxes and looked at her own parcel and felt glad she had kept so free of possessions during her English sojourn."[44]

The film versions of *The Constant Nymph* offer a

Press photograph of Gordon Conway, London, 1933, accompanying articles about her leadership in the British film industry.

variety of options for the analyses of costume art. Though no data have emerged comparing Orry-Kelly's costuming for the 1943 version to Gordon's 1933 designs, *The Constant Nymph* of 1943 spawned news reports, press releases, and advertisements touting the technical expertise behind the Warner Brothers version. Costuming was lauded, as usual, for the Hollywood production but with a consumer and fashion guide emphasis, ignoring the delineation of character development.

An important reason that films like the 1933 *The Constant Nymph* were devalued and Gordon has been forgotten is the fact that many of her movies were labeled "women's pictures." Also, the designing and sewing of the costumes was considered "women's work." *Variety,* joined by other reviewers of the 1943 film, noted that *Nymph* had "women's appeal."[45] A Hollywood memo on the marketing strategy of the 1943 film called it "A women's picture that the fems will enjoy as one of the best dramas in many a moon."

The piece urged sales promotions of an essay contest on "great lovers of history, cooperative ads with florists and department stores. . . . [and] music stores using stills from the picture."[46] If Gordon's health had not failed, she surely would have continued to push for Hollywood types of marketing strategies for British film from the woman's angle, and her 1933 film might still be appreciated today.

Rainbows and X Rays

Some of Gordon's most original and elaborate designs—and ones appealing to female moviegoers—were showcased in the musical comedy *Aunt Sally,* an ambitious film released in December 1933, based on a screenplay coauthored by Guy Bolton. On August 10 Gordon conferred with Tim Whelan, director and originator of the story, on costumes for supporting actresses Phyllis Clare and Ann Hope, and approximately seventy-five chorus girls. She helped dress

Cicely Courtneidge for the title role of "Sally," who masquerades as "Mlle Zaza," a parody of Mistinguett, the celebrated Folies Bergère and Casino de Paris entertainer. Gordon's spangled satin, tulle, and lace costuming accented Alexander Vetchinsky's streamline moderne sets. The sets included three giant rainbows showcasing the cast on tiers of glittering bands against a horizon of twinkling stars. Reminiscent of Hollywood's Busby Berkeley productions, the lively song and dance numbers featured British hit tunes like *You Ought to See Sally on Sunday* and a Courtneidge lifelong specialty, *We'll All Go Riding on a Rainbow.*

Receiving costume credits with Gordon was Norman Hartnell, who would become a favored couturier for the British royal family. Although Gordon did not record the collaboration, she had helped him with commissions early in his career.

Gordon's costumes compare favorably to the best of Hollywood design in the early 1930s. The intricate chorine ensembles accented by elaborate plumed headdresses and starburst picture hats deserve critical recognition, as do dozens of exquisitely gowned guests led by partners in white tie swirling around the ballroom of the nightclub in the film. Costumes play an interesting role in the plot when the nightclub owner in the movie, King Kelly—with his American penchant for merchandising—blares an order for ten thousand posters to "plaster the country. . . . [advertising] Beautiful Girls [in] 500 gorgeous costumes." Original drawings by Gordon actually appear in a close-up shot in the film. These showgirl sketches represent designs that Kelly rejects in the film. He demands, "I want the costumes to display the girls, not the girls to display the costumes. . . . The best chorus costumes are nothing in the back, and hope for the best when they turn around."[47] Typical of Gordon's attention to detail, these sketches are finished to the last belt buckle and pleated ruffle. Though many costume designers produce sketchy renderings without face or finger, Gordon's drawings capture the likeness of the performer down to each rouged cheek, plucked eyebrow, and polished nail.

The precision and polished look of the figures was an aspect of Gordon Conway's oeuvre that appealed to Michael Powell fifty years after their collaboration. He lauded the resemblances, especially the drawings of "Jessie Matthews that looked like her." Powell noted that a fully developed drawing was essential for print-media publication but not required for stage and screen reproduction. He elaborated on the demands on one's time and energy in providing every detail, since a sleeve or waistline might change half a dozen times at the whim of an actress or a director. Powell was startled by the quality and quantity of Gordon's drawings and assumed she had apprentices and sketch artists as did Alfred Junge and other designers with whom he had worked. He queried: "Did she have a studio with several people working for her, like the French do, with only one signature on the drawing? . . . [for] it was common in those days. . . . The French designers, usually, if they had any success at all, they had a studio with several workers."[48] Though Gordon's two known sketch artists had been on staff since mid-1932, no evidence has surfaced of other apprentices during her twenty-two-year career. Nor is there evidence that her signature appears on the artwork of others as in the case of some ateliers. The few tracings and copies of Conway's costume designs that have emerged from costumier collections are mostly unsigned.

As Powell studied dozens of images, he declared the drawings "brilliant. . . . [and] very impressive. . . . Well, you can see from [these] . . . the amount of work she did was prodigious. . . . I should think her contract was probably too embracing and she couldn't get out of having all this work loaded on her. And she was far too fine for that kind of thing quite obviously. . . . I should think she worked herself into a breakdown." On learning Gordon's singular role in sketching, supervising, shopping, and public relations, along with her pleas for staff, Powell appeared shocked. "That's the kind of thing, you see, where Mickey [Balcon] would have a blind spot for that kind of thing. He hadn't much sympathy, really, with artists. And yet, he dreamed of a great British film industry; it's a strange mixture. . . . [because] Michael Balcon . . . [was] the real foundation stone of the new British film industry. . . . [His] *Rome Express* put the studio on the map." Powell then recalled his low-budget Gaumont-British pictures, around £14,400 each—a budget that could not properly showcase Gordon's talent. He turned to the topic of Gordon's film-musical designs such as *The Good Companions*. As though explaining Gordon's work milieu in the early 1930s, Powell exclaimed, "Once you take on musicals, it's murder. Designing clothes for a film is not so bad, and if you've got plenty of money to spend, but designing clothes for . . . film musicals is terrible—a *terrible* thing." [49]

The success of the film musical *Aunt Sally* typified the British production that promised new horizons for aspiring young motion picture talent, like many of Gordon's associates and friends. As in the lyrics on the showgirls' lips, her colleagues were "riding on a rainbow," on an upward climb to fame, whether in Hollywood or in the domestic film industry now perched on the threshold of world acceptance. During 1933 and the years that followed, fellow performers and production colleagues moved into the spotlight, while Gordon was forced by illness to retreat into the shadows. Throughout her remaining twenty-four years, Gordon's untimely retirement at the age of thirty-eight must have been painful, especially since she had sacrificed not only her talent and her time on the demanding altar of the silver screen, but her health as well.

From late summer through the fall, through ailments and exhaustion, Gordon produced sketches for an unidentified film labeled "Runaways," worked with Nancy O'Neil and Tamara Desni on *Jack Ahoy,* and dressed Leonora Corbett and Gwynneth Lloyd for her last film, *Wild Boy.* She sought career advice from motion picture, publicity, and business colleagues. Gordon discussed professional possibilities with Edward Carrick, the art director and son of legendary designer Edward Gordon Craig. Gordon sent sketches and information to Leland Hayward, a friend from the teens in New York who had become a successful agent and producer for stage and screen. Talks with Howard Hughes also took place, but it is hard to trace how much dealt with her film career and how much was social, since the conversations centered around Tommie Conway. (Hughes, Gordon once wrote, was "a young boy mother knows" from Texas.) [50] Hughes may have been responsible for offers from RKO. Most probably Lilly Messinger and the supportive staff of RKO in London played the key role in the studio offer.

German émigré Lothar Mendes, noted UFA and Hollywood director, offered a brief glimmer of hope for a renewal of Gordon's film career. Between September 7 and 25, meetings for his costume spectacle *Jew Süss* rejuvenated Gordon with artistic challenge and creative inspiration. This highly respected Gaumont-British costume drama, however, was not released until October 1934 and features no credit for Gordon Conway, only "costume and period adviser" for Herbert Norris with art direction by Alfred Junge.

The summer's end witnessed the usual pair of doctors at Gordon's bedside. Her health did not improve even with a two-week sojourn to Selsdon Park, where Joyce Murchie, Betty Claire, Miss Taylor, and Miss Watts commuted for daily conferences. In early October a third doctor joined the case, introducing a spate of X rays and blood tests into the daily routine already scheduled with medically prescribed massages and long walks. Though speculation was exchanged between doctors and friends about the tension from eleven-hour days, seven days a week, hospital examinations produced nothing. Medical advice focused again on excursions for relaxation. Yet Gordon interrupted another rest at Frinton-on-Sea and scheduled a studio car in order to complete assignments she deemed urgent. She viewed *Just Smith* on September 30 and *I Was a Spy* on October 5. They were the last premieres she attended as head of the wardrobe department. On October 18 Gordon and Tommie Conway boarded the Golden Arrow for a four-week stay on the Continent. Before she departed, Teddie Holstius offered an avuncular scolding and noted that Gordon was "overworked mentally and physically." He apologized for canceling their R.A.F. Club luncheon, because "I'm being very smart again and going down to the Prince of Wales' at Fort Belvedere tomorrow." During her month abroad, Holstius penned warnings: "You're being sent away for a rest. . . . Take every advantage of this rest to get really fit. All this messing about has taken quite long enough, Gordon, and some change ought to be felt by now. . . . You really should feel better by now."[51]

Gordon briefly regained some strength during reunions with Rita and Kev Essayan that melded into a parade of friends in Paris and Versailles. On her return, though, not even the welcoming surprise at the train station, topped with lilacs and champagne at Bryanston Court, could halt the continuing fatigue, exhaustion, and insomnia. Persistent headaches and back strain combined with the old heart palpitations and stomach pain. Days still found her in and out of bed with repeated appointments for massages, blood tests, and X rays. With hollow eyes, taut muscles, and

weary limbs that robbed her of her natural zest and joie de vivre, Gordon reluctantly traveled to Shepherd's Bush in Lime Grove on Monday, November 27, for a conference with Harold Boxall. Her motion picture executive post and vision of a distinguished costume department had come to an end—and all before her thirty-ninth birthday.

A Small Army of Collaborators

Because there was a living to be made for her mother and herself, Gordon was open to offers from former clients she knew she could work with. She had their lifestyle to maintain, a style of living reflected in certain pastimes and possessions that were determined by Gordon to be expressed in an understated good taste. While this standard of living was neither extravagant nor lavish, it did take money, and she was the sole breadwinner.

Never losing her resourcefulness, drive, and determination, Gordon refused to be defeated by pain, stress, and enervation. Now it was December 1933—Gordon's month of new beginnings. On the first day of the month her creative spirit resurfaced and a long-standing offer from the Tomson Twins was sealed. Scheduled for the spring of 1934, the musical revue *Why Not To-Night?* featured scores of Gordon's most original gowns and her set design for the scene opening the second act. Gordon suggested a unified design scheme—to identify central motifs and channel those concepts into visual messages through the use of costuming, scenery, and illustrative graphic art. However, she discovered that the only common thread interweaving the thirty-one independent vignettes was Herbert Farjeon's book. Nevertheless, Gordon played a major role in overall planning and was rejuvenated by the authority to carry out most of her own ideas. She also liked the production team.

Working tracing and costume design for Why Not To-Night?, *London, 1934. This show was Gordon Conway's last major stage production.*

Within days the new cast of colleagues swarmed into Bryanston Court, glad to be guests again after her film preoccupations. They were ready for a return to the fun, food, and friendly repartee at the Conways' flat. A theater reviewer would refer to this talented assemblage as a "small army of collaborators [who] have worked together very well. . . . [on the] bright revue" at the Palace Theatre.[52] Five meetings took place with the Tomsons before the end of December. Executing all of Gordon's revue designs, Jill Casson and her fitters, seamstresses, and models arrived almost daily to the flat. On December 28, Gordon hosted cocktails for the Tomsons, composer Ord Hamilton, and Greta Nissen, a Norwegian film beauty turned stage star. The evening would be the first of a number of gatherings from January to mid-March that welcomed actresses along with male production team chums like director Romney Brent and scenic designer Reginald Leefe. Gordon returned to the practice from her stage

days of hosting the production executives. Her cocktail conferences at the flat often comprised eight men and Gordon. The ambitious show exploded with colors, textures, and forms. Gordon reveled in the work.

Carefully marked in Gordon's phone-reminder book is the name of the young Agnes de Mille, the ballet choreographer for *Why Not To-Night?* and the only other woman on the production team. She arrived in England in May 1933 for training with Marie Rambert, and over the next six years worked with rising stars of British ballet and choreographers like Antony Tudor. Fifty-three years later de Mille explained her "unusually brief" experience with the revue but, uncharacteristically, did not remember Gordon:

My memories of the show are very sketchy. . . . I must have met her and worked with her but I can remember absolutely nothing. . . . of the show except Gina Malo who later married Romny [*sic*] Brent, took to drink, and died tragically. . . . I was given the job by my good friend Romny Brent [Romolo LaRalde, the Mexican actor and director], then a star in London. I undertook to stage two ballets for the production when I was suddenly summoned to Hollywood by my uncle, Cecil B. De Mille, the first notice he had ever taken of me professionally, to dance in his current production of "Cleopatra." This was a big Hollywood opportunity and Romny released me from the contract so that I could go.[53]

The Manchester premiere on March 21 and the London opening on April 24 pleased the critics and the public. The reviews reserved special accolades for the dancing, mimicry, scenery, and costuming. In the early 1930s, most theater critics across England, unlike most film critics, acknowledged costuming for legitimate theater, musicals, and cabaret. In comparing *Why Not To-Night?* with ideal revue standards, one critique claimed that costuming itself was one of the essential elements used to define the genre of revue: "its episodes should be bright, varied and amusing. . . . [with] tuneful music, a few catchy songs, some pretty girls as a chorus, good team work in the ensemble dances, one or two clever comedians, and attractive and colourful scenery and costumes."[54] The *Star*'s A. E. Wilson agreed that "The Perfect Revue. . . . should have . . . wit . . . lively music, neat dancing, pretty clothes, and a lovely host of girls to wear them." All these elements were present in *Why Not To-Night?*, resulting in "one of the best specimens of its kind that London has had."[55] The *Manchester Guardian* concluded: "As a spectacle the show owes a great debt to Mr. Reginald Leefe, who did the scenery, and Mr. [*sic*] Gordon Conway, who designed the costumes."[56] As usual, women's news articles expanded on the costumes. A regular feature called "Fashions from Stage and Stalls" reported audience reaction to Gordon's designs: Greta Nissen's "up-to-date checked taffetas or early Victorian crinoline skirt and frilled lace pantalettes, or nun-like white robes . . . were watched and applauded enthusiastically on the first night of the new Palace revue."[57]

With this type of news coverage, Gordon must have been puzzled by the scant attention to costuming in motion picture criticism. Costuming served the same purpose on the screen as on the stage: the creation of character, mood, tone, time, and place. Perhaps London movie critics found the practice of apparel marketing distasteful and wanted to separate themselves from what was perceived as blatant commercialization, a charge often aimed at the industry itself. Or perhaps the real reason was the perception of costuming by critics and industry executives as mere "women's work." Costume criticism was confined to theater critics and to women journalists writing about a certain type of New Woman, who aspired to be a modern professional earning money in order to gain freedom to express herself in clothes that fit her dreams of an upscale style of living.

Gordon's exuberance and enthusiasm for work and daily living once again abounded. A bounce in her step and spontaneous laughter signaled to associates that the overcast skies of November had dissipated. Lively images, delectable colors, and supple fabrics crowded her working hours. In December, her seasonal customs, like her birthday soirée at the Savoy, her parents' anniversary, the gala Christmas Eve dinner at the flat, and a joyous Christmas Day at Alice and Percy Lawson-Johnston's home, made her feel that the horizon ahead was bright. The fun of Boxing Day and of Tommie Conway's sixty-third surprise birthday party at Claridges flowed into a New Year's Eve celebration until 2:00 A.M. at the Ambassadors, only hours away from the holiday's usual marathon of bridge and mint juleps.

Before Gordon could catch her breath, winter raced into spring. She and Tommie Conway viewed the collections of Molyneux, Worth, and Schiaparelli between jaunts to L'Apéritif, Nash's, and the Monseigneur Grill, and evenings of dining and dancing at the Blue Train. Rehearsals at the Gaiety Theatre blended into scenery sessions with the set carpenter, stenciler, and curtain decorator—favored chores betraying Gordon's thwarted aspirations to art direction. She long before had discovered that the absence of architecture and engineering schooling hindered the opportunities available to her in art direction, a profession almost totally dominated by men trained in these skills.

A bright spot in the schedule was the March 5, 1934, return of artist and friend Joyce Murchie as Gordon's assistant. Just in time it was, for besides revue changes, work was due in eight days on the first set of original designs for the "Fashion House-Party" tableaux in *"The Daily Mail" Ideal Home Exhibition and Fashion Pageant.* The producers commissioned Gordon for the annual event at Olympia Hall on April 25; it was a revue-type entertainment and a commercial showcase with sixty scenes.

The reappearance of her assistant Murchie raises an interesting point about independent and freelance artists like Gordon. She shunned the production line process that allowed the assistant's work to be stamped with the artist's name. Gordon counted herself among artists, whether fine artists or commercial artists, who avoided coteries of sycophants as well as the respected apprentice system, which would have provided psychological support and increased productivity with legitimate derivative work. Gordon's work formula— her drive toward perfection and compulsive reliability—produced an uneasy alliance with enormous commissions. Attempting to accomplish the work alone was, in Michael Powell's word, "murder." In ad-

dition, Gordon's formula included a sense of civility, courtesy, and plain good manners that was necessary to her creativity and effectiveness. She was not an "autocrat" like Alfred Junge. This combination of attitudes and beliefs caused tension and strain, especially in a profession that served mass-market commercial entertainment, a business much like a battlefield or a boxing ring. Even Erté, a powerful illustrator and designer who managed a successful atelier of apprentices, became frustrated with the modus operandi of the motion picture industry and appalled by the treatment he received in Hollywood. Though provided with a wardrobe department, Erté remained only a few months and "looked forward to being treated considerately on his return to Paris." [58]

During Gordon's film tenure, records are not clear as to whether Gaumont-British or Gordon paid Murchie's salary. Until she sailed home two years later, Gordon continued appointments with former assistants Betty Claire and Miss Taylor, but research offers no answers about their employment and salaries. Perhaps the studio kept one or both on staff, since a semblance of administrative continuity was needed when Gordon resigned. It would have been typical of Gordon to care about what happened in the department and to respond informally to questions about couturiers, costumiers, seamstresses, dressers, maintenance and storage of properties, and files of measurements, patterns, and production costs.

Shedding light on these golden years of costume design that were perceived as glamorous and fun, Gary Chapman, an authority on Dolly Tree and costume design, emphasizes that "the work *was* murder, especially in the movies." [59] A key observation about Hollywood designers is made by Susan Perez Prichard in *Film Costume: An Annotated Bibliography:* "The demands of the job have brought about their casualties. Adrian died in 1959 at the age of 56 from a heart attack. Irene committed suicide in 1962 at the age of 54. Travis Banton lost his job as Paramount's chief designer due to alcoholism." [60] Chapman adds: "Like many others engaged in the dream factories, stress was common amongst the Hollywood costume designers. The pressure of deadlines and increasing output, deficient budgets, competition and the need to maintain creativity, and the continual quest for new ideas and styles exacted its toll. Many suffered in a variety of ways from alcohol abuse and nervous breakdowns to suicide. Travis Banton, Howard Greer, Orry Kelly, Dolly Tree, and Irene, for example, were all reported to have drinking problems. Adrian died an early age, Irene committed suicide, and reports have suggested that Robert Kalloch committed suicide." [61]

As a British newswoman explained in 1933, there was more to the job than just designing dresses. Though Gordon received a Christmas reprieve and benefited from an assistant and the skill of Jill Casson's handworkers, old ailments crept back into her life. On March 20 she "sent Joyce to Manchester to look after the dresses in 'Why Not To-Night?' as I was not well enough to go." After a shaky recovery, in response to Romney Brent's urgent plea for her opinion of the revue, Gordon boarded the train for Manchester but became ill. With the opening of *Why Not To-Night?* in London, Gordon attended the dress parade and participated in a BBC radio interview prior to the dress rehearsal. Along with the Savoy and Embassy Club parties accenting the opening, all the events came and went amid a blur of roses, telegrams, doctors, orchids, fever, missed invitations, phone messages, headaches, hemlines, and headlines. "So tired. . . . feeling rotten," she scrawled across the page. [62]

There it was—the abrupt ending to a brilliant career and all at the age of thirty-nine. Interweaving elements of Conway's career, private life, and personality, Jessie Matthews stated to her biographer Michael Thornton during a 1965 interview at the actress's Northwood home that Gordon "was a lovely person, very sweet and gentle. . . . [but] her mother caused her a great deal of misery. . . . She died much too young after a not very happy life." [63] Though Gordon made half-hearted attempts until 1937 to maintain her stature as a commercial graphic artist and a costume designer, her high-profile career actually ceased in April 1934, during the London run of *Why Not To-Night?*

Remarkable for an illustrator and designer, especially so for a woman in these fields between the world wars, Gordon reached the pinnacle of success and influenced millions along the way. She achieved international fame, earned a good living, and surely experienced a certain level of self-fulfillment. She worked with some of the most talented and celebrated personages on both sides of the Atlantic in the fields of print media, stage, and film production. For women in these fields, she blazed new and difficult trails, though her name had disappeared from the historical record before the middle of the century.

Gordon Conway made a difference, whether as her own New Woman model in her art of image making, or as a consumer and public relations activist in a rising advertising culture, or as an example of female management style, or as the first woman executive in charge of the first wardrobe department in the history of British film. She was a pioneer, an innovator, and an explorer. All the while, however, she never got too far ahead of the public she served. Her images were a major force that shaped the acceptance and rise of the financially independent and career-oriented New Woman of the pre–World War II period. Gordon knew when to adapt and adopt, when to reflect and absorb. Gordon knew what the audience wanted to see and what women's dreams were all about.

CHAPTER NINE

AN ARTIST IN MORE WAYS THAN ONE

We Were with Him All the Time

Before and after the Manchester opening of *Why Not To-Night?*, a retinue of revue stars and *Daily Mail* models descended on Bryanston Court. To Gordon, actresses Florence Desmond, Gina Malo, Greta Nissen, and Polly Luce were delightful guests between fittings that ran as late as 9:00 P.M. Since Gordon was her usual efficient and cordial self, it surprised no one that she "sketched in bed all day. . . . feeling awful. . . . in bed all day, but working." Since Tommie Conway also had not been feeling well, the women counted on two doctors and an occasional night nurse to get them back up to pace. Except for colds and sleeplessness the physicians found nothing serious. Since her mother had fired yet another housekeeper, Gordon scrambled to locate a young woman willing to try a second time. Such was the situation on the weekend of April 7, 1934.[1]

Mr. Fing seemed well enough that Saturday morning, but by 3:00 P.M. he fell gravely ill. Dr. Batts responded immediately, staying by the feline's side from 6:00 P.M. until he died at 9:00 that night. Gordon lamented: "My beloved Mr. Fing . . . We were with him all the time." On Sunday the women never left the flat, refused all calls, and left word for visitors with the doorman that #28 was not to be disturbed. On Monday morning, April 9, the women struggled into their clothes to view the body at 10:00. Gordon confessed to the veterinarian, "Fing looked perfectly beautiful." She wrote in her diary that "we had him cremated in the afternoon . . . and stayed in alone all day." The next day "at 2:00 P.M. we brought Mr. Fing's ashes home."[2]

Gordon placed the ashes of the cat in a marble urn on the drawing room mantle at Bryanston Court; three years later she moved the ashes to Mount Sion and placed the urn on the mantle of the fireplace ennobled for generations by Conway family members and remembered as the backdrop for the wedding of James Madison's parents in 1749. The importance of pets to the psychological well-being of people is widely recognized today, and while Gordon's grief might seem excessive, such a reaction and such profound affection are not unusual. Both Gordon and Tom felt genuine grief.

Gordon stretched her energies during the bereavement, only too glad to have the pressure of deadlines and visits from friends, like Florence Desmond, who stayed for late talks after fittings. Mr. Fing had witnessed her first major commission in Europe, and as it turned out he was witness to her last. Three days after the revue opening, Gordon and Tommie Conway traveled to Cooden Beach at Bexhill-on-Sea for a two-week rest. Mr. Fing's death, however, had left both women depressed. Friends soon flocked to the shore, including Lothar Mendes and Jerry Jackson, who brought quiet pleasures and deep discussions. As

Gordon soaked up fresh air and sunshine, her spirits improved. Regaining her stamina and drive, she attempted to get her career back on track in London. She called on Peter Huskinson at the *Tatler,* conferred with Mlle Apel at her studio, and enjoyed the Palladium performance of Sophie Tucker and the four Mills Brothers as well as a film at the new Curzon Cinema. On May 31 Gordon was a guest at Betty Lawson-Johnston's charity benefit luncheon attended by the Queen. That same evening, she and Tommie Conway applauded Dorothy Dickson in the first night of *The Private Road,* applause repeated two weeks later for Dorothy Hyson in *Touch Wood.* That May the Tomson Twins requested designs for "Carioca," a new scene added to their revue, *Why Not To-Night?* Following the dress rehearsal approval, Gordon's records do not indicate future collaboration with the brothers. Choreographer Agnes de Mille related that the twins went bankrupt after this show.[3]

Gordon sublet the flat for July and August during a six-week trip abroad that included medical consultations. On July 12 Gordon and Tommie Conway boarded the Golden Arrow and converged in Paris with a caravan of friends, who lunched at the Crémerie, took tea at Armenonville, and partied at the Hermitage. Part of the group traveled on to Vittel with Gordon and Tommie to take "the cure" at the Grand Hotel. Gordon felt that the "effervescent and pine oils baths" weakened her almost to a faint, but that the glasses of mineral water had a salutary effect. The entourage retraced the route for Gordon's appointments with Dr. L. S. Fuller, her physician from Paris days, who ordered a series of examinations at the American Hospital. The findings were inconclusive, and he sent Gordon on her way with "nerve medicine." Today, Gordon's chain-smoking would be questioned, but in those days it was a daring and glamorous habit for a New Woman and not considered a health hazard. Another cadre of friends caught the train for Chartres and motored for an hour to visit Gerry Knight and Ben Smith ensconced in their Moulin de Tachainville. Gordon described it as "a paradise," with the old windmill, moonbeams, and perfumed air. Joining her from a nearby site, Romney Brent read his new play aloud during a marathon of late night talks. Back with friends in Versailles, Gordon suffered more unexpected attacks and summoned Dr. Fuller; she stayed behind as friends rushed into Paris to party. The trip ended at an idyllic retreat, the Gulbenkian estate in Saint-Germain-en-Laye.[4]

Refreshed and rehabilitated, Gordon returned to work that fall in London. She focused almost exclusively on magazine and advertising illustration, though Bertie Meyer discussed a stage commission along the way, and the next year she dressed Dorothy Hyson for the stage production of *Ringmaster.* For more than fourteen months not only did she pursue familiar clients at the *Tatler,* the *Bystander,* Selfridges, and Swerlings, as well as Charles J. Lytle's products, but she also met with Alison Settle at British *Vogue* and followed up leads with nine advertising agencies. Posters for Melford Gowns Limited and lipstick display cards typified the fashion and consumer product advertising she created. The pursuit recalled career efforts during her honeymoon arrival in London in 1921.

Motion picture costume design, however, still stirred in her brain. She met with Reginald Fogwell and Jerry Jackson about productions in London. Letters and portfolios of sketches were flown back and forth across the Atlantic. Leland Hayward made suggestions, Bill O'Bryen offered help, and Irvin S. Cobb, at the urging of Bobbie Appleton, did his share to promote Gordon's work in Hollywood. Lilly Messinger with RKO in London arranged Gordon's offer from the studio. These contacts opened doors, but her own talent, experience, reliability, and reputation cinched the RKO job offer. This offer was an important career development because she needed the money, realized that Hollywood held more career opportunity than the British film industry, underestimated her health problems, and was confident she could do the work.

Contemplating the Hollywood offer, Gordon and Tommie accelerated their attendance at American films, informally researching the 1933 and 1934 Hollywood products as soon as they were screened in London. Among her favorites were film classics still admired today: *Queen Christina, The Painted Veil, The Barretts of Wimpole Street, Chained, It Happened One Night, Flying Down to Rio, We're Not Dressing,* and *The Gay Divorcee.* The viewings were intended to anticipate potential assignments and catalyze her imagination. Devotees of early 1930s costuming in American movies often are amazed by Gordon's ideas and styles that predate Hollywood classic apparel. She also responded rapidly to trends in Parisian haute couture, adding her own flair and individuality. Gordon Conway was often a predictor of trends.[5]

The RKO Hollywood job offer was attractive for the salary, the challenge, and the climate. Even the hard work, notoriety, and manufactured glamour appealed to her, for she liked a rapid pace with an avalanche of assignments in a luxurious setting where her name was known. However, something gnawed away at this independent New Woman during the decision-making process. Had *Wild Party,* the popular epic poem she read in the 1920s, implanted its warning in her psyche? Had Gordon listened too long to colleagues damaged by the production system, or was their reaction sour grapes? Had she the hunger and the hubris deep inside to push, prod, and plot to get ahead? Just acknowledging these questions may

have presaged the answer. More important, would her mother like Hollywood and would Hollywood like Tommie Conway? What about Mount Sion, splintering apart without her care? What would her father say? Only these last questions really mattered. Regardless of the salary and the possible fame, Hollywood was not for her, nor for her mother.

Writing seventeen years later from Mount Sion, she commiserated with Teddie Holstius during his second tour in Hollywood: "It burns me up to think of the dirty deal Hollywood gave you. . . . P. G. Wodehouse and Dorothy Parker both were there for about a year without doing anything. . . . but why did it have to happen to our 'T.' I am thankful I did not accept the one offer I had to go there. We were interested to hear in detail . . . your experiences in that wild place. I can now appreciate them. . . . Life would be too hectic for these two country gals."[6]

Gordon's health, of course, was also a factor in turning down the Hollywood offer. In the fall of 1934, in the middle of yet another revived career campaign, insomnia and lethargy overwhelmed her. Gordon agreed with friends that things were at their worst when she abandoned the usual December festivities and went to bed at 9:30 P.M. on New Year's Eve. She began to wonder if she ever would be well, a fear that compounded her discomfort with anxiety about the future. Gordon liked to work and needed to work. She telephoned Dr. Fuller, who ordered a series of "20 injections" administered by Dr. Creighton, and she took long walks, prescribed by the doctors.[7]

In the spring of 1935, Gordon designed Dorothy Hyson's bridal gown and six bridesmaids' dresses for her wedding to Robert Douglas. The sunny roof of Bryanston Court became an alfresco studio for her new advertising assignments. Gordon recorded that she was happy when Kay Hammond invited her to see the new baby and thrilled at the birth of Gerry and Ben Smith's new child. She loved seeing her godson from Annapolis, now on a Navy cruise in British waters. Friends and colleagues were getting married for the second and third times, having more children, building homes, and advancing in their jobs—all elements missing from her own personal life. The Nazi and Fascist threat loomed in the background as she remembered the start of World War I. Some American friends with a feeling of foreboding had already returned to the States. Gordon and her mother made preparations to return to New York. Tenants took up Gordon's lease on the flat for £375 per annum, her first asking price. During December 1935 and into the first month of the new year, friends showered the two women with bon voyage parties, parting gifts, and promises of future visits. As it happened, the royal funeral for George V was held on the day before Gordon and Tom sailed.

Color Was Her Happiness

On January 29, 1936, Gordon and Tommie Conway embarked on their last ocean voyage. Unlike her diary entry on the *Olympic* at the beginning of World War I, Gordon did not venture the same confident farewell to "dear old Europe. . . . but we'll return." The 1914 hope—that the skirmish would be over by Christmas—was not matched in 1936. The political upheaval in Germany looked ominous. Teddie Holstius escorted the two women to Southampton on that "cold and bleak day." He wrote that evening "how sad I was to see Gordon getting further and further away. . . . and me standing on the quayside—helpless." [8] Gordon's diary, though, indicates no such melancholy, for she was not saying good-bye and fully intended to see European friends on trips to the United States.

Though the Conway women regretted that it was

the final voyage of the RMS *Majestic* and their final voyage, they were overjoyed at the sight of New York as the liner steamed into the harbor on February 5. Since their last visit to the United States in 1926 the country had changed. Though New York meant the same friends, plays, movies, floor shows, dinners, and dancing, the Depression projected a different mood. At least Prohibition was over. The women leased an apartment near their old haunts at 45 East 85th Street. The same Manhattan Storage Company delivered the same furniture. Old friends visited. Blake and his wife were in touch. Long Island weekends picked up again at "Nid de Papillon" with Bobbie and Katharine Appleton, who had commissioned Gordon's graphic designs for the Riding Club of East Hampton. Frequent trips commenced to Mount Sion to oversee restoration of the house. Gordon had written Dr. Fuller that she was well, but before she received his reply, the old ailments forced her into a final acknowledgment of her chronic health problems.

Over the next eight months when Gordon attempted to revive professional contacts, she discovered that what she feared was in fact true: the photographic image was replacing drawing—it was now a less expensive medium. Before her very eyes the golden age of illustration that had propelled her to eminence was being eclipsed by photography, especially color photography. Though illustration continued to be used in print media, Gordon found that the demand had decreased and the popularity and prestige once associated with the art had diminished. She also discovered that within illustration itself, the styles of image presentation in magazines and advertising had changed. Perhaps to combat the realism of photography, potential clients shifted to using drawings with a softer edge. They wanted more romantic sketches in a lyrical and impressionistic style that were best represented by Eric, now the rage of Condé Nast publish-

Tear sheet of cartoon, New York American, *October 26, 1936.*

ing. Gordon briefly tried a style change herself, but to no avail. Her career beginnings had seemed so effortless, so promising, and so rewarding. Now Gordon was struggling much harder to find commissions and was barely able to cover living expenses.

Gordon Conway's life seemed destined to travel full circle as she met with Heyworth Campbell, recently associated with *Harper's Bazaar.* She met with Ned Wayburn about assignments for stage costume and promotional graphics. She called on Lee Shubert, Morris Gest, Sam Harris at the Music Box Theatre, and George S. Kaufman at the Winter Garden Theatre. She contacted advertising agencies, took sketches by the Paramount circuit office, and had appointments with Saks Fifth Avenue, Lord and Taylor, and Bonwit Teller. Gordon tried a new field for her—political cartooning. One cartoon published that fall in the *New York American* elicited the editor's promise for more. Another commission with high expectations was an order for wallpaper designs, a job that could be executed long distance, necessary now that she was moving to Mount Sion. That autumn she and

her mother traveled to Mount Sion and found the place in worse repair than they had expected. Over the next year, with a sizable loan from relatives in Texas, she oversaw the restoration of the original eighteenth-century structure and the construction of an addition that included a modern kitchen. She engaged a Virginia architect, a historic preservation authority who had been influenced by the restoration of nearby Colonial Williamsburg since the beginning of the project in 1928. Gordon was now her own art director. The project was the ultimate stage setting. Back and forth between New York and Virginia, she allowed construction duties to take precedence, eclipsing her half-hearted career forays in the city. The days were filled with business duties in both states: banking matters, the sale of timber from the property, buying her first car, subletting the New York apartment, and orchestrating yet another furniture move. As the restoration drew to a close, the two women moved permanently to Mount Sion on December 28, 1937.

At the end of Gordon's 1936 diary, tucked in back of the December entries, Gordon penned poignant autobiographical musings that give insight into her life. She wrote of being "born in the South . . . [and that she was] a disappointment . . . a boy was wanted, but . . . only a girl arrived [with] red hair and blue eyes . . . She was given a boy's name, a family name selected for an heir [but] bestowed upon the daughter in lack of intense enthusiasm." Gordon confessed she was "burdened with thoughts untold. . . . was a dreamer, full of rhythm, song, and dance, and a lover of animals and all nature. . . . graceful as a breeze across a hilltop and color was her happiness." [9]

The two women moved in on the day before Tommie Conway's sixty-seventh birthday. As their black Plymouth sedan passed through the gate, they drove through a dense stand of black walnut, oak, and dogwood trees, and thousands of hollies. They navigated

Wallpaper design, 1937.

the long narrow gravel road that rose slightly to a clearing. Like a stage setting, the mound revealed the Colonial homestead, the smokehouse, and a sprinkling of outbuildings. Gordon's diary indicates that she felt that this move to Mount Sion was yet another new beginning.

Friends soon joined them. Harold Horan and his bride selected Mount Sion for their wedding; Gordon staged the ceremony before the drawing room fireplace where members of the Conway family had pledged their troth and where Mr. Fing rested in peace. Urban sophisticates teased Gordon about her rural revolution, but they rarely turned down an invitation. A half century later, many vividly remember the retreats. Besides Gordon's warmth and charm, the appeal centered on walks and drives through the Virginia countryside, gathering the right herb from the kitchen garden, and marketing in the town of Fredericksburg. There was breakfast in bed, "lunch like a poem," and a gourmet dinner served on blue and white Staffordshire dinnerware, a nuptial gift to a Conway ancestor from Dolley and James Madison. Joan Antill, a colleague and friend from London stage days, and Mary Lutz, a Washington, D.C., friend, testified to Gordon and Tom's hospitality, which seemed custom-designed for each individual. Especially memorable were the conversations that could last all day, through one demitasse, a cordial, and more coffee past midnight. During World War II, when Joan Antill worked for the British Air Command in Washington, she thanked Gordon for a Mount Sion welcome on the day Singapore fell. On that "day of doom," Gordon's spirits kept her guests from despair. Joan Antill wrote that "when all the world is conscious only of the losses and the suffering apparent all around us, among those days that are happy to remember. . . . I like to think of your house with . . . the beauty that is your way of writing poetry. . . . I like to think of . . . flipping ideas backwards and

forwards in a game where neither of us minded losing and neither of us 'specially wanted to win." Friends remembered that although the dialogue may have taken place far from the centers of culture, cosmopolitan pleasures, world politics, and battles, ideas were alive at Mount Sion.[10]

Conversation included discussions of books and poems that Gordon and her intimates read, as well as the movies all had viewed, especially films showcasing talented friends of Gordon's, like Thorne Smith's *Topper* series and *Huckleberry Finn* with Rex Ingram. Guests grieved over George Gershwin's untimely death and took sides in the debate about the marriage of the Prince of Wales to Wallis Simpson. A topic of conversation rarely introduced, though, was Gordon's career. Joan Antill and Mary Lutz shed light on the recollections of other friends: there was

lots of talk. We talked lots. We talked about books and we talked about places and we talked about things, but we never talked about Gordon's famous past. . . . You didn't ask about her past. That was an-

Gordon Conway and "Laddie," Mount Sion, ca. 1937–1939.

other time, another era. She never gave any sign of regret at all. . . . She did not hanker for the bright lights . . . I never got the impression that she thought "Oh what would I give to go to the Café de Paris or the Perroquet". . . . One time we were there, and Mrs. Conway wanted something very grand to happen. . . . Gordon said "Oh mother thinks she's still living at the Ritz.". . . [But] she never talked about that part of her life.[11]

An assortment of associates knew she occasionally sent cartoons to Harold Horan in New York and prepared wallpaper and textile designs for clients. The last public forum anyone remembered, however, was an exhibition of twenty illustrations and designs during Federal Art Week in Fredericksburg in November 1940.

Friends, acquaintances, and employees all remembered Gordon's own kind of animal humane society. Like a female Dr. Doolittle, she increased her menagerie from cats and dogs of all pedigrees to include woodland creatures and ordinary chickens. Joan Antill and Mary Lutz talked about "the flock of cats. . . . seventeen cats at Mount Sion. . . . [they] were a thing with Gordon. . . . Every one of those cats had a name and a personality." Running through Gordon's records are names of special pets like Honey-child, Teto, and Totee. These cats shared Gordon's affection with strays as well as with blue bloods, like Laddie the Airedale and Rex the Boxer. She nursed them through bouts of illness, including a near epidemic of distemper that filled the animal cemetery with her furry friends. One intimate reminisced about Laddie's funeral, for which he served as a pallbearer. He told of hymns on the long trek to the pet graveyard near the Conway family cemetery, with the Episcopal burial service read from *The Book of Common Prayer*. Among friends from Paris to Buenos Aires and from London to the Maghreb, the pets that caused the most astonishment were the flocks of chickens. Rita Essayan wrote from

Paris in the early 1950s that the Gulbenkian family could not imagine their stylish Gordon of Place Vendôme and West End fame out in the hen house feeding chickens.[12]

For two decades Gordon managed the property, tending to business and household details that ranged from road and furnace repair to timber sales and taxes. She defended the land against nature's vagaries, financial hard times, and even the Department of War. In 1940, before the United States entered World War II, Gordon circulated petitions and launched a public awareness and letter-writing campaign to save Mount Sion and nearby historic structures from being swallowed up by Camp A. P. Hill. She enlisted the help of Senator William E. Borah and his wife Mary, friends from her National Cathedral School days in Washington, D.C. She corresponded with columnist Drew Pearson, who raised public consciousness about the Virginia sites. Secretary of War Henry L. Stimson sympathized with the need for preservation. On March 24, 1941, the Army notified Gordon that the acreage would not be needed, and Mount Sion and nearby historic Virginia sites were saved for posterity.

Throughout these years, Gordon continued to have bouts of ill health. In the fall of 1941, a month before Pearl Harbor, her doctors in Richmond, Virginia, conducted an exploratory operation, but they were unable to find a cause for her continuing pain and discomfort. In March 1942 Gordon ceased the lifetime habit of keeping a diary, probably because of her health, the depressing world conditions, and the fact that she did not need the record of dates, commissions, and clients anymore. For the next fourteen years, various malignancies—from breast to uterine cancer—drained her strength, but she never complained. Even those closest to Gordon could not tell when she suffered. Margaret Page Elliott recalled a visit to Mount Sion when Gordon whispered she had breast cancer but begged her not to say anything to Tommie. Joan Antill and Mary Lutz recounted that one weekend at Mount Sion, Gordon confessed, "I don't know what to do; [the doctor] has given me a very bad report. Yes, it's

cancer. . . . but I'll never, never, never let mother know, *never,* because it would distress her terribly." Tommie Conway, however, did know, and in turn, she begged intimates not to let on to Gordon that she knew. The friends expanded on others' recollections: "She just wouldn't go to the doctor, she just let it take her." [13] In 1953 she finally consented to surgery, but by then the malignancy had spread throughout her body, and "there was nothing to be done." [14]

On the afternoon before she died, with great effort Gordon went downstairs for a game of backgammon with her mother. Halfway into the game she sighed and asked to be excused. Uncharacteristically, she crept slowly back to her sickroom. Tommie Conway motioned the housekeeper to join her at the dining room window, and murmured, "Do you see the white car waiting for my darling child?" [15] The woman saw nothing except the front lawn bordered by Gordon's flowers and the forest beyond. In the early morning hours of June 9, 1956, a white ambulance pulled up to

Greetings From Tommy and Gordon Conway—
1952

Illustration for a Christmas card of Mount Sion, 1952, which later appeared on the cover of The Spur, *June 1953.*

the front door at Mount Sion, into the very spot the mother had envisaged. Gordon died on the stretcher at the top of the landing of the stairway as two attendants carried her swollen body to the hospital. Loved ones agreed that it seemed she had orchestrated the very spot to say farewell to Tommie Conway and Mount Sion. To the end Gordon was the quintessential designer, arranging every setting. Earlier she had ordained that, prior to the graveside service in the family plot, her coffin should be placed before the handcarved fireplace in the drawing room of Mount Sion. The Conway family spirits were there to welcome her, and so was Mr. Fing.

Golden Gordon

Gordon's fight for life during those last two decades of life shared a common thread with her struggle against stress and chronic illness during the artist's twenty-two-year career: she fought pain, exhaustion, and sickness by reordering the physical world around her. Order was visible and tangible. Design—both as process and product—was the leitmotif of her life. She gathered whatever materials were at hand and forged them into a form. Using line, color, and texture, her aesthetic sensibility transformed objects into compositions. Other artists organized sounds, words, and movements, but Gordon perceived reality with the eye and created an ordered whole composed of images. Tangible items—whether a film costume, stage setting, fashion sketch, or lipstick advertisement— were assembled to order her own psyche, as well as to send visual messages to the viewer. These abstract conceptions and arrangements of the material world gave Gordon a sense of order. Beauty, design, and function were weapons in the battle to make life more livable and to make the world a pretty but practical place for others. Gordon's father, after all, as mayor of Cleburne,

Texas, had insisted on city parks and public parking space for wagons with their horses in full harness. No matter where, no matter when, Gordon cared deeply about the way things looked. Wood Kahler was right when he wrote in 1930 as part of his novel and in a personal inscription that Gordon Conway was "an artist in more ways than one." [16]

Two of Gordon Conway's legacies evolved from her efforts to create order out of chaos. Both involved arranging life into an artificial construct, into the ultimate tableau. The first legacy was the visual record in paint, print, and celluloid of Gordon Conway's kind of New Woman. The second, more ephemeral, legacy was Gordon's talent for making art out of the fabric of life. [17]

The images portraying New Women on page, stage, and screen, images that both reflected and shaped a certain look and outlook, Gordon stored in the Mount Sion basement during December 1937. Stacked neatly in a mass of trunks, here resided the Gordon Conway oeuvre, a record of an internationally acclaimed commercial graphic artist, costume designer, and New Woman between the two world wars. Examples of her work follow, in Part Two. Gordon's 1920s flappers and 1930s sophisticates dance off the page to recreate an era long forgotten.

The second legacy arose from Gordon's personal philosophy of making art out of life. With her talent for the art of living, she gathered the pieces of everyday existence into a whole, selecting the beautiful and the best while eliminating the ugly and mundane. Whether in a studio in Montparnasse, an Art Moderne flat in London, or an eighteenth-century Colonial home in Virginia, Gordon's formula worked. Her impulse to reconstruct reality, the driving force no matter where she lived, explains her wish to be an art director. At Mount Sion she was her own art director, overseeing the ultimate stage setting. Joan Antill

Self-caricature of Gordon Conway in retirement or drawing of Zina (see Part Two, Image One) at Mount Sion, ca. 1937. Conway's cousin remembered this old, tattered floral-patterned dress that Conway often wore when working in the garden. Two former employees recalled Conway being attacked by a swarm of bees during her work outdoors.

said it well: the beauty and beneficence of Mount Sion was Gordon's "way of writing poetry." She and Mary Lutz expanded on the theme:

I always felt Gordon channeled her creative talent into the whole place. . . . You see, when she came here and had totally retired from everything else, it appeared to me that her project was Mount Sion. Everything she did was just perfect. . . . The whole place was designed to match and to look beautiful. . . . Everything that could be done in needlepoint was done in needlepoint. . . . She didn't really pursue anything to do with the theater or the art part of her life . . . except for Mount Sion itself. . . . She transferred her artistic feelings away from anything commercial and into her own home.

The two friends explained that even one-time visitors were inspired by Gordon's reverence for the place, evident in the awe expressed by a British dignitary when the friends introduced the visitor to Mount Sion: "It's beautiful, it's like a shrine!" [18]

Similar memories were expressed by former employees. Oscar and Thomas Coghill, brothers who worked for Gordon as teenagers, recalled plans and color charts prepared for the flower beds and vegetable rows, like those of a landscape architect. "She'd put on old clothes and dig and dig, then the next season change the placement because of color mostly, and size and height." [19] Gordon experimented and revised everything within her unified design scheme.

Dorothy Dickson, who epitomized the look and outlook of the New Woman between the world wars, was witness to Gordon's art of living: "Everything she did, she did well. She had such flair, such panache, such style. And a smart dresser, very chic, always the latest fashion . . . Her personality, her intelligence, her character, her sense-of-humor, she was A-Okay, that's exactly what she was, A-Okay in every way. . . . Of course she had been brought up right and knew how to do things with taste and charm. She had class." [20] Dorothy Hyson, now Lady Quayle, discussed the artist while perusing photographs and news clippings from Gordon's heyday in New York, London, and Paris: "See what I mean . . . she is very elegant. . . . She's very classy, you see. There's a lot of style." Lady Quayle recalled Gordon's manner at Gaumont-British studio in 1932 when she entered the movie business as a teenager: "She always looked very chic. . . . Some people are a little bit awed by a very sophisticated looking young American. . . . but she got on with everybody. . . . She was so courteous and absolutely delightful with everybody. They couldn't have helped but be charmed by her. I can't ever think now that she would be difficult or make a scene or be awkward in any way. And yet," the actress paused, "she was *very* particular about how things were done. I think she was a perfectionist. I'm sure she'd be wanting the highest standards in her work." [21]

Twenty years after the last public acknowledgment of the impact on style and taste by this image maker, a friend captured the essence of Gordon Conway in a letter written with the knowledge that it might be the last she would send to an ailing Gordon. Longtime friend Rita Gulbenkian Essayan wrote from Lisbon in the spring of 1956 before her trip to Mount Sion to bid a final farewell. She reminded Gordon that "We knew nothing about glamour, shingled hair or cocktails till we met you. I still have your photo in the polka dot dress. . . . that will always be Golden Gordon for us." [22]

PART TWO

IMAGES OF A
NEW WOMAN

MODEL IN YOUR MIRROR

A Carefully Studied Simplicity

In the spring of 1924, the Paris edition of the *New York Herald* featured an illustration of Gordon Conway "as seen by herself" and recognized the artist as a "staunch advocate of freedom for women." The article described Conway's different genres of expression: "The era of Jazz has increased the call upon the imaginative powers of artists who design costumes for the musical play. . . . [like Conway's] costumes for the new Midnight Follies to be established at the Club Daunou. . . . [She] does more than design chorus girls' costumes; she also draws those bewitching heads which adorn magazine covers, sketches posters to show the excellence of this or that play and, besides, draws silhouettes with such a fine touch of resemblance that she has earned the reputation of being one of the best artists of that special school in America." The author recalled Conway's Paris studio, especially "a remarkable sketch on exhibition entitled 'Jazz Lint,' which represents the 1924 model of syncopated art. It depicts magnified microbes in human form, such as might be supposed to have had their origin in the texture of syncopation."[1] This article typified press coverage during her career that acknowledged her versatility and multifaceted talent.

Gordon Conway started out during the golden age of American illustration as a self-taught, freelance commercial graphic artist who worked without models, copyists, and apprentices. Her art focuses primarily on the female figure. Conway's body of work can be divided into two categories. One category comprises highly polished narrative illustrations, silhouettes, and line drawings for graphic reproduction in both the editorial and advertising print media.[2] The other category contains finished working drawings for reproduction in fabric for stage and film costuming. These two sets of drawings are works on paper in pen and ink, gouache, watercolor, tempera, and mixed media. Though beyond the scope of this discussion of illustrative art, Conway's selection and treatment of textiles for costuming as a secondary medium also won accolades for originality and versatility. This creative process parallels an artist's arrangement of materials for a collage, or a sculptor's approach to stone or metal. Materials for Conway's costuming ranged from tucked and clipped oilcloth to wired ruffles of faille, from giant wooden buttons to showy costume jewelry, from finely tailored wool to yards of swirling chiffon.[3] Like most ephemera of stage and film production, Conway's costume art survives only in photographs and on film, or in her artwork, which includes instructional notations and fabric swatches pinned to the drawings.

The major strengths of Conway's illustrative art include a vision of simplicity and a strong sense of composition with bold lines and vibrant color combinations. Noted for clarity, directness, and a clean, uncluttered look, Conway's Art Moderne style combines

Proposal entitled "Three Filigree," for Harper's Bazar, *1917. The drawing shows the influence of Aubrey Beardsley and the Art Nouveau aesthetic.*

sleek, streamlined, and elongated lines that highlight striking forms, which are presented in an asymmetrical balance and enlivened with bold, vivid, and flat planes of color. This style differs dramatically from her first series of drawings executed in early 1914 during brief academic art classes in Rome. They were watercolor portraits representing Western easel painting's chiaroscuro tradition and use of perspective. Whereas these early pictures show her facility for drafting, color, and portrayal of character and personality, there is little indication of the pizzazz and vibrancy subsequently seen in her work. This art from her early classes in Rome later evolved into a style derived from Art Nouveau that featured gently flowing arabesque lines but eschewed the usual Art Nouveau curvilinear extravagances of tangled tendrils and convoluted organic detail. Though Conway often incorporated exotic patterns in her compositions, the decoration

remained restrained and stylized. By the early 1920s, Conway's work reached a mature style with taut, sharp-edged, geometric, and rectilinear characteristics.

Conway's style captured the essence of movement. Her figures spring from the page with energy and verve. They move with ease, displaying a sense of rhythm, pace, agility, grace, and muscular coordination. Conway's brisk, quick-paced motions defy the inert, passive statuary poses drawn by contemporary colleagues like Erté, who rendered female figures as inanimate, decorative objects similar to those on the ancient Greek vases he so admired. His impersonal countenances distance the subject from the viewer, as do the stylized and immobile female figures of illustrators and costume artists like Barbier, Lepape, and Iribe. Even in these male artists' illustrations and designs for dance and sport, they often anchor the legs and feet to the ground without a hint of agility or ac-

Presentation drawing, "Winter Scene," Paris, 1922, shows the influence of Japanese prints and the Japonisme aesthetic on Gordon Conway's Art Moderne style.

tion. (Ironically, Conway's treatment of the few male figures in her work betrays the same inactivity.) Conway expressed female freedom and aspiration through movement and agility, while the male artists portrayed the female in a passive, inactive stance derived from academic classicism or from a reluctance to acknowledge women's ability to move with energy and grace. Though beautiful in composition, color, and design, as well as adequate guides for costume and fashion construction, the drawings by these male artists lack the sparkling vitality of the lively attenuated figures that grace Conway's work.[4] (These male artists' works also lack the personal resemblances and individual charm of Conway's renderings of such actresses as Dorothy Dickson and Jessie Matthews.) This interplay of Conway's lithe and supple shapes makes her drawings come alive with an effect as engaging as the stunning simplicity of the art.

The goal of simplicity was a main tenet espoused by advocates of Japonisme, most prominently the Columbia College teacher Arthur Wesley Dow, who rediscovered traditional Japanese woodblock art, and architect Frank Lloyd Wright. Conway would agree that "the elimination of the inessential" was important in art and design from both an aesthetic and a moral viewpoint. Furthermore, as a practical commercial graphic artist and especially as a poster and billboard designer alert to the "integration of image and text," Conway also valued the Japanese print aesthetic as a device of salesmanship. She joined advertising artists who appropriated "simplified shapes in order to communicate their messages more directly." The Japanese print aesthetic provided "a more powerful means to transmit commercial messages in a two-dimensional format."[5] In 1928, though writing about film design, Conway summarized the central focus of her style in any genre: "My experience . . . has served to strengthen my conviction that the most telling and striking effects are usually secured by carefully studied simplicity."[6]

Harmony of All the Arts

Conway's creative contributions evolved from a cluster of artistic and cultural sources during unprecedented changes in art and design early in the twentieth century. Though Modernism in the fine arts, including Cubism and Fauvism, informed the oeuvre of Gordon Conway, modern movements in the applied arts and architecture actually molded her work to a larger extent. These modern design innovations during the era's visual revolution influenced her work in tandem with new industrial and technical developments, aspirations for economic and social mobility, consumer strategies, and democratic social theories. Conway's eclectic influences ranged from the startling performances and designs of Serge Diaghilev's Ballets Russes to stage art for the Parisian music hall spectacles created by rising young designers like José de Zamora, Dolly Tree, and Erté. These experiences reinforced Conway's study of books on and portfolios of art by Léon Bakst, Georges Lepape, Georges Barbier, and Umberto Brunelleschi. Her print collection included *pochoirs* from Lucien Vogel's *Costumes de Théâtre, Ballet et Divertissements,* which augmented his acclaimed fashion journal, *La Gazette du Bon Ton.* The art reproductions in her collection were sometimes at the opposite end of the aesthetic spectrum from these Russian ballet designers and decorative artists. These reproductions reflected Conway's diverse tastes, for example, Harrison Fisher's lyrical and graceful lines in sharp contrast to Egon Schiele's abrupt and distorted forms.

Conway studied other art and design books in her library that included Walter Schnackenberg's illustrations and graphic designs, Cyril W. Beaumont's *Impressions of the Russian Ballet* (featuring both *Scheherazade* and *Cleopatra*), Paul Louis Victor de Giafferri's volumes of *L'Histoire du costume féminin mondial,* Herbert Norris's *Costume and Fashion,* Alice Morse Earle's *Two Centuries of Costume in America,* Oskar Fischel's *Die Mode,* and G. Woolliscroft Rhead's *Chats on Costume,* a book treasured by Conway because it had been owned and signed by John Singer Sargent. She perused Maurice Raynal's *A. Archipenko,* Fr. Hottenroth's *Le Costume chez les peuples anciens et modernes,* Auguste Wahlen's *Moeurs, usages et costumes de tous les peuples du monde,* William Heinemann's 1921 edition of *The Beggar's Opera, Written by Mr. Gay,* Clive Bell's *Art,* Robert Ross's *Aubrey Beardsley,* and Laurence Housman's *Stories from the Arabian Nights* featuring the celebrated illustrations of Edmund Dulac.[7] (A list of Conway's books is included in Selected Bibliography.)

As part of her self-education, before and after World War I and on both sides of the Atlantic, Conway attended exhibitions at the Galleria Colonna in Rome, at the Victoria and Albert Museum, the Royal Academy, and the Leicester Galleries in London, and at the Louvre, the Salon des Indépendants, and the Musée Guimet dedicated to Asian art in Paris. She viewed frequent displays of Japanese prints and other Oriental art, stage designs of Edward Gordon Craig, caricatures of Max Beerbohm, sculpture of Paul Manship and Jacob Epstein, and paintings of studio artists like Amedeo Modigliani, Federico Beltrán-Massés, Paul Gauguin, and the Cubists, Futurists, and Fauves. Visual and textural stimuli also emanated from the art and artifacts of exotic cultures researched by anthropologists and archaeologists, cinema's lighting effects and ever increasing moving images, new machine aesthetics, trends in layout and typography, and scores of Bauhaus designs.

Conway shared aesthetic insights and exchanged practical information with multitalented transatlantic friends and colleagues including designers Raymond Loewy, Henry C. Beck, and Serge Chermayeff; illustrators Porter Woodruff, Reynaldo Luza, and Edmundo "Mundo" Searle (also known as Ronald Searle); sculptor Seymour Fox; filmmakers like director Victor Saville, cameraman Roy Overbaugh, and Rex Ingram, who was a sculptor as well as a director and actor; and writers who possessed expertise in design like Wood Kahler and Guy Bolton. In New York Condé Nast's art director and Conway's mentor, Heyworth Campbell, guided her to tutors and brief classes at the Art Students League. She was exposed to the popular styles at Condé Nast's magazines, including Helen Dryden's illustrations, line drawings by Anne Harriet Fish, and covers by Eduardo Benito. Conway received encouragement from the modern art advocate and founding editor of *Vanity Fair,* Frank Crowninshield, and from Henry B. Sell, the editor at Nast's rival, the Hearst-owned *Harper's Bazaar,* who introduced Conway to the work of Erté. She witnessed the Broadway spectacles of Joseph Urban and the design work of Robert Edmond Jones, whose *Continental Stagecraft* she studied. Conway discussed the drama initiatives of Eva Le Gallienne with her father, writer Richard Le Gallienne, and continued to be inspired by American jazz rhythms and blues music that were the rage of Continental and London cafés and cabarets. These entertainment venues nurtured rising émigré and transatlantic talent in ballet, modern dance, and exhibition dancing—yet another avenue for cross-fertilization in her art.

In London and on the Continent, editor Peter Huskinson showcased her illustrations and original designs at the *Tatler* and *Eve: The Lady's Pictorial.* Conway worked with business art directors and advertising officers who ordered sketches for such publications as Harrods fashion supplements. She educated herself about textile developments such as synthetic fibers, British tailoring expertise, the embroidery and other exquisite handiwork of Parisian artisans, and the fabric cutting and draping techniques of innovative dressmakers, such as the bias cut technique of couturière Madeleine Vionnet. Conway was inspired by the work of other Paris designers such as the new streamlined, comfortable sports clothes of Jean Patou, and the chic, elegant attire of World War I hero Captain Edward Molyneux, whose lines she both wore and interpreted for the Milan-based *La Donna* magazine.[8]

Conway was especially taken with the revolutionary collections, publications, decorative arts school, and atelier created by couturier Paul Poiret, whose visual and textural innovations she first encountered as a teenager in Paris in 1912. Poiret was inspired by the Wiener Werkstätte and hired such accomplished artists as Raoul Dufy as staff designers for his "objets et décors de Poiret." Conway identified with Poiret's total design concept that honored the beauty and function of handcrafted items from cushions to carpet, from perfume bottles to wallpaper. The integrated concept celebrated the use of these everyday objects created to improve people's private lives and the general visual environment.[9]

This cultural attitude and social ritual, labeled by some practitioners as "making art out of life" and "the good life à la mode," paralleled Conway's aesthetic manner of living that highlighted well-designed surroundings down to the smallest detail. Though operating in separate orbits, Conway shared this secular philosophy with the American expatriate, bon vivant, and accomplished Cubist artist Gerald Murphy and his wife Sara. The Murphys made their life an experiment—a "joint imaginative creation." The Murphys felt that the imagination could triumph in the battle against daily chaos. Indeed, Murphy proclaimed his own personal dictum to be "living well is the best revenge." He appropriated this ancient Spanish proverb as a clarion call to action in life. After all, Murphy reasoned, one could do nothing about sickness, death, and disappointment. Sorrow was the rule of life. Since one could not prevent misfortune, one must take revenge on the tragedy, ugliness, and mediocrity of daily existence. Learn to accept, then fight back. Friends of the Murphys, including avant-garde artists and Modernist intellectuals Pablo Picasso, Ernest Hemingway, Fernand Léger, John Dos Passos, e. e. cummings, Archibald MacLeish, Igor Stravinsky, and F. Scott Fitzgerald, all marveled at the couple's ingenuity in inventing an artistic lifestyle. MacLeish pointed out that "person after person—English, French, American, everybody—met them and came away saying that these people really are masters in the art of living."[10]

Reflecting the Japonisme aesthetic, Conway's views identified with certain elements like the "harmony of all the arts. . . . [and the] universal principles of good design."[11] She became her own kind of design reformer who believed that "nothing need be ugly," that good design raised the artistic standards of the public, and that the consumer goods and services she illustrated were "designs for better living."[12] Conway believed in the democratization of design and in the very concept of style itself, once only the prerogative of aristocratic taste. Her objectives, which were flashier than but similar to the tenets of the Arts and Crafts movement, centered on the arrangement of visual space, on good design with coordinated aesthetic themes and finely handcrafted objects that lifted daily existence out of the ugly and mundane.[13] This impulse for a unified design scheme

also inspired Conway to pursue art direction for the stage and screen, though her access to the predominantly male profession never met her dreams and expectations.

The many modern art and design movements culminated in a landmark twentieth-century design event in 1925, during the time that Conway lived and worked in Paris and commuted to London. The Exposition Internationale des Arts Décoratifs et Industriels Modernes became the inspiration for the popularized and loosely used term of Art Deco, a term often applied to Conway's illustrations and designs. Pointing out the impact of these revolutionary changes, the illustrator of prototypical middle America, Norman Rockwell, recalled that "Paris became the gravitational center for many artists. Not only were Picasso and the Cubists leading the avant-garde, but French artists—Drian, Brissaud, Cassandre and Bernard Boutet De Monvel—were influencing a new look in American publications."[14] Guillaume Apollinaire, avant-garde poet and pioneer in integrating "word and image," added that "catalogues, posters, advertisements of all types, believe me, they contain the poetry of our epoch."[15] Another observer added that there was a natural interchange "between poet and painter, composer, decorator, designer, couturier. . . . The graphic and decorative possibilities of Cubism . . . and a little later of Constructivism, the Bauhaus and De Stijl. . . . [informed] the bobs and shingles, the straight lines, the clean tubes and spheres of the fashion of the later twenties and equivalent qualities in the other disciplines of applied design—architecture, industrial, domestic and graphic."[16] Gordon Conway's oeuvre is an amalgam of these discordant modern forces. Yet, her work possesses its own individual style and cultural statement. She was both a beneficiary of and a contributor to the artistic and cultural legacy of the early twentieth century; she was a symbol of the age.

Untitled drawing, ca. 1936. These three sophisticated ladies—one blonde, one brunette, and one redhead—are emblematic of Gordon Conway's New Woman images.

Modes and Messages

Gordon Conway's art recalls the spirit of an age that honored vitality, speed, exuberance, experimentation, lighthearted rebellion, naive hedonism, and extravagance.[17] These attitudes were reinforced by optimism, hope, and, most of all, a boundless sense of possibilities. Conway's wide range of expression in print, stage, and film media affected cultural attitudes about new glamorous lifestyles and produced thousands of images that inspired and reinforced dreams of a new feminine ideal. These images both reflected and shaped the aspirations of women yearning for economic, political, physical, emotional, sexual, social, and cultural freedom prior to and following legislation awarding suffrage and property rights to women in the United States and Great Britain. Conway's art also includes allusions to various cultures and styles that transcend their surface sophistication. Her women are often "goddesses," reflecting a certain calculated stylishness and intelligent aloofness. Suggesting the multiheaded goddesses of mythology, her drawing of

three sophisticated ladies is representative of Conway's "cool medium" approach that leaves much more to the imagination. These bejeweled heads—one blonde, one brunette, and one redhead—glance in three different directions: the women are self-assured, individualistic, and indifferent to one another.[18]

Credited early in her career as a major image maker, Conway captured the essence of a popular type of woman that emerged prior to World War I in urban areas and consumer centers on both sides of the Atlantic. Her images portrayed tall, sleek, svelte, agile, sophisticated, independent, and self-assured women like Conway herself, who was the quintessential New Woman extolled in upscale publications, consumer advertisements, and female roles showcased in musical comedy, cabaret, and motion picture productions.

These New Women images from the brush of Gordon Conway defy the submissive postures and weighted bodies from the artist's own background, such as the encumbered strollers pictured in a ca. 1905–1907 postcard of Gordon's home in Dallas, a caricature of Conway by a fellow student in Lausanne

Picture postcard of the Conways' Dallas home, ca. 1905–1907. Note women's styles before the revolutionary change in the "look" of women. Text on postcard: "DALLAS, TEXAS. Colonial Style Residence. Ross Ave."

in 1914 (see p. 21), and a prayerful madonna painted by Conway in 1914 in Rome. Conway's New Woman images do not record the radical suffragists and the prohibition crusaders, nor the Marxist labor girls and the salon queens of the fashionable Left elite. Neither do her figures resemble the models pictured in the Sears and Roebuck catalogue, nor the sisters and sweethearts rendered by Harrison Fisher for *Cosmopolitan* and by Norman Rockwell for the covers of the *Saturday Evening Post,* nor the Texas *Oil Field Girls* painted by Jerry Bywaters. Nor do they resemble the New Woman views in Cornelia Barns's cartoons for the *Masses,* the department store shoppers on Kenneth Hayes Miller's canvases, or the daring flappers of John Held, Jr., in the older *Life* magazine.[19]

Conway's images differ, for example, from one

Untitled watercolor from Gordon Conway's art lessons in Rome, 1914. This image of a "prayerful madonna" contrasts sharply with Conway's spritely and sophisticated New Women created one year later.

IMAGE FIVE
Consuming Woman

17. *This drawing is similar to advertisements for Burgher Real Estate, 1917, Dallas, published in Dallas newspapers. Similar ones also were published nationally by the Franklin Motor Car Company in 1917. Both advertising efforts urged women to purchase houses, property, and automobiles.*

18. *Tear sheet of La Donna, 1-Ottobre, ca. 1924–1926. Gordon Conway interpreted the collections of Parisian couturiers for this woman's magazine published in Milan. Her illustrations were a welcomed marketing tool for these design houses.*

19. *Delage advertisement, 1920, appearing in* Town and Country *and* Country Life. *This drawing features a Conway-like sophisticate waiting for a drive in the beautifully designed Delage automobile.*

20. *Another smartly dressed woman graces the Dura car in a cover for* L'Equipement Automobile, *Paris, September 1924. These two automobile advertisements were commissioned by Blake Ozias.*

21. *Cover for* Eve, *February 22, 1928. In the 1920s, European consumers were fascinated by newly discovered African art and archaeological artifacts.*

22. *Tear sheet of* The Tatler, *"The Red Hat," December 18, 1929. Three popular consumer products are evident: cloche hat, cigarette holder, and Art Deco jewelry.*

23. *Proposal for a lipstick advertisement, London, ca. 1934–1936.*

24. *Proposal for a cigarette advertisement, London, 1933.*

25. *Drawing for* The Tatler, *September 24, 1930. The geometric aesthetic and Art Deco motifs inform this drawing from floor tile to braid trim.*

PLATE 26

IMAGE SIX
Working Woman

VANITY FAIR

26. Proposal for a Vanity Fair *cover, ca. 1918. The glamorous nurse, with her sturdy Afghan Hound, is ready for work behind the front lines, though the young woman's illusions will be shattered by the reality of war. This theme of "society-girl-turned-Red-Cross-nurse" was popular with readers of* Vanity Fair.

IMAGE SEVEN
Female Fantasia

27. Presentation drawing, "Diana and the Centaurs," Paris, 1924, celebrates the New Woman as a modern goddess.

28. Costume design for Carl Hyson's dance partner, Vera Lennox, in "China Love" number, Midnight Follies, *London, 1922–1923.*

29. *Costume and small set designs, "Shady Gals" scene,* New Princes' Frivolities, *London, 1923.*

30. *Costume design for "Fan" number, Casino de Paris, Paris, ca. 1923–1924.*

31. *Costume design for Evelyn Laye,* Waltz Time, *1933, later featured in still (see p. 220).*

see p. 220

32. *Costume design for Dorothy Dickson, "Romany Love" scene,* Charivaria, *Liverpool, 1929.*

Drawing by Jon Whitcomb illustrating article "Your Ideal Girl," Good Housekeeping, *August 1953, that subsequently became the cover for Walt Reed's book* Fifty Great American Illustrators. *Photo courtesy of Illustration House, N.Y.C. Compare to Gordon Conway's drawing on p. 190.*

popular ideal as seen in traditionalist Jon Whitcomb's illustration for the story entitled "Your Ideal Girl," published in *Good Housekeeping* magazine. Whitcomb's young woman leans forward, gazing straight into the eyes of the viewer. She emanates pleasure and signals connection on a sensual level in an intimate spot; the background decoration suggests wallpaper design for a bedroom. Though much like Whitcomb's illustration in composition, Conway's drawing of a woman in a sun hat conveys a very different message.[20]

In contrast to Whitcomb's curves that evoke a physical and spontaneously instinctual presence, Conway's stylized and geometric lines convey a streamlined, understated, and poised manner that highlights the woman's consciously created élan. Reinforcing this contrast, the two settings send different signals by pre-senting one woman in an intimate, secluded interior, and the other woman on a beach with a sailboat in the distance. Conway's young woman also leans forward, but slightly to the right, not toward the observer. She too stares at the viewer, but the look is cautious, controlled, and informed. There is an emotional and psychological distance. Conway's female image calls out for connection, but not on a physical level; she invites another kind of communication. Gordon Conway's image is not Jon Whitcomb's message of curvaceous prettiness and calculated naive sexiness. Rather, it reflects direct intelligence, cool independence, and guarded individuality, essential characteristics in Conway's New Woman representations.

The images of Gordon Conway frequently appear as cosmopolitan and slim sophisticates in autobio-

Unpublished drawing, ca. 1936. This New Woman in a sun hat reflects a different attitude and look from that of Whitcomb's "Ideal Girl."

graphical renderings or as whimsical self-caricatures. Both types of silhouettes capture the artist's height, weight, shape, gesture, agility, demeanor, personality, style, and coloring—especially the red hair that became a trademark of her images as well as her own public persona. Seven images emerge from Conway's variegated cache of New Women (see pp. 196–222). That she believed herself to be one, or all, of these seven images is clear.

Model in Your Mirror

While World War I raged, New York clients commissioned an increasing number of Conway's New Women for their advertisements, magazine illustrations, and stage work. Building on experience in a wide variety of commercial art jobs executed before the United States entered the fighting, Conway produced an original and distinctive style by 1917. She created a special female character for which she was known across the country.[21] This character became one of America's dream girls. Thus the images evolving from her budding career provided a prototype for the increasing number of women in public life due to war work.[22] *Vanity Fair* published its first cover by Gordon Conway in the January 1918 issue: a sprightly red-haired gal in a snow storm signals Valentine greetings to a military sweetheart with a pair of semaphore

JANUARY 1918   CONDÉ NAST, Publisher   PRICE 25 CTS.

Cover for Vanity Fair, *January 1918. Gordon Conway's first cover resembles her line drawing parodies for the magazine in the late teens. This red-haired lass introduces "Zina," Conway's public persona and alter ego seen on pages 196–199.*

flags displaying big red hearts. This lighthearted touch and carefree attitude toward war themes may be surprising to a contemporary audience familiar with the death and devastation in France. However, during World War I a naive, detached, and romantic posture predominated in much of American culture. Many soldiers and war volunteers enjoyed reading magazines that treated war activities in a humorous, ironic, and sophisticated manner. Even the irreverent *Vanity Fair* discovered a wide public appeal for its gentle mockery. Indeed, the Condé Nast publications had determined an editorial policy with dual themes: the magazines would be patriotic and fashionable at the same time.[23]

Letters Gordon Conway received from a friend fighting in France were a testament to this public approval. A lonely young lieutenant with the American Expeditionary Forces who survived the fighting at the front wrote from a battlefield twenty miles from Verdun. He wrote, "Today when I ran across this cover in the lonesomeist [*sic*] part of this country, I felt as though I'd wandered into an old home meeting. . . .

Do you draw all your girls with red hair and slim figures like this one?" He wondered if the model was "in your mirror"?[24]

The soldier wrote again to spoof a page of Conway's monthly parodies in *Vanity Fair,* explaining he had not had a chance to R.S.V.P. to the benefit she illustrated, because he had been out of the country and, incidentally, quite busy at the front. He found amusing her interpretation of New York debutantes aiding the war effort in "Isn't It Fun to Get Up a Benefit?" Hard working debutantes revealed an aspect of womanhood previously unknown. Conway's work expressed a teasing treatment of high society's pretensions associated with the war. Another satirical vignette, "The Bitter Truth about the War," included the subtitle "Dream-Shattering Sketches by Gordon Conway." The narrative sequence of line drawings features a young debutante's dream of romance and adventure that awaits her upon entrance into a war job. In another column the scenes are juxtaposed so as to destroy the girl's romantic illusions. The captions explain that the dreams are "the result of hot press-agenting. . . . This war is certainly rough on a young girl's innocent illusions. . . . [when] she is rudely awakened by Truth's unerring little alarm-clock."[25]

After the armistice Conway continued to pair the dream and illusion scenes for *Vanity Fair.* One notable offering, published in mid-1919, was "The New Freedom in Marriage: Sketches of New York Fashionable Life by Gordon Conway," in which marriage was labeled "the greatest lottery of them all." This series of vignettes lampoons the before-and-after experience of marriage, spotlighting four kinds of unsatisfactory husbands. Conway's special talent for delineating bodily movement to convey women's emotions is highlighted in this sequence. She portrays the unhappy wife as immobile and cowed, slumping over a baby

Drawing from "Isn't It Fun to Get Up a Benefit?"   *Proof page for "Dream-Shattering Sketches by Gordon Conway"*

The New Freedom in Marriage

Line drawings, proof pages, and tear sheets of Gordon Conway's monthly parody pages, Vanity Fair, *January 1918–August 1919. See contrasting images of women which often are featured in a "before and after" theme—when illusion and reality collide.*

MADAME LA VIE

Drawn by Gordon Conway

Tear sheet of "Madame La Vie," The Tatler, *November 3, 1926. Note the removal of a youthful and beautiful face mask on this red-haired woman—a gesture that frightens her male suitor.*

bed. In sharp contrast, the recent ex-wife moves with agility and abandon: she stretches and reaches because the world is at those outstretched fingertips. This New Woman persona, according to the caption, is "fed up and disillusioned. . . . she has hung out the red flag . . . bobbed her hair, and invested in a litter of bombs. . . . Her cry now is 'Down with Husbands . . . Down with marriage—up with the flag of freedom.'"[26]

Gordon Conway's awareness of this power to create dreams and fantasies through style, advertising, and marketing was to propel her career upward. She understood the difference between the "Dream-Shattering Sketches" and the art that inspired dreams.[27] Conway possessed a dual talent for producing persuasive cultural images that were in demand and for promoting them. Both abilities would bring two decades of in-

Self-caricature of Gordon Conway, 1920, printed in selected U.S. and Continental newspapers, 1920–1924. Conway's sense of humor triumphs over the pain of "Madame La Vie."

and fantasies for women on page, stage, and screen. She could create "the good life à la mode." She could not, however, prevent illness and stress resulting from an uncompromising work load that forced her into early retirement. Conway's art does not reveal these scenes from real life, nor does the publicity these images and lifestyle attracted. Nevertheless, one image lifts the veil from what appeared to be an enviable fun-filled and glamorous existence. In the November 3, 1926, issue of the *Tatler* was an illustration that was uncharacteristic for both Conway and the magazine. "Madame La Vie" symbolizes the pain and agony Gordon Conway encountered as an overworked commercial graphic artist and costume designer, a female professional struggling to keep pace, a divorcée supporting herself and her mother, and a sensitive woman. This image in the *Tatler* features the usual tall, slim, and smartly clad figure with bright red hair. The red hair, however, encircles a mask—a mask of a pretty young face that the woman jerks from her head, exposing a wrinkled and withered face beneath. She offers the mask to a young man, who cowers in fear and disbelief as he beholds the distorted face before him. The man's terror arises from the unacceptability of age and the fear of ugliness. He expresses the often unspoken dread of a female form other than a culturally programmed image of youth and beauty. For good or for bad, popular culture honors certain images and ideals of feminine beauty. Gordon Conway knew this, both as an artist and as a woman.

Another image of Gordon Conway, however, emerges to challenge this bitter scene when a certain redhead dashes from the wings just in time to rescue the distraught "Madame La Vie." The feisty and fun-loving carrot-topped girl—a caricature of Gordon "as seen by herself"—counterbalances the theme of rejec-

ternational fame to this one-woman dream factory in New York, Paris, and London. The acclaim, however, would be bittersweet.

Gordon Conway paid a price for success. Though she herself was a New Woman among New Women friends and colleagues, creating images of the New Woman that were popular with New Woman consumers, there were circumstances in life she could not control with a sketching pen. She could master dreams

tion and pain in the image of the unmasked woman. The victorious self-caricature is symbolic in more than a visual sense because Gordon's sense of humor bolstered the artist during her travails. In the early 1920s, during an interview in her Paris studio, Gordon Conway told the *New York Herald* journalist that this figure was the way she thought of herself.[28] And it was. Since childhood Gordon Conway had signed letters, funny scribblings, and Christmas cards with the tousled copper-curled lass. The signature figure became a longtime companion and a kind of alter ego for the artist. This silhouette differs little from the self-anointed persona consciously constructed out of the artist's wry wit for publicity purposes during the

teens and early 1920s. The unpublished character of "Zina" was born about the same time that the publicity persona appeared in print. These red-haired relatives mount a festive family reunion in the image section entitled "Zina and Her Cousins."

This madcap miss captures Gordon "as seen by herself." The young woman joins hands at center stage with the chic models of the artist's three sophisticated ladies to celebrate seven images of the New Woman in the artwork of Gordon Conway: Zina and Her Cousins, New Body, New Energy, Night Owl, Consuming Woman, Working Woman, and Female Fantasia.

ZINA AND HER COUSINS
Unconventional and Uninhibited Hilarity

Unpublished autobiographical drawings of Gordon Conway's paper-thin Zinas enliven the pages that follow with whimsical and witty images from the New Woman ethos. Zina could be a female parallel to Charlie Chaplin's comic tramp with her crumpled stovepipe hat, catawampus vest, raggedy sleeves, and straggly hair. These comic redheaded svelte figures tease and taunt, amuse and alarm. Jaunty beanpole girls grin at the poetic ironies of Conway's friend Dorothy Parker. They giggle at shady jobs once taboo in polite society and laugh out loud at their own outrageous antics and practical jokes.

Joining Zina—and created under the tutelage of editor Frank Crowninshield—are Conway's caricatures (e.g., p. 194) and little satires that dare to ridicule the artist's own world, similar to the line drawings of "Fish" and Ethel Plummer. The images capture the fun-loving amateur comediennes like Conway herself along with World War I debutante-volunteers in parodied poses on the pages of *Vanity Fair*. This newly accepted sense of humor topples the taut and tight-lipped "lady" of the "cult of true womanhood" inherited from the nineteenth century and gives permission for the New Woman to be funny.[1]

Presentation drawing, ca. 1920. In this before and after scene, a Zina cousin confronts "Prohibition" in the snow during the dark of night.

Proposal for Vanity Fair, *ca. 1918, featuring a Zina cousin—a red-haired lass distributing flags of the Allies to a soldier.*

Presentation drawing or magazine proposal, ca. 1920–1922. This redhead attracts a foursome of elegant beaus for a night on the town.

Magazine proposal, ca. 1916–1920. This saucy cousin enlists help from an attentive male as she gathers holly for the Christmas season.

Presentation drawing or magazine proposal, ca. 1920–1922. This redhead imp is a piper to the geese.

Presentation drawings, London and Paris, 1921. The slouched and bruised redhead, entitled "Love," was once one of Zina's fun-loving and carefree cousins. Another cousin reacts to this relative's abuse by experimenting with opium, while Zina, as a seductress, lies in wait with a dagger to take revenge on her cousin's abuser.

NEW BODY
Lithe, Limber, and Unconstrained

The sheer joy of movement soars with images of Gordon Conway's friends—the high-kicking Dorothy Dickson and the twirling Jessie Matthews, stage and film favorites who conveyed New Woman aspirations. Unlike their draped, bound, and weighted predecessors, these female visions experience a new freedom in their bodies. Ballroom dancing, sports, driving, and travel, previously frowned upon as unhealthy and immoral, now reign supreme, banishing submissive and static poses of the hourglass torso and corset set. Irene Castle facsimiles glide down Fifth Avenue and through the West End to the Place Vendôme. They waltz on the public stage, sunbathe on the Riviera, climb the Alps, and cross nations and oceans on liners and trains. With an acceptance of exposed skin and a naive sexiness, the New Body adds another dimension to the revolution in healthy and aesthetic dress. Brief bands of cloth reveal curves and bare female parts, allowing the body to move and provoke. Allure becomes the New Body.

See also Plates 1–5 (following page 12).

Costume design for Jessie Matthews in the "Three Wishes" scene in The Good Companions, *1933, later featured in film stills of Matthews with John Gielgud in his first film role. In a letter, Jessie Matthews's biographer Michael Thornton recalled that this "amazing stage dress . . . became her all-time favourite." Matthews remembered the "dazzling sequinned neckline, and cloud upon cloud of floating, transparent chiffon, covered in . . . ostrich feathers. For a dancer, it was a dream of a dress. When I left the piano and began to dance, the dress danced too, almost independently, giving the illusion that I was floating through the air. I think Gordon told me that it cost £500 to make, which was a phenomenal sum for one dress in 1932." Matthews long had thought that Ginger Rogers's famous dress—created three years after* The Good Companions *for her legendary dance scene with Fred Astaire in* Top Hat—*had been based on this Conway gown. Matthews exclaimed: "At the time I was angry for Gordon that her concept was copied without credit, but it proves what a great talent she was that even Hollywood borrowed her ideas." (Quotes from Michael Thornton's letter to author, August 8, 1996.)*

Clown costume design for the Tiller Girls, renamed the Sunny Girls, for the London stage production of Sunny, *1926.*

Drawing for The Tatler, *November 6, 1929. After skiing and hiking in the snow, these New Women pause for a smoke.*

Cover for Eve, *August 8, 1928. The New Woman in Gordon Conway's signature polka-dot-patterned sundress takes a pause in a punt on the River Cam. She has the self-assurance to float alone and turn her back on prying eyes.*

Cover for The Bystander, *August 19, 1931. These athletic New Women revel in strenuous water games.*

Costume design for and film still of Charlotte Greenwood,
Orders Is Orders, *1933. She performs her signature high kick*
with a graceful effect made possible by Gordon Conway's bias-
cut chiffon skirt.

(Top left and bottom) Costume design for and film still of Anne Grey, Just Smith, *1933. She displays a newly accepted nude look for middle-class female consumers.*

(Top right) Possible proposal for The Tatler, *ca. 1936. This New Woman dons a backless gown with a décolletage neckline that shocked the more traditionally dressed women of the era.*

NEW ENERGY
Vitality, Verve, and Velocity

Stepping up the pace of the New Body, the New Energy image celebrates New Year's Eve every night. Streamlined bodies speeding in zigzag acceleration and racing rhythms evoke Art Moderne themes. Jazz Age New Women parade and prance in mass anonymity, popping out of Conway's vast grown-up playground of vivid reds, yellows, greens, and blues. In restless, reckless, and relentless rebellion, these images collide with adult toys: champagne bottles, confetti, cigarettes, dice, serpentine, top hats, playing cards, drums, stars, coins, and horns. As the carefree 1920s crash into the somber 1930s, the Jazz Lint series and the *Wonder Bar* set and costume images give vent to the agitated activity and quickened tempo of the post–World War I era. These escapades testify to a frantic and frenetic spiral of work and play in defiance of time, age, and ennui.

See also Plates 6–10 (following page 12).

(Top) Tear sheet, The Tatler, *June 20, 1928. Jazz Age dance-mad flappers cavort in cabarets till dawn.*

Proposal for set design, Wonder Bar, *London, 1930.*

Presentation drawing or magazine proposal, ca. 1920–1924. A Zina-like figure speeds the pace of daily life, reminiscent of Gordon Conway's own urgent trips to airmail designs across the English Channel.

Cover for Eve, *September 28, 1927. These samba twins capture Latin rhythms that energize dance routines on stage and screen.*

NIGHT OWL
Café Society, Savoir Faire, and Savoir Vivre

The fourth image in Conway's drawings is a New Woman who not only goes out alone, but stays to the wee hours dining and dancing with the likes of Gordon Conway, a New Woman extraordinaire whose life à la mode rivals the era's bon vivants such as Gerald Murphy and his wife Sara or the more daring characters out of F. Scott Fitzgerald's novels. Both Conway and the images grace the threshold of a new social class—café society, the self-claimed invention of Condé Nast, ripe for the pages of glossy magazines. These elegant ladies of "after 5:00" dress for dinner and dancing—white tie or black. The New Women flock to theater openings, catch the final cabaret number, and dance the tango and the Black Bottom till dawn. Unlike their sheltered turn-of-the-century sisters in drab mauve, the unchaperoned and brightly decorated doyennes of Paris fashion ignore warnings of religious tracts and moral caveats about drinking, smoking, and carousing. This all-night party girl defies the old adage that the early bird gets the worm; she crawls into bed at dawn, sleeps through the day, and comes out after dark. This New Woman makes diary entries like Gordon Conway herself: "To bed at 6:00 A.M." and "Up at 2:00 P.M."[1]

See also Plates 11–16 (following page 12).

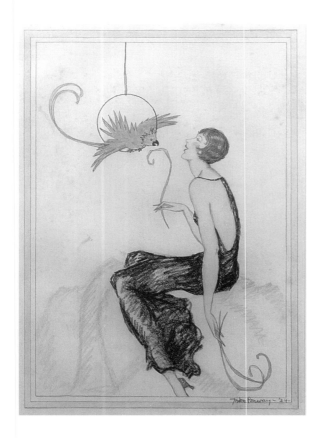

(Opposite, left) Drawing (Paris, 1924) was published in La Donna, *ca. 1924–1926. This New Woman talks to a pet bird about her escapades of the night.*

(Opposite, right) Cover for The Boulevardier, *Paris, July, 1927. New Women and New Men celebrate late night cocktails and dining.*

(This page) Costume for a late evening at home designed for Wendy Barrie, It's a Boy, *1933, that later accented a striking Art Deco set in a film still.*

CONSUMING WOMAN
The Moneyed Market Maker

This New Woman consumes other things than the Night Owl's pleasures and entertainment. She often keeps regular hours and rises at dawn searching for bargains in the local papers—bargains that may be meant for a husband and child as well as herself. She is identified as a customer and a client. This New Woman pays her bills. An image in advertising and in the real world, this woman possesses a newfound power that offers freedom and a certain kind of respect. The more this woman buys, the more goods are manufactured for her consumption and the more services are created to meet her needs. This woman's elevation to consumer queen rivals Conway's own purchasing record. The advertisements featuring the products she consumes give insight into a fashionable world of credit. Whether she is the customer who goes to fittings or the seamstress who does the fittings, the new Consuming Woman tries out the new layaway plan that serves one and all.

Rhetoric from a 1920 advertisement paired with Conway's silhouettes provides a stage for these actresses in the act of trade. The wording in one poster by Conway highlights this landmark appeal to female customers: "'Economy no more means saving money than it means spending money. It means spending or saving to the best advantage,' said Ruskin."[1] Trade could fulfill every wish, every fantasy. What trade cannot provide will be made up in promises. For this New Woman, dreams of things glow on the horizon.

See also Plates 17–25 (following page 188).

Advertisement for Ariel, New York City, ca. 1916–1918, shows the influence of the Art Nouveau aesthetic on Gordon Conway's early work. This New Woman lounges in her lingerie on public pages for all eyes to see.

There is satisfaction in knowing that on certain dates interest is coming to you from well-chosen investment securities. Let us discuss your investment needs with you and suggest suitable securities.

The National City Company
514 Fifth Avenue *at* 43rd Street

One of a series of twenty advertising posters and window display cards for National City Company, New York City, 1919–1920. These women take care of their own business, including loans and stock market investments.

Poster for Lawson stove, Paris, 1921. Gordon Conway's Lawson advertisements were commissioned by Blake Ozias when he worked briefly for the company in Paris.

Cover for The Bystander, *October 28, 1931, captures a sense of active women in the work force, both as busy employees and as avid consumers.*

WORKING WOMAN
The New Professionals and the Volunteers

While the Consuming Woman stands in front of the department store counter, the Working Woman stands behind the counter. The consuming New Woman with money to spend shares much the same image as the Working Woman who earns her keep. The working professional, however, need not ask permission of the male breadwinner in the household. Choices, especially in dress, are her own. Conway once commented that tight skirts serve women of leisure in staged and decorative poses, but that fuller skirts are needed for the employed female. The artist understands the need for comfort in movement, for she is a ten-hour-a-day professional. Conway's specialty—"Nine to Nine" clothes—seems commonplace today but in the 1920s it was a revolutionary concept in women's dress.

Apparel for active volunteers is also featured in Conway's drawings—especially that of the World War I nurse. The demand for appropriate clothing comes from women with a range of charitable duties from hospital auxiliary chores to social work in the city slums to museum clerical jobs. The shift in roles for this New Woman reflects the rise of volunteer service in America and Western Europe accelerated by the Great War.

See also Plate 26 (following page 188).

The Bright Side of the War
Sketches by Gordon Conway

Thrills in the Life of a Red Cross Nurse

Sketches of working women volunteers during World War I in New York. These society women were spoofed in Gordon Conway's parody pages in Vanity Fair, *January 1918–August 1919.*

From Conway's parody page in the September 1918 Vanity Fair: *"A Woman-Hater's Day: Showing That It's a Woman's World, After All": "This thing of women's filling men's positions has really ceased to be a joke. . . . since all the jobs that used to belong exclusively to men are being filled by women. . . . It is particularly rough on the woman-hater. . . . the very doorman is a woman. . . . This is the ultimate straw—the woman bar-tender."*

Drawing for The Tatler, *March 13, 1929. Gordon Conway's images, such as this tailored suit, appealed to working women who aspired to a stylish, understated look to their clothes, which also is featured in the tailored dress for Edna Best in* There's Always Juliet.

Costume design for Edna Best, There's Always Juliet, *with stage productions in both London and New York, 1931.*

Note the New Women images in drawings and film stills of working-women-heroines featured in British films dressed by Gordon Conway, 1931–1933 (pages 214–218):

Drawings and stills from Love on Wheels, *1932 (shot on location at Selfridge's department store): clerk Leonora Corbett with promoter Jack Hulbert; the professional models in the store's sales promotion scheme perform in vignettes entitled "Artist Model" and "Rain."*

Images of Esther Ralston playing a working woman who is a professional actress in Rome Express, *1932.*

Still of Jessie Matthews in There Goes the Bride, *1932, in which she influenced thousands of British working women through sewing patterns and mass media coverage on how to achieve an individual and tailored look by dressing in this practical and chic four-piece ensemble. In a 1965 interview with biographer Michael Thornton, Matthews explained that during the filming "I was very unsure of myself. . . . If it hadn't been for darling Gordon Conway, I don't know how I would have got through it all. . . . she had designed a stunning and very French-looking outfit for my running away. . . . the coat, the day dress had a cut-away jacket with a very clever design with large buttons at the neck and waist." Matthews confessed her own "absolute ignorance about clothes and fashion. Gordon Conway was in fact years ahead of her time as a designer. . . . she put me on to the screen in my first important film looking a pert and authentic young French gamine." (Quotes from Michael Thornton's letter to author, August 8, 1996.)*

Images of Jessie Matthews in The Good Companions, *1933, in which she plays a working woman member of a "concert party."*

Two clusters of images of Jessie Matthews in Friday the Thirteenth, *1933, in which she plays a hard-working chorus girl, opposite Ralph Richardson. Jessie Matthews told Michael Thornton in an interview that "I loved Gordon's designs for me. . . . Gordon had the most important gift a designer can possess: the ability to express a person's essential character and personality through their clothes. . . . [such as] the chorus girl costume for Millie: the tiny skull hat with its enormous peacock-tail halo, which so cleverly accentuated my large eyes, and the full back skirt with no front to show off my other principal asset, my legs." (Quote from Michael Thornton's letter to author, August 8, 1996.)*

Still of Heather Thatcher, who plays a struggling woman novelist, whose male publisher insists she use a male pseudonym, It's a Boy, *1933.*

Still of Constance Cummings, who plays an executive secretary in Channel Crossing, *1933.*

Still of Charlotte Greenwood, who plays a woman film director in Orders Is Orders, *1933.*

Still of nurse Madeleine Carroll with Herbert Marshall, I Was a Spy, *1933.*

Still of Cicely Courtneidge, who plays an aggressive journalist in Falling for You, *1933.*

Still of office girl Renate Müller, Sunshine Susie, *1931 (note the gender "hazards" of being an office girl).*

FEMALE FANTASIA
Dreams, Illusions, and Imaginings

"Female Fantasia" is a composite of the six preceding images that represent the dreams of the New Woman. This final New Woman declares the freedom to dream, the freedom to fantasize. The consumer messages stir her imagination. She openly wishes for "things" beyond her pocketbook. She buys not only clothes and cars but also houses, and she dreams of castles in Spain, chateaux on the Loire, and even real estate in Morocco. Images of health, youth, romance, and beauty pervade her daily musings. Imagined wealth and power radiate from magazine pages and movie screens, fueling female fantasies. The hopes ushered in with the modern era unfold hidden desires. Expectations soar when possibilities abound.

Fantasy bridges the material world with the intangible and the imaginary, with unknown vistas, with flights into imagined lands. The images of the New Woman find new roles, varied beings, and unbridled dimensions. With new perspectives from Freud and Jung, repression seems to disappear. Women dare to fantasize, to play with forbidden personae, and to vicariously live other lives. From Gordon Conway's tableaux in print, stage, and film designs, these images permit women to assume roles as princesses and proletarians, cowgirls and Chinese handmaidens, shooting stars and flower pots, gypsies and ballerinas, hats and fans, swans, nudes, and nymphs. This final image picks up threads from the previous six and is reflected in the dreams of a modern female utopia with futuristic costumes appearing in *High Treason* (1929).

See also Plates 27–32 (following page 188).

Presentation drawing, Paris, ca. 1922–1924. Gordon Conway's New Women are fascinated by the nude female figure.

Costume design for "When" scene, Midnight Follies, *Club Daunou, Paris, 1924.*

Film still of scene from Waltz Time. *See Plate 31 for costume design for Evelyn Laye.*

(Top left) Costume design for Evelyn Laye, in Waltz Time, *1933, later featured in a film still.*

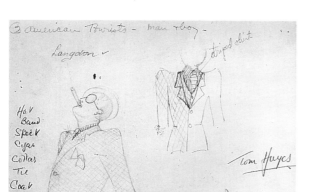

Film still of Esther Ralston with Basil Rathbone, After the Ball, *1932.*

(*Top left*) *Costume designs for* Britannia of Billingsgate, *1933, later featured in a film still.*

Film costume design for Dorothy Hyson, Cicely Courtneidge, and Miss Sempsi, Soldiers of the King, *1933.*

Program cover and promotional graphics for New Princes' Frivolities, *London, 1925.*

Headdress design for chorus girls, Aunt Sally, *1933.*

CONCLUSION
A Streamlined Woman in a Mechanized World

These seven images proclaim not only change for women but hope through a new consumer community. Dreams of a better world abound. That hope reflects the same optimism inherent in the early century's utopian social theories and in modern design itself. From Manhattan to Milan, and from the Bauhaus to Brussels and Buenos Aires, the dreamer-designers joined scientists and technocrats in prophesying a new era and dreaming of an ideal civilization for all. From a period advertisement for synthetic fabric, a typical utopian attitude leaps out at today's skeptical and cynical world: "Where to tomorrow? . . . To a thousand untouched shores. To a land of tomorrow where rain won't wet your clothes . . . where life is easier, happier, and more complete in ways that can't be dreamed of today."[1]

Gordon Conway's own optimistic predictions made headlines in 1929. With no anticipation of the worldwide Depression only a few months away and the mechanized and human horrors of World War II to come, Conway, the prophet, buoyantly shared her dreams. In a 1929 newspaper interview focusing on her futuristic costume designs for the British science fiction film *High Treason,* the designer proclaims a "startling fashion forecast." Bold print emblazons, "What the World Is Coming To: Women in Plus Fours and Rain-Proof Dresses." (Conway was convinced that the comfortable, sporty knickerbockers, made famous on the golf course by the future Duke of Windsor in the 1920s, should be available for active and athletic females. Women also deserved the extra four inches of fabric that added fullness and ease to these breeches—then popular as men's informal daywear.) In the article Conway assures the reader that "women will adopt an eminently practical garb of masculine plus fours for office work, or the type of overalls men wear in factories." She predicted that these loose and easy garments would be made from modern synthetic fabrics. With boundless confidence the designer concludes, "After all . . . we shall live in a mechanised [*sic*] world." The film reinforces the belief that the machine is an answer to humanity's concerns and proclaims that working women should play a key role in achieving world peace.[2]

Until 1956 Gordon Conway survived in an increasingly mechanized world, though not in the sleek, streamlined cities of *High Treason* nor a peaceful world nor a New Woman–promised female utopia. Yet, during Conway's problems with malignancy and money, the artist never lost her capacity for hope. True to that outlook, her images remain redolent with rosy visions, innocent abandon, and cheerful chic. Her images were not a bad inheritance to will to today's terrorist-torn and environmentally challenged world.

Images, dreams, and fantasies imbue the Art Moderne visions in the artwork of Gordon Conway. To answer the World War I soldier's 1918 query—Gordon Conway's model *was* in her mirror. The seven images seined from her drawings highlight major shifts in female roles and signal the multifarious sides of the artist herself—the quintessential New Woman of the early twentieth century.

Drawing and six film stills for High Treason, *1929 (pages 224–226). Note Gordon Conway's costume designs for Benita Hume and the female cast in stunning futuristic attire in this concluding collage of New Women.*

CATALOGUE RAISONNÉ

A Reference Guide to the Artwork and Career of Gordon Conway

Abbreviations Used

ad.	advertising
b&w	black and white image
ed.	editorial
illus.	illustration

FILM LIST ONLY

1   Costume design, shopping, supervision of fittings, wardrobe budget and management.

2   Casting of minor players, still-photography consultation, publicity or public-relations production duties.

3   Set design or properties and art production design duties.

*   Films viewed once or more by the author.

**   Author viewed trailer only.

Notes:

The author reviewed stills from all films in the list. Films are in black and white.

The "Conway Date" is Gordon Conway's working date, which is usually earlier than the publication date or film release date.

Published Work by Gordon Conway

PUBLICATION / BUSINESS / CLIENT	CONWAY DATE	LOCATION	CONWAY WORK
Brentano's bookstore	1915	NYC	drawings for menu & place cards
Heyworth Campbell, art director, *Vogue* & *Vanity Fair*	1915–1920	NYC	b&w illus.-card, silhouettes, line drawings, b&w illus. (ed. and ad.), color covers
Stormberg advertising service	1916	NYC	sketches
Bobbs-Merrill Co.	1916	NYC	sketches
Vanity Fair	1916	NYC	line drawing (ed.)
Vogue	1916	NYC	silhouettes, line drawings (ed.)
Harper's Bazar [sic]	1916–1917	NYC	drawings (ed.)
Malcolm Strauss advertising service	1916–1917	NYC & USA	silhouettes, line drawings, b&w illus. (ad.)
Terrill school publications	1916–1917	Dallas	b&w illus. (ed.)
Ariel undergarments	1916–1918	NYC & USA	color illus. (ad.)
Advertising department of *Vogue* & *Vanity Fair*	1916–1920	NYC	silhouettes, line drawings, b&w illus. (ad.)
Vanity Fair	1917	NYC	silhouettes, line drawings, b&w illus. (ed.)
Allied Charity Ball	1917	Dallas	b&w illus. for program (donation)
Vogue	1917	NYC	silhouettes, line drawings, b&w illus. (ed.)

PUBLICATION / BUSINESS / CLIENT	CONWAY DATE	LOCATION	CONWAY WORK
Neiman-Marcus	1917	Dallas	b&w illus. (ad.)
Dallas Times Herald	1917	Dallas	b&w illus. (ad.)
Dallas Morning News	1917	Dallas	b&w illus. (ad.)
Burgher Real Estate	1917	Dallas	b&w illus. (ad.)
Franklin Motor Car	1917	Dallas & USA	color illus. (ad.), b&w illus. (ad.)
French Wounded Emergency Fund	1917	Dallas	color poster (donation)
Manhattanville Day & Night Nursery	1917	NYC	silhouettes (donation)
Russek's	1917	NYC	b&w illus. (ad.)
Client unknown	c. 1917	NYC	Red Cross color poster
New York Times	1917–1919	NYC	silhouettes, line drawings, b&w illus. (ed.)
Harper's Bazar [sic]	1917–1919	NYC	silhouettes, line drawings, b&w illus. (ed.)
Evening Mail	1918	NYC	line drawing (ed.)
Babies' Ward of the Post Graduate Hospital	1918	NYC	silhouettes (donation)
Vanity Fair	1918	NYC	two color covers & color cover collaboration with "Fish"
Vanity Fair	1918	NYC	b&w illus. (ed.)

PUBLICATION / BUSINESS / CLIENT	CONWAY DATE	LOCATION	CONWAY WORK
Tribune	1918	NYC	Dorothy Dickson sketch (ed.)
Cammeyer Shoes	1918	NYC & USA	b&w illus. (ad.)
Judge	1918–1919	NYC	page: silhouettes (ed.)
Vanity Fair	1918–1919	NYC	monthly pages: line drawing-parodies (ed.)
D. Appleton & Co. / *Piggie* by Eleanor Gates	1919	NYC & USA	silhouettes for book (ed.)
Theatre	1919	NYC	page: b&w illus. (ed.), page: silhouettes (ed.)
The National City Co.	1919–1920	NYC & USA	silhouettes for twenty window cards and posters (ad.)
Delage auto co. / Blake Ozias	1919–1920	NYC & USA	color illus. (ad.)
Town & Country	1920	NYC & USA	color illus. (ad.)
Spur	1920	NYC & USA	color illus. (ad.)
Country Life	1920	NYC	color illus. (ad.)
Vogue	1920	NYC	b&w illus. (ed.)
Metropolitan	1920	NYC	silhouettes (ad.)

PUBLICATION / BUSINESS / CLIENT	CONWAY DATE	LOCATION	CONWAY WORK
Harper's Bazar [sic]	1920	NYC	line drawings (ed. and ad.), b&w illustration series (ed.)
La France	1920	NYC	b&w illus. (ed. and ad.)
Hallmark watches	1920	NYC & USA	silhouettes (ad.)
Barron G. Collier Co.	1920	NYC	color car-card
George H. Doran Co.	1920	NYC	silhouettes (ad.)
YWCA / The Woman's Press	1920	NYC	silhouette (ed.)
The Houston Chronicle	1920	Houston & Texas	b&w illus. (ed.)
R. R. Bowker Co. / The Book Shelf for Boys and Girls	1920–1921	NYC	silhouettes (ed.)
Bubble Books	1920–1921	NYC	silhouettes (ed.)
Huyler's chocolates	1920–1921	NYC & USA	silhouettes (ad.)
Arts & Decoration / Blake Ozias	1921	NYC	b&w illus. (ed.)
Eve: The Lady's Pictorial	1921	London	sketch
The Sketch	1921	London	b&w illus. from poster of Dorothy Dickson
Lawson stove manufacturer	1921–1924	Paris & Europe	color posters, b&w illus. (ad.)

PUBLICATION / BUSINESS / CLIENT	CONWAY DATE	LOCATION	CONWAY WORK
Eve	1921–1924	London	odd (irregular) pages, b&w illus. (ed. and ad.)
Barker's-Loomis poster competition	1922	London	poster
National Assoc. of Book Publishers / The National City Co.	1922–1923	NYC & USA	silhouette for poster
The National City Co.	1923	NYC	silhouettes (ad.)
The Tatler	1923	London	page: color illus. (ed.)
Eve	1923	London	odd (irregular) pages, color illus. (ed.)
The Tatler	1923–1925	London	odd (irregular) pages, b&w illus. (ed. and ad.)
The Tatler	1923–1929	London	odd (irregular) pages, color illus. (ed.)
Eve	1923–1929	London	odd (irregular) pages, color illus. (ed.)
Chicago Tribune / Wood Kahler	1924	Paris	b&w illus. (ed.)
The Graphic	1924	London	cover
New York Herald	1924	Paris	b&w illus. (ed.)
L'Equipment Automobile: Le Chic Français de l'Automobile / Dura Auto Co.	1924	Paris	color cover

PUBLICATION / BUSINESS / CLIENT	CONWAY DATE	LOCATION	CONWAY WORK
Dura Auto Co. / Blake Ozias	1924–1925	Paris & Europe	color posters
La Donna	1924–1926	Milan	monthly pages: color illus. (ed. and ad.), monthly pages: b&w illus. (ed. and ad.)
Red Cross	1925	Paris	color poster
Paris Times	1925	Paris	b&w illus. (ed.)
Eve	1925	London	b&w illus. (ed. and ad.)
Eve	1925–1929	London	weekly pages: b&w illus. (ed. and ad.)
The Tatler	1925–1929	London	monthly pages: color illus. (ed. and ad.)
The Tatler	1925–1930	London	weekly pages: b&w illus. (ed. and ad.)
The New Yorker	1926	NYC	b&w illus.
The Tatler	1926	London	page: color illus. (ed.)
Wood Kahler	1927	Palm Beach, Fla.	newspaper illus. (ed.)
La Saison de Cannes	1927	Cannes	page: line drawing-parodies (ed.)
The Ambassadeurs	1927	Cannes	illus. (ad.)

PUBLICATION / BUSINESS / CLIENT	CONWAY DATE	LOCATION	CONWAY WORK
The Boulevardier	1927	Paris	color cover
Eve	1927–1929	London	odd (irregular) weekly color covers
Eve	1927–1929	London	color covers
Picture Show	1928	London	b&w photos of costumes for *God's Clay* (ed.)
Kinematograph Weekly / Warner Bros.	1928	London	b&w illus. of costumes for *Sir or Madam* (ed.)
Mr. Lawson-Johnston	1928	London	posters
Harrods Ltd. catalogue / supplement in *The Tatler*	1928	London	color illus., b&w illus. (ad.)
Harrods Ltd. advertising dept.	1928–1929	London	line drawings, b&w illus. (ad.)
Burt Lytel advertising	1928–1931	London	ad.
Bioscope British Film Number (1929)	1929	London	b&w illus. of costumes for *The Return of the Rat* (ed.)
The Film Weekly	1929	London	b&w illus. of costume for *The Return of the Rat* (ed.)
Britannia and Eve	1929–1930	London	pages color illus. (ed.)
Harrods Ltd.	1929–1930	London	b&w illus. (ad.)
Selfridges	1929–1930	London	b&w illus. (ad.)
Debenham and Freebody	1929–1930	London	b&w illus. (ad.)

PUBLICATION / BUSINESS / CLIENT	CONWAY DATE	LOCATION	CONWAY WORK
Dickins and Jones	1929–1930	London	b&w illus. (ad.)
Marshall and Snellgrove	1929–1930	London	b&w illus. (ad.)
Swan & Edgar furs	1929–1930	London	b&w illus. (ad.)
Gorringes	1929–1930	London	b&w illus. (ad.)
Gouch hats	1929–1930	London	b&w illus. (ad.)
The Tatler	1929–1930	London	weekly pages: color illus. (ed.)
Merivale Press	1930	London	poster
The Sketch / Black & White Scotch Whiskey	1931	London	color illus. (ad.)
The Bystander	1931	London	color covers, color illus. (ad.)
Program for *Daily Mail Ideal Home Exhibition and Fashion Pageant*	1934	London	b&w illus. (ed.)
Melford Gowns	1935	London	posters
Sterling boat motor co.	1936	NYC	color illus. (ad.)
New York American	1936	NYC & USA	color cartoon
Riding Club of East Hampton / Bobbie Appleton	1936	Long Island, N.Y.	color illus., poster
The Spur	1953	Fredericksburg, Va.	b&w cover

PUBLICATION	PUBLICATION DATE	LOCATION	CONWAY WORK
Costume Design in the Movies	1976, 1991	UK & USA	b&w illus. for *The Return of the Rat* (ed.)
Gordon Conway exhibition catalogue entitled *That Red Head Gal: Fashions and Designs of Gordon Conway, 1916–1936*; accompanying gallery guide and poster with same title*	1980	Washington, D. C., & USA	color cover, color illus., b&w illus. (ed.)
Horizon	1980	USA	color illus., b&w illus. (ed.)
Modern Maturity	1981	USA	color cover, color illus., b&w illus. (ed.)
Alfred A. Knopf book jacket for *Kay Wayfaring in "Avenged"*	1984	NYC & USA	color cover
Gordon Conway exhibition brochure entitled *Red, Hot and Southern: The International Fashions and Designs of Gordon Conway, 1916–1936**	1990	Fredericksburg, Va.	color cover, color illus., b&w illus. (ed.)
Gordon Conway biography in *The New Handbook of Texas*	1996	Austin, Tex.	b&w illus. (ed.)

*Color and b&w illus. (ed. and ad.) also appeared in accompanying feature articles and advertisements in various newspapers and magazines.

Theater/Cabaret Work by Gordon Conway

PRODUCTION / PERFORMER / CLIENT	CONWAY DATE	THEATER / CABARET	WORK
Basil Durant	1916	Hotel Plaza Grill / NYC	silhouettes
Basil Durant & Margaret Hawkesworth / exhibition dancing	1916	NYC: Century Grove Roof Garden, Paradise, Palace Vaudeville	silhouettes for programs, menu card, wine list
Margaret Hawkesworth	1916	Paradise / NYC	silhouette, menu cover
Polynesian Princess	1917	Little Theater / Opera House / Dallas	player, program cover, sketches (ed. and ad.)
Behind a Watteau Picture	1917	Greenwich Village / NYC	silhouette (ed.)
Words and Music	1917	Fulton / NYC	total design concept
Dorothy Dickson & Carl Hyson / exhibition dancing	1917–1918	Biltmore Roof / NYC	sketches
Tiger Rose / Lenore Ulrich	1917–1918	Lyceum / NYC	poster, sketches
Maurice	1917–1920	NYC	costume sketches
Keep It to Yourself	1918	39th Street / NYC	sketches
The Maid of France	1918	Greenwich Village / NYC	silhouette (ed.)
A Marriage of Convenience / Henry Miller & Billie Burke	1918	Henry Miller's / NYC	silhouette (ed.)
Hitchy-Koo of 1918	1918	Globe / NYC	costume sketches, poster

PRODUCTION / PERFORMER / CLIENT	CONWAY DATE	THEATER / CABARET	WORK
Oh, Lady! Lady!!	1918	Princess / NYC	posters
Getting Together / Gitz Rice	1918	Lyric & Shubert / NYC	silhouette (ed.)
Oh, My Dear!	1918	Princess / NYC	posters, billboard
Rock-a-Bye Baby	1918	Astor / NYC	posters, billboard, silhouette (ed.), b&w illus. (ed.)
Sleeping Partners / Irene Bordoni	1918	Bijou / NYC	poster
Ned Wayburn	1918	NYC	costuming
Double Exposure	1918	Bijou / NYC	poster
The Woman on the Index	1918	48th Street / NYC	poster
She Walked in Her Sleep	1918	Playhouse / NYC	silhouette
Going Up / Frank Craven	1918	Liberty / NYC	sketches, silhouette (ed.)
Allegiance	1918	Maxine Elliott's / NYC	poster, sketches
The Maid of the Mountains	1918	Casino / NYC	silhouette (ed.)
Information Please! / Jane Cowl	1918	Selwyn / NYC	program cover, page decorations
Selwyn & Company	1918–1922	Selwyn / NYC	program cover, page decorations
He Didn't Want to Do It	1918	Broadhurst / NYC	sketch

PRODUCTION / PERFORMER / CLIENT	CONWAY DATE	THEATER / CABARET	WORK
The Crowded Hour / Jane Cowl	1918	Selwyn / NYC	program cover, page decorations
Tea for Three	1918	Maxine Elliott's / NYC	program, brochures, fliers, poster, billboard
Forever After / Alice Brady	1919	Central / NYC	b&w illus. (ed.)
Margaret Lawrence	1919	NYC	personal wardrobe
Back Again / Ned Wayburn	1919	Weber & Fields / NYC	costuming
Listen Lester	1919	Knickerbocker / NYC	covers for program & sheet music, posters, billboard
The Riddle: Woman / Bertha Kalich	1919	Harris / NYC	poster, billboard
Mlle Dazie	1919	Coney Island	costume sketches
Mis' Nelly of N'Orleans / M. M. Fiske	1919	Henry Miller's / NYC	poster
A Sleepless Night / Peggy Hopkins	1919	Bijou / NYC	b&w illus. (ed.), poster
Wake Up, Jonathan! / M. M. Fiske	1919	Henry Miller's / NYC	poster
Good Morning, Judge / Mollie King	1919	Shubert / NYC	b&w illus. (ed.), posters
Ziegfeld Midnight Frolic / Ned Wayburn	1919	New Amsterdam Roof / NYC	costume sketches

PRODUCTION / PERFORMER / CLIENT	CONWAY DATE	THEATER / CABARET	WORK
The Royal Vagabond	1919	Cohan / NYC	silhouette (ed.), poster
Molière / Henry Miller	1919	Liberty / NYC	silhouette (ed.)
East Is West / Fay Bainter	1919	Astor / NYC	poster
Toby's Bow	1919	Comedy / NYC	posters
A Prince There Was / George M. Cohan	1919	Cohan / NYC	poster
Dear Brutus / Helen Hayes	1919	Empire / NYC	b&w illus. (ed.)
The Rose of China	1919	Lyric / NYC	poster
Nighty-Night	1919	Princess / NYC	poster
Various performers	1919	NYC	silhouettes (ed.)
Adam and Eva	1920	Longacre / NYC	posters, billboard
Aphrodite / McKay Morris	1920	Century / NYC	poster
As You Were / Irene Bordoni	1920	Central / NYC	poster
Hitchy-Koo / Ned Wayburn	1920	New Amsterdam / NYC	costuming
Buddies	1920	Selwyn / NYC	costume sketches
The Charm School	1920	Bijou / NYC	total design concept
Mary	1920	Knickerbocker / NYC	costume sketches
Wedding Bells	1920	Harris / NYC	silhouette (ed.), costume sketches

PRODUCTION / PERFORMER / CLIENT	CONWAY DATE	THEATER / CABARET	WORK
Dorothy Dickson and Carl Hyson, exhibition dancing	1920	Palais Royal / NYC	costuming, posters
League of Notions	1921	New Oxford / London	costume sketches, poster
Pins and Needles (Hat Scene)	1921–1922	Royalty / Gaiety / London	costume sketches, scene design, posters
London, Paris and New York	1921	Pavilion / London	posters, b&w illus. (ed.)
Sally / Dorothy Dickson	1921	Winter Garden / London	costume sketches, poster (Dickson only)
Alice Brady	1921	European performances	costume sketches, personal wardrobe
Dolly Sisters	1921–1922	London & European performances	costume sketches, personal wardrobe
Folies de Montmartre / Carl Hyson	1921–1922	Queen's Hall Roof / London	costuming
Peggy O'Neil	1921–1922	London	posters
Maurice	1921–1926	Paris	costume sketches
The Cabaret Girl / Dorothy Dickson	1922	Winter Garden / London	costume sketch, poster (Dickson only)
The Island King	1922–1923	Adelphi / London	costume sketches

PRODUCTION / PERFORMER / CLIENT	CONWAY DATE	THEATER / CABARET	WORK
Ruth Draper	1923	RMS *Majestic* / Atlantic crossing	color illus., donation
Lady Butterfly / Ned Wayburn	1923	Globe Theatre / NYC	costume sketches, posters
Shadowland	1923	Brooklyn, N.Y.	sketches
Gladys Cooper & Dolly Sisters	1923	RMS *Berengaria* / Atlantic crossing	color illus., posters, donation (British & American Seamen's Institutions)
Dover Street to Dixie	1923	Pavilion / London	costuming, scene design, posters
Rector's One O'Clock Revue / Percy Athos & Carl Hyson	1923	Rector's Club / London	costuming
Oddenino's / Frank Cavell	1923	Oddenino's Imperial Restaurant / London	poster
Palais Cabaret / Carl Hyson	1923	London	costuming
Odette Myrtil	1923	*The Midnight Follies* / Hotel Metropole / London	posters
The Midnight Follies / Carl Hyson	1923–1924	Hotel Metropole / London	costuming, posters
Midnight Follies / Tomson Twins	1924	Club Daunou / Paris	total design concept
Casino de Paris / "The Hat Shop" tableau / Léon Volterra	1924	Casino de Paris / Paris	costume sketches

PRODUCTION / PERFORMER / CLIENT	CONWAY DATE	THEATER / CABARET	WORK
Frivolities of 1924 / Percy Athos	1924	Princes' Restaurant / London	total design concept
The Odd Spot	1924	Vaudeville / London	costume
Patricia	1924	His Majesty's / London	costuming, posters, billboard
New Princes' Frivolities / Percy Athos	1924–1927	New Princes' Restaurant / London	total design concept
Casino de Paris / Léon Volterra (possibly "Fan" tableau)	1925	Casino de Paris / Paris	costume sketches
Peter Pan / Dorothy Dickson	1925	(unknown theater) / London	hand-painted tunic for Peter Pan role (Dickson only)
Tricks	1925	Apollo / London	costuming
Mercenary Mary	1925	Hippodrome / London	costume sketches
Gordon Conway's "Tricks" dresses	1926	*Homeric* / Atlantic crossing	costume adaptations, personal wardrobe
The Maiden Voyage / Ned Wayburn	1926	unknown / NYC	costuming, silhouette (ed. & ad.)
Tip-Toes	1926	Winter Garden / London	costuming
Princess Charming	1926	Palace / London	costuming

PRODUCTION / PERFORMER / CLIENT	CONWAY DATE	THEATER / CABARET	WORK
Sunny / Tiller Girls	1926	Hippodrome / London	costume sketches (Tiller Girls only)
So This Is the Princes' / Percy Athos	1926	Finsbury Park Empire / London	total design concept
New Princes' Frivolities / European tour / Percy Athos	1927–1928	Berlin	total design concept
Peggy-Ann	1927	Daly's / London	costuming, poster
Their Wife	1927	Little / London	costuming, scene designs
Irene Vanbrugh	1927	London	costume sketches
Charivaria	1929	South Sea & Liverpool in England	costuming
Coo-ee / Dorothy Dickson	1929	Vaudeville / London	costume sketches (Dickson only)
Hold Everything	1929	Palace / London	costume sketches
The Maid of the Mountains / Annie Croft	1930	London	costume sketch (Croft only)
Charlot's Masquerade	1930	Cambridge / London	costuming, casting, scene design
Wonder Bar	1930	Savoy / London	total design concept
There's Always Juliet / Edna Best	1931	Apollo / London and NYC	costuming, program (Best only)

PRODUCTION / PERFORMER / CLIENT	CONWAY DATE	THEATER / CABARET	WORK
The Sign of Seven Dials	1931	Cambridge / London	sketches
The Cat and the Fiddle / Alice Delysia	1932	Palace / London	costuming (Delysia only)
The Daily Mail Ideal Home Exhibition & Fashion Pageant	1934	Olympia Hall / London	costuming, program
Star Dust	1934	London	sketches
Why Not To-Night?	1934	Palace / Manchester, Palace / London	costuming, scene design
The Ringmaster / Dorothy Hyson	1935	Shaftsbury / London	costuming (Hyson only)

Film Work by Gordon Conway

FILM / PERFORMER / CLIENT	CONWAY DATE	PRODUCTION / LOCATION†	WORK
The Danger Mark	1918	Paramount / NJ-NYC	bit player (self-costumed)
Her Final Reckoning	1918	Paramount / NJ-NYC	bit player (self-costumed)
Everywoman	1918	Paramount (Famous Players) / NYC	billboard
Paying the Piper	1920	Famous Players / NYC	bit player (self-costumed)
Nanook of the North / Walter Wanger	1922	London exhibitors	posters
Foolish Wives / Walter Wanger	1922	London exhibitors	posters
When Knighthood Was in Flower / Walter Wanger	1922	London exhibitors	posters
A Bill of Divorcement / Walter Wanger	1922	London exhibitors	posters
Confetti	1927	First National–Pathé	1, 2, 3
Sir or Madam	1928	Foremost at B.I.P.	1
God's Clay	1928	First National–Pathé	1, 2
The Ringer / Annette Benson	1928	British Lion	1 (Benson only)
A South Sea Bubble	1928	Gainsborough	1
The Return of the Rat	1929	Gainsborough	1, 2

†London area if not otherwise indicated.

FILM / PERFORMER / CLIENT	CONWAY DATE	PRODUCTION / LOCATION†	WORK
Express Love / Heather Thatcher	1929	Alpha	1 (Thatcher only)
**High Treason*	1929	Gaumont-British	1, 2
Sleeping Partners / Edna Best	1930	Sageen Prod.	1 (Best only)
Laddie Cliff	1931	Unknown Prod.	costuming
**Sunshine Susie* (USA: *The Office Girl*)	1931	Gainsborough	1, 2
**Michael and Mary*	1931	Gainsborough	1, 2
Lord Babs	1931	Gainsborough	1, 2
The Frightened Lady (USA: *Criminal at Large*)	1931	Gainsborough-British Lion	1, 2
**The Faithful Heart* (USA: *Faithful Hearts*)	1932	Gainsborough	1, 2
White Face	1932	Gainsborough-British Lion	1, 2
**Jack's the Boy* (USA: *Night and Day*)	1932	Gainsborough	1, 2
**Love on Wheels*	1932	Gainsborough	1, 2, 3
**Marry Me*	1932	Gainsborough	1, 2
**There Goes the Bride*	1932	Gainsborough-British Lion	1, 2
**Rome Express*	1932	Gaumont-British	1, 2, 3

FILM / PERFORMER / CLIENT	CONWAY DATE	PRODUCTION / LOCATION†	WORK
The Man from Toronto	1932	Gainsborough	I, 2
**After the Ball*	1932	Gaumont-British	I, 2
The Lucky Number	1932	Gainsborough	I, 2
The Midshipmaid	1932	Gaumont-British	I, 2
The Good Companions	1932	Gaumont-British	I, 2, 3
*Soldiers of the King (USA: *The Woman in Command*)	1932	Gainsborough	I, 2
Waltz Time	1932	Gaumont-British	I, 2
Britannia of Billingsgate	1933	Gaumont-British	I, 2
Falling for You	1933	Gainsborough	I, 2
The Ghoul	1933	Gaumont-British	I, 2
Orders Is Orders	1933	Gaumont-British	I, 2
It's a Boy!	1933	Gainsborough	I, 2
I Was a Spy	1933	Gaumont-British	I, 2
The Prince of Wales (documentary)	1933	Gaumont-British & Gainsborough	studio representative for benefit
Channel Crossing	1933	Gaumont-British	I, 2
Just Smith	1933	Gaumont-British	I, 2

FILM / PERFORMER / CLIENT	CONWAY DATE	PRODUCTION / LOCATION†	WORK
*The Night of the Party (USA: The Murder Party)	1933	Gaumont-British	1
*A Cuckoo in the Nest	1933	Gaumont-British	1, 2
*The Fire Raisers	1933	Gaumont-British	1, 2
*Friday the Thirteenth	1933	Gainsborough	1, 2
*The Constant Nymph	1933	Gaumont-British	1, 2
*Red Ensign (USA: Strike!)	1933	Gaumont-British	1
Jack Ahoy	1933	Gaumont-British	1
*Aunt Sally (USA: Along Came Sally)	1933	Gainsborough & Gaumont-British	1, 2
*Turkey Time	1933	Gaumont-British	1
Wild Boy	1934	Gainsborough	1
*Jew Süss (USA: Power)	1934	Gaumont-British	costume consultant, research

Unidentified Works by Gordon Conway

	DATE	LOCATION	WORK
Patrician	before mid-1921		
Ariel	1924	London	design
A. Rasch	1925	London	costumes
Duramend	1929	London	poster
Roughes Boro	1930	London	
Associated Equipment	1931		
Runaways	1933–1934	London	possible film
Tokalon	1935	London	
Wm. Anderson / Textiles	1937	NYC	wallpaper designs
Match	unknown		

Clients with Whom Gordon Conway Worked and Designers Whose Collections She Was Invited to Sketch, 1915–1937

COUTURIER / COSTUMIER DESIGNER / STORE	LOCATION	COUTURIER / COSTUMIER DESIGNER / STORE	LOCATION
Agnes	Paris	Callot Soeurs	Paris
Madam Aida	Paris	Calotta	Paris
Albert & Johnson	London	Capdeville	Paris
C. Alias, Ltd.	London	Paul Caret	London
Alix (hats)	Paris	Jill Casson	London
Morris Angel & Sons	London	Gabrielle "Coco" Chanel	Paris
Anna	Paris	Chantal	Paris
Maison Arthur	London	Charlotte	Paris
Marie Athos	London	Serge Chermayeff	London
Augustabernard	Paris	Cheruit	Paris
A. E. Barbosa	London	Chez Beth (Beth Miller)	London
Beer	Paris	Willie Clarkson	London
Berman's	London	Cyber	Paris
Bernard	Paris	Daphné	Paris
Boué Soeurs	Paris	Debenham & Freebody	London
Brooks	NYC	Rose Descat (hats)	Paris
Busvine's	London	Dickens & Jones	London

COUTURIER / COSTUMIER DESIGNER / STORE	LOCATION	COUTURIER / COSTUMIER DESIGNER / STORE	LOCATION
Phyllis Dolton	London	Hawes & Curley	London
Jacques Doucet	Paris	Eileen Idare	London
Drecoll	Paris	Idare et Cie	London
A. Dubens	London	Jean	Paris
L'Echo de Paris	London	Madame Jenny	Paris
Edna's	London	Charles Judd	London
Elspeth Fox-Pitt	London	Jeanne Lanvin	Paris & London
Galleries de Lafayette	London	LaRue, Ltd.	London
A. L. Gamba (shoes)	London	Lucien Lelong	Paris & London
Geene Glenny	London	Lucile	Paris & London
Gooch's (hats)	London	Marguerite	London
Gorringes	London	Marks & Spencer	London
Philip Gough	London	Marshall & Snellgrove	London
Madame Gres	Paris	Martial et Armand	Paris
Harrods	London	Mercia & Co.	London
Norman Hartnell	London	Migel (fabrics)	NYC
Hawes & Curtis	London	Mignapouf (children)	Paris

COUTURIER / COSTUMIER DESIGNER / STORE	LOCATION	COUTURIER / COSTUMIER DESIGNER / STORE	LOCATION
Modiste	London or Paris	Rayne	London
Molyneux	Paris & London	Caroline Reboux (hats)	Paris
Lina Mouton	Paris	Redfern	Paris
L. & H. Nathan	London	Morgan & Austin Reed	London
Neiman-Marcus	Dallas	Marthe Régnier (hats)	Paris
Nicole	Paris	Rodier (hats)	Paris
Cornelia O'Connor	Paris	Reville & Rossiter	London
O'Rossen	Paris	Elsa Schiaparelli	Paris & London
Patricia Orwin	London	Edmundo "Mundo" Searle	Paris & London
Joseph Paquin	Paris	Selfridges	London
Madame Paquin	Paris	B. J. Simmons & Co.	London
Jean Patou	Paris	Franklin Simons	NYC
Clifford Pember	London	Mrs. Stubbs	London
Madame Perot	London	Swan & Edgar (furs)	London
Philippe et Gaston	Paris	Swerling (hats)	London
Paul Poiret	Paris	Susanne Talbot	Paris
Premet	Paris	Mrs. Peter Thursby	London

COUTURIER / COSTUMIER DESIGNER / STORE	LOCATION	COUTURIER / COSTUMIER DESIGNER / STORE	LOCATION
Veer	Paris	Madame Wolkowsky	London
Vickers	London	Porter Woodruff	NYC, Paris, London
Madeleine Vionnet	Paris & London	Worth	Paris & London
Victoire	Paris		
White House	Paris		

No Record of Conway Collaboration While Both Were Assigned to the Same Projects

COUTURIER / COSTUMIER DESIGNER / STORE	LOCATION*	COUTURIER / COSTUMIER DESIGNER / STORE	LOCATION*
Adler	NYC	Mary E. Fisher, Ltd.	London
B. Altman & Co.	NYC	Francis, Inc.	NYC
Bechoff	Paris	Nicole Groult	Paris
Henri Bendel	NYC	Joan Magnin	Paris
Louise Boulanger	Paris	Max	Paris
Gladys Calthrop	London	J. Muelle	Paris
Attilio Comelli	London	Herbert Norris	London
Sonia Delaunay	Paris	Dolly Tree	London, Paris
Guy de Gerald	London		
Marcelle de Saint-Martin	London	Max Weldy	Paris, London
Helen Dryden	NYC	Doris Zinkeisen	London

*Principal location during Conway's career. Many worked on both sides of the Atlantic.

NOTES

Abbreviations Used

OJA	Olive Johnson Allen
JA	Joan Antill
HC	Heyworth Campbell
GC	Gordon Conway
TJC	Tommie Johnson Conway
DD	Dorothy Dickson
JD	Julia Dierks
MPE	Margaret Page Elliott
WKE	William K. Everson
DGF	Diana Gibbs Felder
ENH	Edward N. "Teddie" Holstius
KH	Katharine Houghton
WK	Wood Kahler
ML	Mary Lutz
DHQ	Dorothy Hyson (Lady Quayle)
JBW	Jeanne Ballot Winham
NYTFR	*The New York Times Film Reviews*
VFR	*Variety Film Reviews* (*VFR* in New York and London)
HRHRC/UT	Harry Ransom Humanities Research Center, The University of Texas at Austin
Com/Bib/RVA	Comprehensive Bibliography by author deposited at HRHRC/UT

Part One. Biography
INTRODUCTION.
THE ARTIST WHO DRAWS BY EAR

1. Daniel Cohen, "Grand Emporiums Peddle Their Wares in a New Market," *Smithsonian,* March 1993, pp. 122–133. (This is listed in the magazine contents as "For Department Stores, It's Retail Wars.") For insight into "consumerism" and the American female, see Blanche H. Gelfant, "What More Can Carrie Want? Naturalistic Ways of Consuming Women," in *Prospects: An Annual of American Cultural Studies,* 389–417. (See the definition of "consumerism" on 393–394, 408–409.) In addition, for insight into the influence of Condé Nast on female consumers and his concept of "class publication," see Carolina Seebohm, *The Man Who Was "Vogue": The Life and Times of Condé Nast,* 79–81. Authorities credit mass-print pioneer Condé Nast with introducing the concept of the special-interest magazine, which he labeled "class publication" and first applied at *Vogue* early in the twentieth century. The goals for his publishing empire differed from those espoused by publishers of general-interest periodicals, like his friend and former employer at *Collier's,* Robert Collier, and Cyrus H. K. Curtis, publisher of such popular favorites as the *Ladies' Home Companion* and the *Saturday Evening Post.* Nast explained his objectives in a trade-journal article he authored for the June 1913 issue of *Merchants' and Manufacturers' Journal.* Nast wrote, "this vast population divides not only along the lines of wealth, education, and refinement, but classifies itself even more strongly along lines of interest. . . . And a 'class publication' is nothing more nor less than a publication that looks for its circulation *only* to those having in common a certain characteristic marked enough to group them as a class. That common characteristic may be almost anything: religion; a particular line of business; community of residence; common pursuit; or some common interest." Nast was convinced that the consumer market was exploding with members from various classes who aspired to a lifestyle practice known as the art of gracious living. Seebohm pointed out that he targeted the upper classes because they were "a large, hitherto untapped market of people who had more money to spend on consumer goods than any other group." Others who formed a lucrative market were the "readers *who did not yet belong to the class which he had chosen, but who aspired to it.*" The biographer observed that "the fact that advertisers responded as they did is proof enough that such a class was anthropologically and sociologically identifiable, and that their behavior, manners, clothes, and customs could be accurately chronicled in the pages

of a journal." Also see the autobiography of Nast's influential editor, Edna Woolman Chase, written with daughter Ilka Chase, *Always in "Vogue."* For history of the consumer and advertising culture, see Susan Porter Benson, *Counter Cultures: Saleswomen, Managers, and Customers in American Department Stores, 1890–1940;* and Roland Marchand, *Advertising the American Dream: Making Way for Modernity, 1920–1940.*

2. Cleveland Amory and Frederic Bradlee, eds., *"Vanity Fair," Selections from America's Most Memorable Magazine: A Cavalcade of the 1920s and 1930s,* 13.

3. At time of publication, *New Woman* is a popular magazine in the United States.

A selection of publications dealing with the definition and interpretation of this ambiguous and loosely-used term include: Ellen Wiley Todd, *The "New Woman" Revised: Painting and Gender Politics on Fourteenth Street;* June Sochen, *The New Woman: Feminism in Greenwich Village, 1910–1920;* Margaret C. Jones, *Heretics and Hellraisers: Women Contributors to "The Masses," 1911–1917;* and Alice Sheppard, *Cartooning For Suffrage.*

4. Martha Banta, *Imaging American Women: Idea and Ideals in Cultural History.* Banta's landmark study offers an indispensable analysis and guide to various images of women, especially the "New Woman." See "American Girls and the New Woman" in Part One, 45–91. See 82–88 concerning the "new woman" article and sketch in *New York World,* August 18, 1895. Also see a 1913 sketch of female "militants" on 17, as well as the same sketch on 28 in Todd's *The "New Woman" Revised.* For insight into the power of images in the media, see Daniel J. Boorstin, *The Image: A Guide to Pseudo Events in America,* 13, 44–45, 64, 197.

5. Cleveland Amory and Frederic Bradlee, *"Vanity Fair," Selections from America's Most Memorable Magazine,* 259–260. See Frank Crowninshield's comments on magazines, advertising, and American women during a speech delivered to the American Association of Advertising Agencies in 1934. Crowninshield protested legislation introduced in the United States Congress that strove to limit "sin" across the country. He observed that "the measure is devised to prevent the manufacture of, traffic in, and what might be called the 'over-romantic' advertising of certain foods, drinks, drugs, garments, cosmetics and other articles intended to make life a little happier for the ladies." Referring to the supporters of the legislation as "imperial and autocratic," Crowninshield criticized the Washington lawmakers who "drafted a bill of thirty or more pages, the chief purpose of which was to tell, not

one woman, but 50,000,000 women, what they can or cannot eat, what they can and cannot wear, what they may or may not drink. . . . And the laws with regard to modesty, on the stage and on the beaches, which were intended to promote the four-piece dancing suit and the six-piece bathing costume, were so cleverly drafted that naked women now appear nightly in our theaters while women at beaches wear practically no bathing suits at all." Crowninshield's speech concluded, "I have tried to show what an exciting and fascinating realm this world of the magazine advertisements has become, to the average American woman, and how greatly it contributes to her courage and morale, and I am wondering whether Washington will find it in its heart to shatter so much innocent glamour and romance. . . . all we can do is to join together in praying that a majority of Congressmen will turn out to be human beings at heart; that they will not insist upon taking what this bill calls *sin*" from American female citizens who find these beauty and leisure goods and services a benefit to their lives.

6. Zane Grey, *The Call of the Canyon,* 4–5, 42, 142, 149–150, 154–156, 190–192, 197, 204, 222–223, 245–248. Throughout this 1921 novel, Grey excoriated the modern female—a certain kind of New Woman who endangered the moral and social welfare of the United States. Zane Grey protested this "spoiled" woman who "is an ornament, or a toy, to be kept in a luxurious cage. . . . To soil her pretty hands would be disgraceful! . . . the modern devices of science . . . electric dishwasher, clothes-washer, vacuum-cleaner . . . rob a young wife of her house-wifely heritage." He criticized the "abbreviation" of dress, and wrote that "any woman's dress without top or bottom is onnatural [*sic*]." To be "exquisitely gowned in the latest mode . . . [with a] brilliantly tinted complexion was not . . . natural . . . [to] health." For different reasons from those of Zane Grey, this type of New Woman is not without its detractors today. See Naomi Wolf, *The Beauty Myth: How Images of Beauty are Used Against Women,* 9–19, 61–80. One tragic consequence of the pursuit of such Hollywood images is explored in *Constance,* an award-winning 1984 feature film produced in New Zealand. The film is a fictional account of the devastating effects of this type of female image when it dominates one's personal values: a young woman destroys her family financially and emotionally with an obsession about Hollywood fashion and body shape. The film is an important research tool for scholars of Hollywood images. Also see Meriel McCooey, "The Great Fashion Dictators of Hollywood," *Sunday Times Magazine,* September 24, 1947, pp. 60–66, with stills from the John Kobal collection. McCooey points out that Josef von Sternberg made Dietrich "his invention . . . his dream woman," but became

disillusioned when he realized she "was a *hausfrau* at heart."

7. Grey, *Call of the Canyon,* 4–5, 42, 142, 149–150, 154–156, 190–192, 197, 204, 222–223, 245–248.

8. Ibid. Also see Brian Dippie, *Charles M. Russell, Word Painter: Letters 1887–1926,* 226. The author wishes to thank Professor William H. Goetzmann, American Studies scholar and authority on Western art, for pointing out Charles M. Russell's March 1, 1916, drawing and letter that expresses a parallel sentiment of disdain for this kind of New Woman. Delineating a sophisticated young woman dressed for dinner with shoulders, arms, and back exposed, Russell's sketch resembles the type of New Woman that Gordon Conway portrayed in life and art. Russell's writing is faint, but the statement looks like "Maybe you think this lady is [preparing] for a bath, but [you're] wrong. She's at dinner." Dippie states that "this is a classic Russell rap on modern mores. . . . the fashionably dressed women of New York's social scene. . . . [and] the Smart Set. . . . [with] a show of skin."

9. Edna Ferber, *Emma McChesney & Co.,* 64–65, 85, 89, 98–101, 109, 112–113, 120–125, 142–145, 152–168, 172–185, 188–195, 198–205, 210, 216–217, 224–227, 230–231.

10. Seebohm, 92–102.

11. Ferber, *Emma McChesney & Co.,* 64–65, 85, 89, 98–101, 109, 112–113, 120–125, 142–145, 152–168, 172–185, 188–195, 198–205, 210, 216–217, 224–227, 230–231.

12. Ibid.

13. Frederick Lewis Allen, *Only Yesterday: An Informal History of the 1920s,* 85.

14. *Eve: The Lady's Pictorial,* April 19, 1922, London. For a similar observation almost seventy years later, see an article on Hollywood costume design by Carol Troy in *American Film* (June 1989), 6: "Michael Douglas becomes what he wears, and most becomingly."

15. Rufus Gilmore 1915 letter to Heyworth Campbell (hereafter cited as HC).

16. HC's letters, 1915.

17. HC advice reported by Mary K. Brookes in "Texas Lassies Winning Spurs In Great City . . . Gordon Conway of Dallas a Notable Example of Texas Girl Who Won Her Way on Merit," *The Houston Chronicle,* January 16, 1921.

18. *Vanity Fair,* August 1919, p. 15. The phrase probably was written by editor Frank Crowninshield but originally may have been coined by Dorothy Parker before she was fired in early 1920 because of disparaging theater reviews that angered several Broadway producers.

19. Joanna Catron, *Red, Hot & Southern: The International Fashions and Designs of Gordon Conway, 1916–1936.* Exhibition brochure. Fredericksburg, Virginia: Historic Fredericksburg Foundation, Inc., 1990.

1. DECEMBER'S CHILDREN

1. Horace Edwin Hayden, *Virginia Genealogies.* See also T. E. Campbell, *Colonial Caroline: A History of Caroline County, Virginia.* See also Emmie Ferguson Farrar and Emily Hines, *Old Virginia Houses Along the Fall Line,* xvii–xviii. Also, the author gathered family history from records owned by members of Conway's family, especially Olive Johnson Allen (hereafter cited as OJA), who shared the materials with the author during numerous interviews and conversations between 1983 and 1993.

2. Robert A. Rutland, *James Madison and the Search for Nationhood,* 9–10. Also OJA family records and interviews.

3. OJA interviews.

4. Cleburne, Texas, Historical and Architectural Survey, March 1987, and a historic archive, privately owned by Michael Gamble who shared the materials during an interview with the author in 1990.

5. Ibid. See also Gordon Miltenberger, *The Church of the Holy Comforter: A History of the Episcopal Church in Cleburne, Johnson County, Texas,* 40–61, 205. Also see Molly Bradbury, *The History of Johnson County, Texas,* and Mildred Padon, *The History of Cleburne and Johnson County.*

6. William L. McDonald and A. C. Greene, *Dallas Rediscovered: A Photographic Chronicle of Urban Expansion, 1870–1925,* 1–4, 23–26, 169–183, 177.

7. Margaret Page Elliott (hereafter cited as MPE) and Katharine Houghton (hereafter cited as KH) 1983 interviews and subsequent telephone conversations with MPE.

8. *Beau Monde,* a weekly publication in Dallas, ca. 1890–World War I. (Selected issues on microfilm.) Also see the *Dallas Society News,* May 22, 1915.

9. Zula McCauley, *The First Forty Years: A Chronology of Growth,* 2–7. (This is a history of Neiman-Marcus.)

10. Archive of Gordon Conway (hereafter cited as GC) and Tommie Johnson Conway (hereafter cited as TJC) correspondence (1905–1920). Also OJA interviews.

11. Ibid. Also MPE and KH interviews.

12. Ibid. Also MPE interviews.

13. Ibid. Also MPE and KH interviews; GC scrapbook; and the *Dallas Morning News,* fall, 1914.

14. GC 1913–1914 diaries.

15. Ibid.

16. Ibid. During the teens, Conway's male friends from two well-known families in Rome included Don Fabrizio Colonna and Luigi Colonna, as well as the Ruspoli brothers, Constantine, Francesco, and Mariscotti.

17. Ibid.

18. Ibid.

19. Ibid.

20. Ibid.

21. Ibid.

22. Archive of 1920–1960 correspondence to GC and TJC: assorted letters, notes on Christmas cards, and condolence letters to TJC about GC's death.

23. OJA interviews.

24. Interviews with MPE, KH, and Diana Gibbs Felder (hereafter cited as DGF) in 1983–1992, and Julia Dierks (hereafter cited as JD) in 1983.

25. Interviews with Dorothy Dickson (hereafter cited as DD) and Eric Braun, 1983–1989.

26. GC 191? diary.

27. GC 1912–1914 scrapbook with unidentified Rome newspaper clipping. Also OJA interviews.

28. MPE and KH interviews.

29. GC financial records and diaries.

30. JD interview.

31. Banta, *Imaging American Women,* 2, 32, 279, 589, 632–671. Also see Walt Reed, *50 Great American Illustrators,* and Walt Reed and Roger Reed, *The Illustrator in America 1880–1980: A Century of Illustration.* See also Todd's *New Woman Revised.*

2. THE SOUL OF VERSATILITY

1. Other pioneering art organizations are mentioned in HC's business correspondence (1916–1927), privately owned by Walt and Roger Reed of Illustration House, Inc. in New York. For insight into the link between art and advertising, see Sydney R. Jones, *Art & Publicity: Fine Printing and Design* (Special Autumn Number of *The Studio,* 1925).

2. A January 20, 1988, letter from Jacques Barzun to the author describes the atmosphere at the Condé Nast offices. Also Jeanne Ballot Winham (hereafter cited as JBW) interviews in New York, 1983–1985, and references in Seebohm and Chase.

3. Seebohm, *Man Who Was "Vogue",* 60, 165–175, especially 170.

4. JBW interviews.

5. HC 1915–1918 letters to GC.

6. GC 1915–1916 diaries.

7. Ibid. Also OJA interviews. The nickname referred to Edna Ferber's play based on her novels and stories about the fictional character of Mrs. Emma McChesney.

8. HC letters.

9. Ibid.

10. Evelyn Waugh, *Brideshead Revisited,* 152.

11. Nikolaus Pevsner, *Pioneers of Modern Design: From William Morris to Walter Gropius,* 19–39, 21. Also see Lawrence W. Levin, *Highbrow-Lowbrow: The Emergence of Cultural Hierarchy in America.* Also see Michele Bogart, "Artistic Ideals and Commercial Practices: The Problem of Status for American Illustrators," in *Prospects: An Annual of American Cultural Studies,* 1990, 225–281. For data on the revival of Art Deco, see books by Bevis Hillier in Com/Bib/RVA, and the exhibition catalogue, *Les Annees "25": Art Déco/Bauhaus/Stijl Esprit Nouveau* (Paris: Musée des Arts Décoratifs, 3 mars/16 mai, 1966).

12. Interviews with cartoonists and illustrators Harry Haenigsen and Edwina Dumm, as well as with freelance set and costume designer Ann Sheffield, former assistant to designer Tony Walton and theater-design teacher at the University of Oklahoma, Norman, Oklahoma. (Sheffield later acknowledged to the author that from a practical stand-point the signature of a designer was a good idea, though she remained loyal to the idea of the collaborative effort by a group of artists.) Also, the author talked to former assistant art directors at magazine offices and at theaters, who reported incidences of artwork cavalierly tossed into the trash. Employed by *The Tatler* during the 1930s, Mr. Truelove had asked his fellow employees not to destroy the artwork, but to no avail.

13. Wood Kahler, *Smart Setback,* 224–225, 234–235.

14. HC letters.

15. GC 1915 diaries. Also OJA interviews.

16. *Harper's Bazar* was the early spelling of the Hearst magazine's name during the period Gordon Conway worked as a freelance illustrator in New York from 1915–1921. In 1929, the title changed to *Harper's Bazaar.*

17. Captions accompanying GC silhouettes in the National City Bank advertising posters in 1919–1920.

18. GC press books: October 10, 1919, unidentified article possibly from *The Poster.*

19. GC 1918 and 1919 diaries.

20. *Vanity Fair* page of photographs of seven staff members with captions, December 1918.

21. Ibid. Expanding her stage art, Conway created freelance work for such notable New York producers, managers, directors, publicists, and actresses as William A. Brady, George M. Cohan, F. Raymond Comstock, Jane Cowl, William Elliott, Minnie Maddern Fiske and husband H. G. Fiske, Morris Gest, E. Ray Goetz, Sam H. Harris, Raymond Hitchcock, Margaret Lawrence, Robert Milton, the Selwyn Brothers, the Shubert Brothers, Sanford E. Stanton, Ned Wayburn, and Florenz Ziegfeld, Jr. Concerning stage designers of the era see Mary C. Henderson, *Broadway Ballyhoo: The American Theater Seen in Posters, Photographs, Magazines, Caricatures, and Programs,* 21–22, 38, 160; her *Theater in America: 200 Years of Plays, Players, and Productions,* 202, 205, 224–225; and Kenneth MacGowan, *Famous American Plays of the 1920s,* 9.

22. GC 1915–1917 diaries.

23. GC 1910–1914 diaries. Also OJA interviews.

24. Interview with David Schaff, Washington, D.C., 1983. Also in agreement were several authorities interviewed by the author.

25. According to Dolly Tree biographer and costume authority Gary Chapman, Dolly Tree worked alongside Freddy Wittop at the Folies Bergère in the early 1920s in Paris.

26. Guillaume Garnier, *Paul Poiret et Nicole Groult: Maîtres de la Mode Art Déco.* Also see other books on Poiret's ideas like his 1931 autobiography, *King of Fashion,* and a biography by Palmer White, *Poiret.*

27. Alan and Isabella Livingston, *Encyclopaedia of Graphic Design and Designers,* 22.

28. Elizabeth Morano, *Sonia Delaunay: Art Into Fashion,* 8.

29. Alan and Isabella Livingston, *Encyclopaedia of Graphic Design and Designers,* 54.

3. THREE FOR TEA

1. GC 1919–1920 diaries.

2. Explained by costume and set designer Ann Sheffield during a 1992 interview in Newport Beach, Calif., later in Washington, D.C., and in subsequent telephone conversations.

3. GC press books: *New York Telegraph,* October 2, 1918.

4. GC financial records and diaries.

5. GC 1918 diary.

6. DD interviews. Also GC 1918 diary.

7. GC press books.

8. GC 1919 press books: *The Poster,* July 1919.

9. P. G. Wodehouse and Guy Bolton, *Bring on the Girls!: The Improbable Story of Our Life in Musical Comedy, With Pictures to Prove It,* 7, 36. Also informing this study was a 1985 interview with Benny Green, British radio and media luminary, and authority on jazz, musical comedy, and British music hall. Green discussed the influence of both Viennese operetta and African American music on the burgeoning genre of musical comedy. He explained the pioneering role of British-born

P. G. Wodehouse and Guy Bolton in the development of musical comedy during the teens in Britain and the United States. Also see Raymond Mander and Joe Mitchenson, *Musical Comedy: A Story in Pictures,* 6–36; and Ethan Mordden, *Broadway Babies: The People Who Made the American Musical,* 58–63, 72–80.

10. Stanley Green, *The World of Musical Comedy,* 55–59.

11. GC press books: *New York American,* October 19, 1919.

12. Blake Ozias, *A Catalogue of the Highest Grade Prints.*

13. Blake Ozias, *How the Modern Hostess Serves Wine* and *All about Wine.*

14. Albert Lawrence Rohrer, *History of Osio, Osius, Ozias Families,* vii–ix, 1–2, 15–16, 163–164, 186, 249–250.

15. Photos by and four letters from historian Audrey S. Gilbert ("The Archives" of Preble County, Ohio), July 14–30, 1990.

16. GC 1918 diary.

17. GC 1920 diary.

18. Ibid.

19. DD interviews.

20. Interviews with GC friends.

21. GC 1920 diary.

22. Wood Kahler (hereafter cited as WK) 1919–1956 letters to GC and TJC.

23. Jeffrey L. Meikle, *Twentieth Century Limited: Industrial Design in America, 1925–1939,* 60–62.

24. GC 1920 diary. Also OJA interviews.

25. Blake Ozias, December 10, 1920, letter to GC.

26. TJC, February 1, 1921, letter to GC.

27. GC 1921 diary.

4. CHANNEL CROSSINGS

1. Blake Ozias, December 10, 1920, letter to GC.

2. GC 1921 diary.

3. GC 1921–1923 diary.

4. Ibid.

5. Blake Ozias entry in GC 1921–1923 diary.

6. MPE interviews.

7. GC 1921–1927 diaries.

8. GC 1922 and 1923 diaries.

9. Ibid.

10. Ibid.

11. Ibid.

12. Ibid.

13. Ibid.

14. Ibid.

15. Ibid.

16. GC 1920–1923 diaries.

17. Henry Sell, editor at *Harper's Bazar,* 1922–1923 letters to GC.

18. GC 1923 and 1924 diaries.

19. GC 1921–1922 diaries.

5. THAT RED HEAD GAL

1. Geoffrey Moore, "Cabaret Land," *Encore,* September 17, 1925, and October 15, 1925, London.

2. Raymond Mander and Joe Mitchenson, *Revue: A Story in Pictures,* 1–40.

3. Ibid.

4. GC 1923–1926 diaries.

5. GC 1924 diary. Also see GC press books with articles about *Patricia,* including the *Illustrated Sporting and Dramatic News,* December 20, 1924, and the *Evening Chronicle,* October 10, 1924.

6. GC 1924 and 1925 diaries.

7. GC 1923–1926 diaries. Also Dion Titheradge 1923–1926 telegrams and letters to GC.

8. Ibid.

9. J. C. Trewin, Raymond Mander, and Joe Mitchenson, *The Gay Twenties: A Decade of the Theatre,* 71, 10. Also see Sheridan Morley, *Spread a Little Happiness: The First Hundred Years of the British Musical,* 41–63.

10. WK 1919–1955 letters, notes, telegrams, and his March 2, 1924, article in the *New York Herald* in Paris. Also see GC press books: "Texas Girl Wins Fame As Artist in Foreign Nations," by Alice Langelier, columnist for Hearst newspapers/International News Service, Paris, March 21, 1924. Also "Round the Studios in Paris," *New York Herald,* February 15, 1925.

11. Song with same title by Van & Schenck, and Henry Lodge (© Mills Music, Inc., New York, 1923). Also 1980 exhibition catalogue, David Schaff, *That Red Head Gal: Fashions and Designs of Gordon Conway, 1916–1936.*

Two exhibitions of the art and archive of Gordon Conway:

1980–1981 *That Red Head Gal: Fashions and Designs of Gordon Conway, 1916–1936.* Organized by the American Institute of Architects Foundation and supported by Philip Morris, Inc., on behalf of Virginia Slims. Touring exhibition: Washington, D.C., Dallas, Chicago, and Los Angeles.

1990 *Red, Hot and Southern: The International Fashions and Designs of Gordon Conway, 1916–1936.* Sponsored by the Historic Fredericksburg Foundation, Inc., and presented at Belmont, The Gari Melchers Memorial Gallery, Fredericksburg, Virginia.

12. GC 1926 diary.

13. Ibid.

14. Ibid.

15. Ibid.

16. Ibid.

17. Ibid.

18. Ibid.

19. *Eve,* September 1, 1926.

20. Letter to GC from Madame Stella Nathan (of L. & H. Nathan costumiers), September 3, 1926.

21. Three letters to the author between March 2, 1983, and January 29, 1984, from Michael Bolloten, a fan of Dorothy Dickson living in New South Wales, Australia. His remarkable memory of Miss Dickson's costumes greatly informed the author's interpretation of costuming and the process of musical stage production in London during Conway's era. Bolloten's fashion rhetoric represents a popular form of expression among theater costume and clothing enthusiasts.

22. GC 1926 and 1927 diaries.

23. Letters to GC (1924–1926) from the editor of *La Donna: Revue Italienne d'Art et de Modes.*

24. GC 1925 diary.

25. Peter Huskinson of *The Tatler,* January 26, 1925, letter to GC.

26. Claude Lepape and Thierry Defert, *From the Ballets Russes to Vogue: The Art of Georges Lepape,* 42–43, 171–172.

27. GC press books: "Texas Girl Wins Fame As Artist in Foreign Nations," by Alice Langelier, columnist for Hearst newspapers/International News Service, Paris, March 21, 1924.

28. Blake Ozias obituary, October 26, 1967, *Lewisburg Leader,* Ohio.

29. Interviews with GC friends, 1983–1994.

30. GC 1925–1927 diaries.

31. GC 1926 diary, press books, and scrapbooks.

32. GC 1926 diary.

33. Ibid.

34. WK 1929–1930 letters to GC.

35. Reported by Benjamin Faber during 1983–1992 telephone interviews.

36. MPE interviews.

37. Blake Ozias 1927 postcard to TJC.

6. POEMS OF CHIC

1. GC 1927 diary.

2. Stanley Green, *Broadway Musicals: Show by Show,* 54. Also see Green's *The World of Musical Comedy,* 5, 117–118, 413; and Mordden, *Broadway Babies,* 58–64, 72–80, 95–96, 210.

3. DD interviews.

4. Joint interview with Joan Antill (hereafter cited as JA) and Mary Lutz (hereafter cited as ML), 1983, Washington, D.C.

5. GC press files: 1927 clippings about *Their Wife.*

6. GC 1927 and 1928 diaries.

7. Michael Balcon, *Michael Balcon Presents . . . A Lifetime of Films.* Also Brown and Kardish, 13–15, 27, 32.

8. Rachael Low, *The History of British Film: 1918–1929,* 156–160.

9. Michael Balcon, Ernest Lindgren, Forsyth Hardy, and Roger Manvell, *The Literature of Cinema: Twenty Years of British Film, 1925–1945,* 13–15.

10. Ibid. Also see Charles Barr, ed., *All Our Yesterdays: 90 Years of British Cinema,* 47–71.

11. Michael Relph 1983 interview in London, and Michael Powell 1984 interview in New York. At the time of the author's interview, Powell was writing about this period of his career in his autobiography, *A Life in Movies.* He shared recollections and read from his notes. Most of these quotes later appeared in Powell's autobiography.

12. Low, *The History of British Film: 1918–1929,* 160.

13. GC 1927 and 1928 diaries.

14. Low, *The History of British Film: 1918–1929,* 159.

15. GC 1928 diary.

16. Some references list this title as *The South Sea Bubble.*

17. GC 1928 diary.

18. *"Variety" Film Reviews* (hereafter cited as *VFR*), 1928. See also *Kinematograph Weekly,* August 23, 1928.

19. *VFR,* London, April 2, 1930.

20. GC 1929 diary.

21. GC 1928–1929 press books. Speaking of *The Return of the Rat,* Graham Cutts was quoted in "Film Fashions" in the *Evening Standard,* December 6, 1928. These quotes were similar to 1929 news articles based on a Gainsborough Studio press release, November 26, 1928.

22. GC 1928–1929 press books. Also see three articles by Gordon Conway: "Fashions from the Films," *Picture Show,* April 28, 1928,

p. 19; "Frocks for Films," *The Bioscope British Film Number* (1929), pp. 240–241; and "Dressing the Talkies," *Film Weekly,* September 2, 1929, p. 7.

23. GC 1928–1929 press books. Also GC press books: *Film Weekly,* January 7, 1929, and 1929 issues of *The Tatler* about *The Return of the Rat.*

24. GC 1928–1929 press books.

25. GC 1929 diary.

26. GC 1929 press books with many articles on *High Treason* from such periodicals as *Health and Strength.* Also see studio press releases and "Fashions of the Future" in the film program.

27. GC 1929 diary.

28. Ibid.

29. Elizabeth Leese, *Costume Design in the Movies,* 6, 57.

30. GC 1929 diary.

31. Ibid.

32. GC 1930 diary.

33. Ibid.

34. GC 1929–1931 diaries. Also 1985 interview with Ian Grant in London.

35. GC 1930 diary.

36. Ibid.

37. Ibid.

38. Ibid.

39. Cambridge Theatre souvenir brochure, September 3, 1930, pp. 9–14.

40. "The Passing Shows," by "T," *The Tatler,* September 24, 1930. Also see critical acclaim for Beatrice Lillie and the costuming.

41. *The Tatler,* September 4 or 17, 1930.

42. Cambridge Theatre souvenir brochure, 1930.

43. Robert Graves and Alan Hodge, *The Long Week-End: A Social History of Great Britain 1918–1939,* 279–280.

44. *The Play Pictorial* 67, no. 343 (1930): v–vi, 50–64.

45. *The Tatler,* September 17, 1930.

46. *The Star,* September 5, 1930.

47. Celanese advertisement in the program for *Charlot's Masquerade,* 1930.

48. GC 1930 press books: *Birmingham Post,* August 20, 1930.

49. *The Tatler,* September 4, 1930.

50. Morley, *Spread a Little Happiness,* 65–67.

51. Raymond Mander and Joe Mitchenson, *Revue: A Story in Pictures,* 35. Also see statement by celebrated stage artist Gordon Craig in Low, *The History of British Film: 1918–1929,* 310.

52. DD interviews.

53. GC 1930 diary.

54. Ronald Bergan, *The Great Theatres of London: An Illustrated Companion,* 37–39, 157–160.

55. Ibid. (The quote was from a 1929 issue of *Country Life.*)

56. *The Tatler,* December 24, 1930.

57. GC 1931 diary.

58. Raymond Mander and Joe Mitchenson, *Revue: A Story in Pictures,* 33.

59. GC 1931 diary.

60. Ibid.

61. *Picture Show,* April 18, 1928, London.

62. Ibid. Also see John Canaday, *Mainstreams of Modern Art,* 545. Art authority Canaday claims in this landmark study that "The functionalist idea of course is as applicable to pitchers, beds, and razors as it is to buildings."

7. DRESSING THE TALKIES

1. Gordon Conway, "Dressing the Talkies," *Film Weekly,* September 2, 1929.

2. Gordon Conway, "Frocks for Films," *The Bioscope British Film Number,* 1929. The joint acting editor of *The Bioscope* as well as a screenwriter, Frank Fowell, wrote on October 22, 1928, to GC that they were preparing "a special volume of 'The Bioscope' under the title of 'British Films for the World.' . . . [and that] the whole aim of the volume is to increase the supply to Empire screens of films essentially British in their atmosphere, setting and ideals." He requested Conway's "expert advice and opinion" in an article about "the variations between the clothes of artists as they actually appear, and the effect they produce on the screen."

3. Gordon Conway, "Fashions from the Films," *Picture Show,* April 28, 1928. Also see above two articles in notes 1 and 2.

4. Conway, "Fashions from the Films."

5. Carol Troy, "'Can You Imagine Them Making Love?': Ellen Mirojnick and the Inner Game of Costume," *American Film* 14, no. 8 (June 1989): 6, 46–51, 64. This reflects the old debate concerning the origin of ideas about clothing and costume: which comes first, the ideas of the couturiers or the screen designers?

6. Ibid.

7. *VFR,* 1931.

8. Rachael Low, *The History of British Film 1929–1939: Film Making in 1930s Britain,* 177–179.

9. GC 1931 diary.

10. Ibid.

11. Ibid.

12. Ibid.

13. Geoff Brown and Laurence Kardish, eds., *Michael Balcon: The Pursuit of British Cinema,* Balcon film retrospective catalogue for New York's Museum of Modern Art, 1984, 17–19, 27, 53, 73. Also 1983 interview with Michael Relph in London.

14. GC 1931 and 1932 diaries.

15. Ibid. For data on Conway's assistants, the author's search included letters and advertisements in British trade periodicals. British film costume historian Catherine Surowiec discussed in letters and in telephone conversations with the author information about award-winning costume designer Margaret Furse. Margaret Furse must be the "Miss Watts" of Conway's diary entry. According to Surowiec, Furse's maiden name was Watts; she was the daughter of *Punch* cartoonist Arthur Watts. In late 1936 she married artist and designer

Roger Furse, whom she divorced in 1951. In 1952 she married stage and film critic Stephen Watts, who told Surowiec in an interview on April 1, 1993, that Margaret Watts had been hired by Conway for six months in 1932 as an "assistant modern costume designer" and lost this job due to "budget cuts at Gaumont-British."

16. Michael Powell, November 1984, interview in New York.

17. Balcon, *Michael Balcon Presents . . . A Lifetime of Films,* 55–99.

18. Ibid., 117. Also see Brown and Kardish, *Michael Balcon.*

19. *VFR,* late June 1932.

20. Balcon, *Michael Balcon Presents . . . A Lifetime of Films,* 55–99. Also see Brown and Kardish, *Michael Balcon,* 13–15, 27, 32.

21. GC 1932 diary.

22. Ibid.

23. Ibid.

24. *VFR,* 1930–1933.

25. GC 1932 diary.

26. Letter from Paul Caret (Lenôtre, Ltd.) to GC, April 7, 1932. Also GC 1932 diary.

27. Brown and Kardish, *Michael Balcon,* 19.

28. GC press books: *The Daily Film Renter,* May 18, 1932.

29. Brown and Kardish, *Michael Balcon,* 19.

30. Morley, *Spread a Little Happiness,* 76.

31. GC press books: *Financial News,* July 4, 1932.

32. GC press books: "Film Stars Who Never Act: Women with Big Jobs in British Studios," by Mary Power, *Pearson's Weekly,* July 22, 1933. The official position of Gordon Conway at both Gaumont-British and Gainsborough studios should be distinguished from the public's perception of her job, and even from her own interpretation of the job. Conway carried out duties generally attributed to the head of a Hollywood costume department in the early 1930s. The terms describing her job in official Gaumont-British documents often are misleading and do not indicate the depth of her executive responsibilities, some officially assigned and others self-imposed. For example, the 1932

Gaumont-British commemorative brochure honoring the reopening of the studio lists Conway as "Dress Designer," yet her name is included under the "Combined Executive." Also, Conway's contract, dated May 31, 1933, but representing the period from January 1, 1933, defines her job as "Costume designer and Supervisor on films." The ambiguity of terms and job description betray a company in search of a policy about the priority of costume design in film production and the company's ambivalent acceptance of Conway's vision.

Press releases from the studio, on the other hand, along with subsequent news reports, were more definitive and positive and generally credited Conway as head of costuming efforts like her highly publicized colleagues in Hollywood. Conway viewed herself in such a role because she was performing the duties of an executive head well over a year before the *Sunday Referee* announced on September 10, 1933, that she would be serving in "a New Post in British Film: First Studio Dress Department."

33. Gaumont-British 1932 commemorative brochure.

34. Michael Powell, November 1984 interview.

35. Michael Balcon, *Michael Balcon Presents . . . A Lifetime of Films,* 124–125.

36. Reported by British stage and film actresses during 1983–1993 interviews in Great Britain. Though Conway did not design for Anna Neagle and Mary Ellis, the two actresses were informative and helpful about the stage and film milieu of the era.

37. Low, *The History of British Film: 1918–1929,* 243–248; and *The History of British Film 1929–1939: Film Making in 1930s Britain,* 124. Also see the index to both of these books.

38. Clarence Winchester, ed., *The World Film Encyclopedia: A Universal Screen Guide,* 18–21. A still (plate 12) of Cicely Courtneidge in *Jack's the Boy* appears in this book, but Courtneidge wears a traditional Scottish garb, not a Conway original gown. Though Conway supervised the costuming, the still and text do not include credits for the work.

39. *THE PICTUREGOER's Who's Who and Encyclopaedia of the Screen To-Day,* 107, 117, 119, 258, 449–457, 467, 469, 494–497, 507–508. This encyclopedia contains a crowd scene shot at Selfridges for *Love On Wheels,* but the dresses designed by Conway are difficult to see and are not credited.

40. Susan Perez Prichard, ed., *Film Costume: An Annotated Bibliography*, 2–3, 74, 109, 168. This bibliography covers almost four thousand books and articles written over a seventy-year period. Another annotated bibliography that is essential to costume research is Bobbi Owen, ed., *Costume Design on Broadway: Designers and Their Credits, 1915–1985.*

41. GC press books: *Sunday Referee*, September 10, 1933.

42. GC press books: *Pearson's Weekly*, July 22, 1933.

43. See appendix in Leese.

44. C. A. Lejeune, *The Observer*, February 19, 1933.

45. *VFR*, London, February 28, 1933.

46. GC 1932 diary.

47. GC press books: *The Era*, October 19, 1932.

48. Advertisements and a blurb on Kahler's book jacket cover.

49. GC 1932 diary.

50. DHQ interviews.

51. *VFR*, 1932.

52. *VFR*, New York, 193?.

53. GC press books: "Frocks of the Film Stars," *Weldon's Ladies Journal*, October 1933.

54. GC press books: *Sunday Chronicle*, November 27, 1932.

55. *VFR*, London, November 20, 1932.

56. *VFR*, New York, February 24, 1933.

57. *New York Times Film Reviews* (hereafter cited as *NYTFR*), December 1933.

58. C. A. Lejeune, *The Observer*, November 20, 1932.

59. GC press books: "Moderns To Follow," *Modern Weekly*, June 23, 1928.

60. GC press books: Denning, Vere. "The Women Who Help to Make British Films," *Modern Woman*, April 1, 1933.

61. Ibid.

62. Ibid.

63. GC press books: "Magnificent Gowns: Evelyn Laye's Luck in Film of an Opera," *The Star*, December 3, 1932.

64. GC 1932 diary. Conway spelled his nickname as "Chan," though other associates spelled it "Shan." She recently had worked with Philip C. Samuel, the Shepherd's Bush studio manager, when he acted as associate producer for *Rome Express.*

65. See Aileen and Michael Balcon Collection in the Special Materials Unit of the Library and Information Services, British Film Institute, London. (Permission granted to the author by Jonathan Balcon.) A memo from Michael Balcon earlier that year to "Shan" expressed concern about Conway keeping up with the production duties at the studio. A longtime champion of Gordon, "Shan" Balcon believed in Conway's ability to create and produce.

66. Edward N. "Teddie" Holstius (hereafter cited as ENH), 1930–1956 letters to GC.

67. ENH (Mr. and Mrs.) 1932 note to GC.

68. GC 1932 diary.

69. Ibid.

70. GC 1932 and 1933 diaries.

8. AN ARTIST IN CLOTH

1. GC 1933 diary.

2. *VFR*, New York, 1933–1934.

3. Low, *The History of British Film 1929–1939: Film Making in 1930s Britain*, 134–135, 160. Many observers of Conway's images comment on stills that feature heavy actresses. (See list of interviews.) Pointing out Marie Ault in *The Return of the Rat* and Martita Hunt in *Friday the Thirteenth*, film authority Eric Braun explained that these stout actresses often are called the "black bombazine" ladies, in reference to the fabric that concealed and bolstered the hefty bodies. During a 1985 interview, another viewer of Conway's work, Benny Green, exclaimed, "Say, look here . . . she [Conway] should have been designing for actresses like Katharine Hepburn in *The Philadelphia Story*, not that slapstick Cicely Courtneidge." In 1933 Carol Goodner had gained so much weight that she looked stout and matronly in the film stills of *Just Smith*. On viewing these stills during a 1984 interview, Michael Powell recalled that Carol Goodner was "a lovely actress and a lovely

woman. . . . She would have been very beautiful if she hadn't been overweight. . . a bit lumpy, but a beautiful woman." Concerning weight and shape, Gary Chapman observed that two comediennes dressed by Dolly Tree had different images: the slim and agile Rosalind Russell was thought chic, but Margaret Dumont, the stout actress in the Marx Brothers movies, was derided in the films for her size, shape, and bearing. Conway's slim images on paper that contrast with the heavy images in production photographs and stills represent the reverse to the images of Léon Bakst's figures on paper and in photographs. See examples of large buxom images created by Bakst, such as "Danse Syrienne" for *Cleopatra* in 1909, "Odalisque" for *Schéhérazade* in 1910, and "Bacchante" for *Narcisse* in 1911. (These drawings are reproduced in Charles Spencer's *Léon Bakst*, 61, 93, 65.) Interestingly, the reverse of Conway's images in drawings and in photographs, these production photographs reveal thinner figures of these Bakst-costumed ballet dancers. Even the most glamorous of film goddesses had shapes, movements, and mannerisms that had to be remedied by the artfulness of the camera. See McCooey, 60–66: for instance, Greta Garbo was considered by some as "a big girl to dress," and late in her career, others thought "her shoulders looked awkward . . . [and] her feet too big." For researchers concerned with size and shape, see the three body types that were reproduced by Susan Meyerott in the April 1989 issue of *Idea Today*, 1, 16, 18–19. The charts do not portray fat women as such but feature bone structure and muscle with a propensity for fat. Offering insight into the stigma of women with weight is Wolf's *The Beauty Myth*, 94, 98–102. Recent cultural indications point to a more realistic and positive attitude about heavy women. An editor of the New York–based *Big Beautiful Woman*—a magazine that boasts 200,000 subscribers nationally—was quoted in an August 17, 1991, article (p. D-10) in the *Washington Post*: "a lot more people are realizing that Earth does not shatter or stop due to size. . . . The large-size woman now accepts themselves for who they are. . . ." *Washington Post* columnist, Kara Swisher, reports: "more high-fashion designers, who most often cater to the stick-thin set," are producing lines for the women with a healthy attitude about size.

4. Trewin, Mander, and Mitchenson, *The Gay Twenties*, 18. Just as the shape and actions of Cicely Courtneidge differed from those of Rosalind Russell, so did the shape and actions of Charlotte Greenwood differ from those of Dorothy Dickson.

5. *Woman's Life*, March 25, 1933, and unidentified paper, January 19, 1933.

6. *VFR*, 1933 (*It's a Boy*).

7. *VFR*, March 14, 1933. Also see *NYTFR*, October 1933.

8. C. A. Lejeune, *The Observer*, February 20 or 26, 1933.

9. William K. Everson (hereafter cited as WKE), 1984 interviews in New York and Washington, D.C. From his private film collection, WKE screened in New York for the author his print of *The Ghoul* and loaned two reels of *Confetti* for the author to view at the American Film Institute, John F. Kennedy Center for the Performing Arts, Washington, D.C.

10. DHQ interviews.

11. GC 1934 diary.

12. *VFR*, New York, 1933 (*I Was a Spy*).

13. Low, *The History of British Film 1929–1939: Film Making in 1930s Britain*, 165–169, 188.

14. *VFR*, New York, February 12, 1937.

15. GC press books: *The Sunday Referee*, September 10, 1933. (Letter to the editor from Harold Alexander of "New Cross.")

16. John Kobal, *Hollywood Glamor Portraits: 145 Photos of Stars 1926–1949*, v–xii.

17. GC 1933 diary.

18. *NYTFR*, review by Mordaunt Hall, May 24, 1935.

19. *Woman's Own*, April 15, 1933.

20. GC press books: "A Woman Prophet of Film Fashions, New Post in British Films: Studio's First Dress Department," by Nerina Shute, *The Sunday Referee*, September 10, 1933.

21. GC 1933 contract with Gaumont-British.

22. Low, *The History of British Film 1929–1939: Film Making in 1930s Britain*, 175, 180.

23. GC press books: Shute, *The Sunday Referee*, September 10, 1933.

24. GC press books: "Dressing Up the Stars," *Picture Show*, March 24, 1934.

25. GC press books: "Our British Studios," *Picture Show*, November 18, 1933.

26. GC press books: Shute, *The Sunday Referee,* September 10, 1933.

27. GC 1933 diary.

28. *Daily Mirror* reprint, 1933 official program for *Waltz Time.*

29. Marguerite Tazelaar in *New York Herald Tribune,* 1933.

30. C. A. Lejeune, *The Observer,* two reviews: 11 and 18(?) June 1933.

31. *VFR,* London, June 27, 1933.

32. Low, *The History of British Film 1929–1939: Film Making in 1930s Britain,* 166–170.

33. Brown and Kardish, *Michael Balcon,* 19.

34. Robert Graves and Alan Hodge, 354–356.

35. *The Prince of Wales,* film and benefit souvenir program, June 22, 1933. Also GC 1933 diary and scrapbook.

36. Emlyn Williams interview.

37. *VFR,* Fall, 1933 (Two film reviews).

38. Michael Powell, November 1984 interview in New York. Also see Michael Powell, *A Life in Movies: An Autobiography,* 224–227.

39. Ibid., 343.

40. Ibid., 227–228.

41. Ibid., 231–236.

42. Margaret Kennedy, *The Constant Nymph.* For fiction's use of dress to describe character, see Valerie Steele, *Paris Fashion: A Cultural History,* 9–13, 147–149, 195–216. Calling attention to department store window-shoppers in Zola's novel *Au Bonheur des Dames,* Steele adds that in *Remembrance of Things Past (A la recherche du temps perdu),* "fashion references occur so often that, were they collected, they would make a small book of their own. Like Balzac . . . Marcel Proust frequently refers to the clothing his characters wear, and to the idea of fashion as a social force. . . . If Proust is indebted to Balzac for much of his social and psychological analysis of fashion, his philosophy of fashion seems to have come from Baudelaire." Steele asserts that Proust's novel includes an "analysis of the world of fashion" and combines "the *vestignomonie* of Balzac and the dandyisme of Baudelaire."

43. *VFR,* New York, April 10, 1933. Also see the critical acclaim in New York periodicals: William Boehnel in the April 7, 1934, *New York World;* and Otis Ferguson in the May 2, 1934, *New Republic.*

44. Kennedy, 64–65, 94, 102, 200–201.

45. *VFR,* 1943.

46. Studio promotional memo: press release entitled "*Constant Nymph* Production Story," 1943, Warner Bros. Pictures, New York. Also *VFR,* June 26–27, 1943, and *NYTFR,* September 15, 1943.

47. Dialogue notes during author's three viewings of *Aunt Sally.*

48. Michael Powell, November 1984 interview.

49. Ibid.

50. GC diaries.

51. ENH 1930–1956 letters to GC.

52. GC press books: *The Independent,* May 5, 1934. Also see *Stage,* April 26, 1934; and *Everyman,* May 4, 1934.

53. Agnes de Mille July 1, 1987, letter to author.

54. GC press books: *Manchester Evening News,* March 22, 1934.

55. GC press books: A. E. Wilson, "The Perfect Revue," *The Star,* April 25, 1934.

56. GC press books: *The Manchester Guardian,* March 22, 1934.

57. GC press books: "Fashions from Stage and Stalls," a regular feature by Florence Roberts in the *Illustrated Sporting and Dramatic News,* May 4, 1934.

58. Prichard, 123–124, 432.

59. Gary Chapman 1985–1993 interviews and letters, London, New York, Austin, Texas, and Washington, D.C.

60. Prichard, x–xi.

61. Gary Chapman 1985–1993 interviews and letters.

62. GC 1934 diary.

63. Letter from Michael Thornton to the author, August 8, 1996.

9. AN ARTIST IN MORE WAYS THAN ONE

1. GC 1934 diary.

2. Ibid.

3. A letter from Agnes de Mille to the author, July 1, 1987. Describing the aftermath of *Why Not To-Night?,* Agnes de Mille shed light on the possible unfortunate financial outcome: the "Thompson [*sic*] Twins wanted to do a second show and wanted to star me in it and I was very happy at this idea, but they went bankrupt. They were highly unreliable and I believe they left debts in every direction. Romny told me that in lieu of payment they offered him the office furniture, but he said he declined having seen it." Since Gordon usually required a partial payment made in advance of an assignment, the Twins' financial problems may not have resulted in a total loss of fee.

Additional comments by Agnes de Mille inform the cultural circumstances surrounding the revue, *Why Not To-Night?:* "I left my work in charge of an assistant to whom I paid three guineas a week and it was Antony Tudor, who later became one of the three greatest ballet choreographers in the world. My work was in superb hands. . . . [but] there was no one to take care of the work after it opened. When I returned to London in May my work hadn't been polished. I found the dancing in terrible disarray. The ballets were designed as vehicles for two remarkably unsuited performers. . . . paired in one pretty dreadful ballet about the wind called 'Tourbillon.' . . . [a]nd another ballet, devised for me by an English friend, Ramon Reid, called 'Three Virgins and a Devil.' This was rather fun and made a hit. . . . Eight years later I revised it in New York for the American Ballet Theater and danced the lead myself with Lucia Chase and . . . two other maidens and we had a smash. It has been in repertories ever since."

4. GC 1934 diary. Conway records do not specify the medicine.

5. This reflects the old debate concerning the origin of ideas about clothing and costume: which comes first, the ideas of the couturiers or the screen designers?

6. GC draft-letter to ENH, February or March 1951.

7. GC 1934 diary. Conway records do not specify the medicine.

8. ENH, January 12, 1951, letter to GC. The letters (1930–1956) exchanged between ENH and GC include interesting film history. ENH

tells of his first trip to Hollywood disguised as a hobo that he later described in the 1936 and 1937 editions of his book, *Hollywood Through the Back Door.* ENH also wrote of his subsequent five-year ordeal with MGM concerning his novels and screenplays.

9. GC notes in back of 1936 diary.

10. Joan Antill (JA) and Mary Lutz (ML) 1983 joint interview in Washington, D.C. Also December 12, 1943, letter from JA to GC. Also OJA interviews.

11. Ibid.

12. Ibid. Also see list of interviews with Conway's friends and employees during 1983–1993 in Fredericksburg, Va., Washington, D.C., and Dallas, Tex. Also Rita Gulbenkian Essayan 1922–1956 letters to GC.

13. Interviews with MPE, JA, ML, and friends referred to in note 12.

14. OJA interviews.

15. Interview in 1987 with former employees, Virginia Jones and Maude Fortune, Corbin, Va. Also OJA interviews.

16. Kahler, *Smart Setback,* 1930, 235.

17. Calvin Tomkins, *Living Well Is the Best Revenge.* The book on Gerald and Sara Murphy focuses on the couple's talent for the "art of living." A comparison of Conway's outlook with the Murphys' philosophy of life is important to themes explored in this illustrated biography.

18. JA and ML interview.

19. Interviews with brothers and former employees, William Thomas Coghill and Oscar C. Coghill in Fredericksburg, Va., and Washington, D.C. Also interviews with nine of Conway's friends.

20. DD interviews.

21. DHQ interviews.

22. Rita Gulbenkian Essayan 1922–1956 letters to GC.

Part Two.
Images of a New Woman
INTRODUCTION:
MODEL IN YOUR MIRROR

1. *New York Herald,* Paris edition, March 2, 1924.

2. Gordon Conway's print-media art featured various styles that ranged from parody vignettes and book illustrations to advertising and fashion illustrations. Reinforced by upbeat and dream-creating captions, the advertising and fashion drawings showcased Conway's flair for fantasy, persuasion, and subtle manipulation through a style appealing to different levels of the imagination. (As an interesting parallel, see again Lepape's outline on pages 42–43 and 171–172 in *From the Ballets Russes to Vogue: The Art of Georges Lepape.*) Conway informed, entertained, and seduced consumers with three methods of presentation: (a) Using a vignette format, Conway staged scenes with elegant motifs in rich colors and dramatic settings. Offering the promise of a glamorous lifestyle, her drawings spotlighted striking females in original ensembles amidst tony, upscale appointments. This New Woman became the centerpiece of narrative scenes filled with places and things made famous by the aristocracy and beau monde in the mass media and popular entertainment. With these subtle visual instructions on how to dress and behave in daily life, Conway provided a guidepost for middle-class aspirations. (b) In contrast to these affluent settings and top-quality clothes, Conway interpreted moderately priced garments produced by other designers or manufacturers for sale in department stores like Harrods and Selfridges. Using limited backgrounds, she sketched accurate details of these garments with modest lines to accompany the captions that carried practical information like price and size along with flowery descriptions. However accurate the clothing detail, Conway's sketches display female figures that lack the usual personality and movement. (c) Combining elements of both stylistic approaches, she designed clothes to be copied at home or adapted by the neighborhood dressmaker at a reasonable cost. Conway was an expert seamstress and hatmaker who exploited the popularity of the sewing machine and mass-print patterns—such as those published by Condé Nast. Her designs offered the option of fabric at varying prices. She produced exact lines and careful detailing, accompanied by instructional captions for the sew-it-yourself designs. Conway produced simplified, understated, and chic original designs for everyday apparel. She imbued these illustrations with a sense of the real and a no-nonsense

Yankee practicality. Talented in dancing and active in sports, Conway transposed knowledge of her own body to renderings for energetic women who sought both comfortable and stylish attire that moved easily with each gesture. Conway's style reflected a democratic bias to provide women with good design at a wide range of price. Before designers and manufacturers launched the ready-to-wear industry (prêt-à-porter), Conway anticipated the business trend by furnishing women of different economic classes with stylish modes and know-how in the use of accessories. Conway had the talent, business sense, and promotional flair to pursue haute couture as well, but opportunities were scarce. For example, in the spring of 1924, after her style show presented during the Club Daunou *Midnight Follies,* she received requests for custom design work. Conway did not consider such work because she lacked the financing to establish a couture house, and competition within the French-dominated profession was intense. Between 1926 and 1928 the London fashion house of Chez Beth hired Conway to create original designs. This brief arrangement had the potential to establish Conway as a full-time couturière but dissolved due to management and funding problems. Not intended for reproduction in the print-media, these original fashion drawings had a similar format to her working drawings for stage and film costuming. (Chez Beth executed Conway's designs for two prominent 1927 productions—the film *Confetti* and the stage production of the musical-comedy *Peggy-Ann.*)

3. Martin Battersby, *The Decorative Twenties,* 145. For stage and film costuming, Conway used many fabrics, including one that resembled oil-cloth and patent leather, called "American cloth," which she labeled as "A. C." on her drawings. (Also see Battersby's book *The Decorative Thirties.*)

4. Ibid., 51.

5. Julia Meech and Gabriel P. Weisberg, *Japonisme Comes to America: The Japanese Impact on the Graphic Arts, 1876–1925,* 162, 191–92, 75, 37–38, 9. Also see Julian Robinson, *The Golden Age of Style: Art Déco Fashion Illustration,* 9–29. See comments about the influence of Japanese prints and art that influenced artists like Conway.

6. Gordon Conway, "Fashions from the Films," *Picture Show,* April 28, 1928, London.

7. See complete list of Conway's books in the bibliography. In preparing this list, the author reviewed the unpublished "Inventory of The Gordon Conway Collection" assembled by OJA and Jacqueline Downs in 1982–1983 in Orange, Va.

8. Both as a designer and customer, Conway was loyal to Jean Patou, who was a bitter rival of Gabrielle Chanel. Conway credited Patou with much of the comfort and construction of the new sports-clothes phenomenon—a contribution that Chanel was loathe to admit to her customers and the press. For example, Patou was instrumental in creating the stylish image, both on and off the court, for tennis-star Suzanne Lenglen. Though Conway interpreted a few of Chanel's designs for *La Donna,* she portrayed mostly Patou's and Molyneux's designs for the Italian magazine. Reflecting the importance of the couture industry to the economic and cultural well-being of France see Susan Train, ed., *Théâtre de la Mode* (Exhibition Catalogue).

9. Garnier, *Paul Poiret et Nicole Groult: Maîtres de la Mode Art Déco,* 108. Also see other books on Poiret's ideas like his 1931 autobiography, *King of Fashion,* and the biography by Palmer White, *Poiret.* For a view of "aesthetic unity" related to this total design concept, see Walter A. Fairservis, Jr., *Costumes of the East,* 130.

10. Tomkins, 5–7, 11–12, 14, 18–19, 25, 29, 59, 89, 94–95, 106–107, 122–123. See the Murphys' philosophy of "the art of living." Conway's salon shared a similar philosophy. A quarter of a century after their heady salon days before World War II, Guy Bolton and Teddie Holstius often reminisced about the convivial gatherings in the stunning setting at Bryanston Court on Upper George Street. The men wrote to Conway at Mount Sion that they missed her hospitality and the collection of friends from the stage, screen, publishing, and social worlds of London. Though the writers still saw some of the same people, Bolton and Holstius reported that friends were scattered—things had not been the same since the war. These festive occasions in Conway's flat in the late 1920s and early 1930s were replete with talk of the arts, entertainment, and leisure pursuits. The sartorial events included a wealth of games, like ten-hour bouts of bridge—from contract to three-handed bridge—that reached epidemic proportions. And there was poker, backgammon, Russian Bank, speculation, fan-tan, Slippery Sam, and rummy squeezed between dancing to the radio and records, and accented by Texas chili suppers and mint juleps with all that "good Kentucky bourbon." Most of all, though, Bolton and Holstius remembered the warmth of friendship and the excitement of those lively conversations. See related lifestyle concepts in Seebohm, *Man Who Was "Vogue",* 3–10, 36, 46–47, 79–82, 114–118, 171, 232–245, 279. See references to Nast's dream of transforming the look and behavior of American women. Welcomed by millions of middle-class women, his grand sweeping ideas brought Nast profits not only from subscriptions but especially from upscale advertising. The book is related to Con-

way's New Woman images and to the concepts of "the mode" and "the art of living." Nast's publications promised new lifestyles, both real and imagined, for women's public and private life. They tantalized with images of swank environs, and elevated the status of aspiring females to members of the "consumption community," like the burgeoning "café society." Though there were other economic, social, and cultural forces leading to the establishment of café society, Condé Nast deserves credit for much of its origin and popularity. In Nast's magazines, every setting and detail counted, whether in an illustration or photograph, not only for artistic composition but as a marketing tool. One of Nast's distinguished art directors, Mehemed Fehmy Agha once revealed, "*Vogue* readers want to see elegant backgrounds and furniture and smart ladies gracefully wearing smart dresses against these backgrounds." Condé Nast consciously created these images based on a "painstakingly constructed dream." Much like the Hollywood moguls—though with very different taste—Nast was "driven by a vision" to create the ultimate consumer's paradise through his magazines, dress patterns, and staged events. His September 1942 obituary in the *New York Herald Tribune* stated that Nast was acknowledged for teaching the American woman the art of gracious living. I suggest that "the mode" was a concept of beauty and style that blossomed in Paris early in the twentieth century, but had roots in the attitudes and practices of the eighteenth-century French court, especially of Louis XIV. Often judged purely commercial and used only as a marketing tactic, "the mode" suggests a more complex definition. The term is associated with a cluster of fashionable ideas and practices emanating from the custom-design ateliers of Parisian couturiers like legendary avant-garde designer Paul Poiret. Yet it stood for more than a revolution in dress. "The mode" represented a new way of living—a consciously created lifestyle. Indeed, it encompassed an artistically inspired experience, an artificial reality, and a tableau carved out of everyday life. The concept provided the New Woman, as well as the New Man, with an aesthetic reason for being. Also see Annette Tapert and Diana Edkins, *The Power of Style: The Women Who Defined The Art of Living Well.*

11. Meech and Weisberg, *Japonisme Comes to America,* 37, 181.

12. Ibid., 163–164; Alan and Isabella Livingston, *Encyclopaedia of Graphic Design and Designers,* 54.

13. Alan and Isabella Livingston, *Encyclopaedia of Graphic Design and Designers,* 54. Concerning this design revolution, see Meech and Weisberg, *Japonisme Comes to America,* 37–38, 163–64, 181; and Robinson, *The Golden Age of Style,* 111–112. Many exhibitions, publications, and

news reports explained "the new aesthetic theories and how these could be applied to modern life. . . . all the resources of the new age [were] to make life more convenient, comfortable and congenial." Related to these objectives of design in society and to "the art of living," also see Lloyd Rose, *Washington Post,* "Chairway to Heaven: Can a Perfect Piece of Furniture Lead Us to a Perfect World," Washington, D.C., March 14, 1993, p. G-5.

14. Walt Reed and Roger Reed, *The Illustrator in America: 1880–1980,* 112.

15. Alan and Isabella Livingston, *Encyclopaedia of Graphic Design and Designers,* 16.

16. William Packer, *Fashion Drawing in Vogue,* 13.

17. Robinson, *The Golden Age of Style,* 14–17. Before the Jazz Age in the 1920s, an almost demonic attraction to speed and activity captivated Conway and her contemporaries in the arts. Providing insight into the teens, Sidonie Gabrielle Colette reported in a Paris newspaper about "the feverish craze for the tango" and described how one woman had danced herself to death from peritonitis: "*She* finally confessed that for two and a half months, and almost without noticing it, she had danced the tango for seven, eight and sometimes eleven hours a day, always wearing fairly tight shoes with high heels." As early as 1910 André Gide noted in his diary that an annoying characteristic of the period was the preoccupation with "the extreme and exaggeration." Before the Great War, famed couturier Jean Worth regretted the abandonment of "former standards in dress. . . . [the change] seems to synchronize with the growing restlessness of this age, an age of fast motors and flying machines and feverish craze for excitement and distraction."

18. Marshall McLuhan, *Understanding Media: The Extensions of Man.* See references to the "cool" medium on vii–xi, 36–45. As to "goddesses" in Conway's art, see James Hall, *Dictionary of Subjects and Symbols in Art,* 254–255. An unpublished drawing of three sophisticated ladies is the epitome of Conway's New Woman message. It relates to such mythological goddesses as "Prudence with three faces," representing the virtues of "memory, intelligence and foresight," attributes that Conway admired in women. Probably created between 1934 and 1936, the drawing displays a fresh concept of beauty and style, and broadcasts a message of "measured judgement." This trio presents a shrewd, independent nature along with a sense of expectation. This drawing serves as a symbolic link and introduction to seven images of the New Woman in the art of Gordon Conway. Also see Conway's "Diana and the Centaurs" from 1924, which suggests one type of the mythical "Diana"—the woman as "Civilization" triumphs over "Barbarism" as represented by the centaurs. (An interesting parallel is the theme of the modern-woman-as-civilizer in the Conway-dressed, futuristic film *High Treason* in 1929.) The goddess Diana was also known as the "protectress of women." See references to goddesses like "Diana the Huntress" in James G. Frazer's *The Golden Bough,* in James Hall's *Dictionary of Subjects and Symbols in Art,* and in *Bulfinch's Mythology* by Thomas Bulfinch.

19. Todd, xxv–xxvii, 24, 36, 98, 136–138, 161, 178, 319–320. Also see contrasting images in: Stella Blum, *Everyday Fashions of the Twenties as Pictured in Sears and Other Catalogs.* Conway's images differ dramatically from a grab bag of looks over the past one hundred years like the ladies of the Gilded Age, the Edwardian Age, and La Belle Epoque, and the Gibson Girl at the turn of the century. Conway's work shows little resemblance to images of subsequent decades like the den mother and dishwasher on covers of mass-print magazines, and sexpot ideals like the World War II pin-ups of the Vargas, Petty, and Whitcomb "Girls," and later the *Playboy* "Bunnies." These historic images exemplify a variety of ideal female types that continue to attract a large following today. If Conway had applied strategies from "the politics of fame" in the same manner as these male illustrators, her New Women might be labeled today as the "Conway Girls." Speculation suggests that Conway neglected to provide for her artistic legacy. She lacked a loyal coterie of followers after her retirement and overlooked plans with publicity agents and gallery dealers to present her art in the years to come. Consequently, Conway's once-popular artwork is unheralded today. For an important analysis of the strategies used to achieve success and fame, see *High Visibility* by Irving Rein, Philip Kotler, and Martin Stoller.

20. Walt Reed, *50 Great American Illustrators.* The cover of Reed's book was Jon Whitcomb's drawing that originally illustrated Eileen Herbert Jordan's story "Your Ideal Girl" in the August 1953 *Good Housekeeping.* An unpublished drawing by Conway of a lady in a sun hat, executed in London around 1934, is both similar and dissimilar to the Whitcomb female image. Though almost two decades separate the two pictures, they nevertheless represent two different ideals of feminine beauty that need to be examined. The drawings differ in tone and intent, yet the similarities of composition are startling: the heads and bare shoulders are posed similarly with a three-quarters view of the left side of the faces. No clothing is visible save one halter strap on each model. The two wear stunning floral decorated picture hats that cast a shadow

across the eyes, highlighting part of the cheek, chin, and lips. The shaped eyebrows accent a sophisticated makeup job on each face. Both women have swept-back short dark hair, yet there is a dramatic difference in the messages broadcast by the two styles of drawing.

21. A 1919–1920 nationwide advertising campaign by the National City Co. featured twenty different posters and window cards that featured Conway's New Woman silhouettes. This campaign was a major marketing effort to attract female customers.

22. During World War I, a large number of women worked as volunteers or received minimal pay for patriotic jobs.

23. Seebohm, *Man Who Was "Vogue"*, chapter "War à la Mode," 83–102.

24. Dodderidge Farrell 1918 letters to GC.

25. *Vanity Fair,* January 1918 and August 1918.

26. Ibid., August 1919. These drawings were executed well over a year before Gordon married Blake Ozias. The attitude expressed in "Down with Husbands" differs greatly from her later treatment of men in "Madame La Vie," a drawing with a less cavalier treatment of the male, which was created after marital difficulties in 1923, though not published until 1926.

27. Ibid., August 1918.

28. *New York Herald,* Paris edition, March 2, 1924.

IMAGE ONE. ZINA AND HER COUSINS

1. See Barbara Welter, "The Cult of True Womanhood: 1820–1860," in *The American Family in Social-Historical Perspective,* ed. Michael Gordon.

IMAGE FOUR. NIGHT OWL

1. Assorted Conway diary entries, 1911–1937.

IMAGE FIVE. CONSUMING WOMAN

1. Advertising text copy from one of a set of 1920 posters for the National City Company, which featured Conway's silhouettes.

CONCLUSION. A STREAMLINED WOMAN IN A MECHANIZED WORLD

1. Henry Allen, "Their Stocking Feat: Nylon at 50 and the Age of Plastic," *Washington Post,* January 13, 1988, p. D-10.

2. Gordon Conway 1929 press books.

A NOTE ON SOURCES

This book is based on materials which include an enormous number of printed texts and reproduced images. It is not possible to present here my list of more than nine hundred entries consulted, especially the secondary texts or books by authorities. For the serious researcher, I plan to deposit this Comprehensive Bibliography (Com/Bib/RVA) in the Theatre Arts Collection of the Harry Ransom Humanities Research Center, University of Texas at Austin (hereafter cited as HRHRC/UT). (Some of these works appear in the Notes and the Selected Bibliography.) This Com/Bib/RVA is divided according to the various career concerns of Gordon Conway: illustrative and advertising art; fashion illustration and design; stage and film costume design; consumer product and service promotion; and women's studies and cultural history between the world wars. These career interests determined my search for primary sources, which were often located in privately owned archives of unpublished materials.

The function of the notes to follow is to present as complete a guide as possible to the primary sources I consulted, since these are the most difficult for researchers to locate. The major holdings of primary sources on Gordon Conway are located in the following collections:

1. The Theatre Arts Collection of the Harry Ransom Humanities Research Center, University of Texas at Austin, Gordon Conway Collection: original Conway drawings and graphic reproductions, posters, programs, advertisements, film stills and scripts, press books, scrapbooks, photograph albums, business-related letters, and memorabilia.

2. Private collection of Dr. and Mrs. Harvey Waldo Allen of Fredericksburg, Virginia, donors of the Gordon Conway materials to the HRHRC/UT (no family relation to author). (Dr. and Mrs. Allen have continued the research agreement with the author first granted by the late Olive Johnson Allen.) Small selection of Conway's drawings, graphic reproductions, personal diaries, letters, photographs, clothing, memorabilia, and Conway's library of books.

3. The Drawings and Prints Department of the Metropolitan Museum of Art, New York: original drawings and graphic reproductions donated by Mr. and Mrs. Marshall E. Allen in 1971.

4. Author's collection: (a) Reproductions and photographs of original Conway drawings, photographs of costumes, and duplicate stills from Conway-dressed films. (b) Small number of original drawings, *pochoirs*, and reproductions of artworks by illustrators and designers of the era, as well as cultural ephemera of the period like programs, sheet music, magazines, and advertisements from Gordon Conway's era.

Though much primary material is located in archival collections in public institutions, I found a wealth of valuable data—pictorial ephemera and material culture—through informal and unconventional sources. Indeed, I have spent eleven years on a continuous cultural scavenger hunt in the United States, Great Britain, and Europe—mostly in the locations where Gordon Conway lived and worked. Informal venues and commercial establishments located include jumbles, film memorabilia fairs, and Ephemera Society shows in London; flea markets and shops in Paris; and antique shows, collectibles fairs, and street and yard sales in New York City and Washington, D.C. Beside the mass of visual material and ephemera viewed or purchased by the author, a network of people—amateur historians and collectors—informed the research and often led to interviews and private collections.

United States

NEW YORK CITY

The Art Students League of New York

The Condé Nast Publications Library: *Vogue* and *Vanity Fair* issues, and selected *House and Garden* issues, 1914–1925

Cooper-Hewitt Museum of Design

Fashion Institute of Technology
    Shirley Goodman Resource Center

Illustration House, Inc., New York

The Metropolitan Museum of Art
    Costume Institute Library
    Drawings and Prints
    Photograph and Slide Library
    Thomas J. Watson Library

The Museum of the City of New York
Costume Collection
Theatre Collection

The Museum of Modern Art
Film Study Center
Stills Collection
Department of Film and Video
Selected film series/program notes/lectures

New York Public Library for the Performing Arts at Lincoln Center, The Billy Rose Theatre Collection

The Shubert Archive

The Society of Illustrators

The Walter Hampden–Edwin Booth Theatre Collection and Library at The Players Club, New York

Brooklyn Museum Library

NEW YORK STATE

East Hampton Library, Long Island

The International Museum of Photography at George Eastman House, Rochester

WASHINGTON, D.C.

American Film Institute in the John F. Kennedy Center for the Performing Arts
Selected film series/program notes

American Institute of Architects Foundation, Inc. and The Octagon House Museum
Research Library and Audio Visual Department

Art Deco Society of Washington, D.C.

Library of Congress, Divisions of
Copyright Office: Certification and Documents
Local History and Genealogy
Motion Picture, Broadcasting and Recorded Sound
Selected film series/program notes/lectures
Music
Newspapers and Current Periodicals
Prints and Photographs

Martin Luther King Library, Georgetown Branch

National Gallery of Art
Selected film series/program notes/lectures

National Museum of Women in the Arts
Library and Research Center
Education Department
Programs on women artists: selected films, mini-courses, gallery talks, symposia, and lectures

Smithsonian Institution
Archives of American Art
National Museum of American Art
Renwick Gallery
National Museum of American History
Clothing and Costume Collection
National Portrait Gallery
Residents Associates Program: selected mini-courses, gallery talks, symposia, and lectures

TEXAS

Austin
The University of Texas at Austin Libraries
Harry Ransom Humanities Research Center, Theatre Arts Collection
B. J. Simmons and Company Collection
Gordon Conway Collection

Fine Arts Library

Cleburne
Cleburne City Library
Layland Museum

Dallas
Dallas Historical Society
Dallas Public Library
Texas/Dallas History and Archives Division

Temple
Temple Public Library, Reference Department

Waco
Baylor University Libraries, Moody Memorial Library

FREDERICKSBURG, VIRGINIA

Historic Fredericksburg Foundation, Inc.

Belmont, The Gari Melchers Memorial Gallery

OHIO

"The Archives" of Preble County

CALIFORNIA

Los Angeles County Museum of Art, Costume Institute

M. H. de Young Memorial Museum of The Fine Arts Museums of San Francisco

Western Costume Company, Los Angeles

OTHER

*University of Georgia Library, Athens
    Prints and Drawings
        Max Weldy Collection

Baltimore Museum of Art

Delaware Art Museum, Wilmington

Great Britain

LONDON

British Film Institute
    Library and Information Services
        Special Materials Unit
            Aileen and Michael Balcon Collection
    Museum of the Moving Image
        Education Department lectures
    National Film and Television Archive
        Stills, Posters and Designs
        Viewing Services (selected British films, 1925–1937)
    National Film Theatre
        Selected film seasons/program notes

British Museum
    Prints and Drawings

British Museum Library
    Newspaper and Periodical Library

Courtlaud Institute of Art

The Fine Art Society

*Hulton Deutsch Picture Library and Collection

Illustrated London News Picture Library

Museum of London
    Later London History and Collections (film archive and costume collection)

The Raymond Mander and Joe Mitchenson Theatre Collection

Victoria and Albert Museum
    Costume Collection
    Library
    Prints and Drawings
    Theatre Museum at Covent Garden

Westminster Central Reference Library

BATH

Museum of Costume and Fashion Research Centre

Europe

LAUSANNE, SWITZERLAND

Les Archives de la Ville de Lausanne

Bibliothèque Cantonale et Universitaire

Musée Historique de Lausanne

GINGINS, SWITZERLAND

Fondation Neumann

PARIS, FRANCE

*Bibliothèque de l'Arsenal

*Musée des Arts de la Mode

*Musée de la Mode et du Costume, Palais Galliera

Auction Houses

(Sources include the catalogues and print ephemera of the auctions proper as well as exhibitions prior to auction.)

NEW YORK AND/OR LONDON

*Bonham's

Christie's

Phillips

Sotheby's

WASHINGTON, D.C.

Adam A. Weschler and Sons

C. G. Sloan and Co., Inc.

*Author's research in collaboration with Gary Chapman of London, stage and film costume authority and biographer of Dolly Tree.

SELECTED BIBLIOGRAPHY

Articles by Gordon Conway

"De Life and de Ladies de Luxe: Impressions by Gordon Conway." *La Saison de Cannes,* 1927.

"Dressing the Talkies." *The Film Weekly* (London), September 2, 1929, p. 7.

"Fashions from the Films." *Picture Show* (London), April 28, 1928, p. 19.

"Frocks for Films." *The Bioscope British Film Number (1929),* pp. 240−241. (London.)

"Mount Sion." *The Spur: Life in Virginia, Past and Present* (Fredericksburg, Va.) 4, no. 3 (June 1953).

For selected periodicals containing graphic reproductions of Conway's artwork, see Catalogue Raisonné: A Reference Guide to the Artwork and Career of Gordon Conway.

Catalogues, Periodicals, and Articles about Gordon Conway

Allen, Raye Virginia. "Conway, Gordon." In *The New Handbook of Texas,* 2: 299−301. Austin: Texas State Historical Association, 1996.

Bauer, Allison. "Gordon Conway: That Red Head Gal." *Texas Historian* 50, no. 1 (September 1989): 1−3. Austin: Texas State Historical Association and Junior Historians, Burleson Junior High School.

Becker, Carolus, ed. "In Memoriam." *The Spur: Life in Virginia, Past and Present* 7, no. 4 (July 1956): 5.

Catron, Joanna. *Red, Hot & Southern: The International Fashions and Designs of Gordon Conway, 1916−1936.* Exhibition brochure. Fredericksburg, Va.: Historic Fredericksburg Foundation, Inc., 1990.

Hotline: Newsletter of The Handbook of Texas. Austin: Texas State Historical Association, Winter 1993, 2−3.

Jewell, Dorothy. "Those Jazz-Age Fashions." *Modern Maturity* 24, no. 4 (August−September 1981): 38−42.

Kery, Patricia Frantz. *Great Magazine Covers of the World,* 65, 163. New York: Abbeville Press, 1982.

Leese, Elizabeth. *Costume Design in the Movies.* New York: Frederick Ungar, 1976. (See other editions of this book with updated information by Leese in Com/Bib/RVA.)

Miller, Melissa. "From Process to Product." In *"Mirror, Mirror . . .": Costume Design for the American and British Stage, 1870s−1970s,* 16−17. Austin: Harry Ransom Humanities Research Center, University of Texas at Austin, 1995.

Owen, Bobbi, ed. *Costume Design on Broadway: Designers and Their Credits, 1915−1985,* 39−40. New York: Greenwood Press, 1987.

Petteys, Chris, ed. *Dictionary of Women Artists: An International Dictionary of Women Artists Born before 1900,* 156. Boston: G. K. Hall & Co., 1985.

Reid, Beryl. *The Cat's Whiskers.* London: Ebury Press, 1986.

Rubinstein, Charlotte Streifer. *American Women Artists from Early Indian Times to the Present,* 163. Boston: G. K. Hall & Co., 1982.

Schaff, David. "Gordon Conway." *Horizon: The Magazine of the Arts* 23, no. 5 (May 1980): 20−29.

———. *That Red Head Gal: Fashions and Designs of Gordon Conway, 1916−1936.* Exhibition catalogue and accompanying gallery guide. Washington, D.C.: American Institute of Architects Foundation, Inc., 1980.

Society of Illustrators. *America's Greatest Women Illustrators, 1850−1950.* Exhibition catalogue. New York: Society of Illustrators, 1985.

Surowiec, Catherine, ed. *Cinema Design.* London: British Film Institute Publishing, forthcoming. To include entry on Gordon Conway.

Works Cited: Books, Catalogues, and Journals

Allen, Frederick Lewis. *Only Yesterday: An Informal History of the 1920s.* New York: Perennial, 1964.

Amory, Cleveland, and Frederic Bradlee, eds. *"Vanity Fair," Selections from America's Most Memorable Magazine: A Cavalcade of the 1920s and 1930s.* New York: Viking Press, 1960.

Anscombe, Isabelle. *A Woman's Touch: Women in Design from 1860 to the Present Day.* New York: Viking Penguin, 1984.

Balcon, Michael. *Michael Balcon Presents . . . A Lifetime of Films.* London: Hutchinson of London, 1969.

———, Ernest Lindgren, Forsyth Hardy, and Roger Manvell.

The Literature of Cinema: Twenty Years of British Film, 1925–1945. London: Falcon Press, 1947; reprint, New York: Arno Press, 1972.

Banta, Martha. *Imaging American Women: Idea and Ideals in Cultural History.* New York: Columbia University Press, 1987.

Barr, Charles, ed. *All Our Yesterdays: 90 Years of British Cinema.* London: British Film Institute, 1986.

Battersby, Martin. *The Decorative Thirties.* New York: Walker and Co., 1971.

———. *The Decorative Twenties.* London: Studio Vista, 1971.

Benson, Susan Porter. *Counter Cultures: Saleswomen, Managers, and Customers in American Department Stores, 1890–1940.* Urbana: University of Illinois Press, 1988.

Bergan, Ronald. *The Great Theatres of London: An Illustrated Companion.* London: Multimedia Books, 1987.

Blum, Stella. *Everyday Fashions of the Twenties as Pictured in Sears and Other Catalogs.* New York: Dover Publications, 1981.

Bogart, Michele. "Artistic Ideals and Commercial Practices: The Problem of Status for American Illustrators." In *Prospects: An Annual Journal of American Cultural Studies,* vol. 15. New York: Cambridge University Press, 1990.

Boorstin, Daniel J. *The Image: A Guide to Pseudo Events in America.* New York: Harper Colophon, 1964.

Bradbury, Molly. *The History of Johnson County, Texas.* Cleburne, Tex.: Johnson County History Book Committee, 1985.

Brown, Geoff, and Laurence Kardish, eds. *Michael Balcon: The Pursuit of British Cinema.* Film retrospective catalogue. New York: Museum of Modern Art, 1984.

Bulfinch, Thomas. *Bulfinch's Mythology.* New York: Thomas Y. Crowell, n.d. (ca. 1958).

Campbell, T. E. *Colonial Caroline: A History of Caroline County, Virginia.* Richmond: The Dietz Press, 1954.

Canaday, John. *Mainstreams of Modern Art: David to Picasso.* New York: Simon and Schuster, 1959.

Chapman, Gary. "Atlantic Crossing: The Work of Costume Designer Dolly Tree." *The Passing Show: Newsletter of the Shubert Archive* (New York) 14, no. 2 (Fall 1991): 7–12.

Chase, Edna Woolman, and Ilka Chase. *Always in Vogue.* New York: Doubleday and Co., 1954.

Cohen, Daniel. "Grand Emporiums Peddle Their Wares in a New Market." *Smithsonian,* March 1993. (This is listed in the magazine contents as "For Department Stores, It's Retail Wars".)

Cutrer, Emily Fourmy. *The Art of the Woman: The Life and Work of Elisabet Ney.* Lincoln: University of Nebraska Press, 1988.

Dippie, Brian. *Charles M. Russell, Word Painter: Letters 1887–1926.* New York: Harry N. Abrams and Fort Worth: Amon Carter Museum, 1993.

Fairservis, Walter A., Jr. *Costumes of the East.* Riverside, Conn.: Chatham Press, 1971.

Farrar, Emmie Ferguson, and Emily Hines. *Old Virginia Houses along the Fall Line.* New York: Hastings House, 1976.

Ferber, Edna. *Emma McChesney & Co.* New York: Frederick A. Stokes Co., 1915.

Frazer, James G. *The Golden Bough.* New York: Macmillan Co., 1922.

Garnier, Guillaume. *Paul Poiret et Nicole Groult: Maîtres de la Mode Art Déco.* Paris: Musée de la Mode et du Costume, Palais Galliera, 1986.

Gelfant, Blanche H. "What More Can Carrie Want? Naturalistic Ways of Consuming Women." In *Prospects: An Annual Journal of American Cultural Studies* 19: 389–417. New York: Cambridge University Press, 1994.

Goetzmann, William H., essay, and exhibition catalogue by Becky Duval Reese. *Texas Images and Visions.* Austin: University of Texas Press and U.T. Huntington Gallery, 1983.

Graves, Robert, and Alan Hodge. *The Long Week-End: A Social History of Great Britain 1918–1939.* London: Faber and Faber, 1941.

Green, Stanley. *Broadway Musicals: Show by Show.* Milwaukee: Hal Leonard Books, 1985.

———. *The World of Musical Comedy.* New York: Da Capo Press, 1980.

Grey, Zane. *The Call of the Canyon.* New York: Grosset and Dunlap, 1952.

Hall, James. *Dictionary of Subjects and Symbols in Art.* London: John Murray, 1985.

Harris, Ann Sutherland, and Linda Noclin. *Women Artists: 1550–1950.* Exhibition catalogue. New York: A. A. Knopf and Los Angeles County Museum of Art, 1977.

Hayden, Horace Edwin. *Virginia Genealogies.* Baltimore: Genealogical Publishing Co., 1979.

Heller, Nancy G. *Women Artists: An Illustrated History.* New York: Abbeville Press, 1987.

Hemingway, Ernest. *A Moveable Feast.* New York: Charles Scribner's Sons, 1964.

Henderson, Mary C. *Broadway Ballyhoo: The American Theater Seen in Posters, Photographs, Magazines, Caricatures, and Programs.* New York: Harry N. Abrams, 1989. (This book contains two Conway drawings, which are not credited.)

————. *Theater in America: 200 Years of Plays, Players, and Productions.* New York: Harry N. Abrams, 1986.

Hollander, Anne. *Seeing through Clothes.* New York: Viking Press, 1978.

Hollis, Richard. *Graphic Design: A Concise History.* London: Thames and Hudson, 1994.

Holstius, Edward N. *Hollywood through the Back Door.* London: Longmans, 1936–1937. (See other Holstius novels in Com/Bib/RVA.)

Jacobson, Lori, and Charles Spencer. *Erté and His Contemporaries: Costume Designs in the Early Twentieth Century Music Halls in Paris.* Exhibition catalogue. McAllen, Tex.: McAllen International Museum, 1988.

Jones, Margaret C. *Heretics and Hellraisers: Women Contributors to THE MASSES, 1911–1917.* Austin: University of Texas Press, 1993.

Jones, Sydney R. *Art & Publicity: Fine Printing and Design.* Special Autumn Number of *The Studio.* London, 1925.

Jordan, Eileen Herbert. "Your Ideal Girl." *Good Housekeeping* 137, no. 2 (August 1953): 50. Illustration of same title by Jon Whitcomb.

Kahler, Wood. *Smart Setback.* New York: Alfred A. Knopf, 1930. (See other Kahler novels in Com/Bib/RVA.)

Kellenberger, Eric. *L'Affiche miroir du temps.* Exhibition catalogue. Gingins, Switzerland: Fondation Neumann, 1995.

————. *La Femme s'affiche.* Exhibition catalogue. Montreux: Commission d'Animation de l'Office du Tourisme de Montreux, 1990.

Kennedy, Margaret. *The Constant Nymph.* London: William Heinemann, 1945.

Kidwell, Claudia, and Valerie Steele, eds. *Men and Women: Dressing the Part.* Book accompanying exhibition, Smithsonian Institution. Washington, D.C.: Smithsonian Institution Press, 1989.

Kobal, John. *Hollywood Glamor Portraits: 145 Photos of Stars, 1926–1949.* New York: Dover Publications, 1976.

Laver, James. *Women's Dress in the Jazz Age.* London: Hamish Hamilton, 1964.

Lepape, Claude, and Thierry Defert. *From the Ballets Russes to VOGUE: The Art of Georges Lepape.* New York: Vendome Press, 1984.

Les Années "25": Art Déco/Bauhaus/Stijl Esprit Nouveau. Exhibition catalogue. Paris: Musée des Arts Décoratifs, 1966.

Levin, Lawrence W. *Highbrow-Lowbrow: The Emergence of Cultural Hierarchy in America.* Cambridge, Mass.: Harvard University Press, 1988.

Livingston, Alan, and Isabella, eds. *Encyclopaedia of Graphic Design and Designers.* London: Thames and Hudson, 1992.

Low, Rachael. *The History of British Film: 1918–1929.* London: George Allen and Unwin, 1971.

————. *The History of British Film 1929–1939: Film Making in 1930s Britain.* London: George Allen and Unwin, 1985. (See other volumes of Low's monumental history of British film in Com/Bib/RVA.)

MacGowan, Kenneth. *Famous American Plays of the 1920s.* New York: Dell Publishing, 1983.

McCauley, Zula. *The First Forty Years: A Chronology of Growth.* Dallas: Neiman-Marcus, 1947. (This is a history of Neiman-Marcus.)

McCooey, Meriel. "The Great Fashion Dictators of Hollywood." *The Sunday Times Magazine,* September 24, 1947. (Stills reproduced from the John Kobal collection.)

McDonald, William L., and A. C. Greene. *Dallas Rediscovered: A Photographic Chronicle of Urban Expansion, 1870–1925.* Dallas: Dallas Historical Society, 1978.

McLuhan, Marshall. *Understanding Media: The Extensions of Man.* New York: Signet Books, 1964.

Mander, Raymond, and Joe Mitchenson. *Musical Comedy: A Story in Pictures.* New York: Taplinger Publishing Co., 1970.

————. *Revue: A Story in Pictures.* London: Peter Davies, 1971. (See other Mander and Mitchenson books on the theater in Com/Bib/RVA.)

Marchand, Roland. *Advertising the American Dream: Making Way for Modernity, 1920–1940.* Berkeley: University of California Press, 1985.

Meech, Julia, and Gabriel P. Weisberg. *Japonisme Comes to America: The Japanese Impact on the Graphic Arts, 1876–1925.* New York: Harry N. Abrams, 1990. (See other books on the influence of Japanese prints in Com/Bib/RVA.)

Meikle, Jeffrey L. *Twentieth Century Limited: Industrial Design in America, 1925–1939.* Philadelphia: Temple University Press, 1979.

Miltenberger, Gordon. *The Church of the Holy Comforter: A History of the Episcopal Church in Cleburne, Johnson County, Texas.* Cleburne, Tex.: Cleburne Episcopal Church, 1971.

Morano, Elizabeth. *Sonia Delaunay: Art into Fashion.* New York: George Braziller, 1986.

Mordden, Ethan. *Broadway Babies: The People Who Made the American Musical.* New York: Oxford University Press, 1983.

Morley, Sheridan. *Spread a Little Happiness: The First Hundred Years of the British Musical.* London: Thames and Hudson, 1987.

Ozias, Blake. *All about Wine.* New York: Thomas Y. Crowell Co., 1967. Revised by Frederick Ek in 1973.

———. *A Catalogue of the Highest Grade Prints.* Darien, Conn., 1914.

———, ed. *How the Modern Hostess Serves Wine.* New York: Epicurean Press, 1934.

Packer, William. *Fashion Drawing in* VOGUE. New York: Coward-McCann, 1983.

Padon, Mildred. *The History of Cleburne and Johnson County.* Cleburne, Tex.: Layland Museum, 1985.

Pevsner, Nikolaus. *Pioneers of Modern Design: From William Morris to Walter Gropius.* New York: Penguin Books, 1978.

THE PICTUREGOER'S *Who's Who and Encyclopaedia of the Screen To-Day.* London: Odhams Press, 1933.

Poiret, Paul. *King of Fashion: The Autobiography of Paul Poiret.* Philadelphia: J. B. Lippincott Co., 1931.

Powell, Michael. *A Life in Movies: An Autobiography.* New York: Alfred A. Knopf, 1987.

Prichard, Susan Perez, ed. *Film Costume: An Annotated Bibliography.* Metuchen, N.J.: Scarecrow Press, 1981.

Reed, Walt. *Fifty Great American Illustrators.* New York: Abbeville Press, 1979.

———, and Roger Reed. *The Illustrator in America 1880–1980: A Century of Illustration.* New York: The Society of Illustrators and Madison Square Press, 1984.

Rein, Irving, Philip Kotler, and Martin Stoller. *High Visibility.* New York: Dodd, Mead & Co., 1987.

Robinson, Julian. *The Golden Age of Style: Art Déco Fashion Illustration.* New York: Gallery Books, 1976.

Rohrer, Albert Lawrence. *History of Osio, Osius, Ozias Families.* Ann Arbor, Mich.: Edwards Bros., 1943.

Rutland, Robert A. *James Madison and the Search for Nationhood.* Washington, D.C.: The Library of Congress, 1981.

Seebohm, Caroline. *The Man Who Was* VOGUE: *The Life and Times of Condé Nast.* New York: Viking Press, 1982.

Seldes, Gilbert. *The Seven Lively Arts.* New York: Harper, 1924.

Sheppard, Alice. *Cartooning for Suffrage.* Albuquerque: University of New Mexico Press, 1994.

Sochen, June. *The New Woman: Feminism in Greenwich Village, 1910–1920.* New York: Quadrangle Books, 1972.

Spencer, Charles. *Léon Bakst.* London: Academy Editions, 1978.

———. *Erté.* New York: Clarkson N. Potter, 1981.

———. *The World of Serge Diaghilev.* New York: Penguin Books, 1979.

Steele, Valerie. *Paris Fashion: A Cultural History.* New York and Oxford: Oxford University Press, 1988.

Stein, Gertrude. *Paris France.* London: B. T. Batsford, 1940.

Tapert, Annette, and Diana Edkins. *The Power of Style: The Women Who Defined the Art of Living Well.* New York: Crown Publishers, 1994.

Thornton, Michael. *Jessie Matthews: A Biography.* London: Hart Davis, MacGibbon, 1974.

Todd, Ellen Wiley. *The "New Woman" Revised: Painting and Gender Politics on Fourteenth Street.* Berkeley: University of California Press, 1993.

Tomkins, Calvin. *Living Well Is the Best Revenge.* New York: E. P. Dutton, 1982.

Train, Susan, ed. *Théâtre de la Mode.* Exhibition catalogue. New York: Rizzoli, 1991.

Trewin, J. C., Raymond Mander, and Joe Mitchenson. *The Gay Twenties: A Decade of the Theatre.* London: Macdonald, 1958.

———. *The Turbulent Thirties.* London: Macdonald, 1960.

Troy, Carol. "'Can You Imagine Them Making Love?': Ellen Mirojnick and the Inner Game of Costume." *American Film* 14, no. 8 (June 1989): 6, 46–51, 64.

Tufts, Eleanor. *American Women Artists: 1830–1930.* Book accompanying exhibition. Washington, D.C.: The National Museum of Women, 1987.

Warkel, Harriet G. *Images of Women in American Illustration.* Exhibition brochure. Indianapolis: Indianapolis Museum of Art–Columbus Gallery, 1991.

Waugh, Evelyn. *Brideshead Revisited.* Boston: Little, Brown and Co., 1945.

Welter, Barbara. "The Cult of True Womanhood: 1820–1860." In *The American Family in Social-Historical Perspective,* edited by Michael Gordon. 3d ed. New York: St. Martin's Press, 1983.

White, Palmer. *Poiret.* London: Studio Vista, 1973.

Winchester, Clarence, ed. *The World Film Encyclopedia: A Universal Screen Guide.* London: Amalgamated Press, 1933.

Wodehouse, P. G., and Guy Bolton. *Bring on the Girls!: The Improbable Story of Our Life in Musical Comedy, with Pictures to Prove It.* New York: Limelight Editions, 1984. (See Wodehouse novels in Com/Bib/RVA.)

Wolf, Naomi. *The Beauty Myth: How Images of Beauty Are Used against Women.* New York: William Morrow and Co., 1991.

Zvonchenko, Walter. "Dazzling Color and Mass Movement: Spectacle on the Presentation House Stage." *Library of Congress Performing Arts Annual, 1989,* pp. 24–49. Washington, D.C., 1990.

Special Collections

Aileen and Michael Balcon Collection. British Film Institute, Library and Information Services, Special Materials Unit. London. (Permission granted to the author by Jonathan Balcon.)

Archive of Heyworth Campbell. Business correspondence, 1916–1927. Privately owned by Walt and Roger Reed of Illustration House in New York.

Cleburne, Texas, Historical and Architectural Survey, March 1987. Archive of historic photographs, news clippings, and research notes. Privately owned by Michael Gamble.

"*Constant Nymph* Production Story," a 1943 Warner Brothers studio press release. Museum of Modern Art Film Studies Center, New York.

Letters to the Author

Barzun, Jacques. New York, January 20, 1988.

Bolloten, Michael. New South Wales, Australia, three letters between March 2, 1983, and January 29, 1984.

de Mille, Agnes. New York, July 1, 1987.

Gilbert, Audrey S. "The Archives" of Preble County, Ohio, four letters with photographs, July 14–30, 1990.

Surowiec, Catherine. London, September 20, 1993. (Information in letter supplemented by research memos and telephone conversations, 1994–1996.)

Thornton, Michael. London, August 8 and 11, 1996.

Interviews

Interview topics included remembrances by colleagues, friends, and employees of Gordon Conway (GC); recollections of persons working in the same fields as GC; and comments and analyses by authorities on the period and/or on illustration and costume design for print media, stage, and film during the first part of the twentieth century in New York, Paris, and London. Interviews mostly were conducted in person and recorded on audio tape by the author (RVA) between January 1983 and March 1993. These tapes were supplemented by notes taken during subsequent conversations with the same source, both in person and over the telephone. After the date of the first interview, the comprehensive dates of discussion are indicated by year. The abbreviations Intrv/RVA, Tel/RVA, and Tel/EB indicate interviews that were not taped.

ABBREVIATIONS AND SYMBOLS USED IN INTERVIEWS

Intrv/RVA   Interview in person with notes by RVA.

Tel/RVA   Telephone interview with notes by RVA.

Tel/EB   Inquiry on behalf of RVA conducted on the telephone by Eric Braun, British author and theater/film critic.

*   Stage/film performer, illustrator/designer, or authority in these fields.

† Friend, family member, employee, or commentator with informed personal observations.

*Allan, Elizabeth. England, spring 1984. (Tel/EB)

†Allen, Olive Johnson (OJA). (Also listed as Mrs. Marshall Allen.) Orange and Fredericksburg, Va., November 1982–March 1993. (Intrv/RVA)

*†Antill, Joan (JA). Washington, D.C., joint interview with Mary Lutz (ML), January 10, 1983.

*Ayer, Nat D. London, February 16, 1983.

*Baxter, Jane. London, September 5, 1984.

†Becker, Naomi. Fredericksburg, Va., September 5, 1987.

*Braun, Eric (EB). London, February 20, 1983; 1983–1989. (Interviews supplemented with Braun's letters and research notes.)

*†Butler, Jeanne. Washington, D.C., 1983–1992. (Intrv/Tel/RVA)

†Carter, Edith. Fredericksburg, Va., September 4, 1987.

*Chapman, Gary. London, New York, Washington, D.C., and Austin, Tex., September 20, 1985; 1985–1993. (Interviews supplemented with Chapman's letters and research notes.)

†Coghill, Oscar C. Washington, D.C., October 6, 1987.

†Coghill, William Thomas. Fredericksburg, Va., September 4, 1987.

*Crane, William H. Fredericksburg, Va. and Austin, Tex., June 21, 1990; 1990–1992.

*Cummings, Constance. England, spring 1985. (Tel/EB)

*Cushman, Wilhela. Washington, D.C., March 19, 1993. (Tel/RVA)

*†Dickson, Dorothy (DD). London, February 15, 1983; 1983–1989. (Interviews supplemented by Dickson's press books.)

†Dierks, Julia (JD). Charlottesville, Va., February 15, 1983.

*Dumm, Edwina. New York, October 10, 1986.

†Elliott, Margaret Page (MPE). Dallas, Tex., March 4, 1983; 1983–1985.

*Ellis, Mary. London, August 23, 1984.

*Everson, William K. (WKE). New York, November 8, 1984; and Washington, D.C., December 3, 1984.

†Faber, Benjamin. Washington, D.C. and Paris, Tex., 1983–1992. (Tel/RVA)

†Felder, Diana Gibbs (DGF). Dallas, Tex., March 4, 1983; 1983–1992.

†Fortune, Maude. Corbin, Va., joint interview with Virginia Jones, September 4, 1987.

†Gamble, Michael. Cleburne, Tex., March 29–30, 1990.

*†Garland, Madge. London, February 1983. (Tel/RVA)

*Gielgud, Sir John. England, fall 1987. (Tel/Letter/EB)

*Ginsburg, Cora. New York, January 26, 1983.

*Grant, Ian. London, September 24, 1985.

*Green, Benny. London, September 13, 1985.

*Haenigsen, Harry. Ewing, N.J., July 7, 1986.

*Harrison, Kathleen. England, spring 1985. (Tel/EB)

†Holcomb, Ray and Margaret. Fredericksburg, Va., September 2, 1987.

†Houghton, Katharine (KH). Dallas, Tex., March 3, 1983.

†Houston, Levin and Betsy. Fredericksburg, Va., September 3, 1987.

*†Hyson, Dorothy (DHQ). (Also listed as Lady Quayle.) London, August 17 and August 30, 1984; 1984–1989.

*†Jeans, Isabel. London, February 1983. (Tel/RVA)

*Jones, Grace. Salado, Tex., Austin, Tex., and New York, 1983–1993.

†Jones, Virginia. Corbin, Va., joint interview with Maude Fortune, September 4, 1987.

†Korth, The Hon. Fred. Washington, D.C., August 7, 1986.

†Lanier, Bess. Fredericksburg, Va., September 4, 1987.

*†Laye, Evelyn. London, August 25, 1984.

*Leese, Elizabeth. London, September 2, 1984 and September 20, 1985. (Interviews supplemented with Leese's letters and research notes.)

Linz, Joe.

*Lockhard, Freda Bruce. London, February 2, 1983.

†Lutz, Mary (ML). Washington, D.C., joint interview with Joan Antill (JA), January 10, 1983.

*Macdonald, Nesta. London, February 18, 1983.

*Mills, Sir John. England, fall 1987. (Tel/RVA)

*Milton, Billy. London, August 18, 1984; 1984–1986.

*Neagle, Dame Anna. London, August 27, 1984.

*Nesbitt, Robert. London, September 11, 1985.

*Newton, Stella Mary (OBE). London, September 10, 1985; 1985–1989.

*Pollock, Ellen. England, spring 1986. (Tel/RVA)

*Powell, Michael. New York, November 9, 1984.

*Pleasants, Rodney. New York, January 27, 1983.

*†Quayle, Lady (See Dorothy Hyson) (DHQ).

*Rachow, Louis. New York, April 11, 1986.

*Reid, Dame Beryl. London and her home on the Thames, 1984–1988.

*Relph, Michael. London, February 16, 1983.

*Ripley, Valerie. London, September 11, 1985; 1985–1989.

*Robson, Christopher. London, August 17–20, 1983 and September 6, 1985; 1983–1989.

†Rose, Joe. Fredericksburg, Va., September 5, 1987.

†Russell, John. Fredericksburg, Va., September 2, 1987.

†Sefton, Kenneth. London, August 21, 1984.

*Schaff, David. Washington, D.C., February 4, 1983.

*Scott, Gary. Washington, D.C., December 7, 1989.

*Sheffield, Ann. Newport Beach, Calif., Washington, D.C., and subsequent telephone conversations, mid-July 1989; 1989–1992.

*Spencer, Charles. London, February 16, 1983.

*Swinburne, Nora. London, joint interview with husband-actor Esmond Knight, August 29, 1984.

*Sylva, Elena. London, September 3, 1984.

*Terrell, St. John. Ewing, N.J., July 7–8, 1986.

*†Thatcher, Heather. London, February 1984. (Tel/RVA)

*Truelove, Mr. London, August 27, 1984. (Tel/RVA)

*Welch, Frankie. Alexandria, Va., December 14, 1989.

†Werley, Helen. London, March 16, 1988.

*Williams, Sir Emlyn. England, fall 1987. (Tel/EB)

*Winham, Jeanne Ballot (JBW). New York, September 7, 1983; 1983–1985.

Books, Portfolios, and Catalogues Owned by Gordon Conway (1894–1956)

Alex Rzewuski. France, 1925. Exhibition catalogue.

Andersen, H. C. I. Bilder av Einar Nerman. *Per Svinaherde Saga.* Stockholm: Centraltryckeriet, 1912.

Ariel. BBC staff magazine, no. 7 (1937).

Arno, Peter. *Man in the Shower.* New York: Simon and Schuster, 1944.

Batchelder, Ernest Allen. *The Principles of Design.* Chicago: Inland Printer Co., 1918.

Beaumont, Cyril W. *Children's Tales.* London, 1919. (Illustrations by Michel Sevier and C. W. Beaumont.)

———. *Cleopatra: Impressions of the Russian Ballet.* London, 1918. (Illustrations by A. P. Allinson.)

———. *Sheherazade: Impressions of the Russian Ballet.* London, 1919. (Illustrations by A. P. Allinson.)

Bell, Clive. *Art.* London: Chatto and Windus, 1921.

Beltran-Masses, Federico. Art Exhibition Catalogue. London, 1929.

———. *L'Oeuvre de Federico Beltran-Masses.* Art catalogue. 1921.

Bie, Oskar. *Schnackenberg-Kostume, Plakate und Dekorationen.* Munchen: Musarion-Verlag, 1920.

The Book of Common Prayer. C. J. Clay & Sons, 1934.

Branksome Tower Hotel Brochure, Boumeworth West, Branksome Park, 1934.

Calthrop, Dion Clayton. *English Costume.* London: A. & C. Black, Ltd., 1926.

Carteret, John Grand, and Albin Michel. *Les Elegances de la Toilette.* Paris, n.d.

Costumes de Théâtre, Ballet et Divertissements. Paris: Editions Lucien Vogel, 1923.

Cupid's Game with Hearts—A Tale Told by Documents. 1897. (Illustrations by Stella Alys Witram.)

Ckazkn A. Nywknha (?). Catalogue. ca. 1924.

Devambez. *Deauville.* France, 1930.

Drawings from the Old Masters. London: British Museum Drawings, 1909.

Earle, Alice Morse. *Two Centuries of Costume in America.* New York: Macmillan Co., 1903.

Egan, Beresford. *The Sink of Solitude.* London: Hermes Press, 1928.

Egan, Beresford, and C. Bower Alcock. *Baudelaire, Fleurs du Mal.* London: The Sophisticated Press and T. Werner Laurie Ltd., 1929.

Egon Schiele. Art Catalogue. n.d.

Fischel, Oskar. *Die Mode.* Munchen: Bei F. Bruckmann A.G., 1858.

Fisher, Harrison. *A Dream of Fair Women.* Indianapolis: Bobbs-Merrill, 1907. [This book was once in GC's collection, as indicated in her diary.]

Fleming, Tom. *The Capital.* Capital Cartoon Syndicate, 1913.

Galerie Colonna. Art collection catalogue. Rome, 1913.

Gay, John. *The Beggar's Opera, Written by Mr. Gay.* London: William Heinemann, 1921.

Giaferri, Paul Louis Victor de. *L'Histoire du costume féminin mondial.* Paris: Editions Nilsson, n.d.

Grahame, Kenneth. *The Wind in the Willows.* London: Methuen and Company Ltd., 1932.

Gribble, Francis H. *Lausanne.* London: Adam and Charles Black, 1909.

Herschel, John. *Treatise on Astronomy.* 1841.

Holme, Geoffrey, ed. *Design in the Theatre.* The Studio Ltd., 1927.

Holscher, Eberhard. *Geore Salter.* Jahrang, 1930.

Hottenroth, Fr. *Le Costume chez les peuples anciens et modernes.* Paris: Armand Guerinet, n.d.

Housman, Laurence, ed. *Stories From the Arabian Nights.* New York: Hodder and Stroughton, 1911. (Illustrations by Edmund Dulac.)

Hoyt, Harlowe R. *Town Hall Tonight.* n.p., n.d. (Illustrations by Ed Keukes.)

The Hymnal, University Press, 1889.

International Theatre Exhibition. Catalogue. London: Victoria and Albert Museum, 1922.

Kipling, Rudyard. *The Pocket Kipling/Departmental Ditties and Ballads and Barrack Room Ballads.* Doubleday/Page & Co., 1918.

Lac Léman Album Avec 32 Vues. Genfer-See, n.d.

Lafenestre, Georges, and Eugene Richttenberger. *The National Museum of the Louvre.* Paris: Libraries-Imprimaries Reunies, 1893 & 1907.

Les Châteaux de la Loire. n.d.

Levinson, André. *Bakst: The Story of Leon Bakst's Life.* London: Bayard Press, 1923.

Louys, Pierre. *Aphrodite. A Novel of Ancient Morals.* London: The Fortune Press, n.d. (Illustrations by Beresford Egan.)

Macgowan, Kenneth, and Robert E. Jones. *Continental Stagecraft.* New York: Harcourt, Brace, 1922.

Male, F. E. *What Men Know about Women.* n.d. (Book of blank pages.)

Marvel, Ik. *Dream Life—A Fable of Seasons.* Thomas Y. Crowell & Co., 1900.

Michaud, Jean Ajalbert Louis, ed. *Chansons de Sao Van Di.* Paris, n.d.

Norris, Herbert. *Costume and Fashion.* Vol. 2. London: J. M. Dent and Sons, Ltd., 1927.

Ozias, Blake, ed. *A Catalogue of Highest Grade Prints.* Darien, Conn.: Blake Ozias, 1914.

Perkins, J. R. *A Thin Volume.* Ohio: Saalfield Publishing Co., 1917.

Phelps, Elizabeth Stuart. *Loveliness.* Houghton, Mifflin and Co., 1899. (Illustrations by Sarah Stillwell.)

Phillips, Stephen. *Marpessa.* London: John Lane the Bodley Head, 1914. (Illustrations by Philip Connard.)

Porgy and Bess. Program. n.d.

Propert, Walter Archibald. *The Russian Ballet, 1921–1929.* London: John Lane the Bodley Head Ltd., 1931.

Raynal, Maurice. *A. Archipenko.* Rome, 1923.

Réau, Louis, Denis Roche, V. Svietlov, and A. Tessier. *Bakst: Inedited Works of Leon Bakst; Essays on Bakst.* New York: Brentano's, 1927.

Rhead, G. Wolliscroft. *Chats on Costume.* London: T. Fisher Unwin, 1906. (Once owned and signed by John Singer Sargent.)

Ross, Robert. *Aubrey Beardsley,* 1st ed. Edinburgh: Turnbull and Spears, n.d. (Second edition published New York and London: John Lane the Bodley Head, 1921.)

Sayler, Oliver M. *Our American Theatre.* New York: Brentano's, 1922.

———. *The Russian Theatre.* New York: Brentano's, 1922.

———, ed. *The Moscow Art Theatre.* New York: Brentano's, 1922.

Schnitzler, Arthur. *Fraulein Else.* London: Constable Publishers, 1929. (Illustrations by Donia Nachsen.)

Sherwood, Robert, ed. *The Best of H. T. Webster: A Memorial Collection,* 1953.

Van Loon, Hendrik Willem. *The Story of Wilbur the Hat.* New York: Horace B. Liveright, 1925.

Vanderpoel, John H. *The Human Figure.* Chicago: The Inland Printer Co., 1916.

Wahlen, Auguste. *Moeurs, usages et costumes de tous les peuples du monde.* Brussels: Librairie Historique-Artistique. Vol. 1 (Asie), 1843; vol. 2 (Afrique-Amérique), 1844; vol. 3 (Europe), 1844; vol. 4 (Oceanie), 1843.

Watt, Hansard. *Back Numbers.* London: Cassell and Company, Ltd., 1914.

Weicher, Verlag Von Wilhelm. *Die Meisterbilder, Van Frans Hals.* Berlin, 1910.

Wickham Court Hotel Brochure. Kent: Central Publicity Services, Ltd., n.d.

Yale University School of Fine Arts. Catalogue. 1915, 1916.

INDEX

Gordon Conway is abbreviated as GC. For Gordon Conway artwork not mentioned in the text, and therefore not listed in the Index, see Catalogue Raisonné on pages 227–255.

GORDON CONWAY

Designed by Heidi Haeuser

Typography in Adobe Garamond and Insignia
by G & S Typesetters, Inc.

Printed and bound by Thomson-Shore, Inc.
Dexter, Michigan